STYLE AND RHETORIC IN PINDAR'S ODES

American Philological Association
American Classical Studies

The Harmonics of Nicomachus and the Pythagorean Tradition	Flora R. Levin
The Etymology and the Usage of ΠΕΙΡΑΡ *in Early Greek Poetry*	Ann L. T. Bergren
Two Studies in Roman Nomenclature	D.R. Shackleton Bailey
The Latin Particle Quidem	J. Solodow
On the Hymn to Zeus in Aeschylus' Agamemnon	Peter M. Smith
The Andromache of Euripides	Paul David Kovacs
A Commentary on the Vita Hadriani in the Historia Augusta	Herbert W. Benario
Creation and Salvation in Ancient Orphism	Larry J. Alderink
Eros Sophistes: Ancient Novelists at Play	Graham Anderson
Ancient Philosophy and Grammar: The Syntax of Apollonius Dyscolus	David Blank
Autonomia: Its Genesis and Early History	Martin Ostwald
Language and Metre: Resolution, Porson's Bridge, and Their Prosodic Basis	A. M. Devine
Descent from Heaven: Images of Dew in Greek Poetry and Religion	Deborah Boedeker
Iamblichus and the Theory of the Vehicle of the Soul	John F. Finamore
Epicurus on the Swerve and Voluntary Action	Walter G. Englert
Seneca's Anapaests	John G. Fitch
Xoana and the Origins of Greek Sculpture	A. A. Donohue
ANAΓKH in Thucydides	Martin Ostwald
Old Comedy and the Iambographic Tadition	Ralph M. Rosen
EKΩN and AKΩN in Early Greek Thought	GailAnn Rickert
Hekate Soteira	Sarah Iles Johnston
The Decrees of the Demotionidai	Charles W. Hedrick, Jr.
Alexandrian Citizenship during the Roman Principate	Diana Delia
Style and Rhetoric in Pindar's Odes	William H. Race

William H. Race

STYLE AND RHETORIC IN PINDAR'S ODES

Scholars Press
Atlanta, Georgia

STYLE AND RHETORIC IN PINDAR'S ODES

William H. Race

© 1990
The American Philological Association

Library of Congress Cataloging in Publication Data

Race, William H.
Style and rhetoric in Pindar's odes / William H. Race.
    p. cm. -- (American Classical Studies / American Philological Association : no. 24)
    Includes bibliographical references and index.
    ISBN 1-55540-490-1 (alk. paper). -- ISBN 1-55540-491-X (pbk.: alk. paper)
1. Pindar--Style. I. Title. II. Series: American Classical Studies. American Philological Association) ; no. 24.
PA4276.Z5R3 1990
884'.01--dc20   90-40137
                                              CIP

Printed in the United States of America
on acid-free paper

in memoriam

Elroy L. Bundy

1920-1975

TABLE OF CONTENTS

Preface ix
Introduction 1-8
Chapter 1: Climactic Elements in Pindar's Verse 9-40
Chapter 2: Elements of Style in Break-Offs 41-57
Chapter 3: Negative Expressions 59-84
Chapter 4: Style and Rhetoric in Opening Hymns 85-117
Chapter 5: Forms and Functions of Prayers 119-140
Chapter 6: An Analysis of *Olympian* 8 141-164
Appendix 1: Climactic Pairs 165-180
Appendix 2: Bakchylides' Opening Hymns 181-186
Appendix 3: Variations on Two Topics 187-195
Bibliography 197-202
Index Locorum 203-213
General Index 215-217

Preface

This book is dedicated to the memory of Elroy L. Bundy, who for the last three years of his life was for me an inspiring mentor, colleague, and friend, and whose published works, *Studia Pindarica* (1962) and "The 'Quarrel Between Kallimachos and Apollonios'" (1972), provide the basis for the present study. In accord with the principles expounded in his works, I too regard the primary function of Pindar's epinician odes to be "ἐσλὸν αἰνεῖν" ("praise the good") and maintain that their style and rhetoric consistently contribute jointly to that goal. I also believe in the importance of reading them sequentially. They were performed and heard from beginning to end, and close attention to the fine points of style and rhetoric can recapture some of the movement—what Bundy aptly called "crescendo" and "decrescendo"—which were meant to guide the understanding and feelings of the original audiences.

My interest in Pindaric style began with an article entitled "Negative Expressions and Pindaric ποικιλία," published in *Transactions of the American Philological Association* 113 (1983). It forms the basis for *Chapter 3*. The book itself first took shape during tenure of a grant from the National Endowment for the Humanities in 1985, to which agency I am profoundly indebted. Preliminary sketches of the first two chapters were presented in a James Loeb Classical Lecture at Harvard in April 1986 and were subsequently published as "Climactic Elements in Pindar's Verse" in *Harvard Studies in Classical Philology* 92 (1989) and as "Elements of Style in Pindaric Break-Offs" in *American Journal of Philology* 110 (1989). I am grateful to the American Philological Association, the President and Fellows of Harvard University, and the *American Journal of Philology* for permission to reuse material that appeared in their publications. I also wish to thank the APA Monographs Committee and the two anonymous readers for much cooperation and helpful criticism. In particular I wish to thank two individuals, David Young, whose own example and support have been a constant inspiration, and Andrew Miller, whose generous and acute criticisms I always disregard to my own harm. Finally, I wish to acknowledge my gratitude to Vanderbilt University for a leave in Fall 1988 and to its University Research Council for a grant during Spring 1989 that enabled me to complete the work.

INTRODUCTION

Basil Gildersleeve, the doyen of American Pindarists and one of the most careful readers of Pindar, made the following observations about Pindar's style:

> In the fine feeling of language few poets can vie with Pindar; and though he is no pedantic synonym-monger, like a true artist he delights in the play of his own work. There is danger of over-subtilty in the study of antique style; but Pindar is a jeweller, his material gold and ivory, and his chryselephantine work challenges the scrutiny of the microscope, invites the study that wearies not day or night in exploring the recesses in which the artist has held his art sequestered—invites the study and rewards it.[1]

In calling Pindar a jeweler, Gildersleeve refers to the passage in *Nem.* 7, where the poet compares the craft of his Muse to the work of a jeweler and says (77-79):

> Μοῖσά τοι
> κολλᾷ χρυσὸν ἔν τε λευκὸν ἐλέφανθ' ἁμᾶ
> καὶ λείριον ἄνθεμον ποντίας ὑφελοῖσ' ἐέρσας.

> The Muse, you know,
> binds gold together with white ivory
> and the lily flower she takes from the dew of the sea.

This very passage, as will become clearer by the end of the first chapter, exemplifies stylistic principles, found throughout the odes, whereby Pindar constructs syntactical units with ever-increasing weight and emphasis. In the following pages I wish to take a microscopic look at certain features of Pindar's style in order to explore some of the recesses in which, as Gildersleeve says, he sequesters his art.

Stylistic analysis, however, is deficient if it does not take into account the reasons for each stylistic trait; it is therefore the aim of this book to analyze some of the most important features of Pindar's style by trying to determine their rhetorical functions in their odes. By "style" I mean the poet's selection and

---

[1] Gildersleeve, *Pindar* xlii.

placement of words;[2] by "rhetoric" I mean his use of language to fulfill his generic purpose, "ἐσλὸν αἰνεῖν."[3] *Chapter 1* determines the principles of composition that underlie rhetorically climactic passages; *Chapter 2* investigates the ways in which stylistic features interact with rhetoric as the poet breaks off from one topic and turns to another; *Chapter 3* explores the use of negative expressions to provide stylistic variation, rhetorical emphasis, and ethical proof; *Chapter 4* examines the interaction of style and rhetoric in opening hymns; *Chapter 5* surveys the forms and functions of prayers; and *Chapter 6* presents a close analysis of *Ol.* 8, in order to demonstrate how the preceding analyses serve to illuminate a particular ode. Finally, three appendices examine climactic pairs, compare Bakchylides' stylistic techniques in his hymns with those of Pindar, and examine Pindar's variations on two topics frequently recurring in the odes, "appearance and action" and "the limits of human success."

Previous Studies of Pindaric Style

A brief survey of previous work on Pindar's style will help to distinguish what is new in this book. One strand of stylistic analysis began with Mezger (1880), who closely studied the recurrence of words in the same metrical position in each ode. In his Cambridge commentaries, Fennell (1879; new ed. 1893 and 1883; new ed. 1899) expanded upon his work, conveniently listing the "recurrent words," "echoes," and "responses" in the introductions of each ode. Bury (1890 and 1892) in turn claimed to find in them keys to the interpretation of passages and entire odes. The legacy of their work is apparent in subsequent studies, including those of Norwood (1945), Stockert (1969), Schürch (1971), Lefkowitz (1976), Greengard (1980), and the Newmans (1984). Taken together, these studies succeed in demonstrating the *existence* of numerous and various "echoes" (Fennell lists over sixty in *Ol.* 1 alone), but the main problem that confronts the critic is determining their *significance*. Are they simply a feature of Pindar's exuberant use of language or are they serious indicators of meaning? Since there are so many instances, how can one determine which ones are significant and which not? Judging from the unconvincing attempts of the above-mentioned scholars (and many others) to discover meaning in such recurrences, one must conclude that the more the reins of rhetoric are slackened, the more easily exclu-

---

[2] The present study does not treat Pindar's use of imagery and metaphor, on which see Silk, *Interaction in Poetic Imagery* (1974); Péron, *Les images maritimes* (1974); Steiner, *Crown of Song* (1986); and Stoneman, "Metaphor."
[3] Cf. the fuller statement of purpose at *Nem.* 8.39: αἰνέων αἰνητά, μομφὰν δ' ἐπισπείρων ἀλιτροῖς, which presents the positive and negative functions of epideictic poetry.

sive concentration on "echoes" of words, images, or ideas leads to run-away associationism.[4]

A more traditional strain of stylistic analysis, which stems from ancient rhetorical classifications of tropes and figures, comes to fruition in F. Dornseiff's study (1921), which remains the only general survey of Pindar's style. It touches on many facets of Pindar's language, including vocabulary, tropes, figures of speech and thought, metaphor, kenning, circumlocution, unstated comparison ("Vergleich ohne wie"), priamel, personification, and enjambment. Although it contains valuable insights (for example, it was the first work to recognize the existence of priamels in Pindar), it is far from comprehensive and contains no discussion of the function of the various figures within their odes.[5]

Although W. Schadewaldt (1928) does not deal directly with Pindaric style, in analyzing the "Aufbau" and "Programm" of epinician odes, he identifies many of the rhetorical topics and motifs that have a direct bearing on vocabulary and style, including adaptations of hymnic language, χρέος-Komplex, Abbruchsformel, κόρος-Motiv, and Charismotiv.

The dissertation of R. Nierhaus (1936), directed by Schadewaldt and relying on his earlier work, presents a helpful analysis of the placement of the parts of an ode with respect to strophic arrangement. In particular, he studies strophic enjambment (which he calls "Überbrückung"), climactic statements occurring at the beginning of strophes, and the frequent use of γάρ and relative pronouns at

---

[4] For example, Skulsky, "Language and Meaning" claims that Pindar's works consist of "an organic system of echoes and collocations that comprise his poetic language" (30-31) and that individual odes are "parts of a continuous fabric of interrelated ideas and images extending throughout the poet's *oeuvre*" (28). Her purpose is to reveal "the semantic infrastructure" (28, 31 note 8) of Pindar's language, and in the course of her analysis the recurrence of such verbs as "echoes," "recalls," "corresponds to," "anticipates," "assimilates," "is similar to," "is associated with," "is connected with" reveals the associative basis of the procedure. By extending Mezger's verbal recurrences to include "interrelated ideas and images" the ground is laid for the more radical structuralist program outlined by Hubbard, *Pindaric Mind* 164:

> If criticism is to continue as a viable and dynamic scholarly activity, it must turn its attention to the generative deep-structures behind the text. Once the obvious has been stated and even restated, it becomes necessary to illuminate what is not obvious, to render explicit what is implicit, to unravel the variegated fabric of mental-conceptual-verbal relations which constitute the text and each sentence, phrase, and word within the text. Webs of connotation, implication, and association branch out indefinitely in every direction; it remains for generations of future critics to chart their way through this ever more complex hermeneutic labyrinth.

Although it does not appear in the index, the operative word throughout his study is "ambiguity," which occurs seven times on one page alone (149). Even further in this line is the work of Segal, *Pindar's Mythmaking*. See the review of Köhnken, *JHS* 108 (1988) 223-224, who refers to him as "a radical symbolist."

[5] Other surveys of Pindar's language and figures of speech before and after Dornseiff include Jebb, "Pindar" 166-173, Gildersleeve, *Pindar* xxxiv-xliv, Fennell, *Olympian and Pythian Odes* xxi-xxv, Thummer, *Die Isthmischen Gedichte I* 138-158, and Braswell, *Fourth Pythian* 30-37.

the beginning of a strophe to add details. Throughout the study he is careful to note exceptions and is sensitive to the rhetorical purposes of the poet. Although his attempt to demonstrate development from (supposed) early poems to late ones is unconvincing, his is a sensible and worthwhile study.[6]

S. Lauer's dissertation (1959) consists of a very detailed description (much of it in tabular form) of the syntax and its relationship to cola and strophes in three odes, *Pyth.* 10, *Nem.* 1, and *Pyth.* 8. Although he observes that Pindar occasionally employs "Wachstum der Glieder," he limits himself to examples that are syntactically similar. Thus he cites χερσὶν ἢ ποδῶν ἀρετᾷ at *Pyth.* 10.23 and ὅσσους μὲν ἐν χέρσῳ κτανών, | ὅσσους δὲ πόντῳ θῆρας ἀϊδροδίκας at *Nem.* 1.62-63, but does not discern that they are part of even larger complexes of increasing elements.

A.-I. Sulzer's study (1961; repr. 1970) is concerned with the syntactical arrangement of clauses and sentences, particularly those containing separated and overlapping elements which she calls "framing" and "chiasmus." The study is useful for revealing the intricate interweaving of Pindaric syntax, but too many passages are forced to fit preconceived patterns and no effort is ever made to discover why Pindar constructed a given sentence as he does or what rhetorical effects were intended.[7]

A. Kambylis (1964) presents an extremely detailed, but loosely organized, listing of all the forms of address in Pindar, including points of grammar, syntax, vocabulary, and style. Of particular importance for the present study are the discussions of hymnal addresses scattered throughout this work and his brief treatment of "das Gesetz der wachsenden Glieder" (177-179), although he uses word-count to measure increases, which, as we shall see, is untenable. Many good observations are embedded in the mass of examples and statistical summaries.

W. Stockert's dissertation (1969) is little more than a catalogue of examples of alliteration, assonance, rhyme, anaphora, and various forms of repetition (or near-repetition). No attempt is made to explain what purpose the examples serve.

P. Schürch's study (1971) consists of lists of recurring words or ideas, including many that manifest only superficial resemblances of sound or rhythm. He includes so many far-fetched examples and offers so little critical analysis that he does not advance the work of his predecessors, Mezger, Fennell, and Bury.[8]

E. Thummer (1969), following in the path of Schadewaldt and Bundy, makes a number of good observations on Pindar's style in the section entitled "Stilistische Mittel zur Verstärkung des Lobes" in *Die Isthmischen Gedichte I*

---

[6] Mullen, *Choreia* 93-96 provides an impressionistic overview of strophic enjambment and argues that epodic enjambment has a special significance. For a critique of his procedure see the review of Burnett, *CP* 79 (1984) 154-160.

[7] See the review of Radt in *Gnomon* 35 (1963) 245-247, who points out that her use of word-count to determine symmetry leads to absurd excesses.

[8] See the review of Slater in *Gnomon* 45 (1973) 490-492.

138-158. In particular, he briefly discusses "das Gesetz der wachsenden Glieder" (148-149) and provides examples from the *Isthmian Odes*.[9]

C. Greengard (1980) draws on various strands of formal analysis, including ring-composition, association of ideas, use of imagery and metaphor, verbal recurrences, framing (by means of a word, motif, or metaphor), and symmetry. She contends that these "technical devices" exist independently of "the linear arrangement of topics," and that her reading is "from an aesthetic rather than from a philosophical or topical point of view."

J. K. and F. S. Newman (1984) base their analyses on recurring words, tautometric phrases, puns, imagery, and symbolism, combined with associationism and formalism—aspects of what they call the "carnival style." In particular, they attempt to find symmetrical patterns in such repetitions in various odes by counting words. Not only do their schemes exhibit the excesses of similar efforts to find symmetrical patterns in Latin poetry, but the use of "words" as a measurement cannot possibly yield any sure results (is δέ a word? then what about δ'? how could either have the same weight as τρισολυμπιονίκαν?).[10] Furthermore, a listening audience could hardly have counted words.

The Present Study

The present work differs from all preceding studies of style by concentrating on the *rhetorical purpose* served by each stylistic feature under discussion. In attending closely to Pindar's choice and placement of words and phrases, particularly in relationship to versification and strophic arrangement, the following questions will be constantly asked: "*Why* did the poet use this particular word here?" "*Why* does this sequence culminate in this particular item?" "*How* does this passage function in the ode as a whole?" The study of style cannot be conducted in a vacuum or as an end in itself. Style serves a purpose (which I have called rhetorical), and that purpose in turn provides a rationale for stylistic characteristics. In

---

[9] He is, however, inconsistent in measuring the increments. For example, he counts lines to show an increase of elements at *Isth.* 5.1-10, by noting that one line is devoted to the invocation, two lines to gold, three to ships and chariots, and four to athletics. The passage is indeed climactic, and I think that we are meant to sense an increasing weight in the four examples, but the line as a unit of measurement is suspect, for one of the three lines in the third item is extremely long (25 syllables; the longest, in *Pyth.* 1, has 30 syllables). Only by counting lines is the letter of the law fulfilled: the third unit actually consists of nineteen words, the fourth of seventeen words (even counting τ'), while both contain forty-four syllables. Then, in the same discussion, in using word-count to demonstrate an increase of elements at *Isth.* 5.61-62, he is forced to count δ' as a word.

[10] They justify counting words by referring to Thummer, *Die Isthmischen Gedichte I* 149, but we have already reviewed the problems inherent in his procedure. See the critique of Verdenius, *Commentaries I* 121, especially his remark on word-count: "The whole idea of taking 'word' as a unit and a kind of module is absurd."

short, I seek to elucidate those passages where, in the words of Wilamowitz (*Pindaros* 459), "Meaning and style are in complete agreement."

In his *Studia Pindarica* Bundy made use of three related concepts in analyzing Pindaric odes: "linear development," "crescendo," and "climax." Many scholars, including those most sympathetic to Bundy's approach such as Young and Thummer, have found fault with the concept of "linear development."[11] I do not intend to defend here Bundy's use of the term, but I do maintain that *sequential reading* is a necessary foundation for interpreting any ode. Common sense tells us that the audience heard the odes performed one word after another, as they did dramas in the theater or speeches in the assemblies or courts. The fact that each re-reading may reveal hidden depths of meaning or previously unnoticed cross-references does not call into question the fact that the odes must *first* be studied

---

[11] Cf. Thummer, *Die Isthmischen Gedichte I* 11, 20 note 1 and Young, "Pindaric Criticism" 87-88:

> It is impossible to travel 'lineally' from start to finish of a Pindaric ode, dismissing what has been heard the while, and not to miss most of what Pindar has to say, for as I have already said and as may be shown from close analyses of the poems, the coherence of Pindar's poems depends primarily upon the cross-references of one part of the poem to other parts. The unity thus created is formed by the aggregate of all passages, and the beginning is still very important at the end of the poem and, ultimately, the end is important at the beginning.

In the context of his study, Young's assessment has some point, but Bundy did not intend the notion of "linear development" to be the end-all of Pindaric criticism, as his constant use of comparative material in *Studia Pindarica* and "Quarrel" amply demonstrates. But some notion of linear sequence is a necessary starting-point toward the goal Young himself has in mind and which he himself adheres to in his very successful studies of *Pyth.* 3, *Pyth.* 11, and *Isth* 7.

Most, *Measures of Praise* 32 counters Bundy's "curious notion of linear unity" with his own concept called "immanent compositional unity" (42), which turns out in practice to include "symmetry" (52) expressed in implausibly complex diagrams (56, 69-70, 135-136) and in images that are said to organize a poem. Thus in *Isth.* 1 the metaphor (or image) of "yoking," which occurs only in the verb ζεύξω (6)—but is claimed (following Bury) to be present also in ἐναρμόξαι (16)—supposedly explains the organization of the poem (59):

> It is no accident that Pindar has chosen images of *yoking* to thematize the activity of *yoking* which organizes his poem on the level of its form . . . Pindar has taken the cue for his poem from the event which provided its occasion: thinking about what it means to gain a chariot victory by *yoking* horses properly and guiding them well, the poet has chosen to emulate Herodotus' success by repeating his actions within his own poem . . . If Pindar has imitated Herodotus' *yoking*, it is because the athlete's *yoking*, with the help of the gods, has achieved success. Pindar expresses the hope in lines 6-10 that, with the help of the gods, his own *yoking* will prove to be equally successful. (emphasis mine)

All this "yoking" results from the single verb ζεύξω in line 6. W. R. Johnson, *Lyric* 70 approves of Young's critique of linear analysis in order to support his claims that "Pindar's poetry is chiefly about eternity and our feelings about eternity, about the rhythm that is over and beneath our experience, about what we have come to feel and to think (but not to know) about ourselves and the world . . . Beginnings and ends have little meaning and little use here. We are dealing, rather, with parabolas, helixes, crystals, with continuities of metaphors that shape feelings."

sequentially. The very forms that Pindar inherited, such as hymns, contain successive development, as do such devices as priamels and break-offs. The fact that "foil" is "dismissed" should not be construed to mean that it is forgotten or totally irrelevant. "Foil" is a relative word: there are varying shades and degrees of backgrounds. What, really, do winds and drenching rains have to do with athletic victory? And yet they are of essential importance in the sequential reading of *Ol.* 11, for Pindar establishes a logical link between them and the victory song.[12] The progressive specification and relevance that one sees operating throughout the odes shows that Pindar conceived of his poems as moving in time. Again and again in this study we shall see that Pindar constructs his language in climactic order, the very perception of which requires sequential reading.

In his analysis of *Isth.* 1, Bundy divided the ode into four sections, which he called "crescendos," a particularly apt term in view of the fact that Pindar's odes were musical compositions. But in the present study his term "climax" proves more useful in designating progressions to emphatic, final elements. The more one reads the odes with an ear to performance, the more manifestly the arrangements of cola and periods and the structure of sentences and strophes carefully prepare for climactic moments. To follow the poet as he builds from phrase to phrase by means of various procedures, including increasing length,[13] greater specification, increasing relevance, intensification, and emphatic word placement,

---

[12] The link is logical and rhetorical, not imagistic, as Skulsky, "Language and Meaning" 31 note 28 argues. The application of the modern notion of imagery as a means for interpreting a Pindaric ode is doomed from the start because meaning and structure do not inhere in images. To take three examples, the *Agamemnon* frequently mentions nets and yokes, the language of *Hamlet* is full of references to animals, and Milton's "Lycidas" abounds in allusions to water. These observations are interesting in their own right and the images are certainly appropriate to the themes of these works. But these images do not "organize" their works or by themselves provide meaningful interpretations. As in the case of other features of style, their importance lies in supporting themes, not in creating them. It is telling that Young's interpretation of *Ol.* 7 in terms of "natural" imagery is the least convincing portion of his brilliant *Three Odes*. Cf. Gerber, "Studies in Greek Lyric" 135: "his imagistic interpretation of *O.* 7 is hardly supported by the language of the ode."

[13] In the brief survey of previous work, I have indicated that lines and words are inadequate units for measuring climactic progressions. The logical unit to use is the syllable, for it is measured by time, and the ear easily hears a difference between, say, five and seven syllables, whereas it cannot distinguish between five and seven words (which may vary in length by many syllables) or between five and seven irregular lines of lyric verse. For example, at *Isth.* 1.32-33 (an example mentioned by Thummer) the listener can hear an increase of length from Ἰσθμῷ τε ζαθέᾳ to Ὀγχηστίαισίν τ' ἀιόνεσσιν, not because the second element has more words (which it does not), but because it has four more syllables. Strictly speaking, one should distinguish between long and short syllables in counting the length of elements, but in practice it proves unnecessary because the distribution of longs and shorts remains quite constant and affects only a very small number of cases where such accuracy becomes pedantic. Throughout the study I have simply counted syllables.

is to recapture some of the spirit with which the ode was meant to affect its original listeners.[14]

I have always maintained that the proof—and justification—of any literary approach lies in its ability to illuminate particular passages in relation to their poems and, ultimately, to all the poet's works. For that reason I have provided an abundance of examples and cross-references. Where appropriate I have analyzed long passages, and the final chapter is devoted to the close analysis of an entire ode. To facilitate the readers' task in following the discussion of fine points of style, I have provided translations for each passage under discussion that adhere as closely as possible to the plain sense and lineation of the original.[15]

---

[14] A result of this study—one not envisioned when I began—is the continual validation of Boeckh's colometry.

[15] On the whole, I have used the text in the eighth edition of S-M (1987), which contains a number of orthographical changes from earlier editions (e.g., ἴυγγι instead of ἴϋγγι at *Nem.* 4.35). In some cases, however, I have maintained the text of previous editions (e.g., ἦτορ instead of ἆτορ at *Nem.* 4.35; Σωκλείδα᾽ instead of Wilamowitz' Σαοκλείδα᾽ at *Nem.* 6.21; and the comma after, not before, αὐτᾷ at *Ol.* 13.53). In addition, I treat *Isth.* 3 and 4 as separate poems and read ἀφροσυνᾶν (e pap.) at *Ol.* 2.52, τετράτοις at *Ol.* 8.46, εὐκλέϊξας at *Pyth.* 9.91, and ἄλλος at *Nem.* 4.39.

CHAPTER 1
CLIMACTIC ELEMENTS IN PINDAR'S VERSE

Scholars have devoted attention to many individual features of Pindaric style, but none has studied in any detail the subtle interplay between style, rhetoric, and colometry that is a regular feature of Pindar's verse. In this chapter I will address one of the most important manifestations of that interplay in what may be called "rising" elements, where groups of three or more units are marked by an effect of climax. This climactic progression results from five principles which often work in concert: increasing length, greater specification, intensification,[1] increasing relevance, and emphatic placement. Although these principles apply throughout the odes, they can best be seen in three types of passages: priamels, hymnal addresses, and catalogues. We shall conclude by examining one particularly impressive series at *Pyth.* 3.61-76.

Priamels

We shall begin with four examples composed in the same year, 476. The opening of *Ol.* 1 provides a good model:

> (1)Ἄριστον μὲν ὕδωρ, (2)ὁ δὲ χρυσὸς αἰθόμενον πῦρ
> ἅτε διαπρέπει νυκτὶ μεγάνορος ἔξοχα πλούτου·
> (3)εἰ δ' ἄεθλα γαρύεν
> ἔλδεαι, φίλον ἦτορ,
> 5 μηκέτ' ἀελίου σκόπει
> ἄλλο θαλπνότερον ἐν ἁμέρᾳ φαεν-
> νὸν ἄστρον ἐρήμας δι' αἰθέρος,
> μηδ' Ὀλυμπίας ἀγῶνα φέρτερον αὐδάσομεν.

---

[1] As we shall see, intensification can be achieved by a variety of means, including emphatic words, such as particles (e.g., δέ), adjectives (e.g., θαυμαστός, αἰνός), adverbs (e.g., ἐξόχως), imperatives (e.g., γεγωνητέον), finite verbs (e.g., ἕλκομαι), or nouns connoting preeminence (e.g., ἀέλιος). Demetrios, περὶ ἑρμ. 50-51 notes that in the elevated style more vivid words (ὀνόματα ἐναργέστερα) are placed last.

>   (1)Best is water, (2)but then gold, like fire gleaming at night,
>   shines preeminent in lordly wealth;
>   (3)but if it is athletics
>   you wish to sing of, dear heart,
> 5   then look no further than the sun
>   for another daytime star shining
>   more warmly through the empty sky,
>   nor let us proclaim a contest greater than Olympia.

This priamel consists of three blocks. The first is extremely concise and contains only 6 syllables, Ἄριστον μὲν ὕδωρ; the second consists of 26 syllables, while the third is more than twice as long with 58 syllables. We see here what German scholarship has labeled in another context *das Gesetz der wachsenden Glieder* (the law of increasing elements).[2] Although its existence has occasionally been noted, particularly in Kambylis' analysis of hymnal style, we shall see that it is found throughout the odes and constitutes one of the most distinctive features of Pindar's style.

But much more is going on in this passage than a simple increase in the length of each part. In addition, there is what might be called the "principle of greater specificity." The first element, "best is water," is so general as to be open to many interpretations.[3] The second element specifies gold as the greatest kind of wealth, but still remains on a generic level,[4] whereas the third is the most specific of all, for it singles out a unique entity with a proper name, the Olympic games.

Also operating in this passage is a "principle of intensification," which is first apparent in the second member, where a simile asserts the superiority of gold by comparing it with fire gleaming in the night, but is clearest in the syntax of the third element with the direct address, the personal expression "dear heart" (φίλον ἦτορ), the imperative (μηκέτ'... σκόπει), and the first person in αὐδάσομεν.[5] But this increasing intensity can also be seen in the comparisons in the last two elements. In the second, gold stands out "like (ἅτε) fire gleaming at night," but in the third the ἅτε disappears and the simile is intensified into a "Vergleich ohne wie": "then look no further than the sun for another daytime star shining more warmly through the empty sky."[6] The fire gleaming at night is surpassed by the

---

[2] The term comes from Behaghel, "Satzgliedern" 110-142. Subsequent notices appear at Lauer, *Zur Wortstellung* 71-77, Fraenkel, *Agamemnon* 3.574, Wilkinson, *Golden Latin Artistry* 175-178, Kambylis, "Anredeformen" 177-179, Thummer, *Die Isthmischen Gedichte I* 148-149, Maehler, *Bakchylides I*. ii 86, 160, 208, and 283, and Gerber, *Olympian One* 4.

[3] See Race, "Best is Water" 119-124.

[4] While water is of use to all creatures, gold and wealth are valued only by humans (cf. *Isth.* 5.2-3: μεγασθενῆ νόμισαν χρυσὸν ἄνθρωποι περιώσιον ἄλλων).

[5] As we shall see, imperatives and first-personal expressions regularly mark a climax, as do proper names and words connoting affection or love.

[6] Demetrios, περὶ ἑρμ. 78-80 points out that metaphors are a mark of grandeur and employing them is riskier (κινδυνωδέστερος) than using a simile.

warm sun in the daytime alone visible in the sky. There is even a considerable increase of length in these two comparisons: the first consists of 9 syllables, the second of 26 syllables. Finally, the last member, emphatically introduced at the beginning of its verse (or period), contains the relevant item, the Olympic games.[7] All of these principles of increasing length, specificity, intensity, relevance, and emphatic position operate together to sculpt this magnificent passage.

An abbreviated form of this priamel occurs in another ode written in the same year, *Ol.* 3.42-44:

> (1)εἰ δ' ἀριστεύει μὲν ὕδωρ, (2)κτεάνων δὲ
>   χρυσὸς αἰδοιέστατος,
> (3)νῦν δὲ πρὸς ἐσχατιὰν
>   Θήρων ἀρεταῖσιν ἱκάνων ἅπτεται
> οἴκοθεν Ἡρακλέος σταλᾶν.

> (1)If water is preeminent, (2)but gold
>   the most honored of possessions,
> (3)now in fact Theron by his achievements
>   comes to the limit
> and from his home reaches the Pillars of Herakles.

This example adheres to precisely the same principles we saw in *Ol.* 1. Each additional member is longer than the preceding one, especially the last. There is increasing specificity from the very generalized "water is preeminent" to the slightly more qualified "gold is the most honored of possessions" to the individual man, Theron. Pindar uses a syntactical means to secure the rise in intensity towards the end of the series, for the first two elements are hypothetical, whereas the last, signalled by the prominent νῦν δέ, gives the apodosis, to which the first two elements are logically subordinated. This example also shows the remarkable ability of Pindar to give variety to standard topics.[8]

Another example of this tripartite structure occurs in *Ol.* 2, in answer to the opening rhapsodic question: "Lyre-ruling hymns, what god, what hero, and what man shall we celebrate?" The three questions themselves adumbrate the climactic order of the forthcoming answers:[9]

---

[7] The last-mentioned item in a series naturally receives emphasis. See Demetrios, περὶ ἑρμ. 39: "We all remember in a special degree, and are stirred by, the words that come first and the words that come last, whereas those that come between them have less effect upon us, as though they were obscured or hidden among the others" (W. R. Roberts, trans.). For examples in Hesiod, see West, *Theogony* 204. For the last item in a priamel, see Bundy, "Quarrel" 78.

[8] For further examples, see *Appendix 3*.

[9] Note the emphatic δ' (2) and the ringing first personal verb in the third element of the question, κελαδήσομεν. τίνα δ' ἄνδρα (2) is specified by Θήρωνα δέ (5) and κελαδήσομεν (2) is intensified by γεγωνητέον (6).

Ἀναξιφόρμιγγες ὕμνοι,
τίνα θεόν, τίν' ἥρωα, τίνα δ' ἄνδρα κελαδήσομεν;
(1)ἤτοι Πίσα μὲν Διός· (2)Ὀλυμπιάδα
δ' ἔστασεν Ἡρακλέης
ἀκρόθινα πολέμου·
5 (3)Θήρωνα δὲ τετραορίας ἕνεκα νικαφόρου
γεγωνητέον, ὅπι δίκαιον ξένων,
ἔρεισμ' Ἀκράγαντος,
— εὐωνύμων τε πατέρων ἄωτον ὀρθόπολιν.

Lyre-ruling hymns,
what god, what hero, and what man shall we celebrate?
(1) Yes, Pisa belongs to Zeus, (2) and the Olympic contest
was established by Herakles
from spoils of war;
5 (3) but Theron, because of his victorious four-horse chariot,
must be proclaimed, just in his regard for guests,
bulwark of Akragas,
— and chief among famous ancestors as upholder of his city.

These three elements are clearly of increasing length—respectively of 7, 19, and 48 syllables. The first, Πίσα μὲν Διός, is very brief; like ἄριστον μὲν ὕδωρ, it contains no verb. The second member contains a miniature plot that recounts the founding of the games. The third element, by far the longest of the three, celebrates Theron for his victory and his noble qualities.[10] Although it might at first seem odd to speak of the progression of god, hero, and man as one of increasing specificity, I think that this is indeed the case. The gods are more distant and more universal; they are immortal, and therefore atemporal. The hero, Herakles, is distant in time. But Theron is a specific, historical man, a citizen of Akragas, and present in the *hic et nunc* of the ode. There is concomitant intensification in the syntax, particularly in regard to the verbs. In the first member, an ἐστί must be supplied; in the second, the finite verb ἔστασεν merely states a fact in the past; the third contains a forceful imperative: γεγωνητέον. Also, there is a small matter of style in the arrangement of names. In the first two elements, the place and festival come first (Πίσα μὲν Διός and Ὀλυμπιάδα δ' ἔστασεν Ἡρακλέης),

---

[10] The three qualities for which Theron is praised (6-7) also rise to a climax with the third and longest element, which is introduced at the beginning of its line and completes the strophe:

(1)ὅπι δίκαιον ξένων,
(2)ἔρεισμ' Ἀκράγαντος,
— (3)εὐωνύμων τε πατέρων ἄωτον ὀρθόπολιν.

Appropriately it is the last item which is elaborated in the antistrophe: καμόντες οἳ [viz. πατέρες] πολλά (8).

whereas the last opens at the beginning of the line with the prominent personal name, Θήρωνα, followed by the place-name 'Ακράγαντος. Finally, the climactic item gains a sense of finality by completing the strophe.

The fourth example is the opening of *Ol.* 11:

>   (1)Ἔστιν ἀνθρώποις ἀνέμων ὅτε πλεῖστα
>   χρῆσις· (2)ἔστιν δ' οὐρανίων ὑδάτων,
>   ὀμβρίων παίδων νεφέλας·
>   (3)εἰ δὲ σὺν πόνῳ τις εὖ πράσσοι, μελιγάρυες ὕμνοι
> 5 ὑστέρων ἀρχὰ λόγων
> — τέλλεται καὶ πιστὸν ὅρκιον μεγάλαις ἀρεταῖς.

>   (1)There is a time when men's greatest need
>   is for winds; (2)there is a time when it is for heavenly waters,
>   drenching children of the cloud;
>   (3)but if through toil someone succeeds, honey-sounding hymns
> 5 become the basis for later words of renown,
> — and a sure pledge for great achievements.

Once again the three elements are of increasing length. The first item of need is named outright, ἀνέμων. The second is more elaborately described and provided its genealogy. One may wonder at this point just why Pindar goes out of his way to add the decorative epithets, ὀμβρίων παίδων νεφέλας (3), to the words οὐρανίων ὑδάτων, which are themselves sufficient for conveying the sense of rainwater. But by keeping in mind the principles we have been observing, we can see that these epithets provide at least three stylistic advantages. First, they give the weight of extra syllables and impressive sound to the second member. They also contribute a sense of specificity: in contrast to the mere mention of winds (ἀνέμων), these children of the cloud are more precisely described. Finally, the epithet ὀμβρίων ("drenching") adds an element of intensity—this is not just a sprinkle, but a cloud-burst. There is also a suggestion that, since there is need for such a cloud-burst, the lack is all the greater.

After this stylistic build-up, the climactic term exhibits, as so often in priamels, a change of syntax. The prominent σὺν πόνῳ τις εὖ πράσσοι (4) indicates a switch from the realm of nature (and of natural needs) to the realm of human effort and achievement.[11] There is also a subtle shift of emphasis from men in general (ἀνθρώποις, 1), who depend upon wind and rain for transportation and farming, to an individual τις (4) who may succeed (εὖ πράσσοι). The

---

[11] The movement from natural, divine, or merely external considerations to successful human action occurs frequently in climactic passages. Cf. *Ol.* 1.3 (ἄεθλα), *Ol.* 2.5 (νικαφόρου), *Ol.* 3.43 (ἀρεταῖσιν), *Ol.* 4.8 (Οὐλυμπιονίκαν), *Pyth.* 2.2 (ἀνδρῶν), *Pyth.* 2.51 (βροτῶν), *Pyth.* 8.5 (Πυθιόνικον), and *Nem.* 8.38 (ἀστοῖς ἁδών), to mention just some of those analyzed in this chapter.

emphatic σὺν πόνῳ suggests that Pindar is contrasting those times when men are dependent upon external things (winds and rains) with those times when it is through his own effort that a person succeeds. And then, of course, after his success, he is once again dependent upon external support from poets to commemorate his deeds and perpetuate the accounts of them (ὑστέρων λόγων, 5). As in the previous example, the climactic entry completes the strophe.

There is a further important stylistic feature in the passages we have examined in these four Olympian odes: the two preliminary elements are linked in midverse, whereas the climactic one is introduced at the beginning of its line. Although Pindar does not always follow this arrangement, its occurrence is so frequent and striking that it constitutes a regular feature of his style. The fact that these four examples were written the same year may suggest that Pindar was particularly attracted to this type of composition at the height of his career, but, as we shall see, there are many other Pindaric passages constructed on the same principles.[12]

Pindar, however, is no slave to a mere pattern, and shows great ingenuity in variation, as at *Ol.* 9.67-70, where he reviews the numerous immigrants who came to Opous before singling out the most important one:

ἀφίκοντο δέ οἱ ξένοι
(1a)ἔκ τ' Ἄργεος (1b)ἔκ τε Θη-
βᾶν, (2a)οἱ δ' Ἀρκάδες, (2b)οἱ δὲ καὶ Πισᾶται·
(3)υἱὸν δ' Ἄκτορος ἐξόχως τίμασεν ἐποίκων
70 Αἰγίνας τε Μενοίτιον. τοῦ παῖς . . .

And foreigners came to him
(1a)from Argos (1b)and from Thebes,
      (2a)and some were Arkadians, (2b)and still others Pisans.
      (3)But of the settlers he most honored the son of Aktor
70 and Aigina, Menoitios. His son . . .

Here each of the first two members is divided into two parts, with subtle variation in each. The first pair (consisting of ἐκ with the name of the city) is connected with the merely additive τε . . . τε. The second pair (which names the inhabitants of their cities) is joined at mid-line and achieves a slightly more climactic effect with the rising δ' . . . δὲ καί and with the weight of two more syllables. The final, climactic term is introduced emphatically at the beginning of its line, is far more

---

[12] For examples of climactic items introduced at the beginning of a line and preceded by two rising elements linked at mid-line, cf. *Ol.* 1.3-7, 31-32, 37-40; 2.5-7, 7; 3.43-44; 4.8-10; 8.15-18; 9.69-70; 11.4-6; *Pyth.* 1.15-16, 79-80; 2.88; 10.59; 11.2; *Nem.* 3.56-58; 5.52-54; 7.79; 11.14; *Isth.* 1.33-34; and 5.63. For other instances of climactic elements at the beginning of lines, cf. *Ol.* 4.16; 11.19; *Pyth.* 1.40; 4.90-92; 10.25-26; *Nem.* 4.27, 35, 54-58; 8.3; and *Isth.* 7.12-15.

specific (υἱὸν Ἄκτορος... Αἰγίνας τε), intense (ἐξόχως, 69), and contains more syllables than all of the foil terms combined.[13] It is obviously of relevance in an ode for Opountians, who prided themselves on Menoitios (whose name is reserved for climactic effect until the very end of its member)—and on his son (τοῦ παῖς, 70), Patroklos, whom Pindar goes on to praise extensively (70-79).

At *Nem.* 8.37-39 a climactically arranged priamel highlights Pindar's poetic program.

(1)χρυσὸν εὔχον-
ται, (2)πεδίον δ' ἕτεροι
ἀπέραντον, (3)ἐγὼ δ' ἀστοῖς ἁδὼν καὶ χθονὶ γυῖα καλύψαι,
αἰνέων αἰνητά, μομφὰν δ' ἐπισπείρων ἀλιτροῖς.

(1)Some pray for
gold, (2)others for land
without end, (3)but I pray to please my townsmen until earth covers me,
praising what is praiseworthy, and casting blame on evildoers.

The first element simply names gold. The second item, land, is qualified by the emphatically enjambed adjective ἀπέραντον (38) "without end," which suggests the limitless greed of those who desire material possessions. In contrast, the poet prays to conduct himself honorably by maintaining a proper relationship with his fellow townsmen (note the emphatic collocation of ἐγὼ δ' ἀστοῖς, 38). The final line, which ends the strophe, emphatically states the two functions of Pindar's epideictic poetry: to praise and to blame.[14]

The final priamel for consideration is the roll call of the battles in 480 and 479 in which the Greeks defeated armies invading from east and west (*Pyth.* 1.75-80):

75   ἀρέομαι
(1)πὰρ μὲν Σαλαμῖνος Ἀθαναίων χάριν
μισθόν, (2)ἐν Σπάρτᾳ δ' ⟨ἀπὸ⟩ τᾶν πρὸ Κιθαιρῶ-
νος μαχᾶν,
ταῖσι Μήδειοι κάμον ἀγκυλότοξοι,
(3)παρ⟨ὰ⟩ δὲ τὰν εὔυδρον ἀκτὰν
Ἱμέρα παίδεσσιν ὕμνον Δεινομένεος τελέσαις,
80   τὸν ἐδέξαντ' ἀμφ' ἀρετᾷ, πολεμίων ἀνδρῶν καμόντων.

---

[13] Note also the shift from ξένοι (67) to ἐποίκων (69).
[14] In these two rising elements Pindar emphasizes blame in order to round off the preceding ψόγος of the Greeks for their treatment of Aias (26-34). In the next sentence at the beginning of the antistrophe he reasserts the positive function of poetry: ἀίσσει δ' ἀρετά ... (40).

```
75                                    I shall earn
    (1)from telling of Salamis the Athenians' favor
        as my reward, (2)and the Spartans' by telling of the battles
        before Mt. Kithairon,
        in which the curve-bowed Medes were beaten;
    (3)but beside the well-watered bank of the Himeras
        I shall pay to Deinomenes' sons the tribute of my hymn,
80      which they earned by their valor, when their enemies were defeated.
)—
```

Each element is longer than the preceding one, with greatest weight given to the last-mentioned. The first two, Salamis and Plataia, come in chronological order, and the second is given greater emphasis and precision by the relative clause, "in which the curve-bowed Medes were beaten." This clause also separates these two victories over the Persians from the climactic battle of Himera against the Carthaginians. The increased specificity of the last item begins with the descriptive epithet εὔυδρον (79), but is most apparent in the fact that individuals are singled out by name (παίδεσσιν Δειμονένεος, 79). Once again the foil terms are linked together in mid-line, whereas the climactic example of Himera is introduced at the beginning of its line and continues until the end of the triad. Although Pindar does not actually say that the battle of Himera is of greater importance than the other two, the formal emphasis that it receives puts it at least on a par with them. Of course, it is the most relevant item in an ode for Hieron, tactfully included among "Deinomenes' sons."

Hymnal Invocations and Requests

The principles we have been tracing are very much in evidence in Pindar's hymns and prayers,[15] though in his use of rising cola in hymnal invocations, Pindar was drawing on a tradition at least as old as Homer.[16] The prayer at *Ol.* 2.12-15 provides a good starting point for Pindaric practice:

---

[15] For a very brief survey of increasing elements in hymnal invocations, see Kambylis, "Anredeformen" 177-179.

[16] For example, Chryses opens his prayer at *Il.* 1.37 with a rising tricolon:

(1)κλῦθί μευ, (2)ἀργυρότοξ', (3)ὃς Χρύσην ἀμφιβέβηκας.

This line, similar to what Kirk, *Iliad I* 20 calls a "rising threefolder," is especially well suited to addresses, as at *Il.* 2.8: (1)βάσκ' ἴθι, (2)οὖλε ὄνειρε, (3)θοὰς ἐπὶ νῆας Ἀχαιῶν (cf. *Il.* 2.110, 246, 3.276, 277, etc.). The remainder of Chryses' prayer consists of rising pairs: Κίλλαν τε ζαθέην → Τενέδοιό τε ἶφι ἀνάσσεις (38) and εἴ ποτέ τοι χαρίεντ' ἐπὶ νηὸν ἔρεψα → ἢ εἰ δὴ ποτέ τοι κατὰ πίονα μηρί' ἔκηα ταύρων ἠδ' αἰγῶν (39-41). The request is also introduced at the beginning of its line (42).

(1)ἀλλ' ὦ Κρόνιε παῖ 'Ρέας, (2)ἕδος 'Ολύμπου νέμων
ἀέθλων τε κορυφὰν πόρον τ' 'Αλφεοῦ,
(3)ἰανθεὶς ἀοιδαῖς
εὔφρων ἄρουραν ἔτι πατρίαν σφίσιν κόμισον
15   λοιπῷ γένει.

(1)But, O son of Kronos and Rhea, (2)ruling over your abode on Olympos
and over the pinnacle of contests and over the ford of Alpheos,
(3)cheered by my songs
willingly preserve their native land for their
15   offspring yet to come.

The first and shortest element names Zeus through his genealogy. The second, a participial clause (*Partizipialstil*), gives his *sedes* (cf. ἕδος, 12), beginning with the most distant (Olympos), adding the programmatic word ἀέθλων at the beginning of the verse, and ending with the most relevant place name (Alpheos). The third member contains the request; the imperative naturally gives it a sense of climax and completion.[17]

The prayer at *Pyth.* 1.39-40 provides an even better example of increasing geographical relevance (along with increasing length, precision, and intensity):

(1)Λύκιε (2)καὶ Δάλοι' ἀνάσσων
Φοῖβε (3)Παρνασσοῦ τε κράναν Κασταλίαν φιλέων,
40   (4)ἐθελήσαις ταῦτα νόῳ τιθέμεν εὔανδρόν τε χώραν.
)—

(1)Lord of Lykia (2)and you, Phoibos, who rule over
Dalos (3)and who love Parnassos' Kastalian spring,
40   (4)willingly take these things to heart and make this a land of brave men.
)—

The first element, an epithet of three syllables, refers to Apollo's *sedes* in Lykia, the geographical location furthest from the site of the games.[18] The second element is longer, the island of Delos is closer to mainland Greece, and the participle ἀνάσσων adds a degree of intensity lacking in the lone epithet Λύκιε. The third element, however, is the longest and contains the most specific location (κράναν Κασταλίαν, 39); in addition, the participle φιλέων conveys greater warmth than ἀνάσσων. The passage moves progressively from the district of

---

[17] For the rhetorical purpose served by the geographical features in this prayer, see below pages 130-131.
[18] Sulzer, *Zur Wortstellung und Satzbildung* 18 tries to force the sentence into a chiastic scheme by making a unit of Λύκιε Φοῖβε and claiming that "Das καί entspricht dem folgenden τε." But the only way to make sense of the καί is to take Λύκιε and Φοῖβε as separate titles: it is Phoibos who rules over Delos and Delphi. Cf. Φοῖβ' ἄναξ Δήλιε at Aristoph. *Nub.* 595.

Lykia, to the small island of Delos, to the mountain Parnassos, and to the specific spring, Kastalia. This geographical survey of Apollo's *sedes* occupies one long period; the emphatic position at the beginning of the following line is reserved for the request (4), which completes the triad.[19]

Ol. 4.6-10 provides a further variation:

> (1)ἀλλὰ Κρόνου παῖ, (2)ὃς Αἴτναν ἔχεις
> ἷπον ἀνεμόεσσαν ἑκατογκεφάλα
> Τυφῶνος ὀβρίμου,
> (3)Οὐλυμπιονίκαν
> — δέξαι Χαρίτων θ' ἕκατι τόνδε κῶμον,
> 10 χρονιώτατον φάος εὐρυσθενέων ἀρετᾶν.

> (1)But, son of Kronos, (2)you who rule Aitna,
> windy burden for hundred-headed
> Typhos the mighty,
> (3)receive an Olympic victor
> — and, for the sake of the Graces, this celebration,
> 10 longest-lasting light for achievements of great strength.

Although this example contains the same three formal elements as the prayer at *Ol*. 2.12-15 (name and genealogy, *sedes*, and request), there are subtle differences. The second member, which provides the *sedes*, is a relative clause (*Relativstil*). The choice of Mt. Aitna is obviously relevant in an ode to a Sicilian, but the further details about Typhos' imprisonment under the mountain serve as a *hypomnesis* that recalls Zeus' victory over the monster and disposes him toward favoring another victor's mighty deeds (cf. εὐρυσθενέων ἀρετᾶν, 10). The request comes at the beginning of its line with the emphatic Οὐλυμπιονίκαν (8) and focuses attention on this specific celebration (τόνδε κῶμον, 9).

A similar increase of elements occurs at *Ol*. 7.87-89, where the request is divided into two parts:

---

[19] Cf. the invocation which opens the Pythian section of the Homeric *Hymn to Apollo* 179-181:

> (1)ὦ ἄνα, (2)καὶ Λυκίην (3)καὶ Μῃονίην ἐρατεινὴν
> 180 (4)καὶ Μίλητον ἔχεις ἔναλον πόλιν ἱμερόεσσαν,
> (5)αὐτὸς δ' αὖ Δήλοιο περικλύστου μέγ' ἀνάσσεις.

Note the geographical progression from Lykia to Lydia, to the maritime city of Miletos (all introduced by καί), and, climactically (cf. δ' αὖ, 181), to the island of Delos, over which Apollo himself "rules in power." For an analysis of these climactic elements, see Miller, *Hymn to Apollo* 66.

(1)ἀλλ' ὦ
Ζεῦ πάτερ, (2)νώτοισιν Ἀταβυρίου
μεδέων, (3a)τίμα μὲν ὕμνου τεθμὸν Ὀλυμπιονίκαν,
(3b)ἄνδρα τε πὺξ ἀρετὰν εὑρόντα.

(1)But, O
father Zeus, (2)you who rule Atabyrion's
slopes, (3a)honor this hymn's due praise of an Olympic victor
(3b)and the man who has won achievement at boxing.

The invocation and request exhibit increasing specificity: from Zeus, father of all, to his *sedes* on Mt. Atabyrion on Rhodes, to the celebratory song, to the man who has succeeded at boxing. As usual, the invocatory elements are joined in mid-line, but so too is the first part of the request. Pindar gives careful weight to these two parts. On the one hand, the first (3a) is longer and ends with the ringing Ὀλυμπιονίκαν; on the other hand, the μὲν ... τε construction slightly shifts the weight to the second part (3b), which is introduced by the emphatic ἄνδρα at the beginning of the epode and mentions the specific event.

We shall conclude this brief survey of hymnal addresses with the hymn to Hesychia that opens *Pyth.* 8, in which Pindar creates an additional element in the invocation by separating the goddess' name from her genealogy:

(1)Φιλόφρον Ἡσυχία, (2)Δίκας
ὦ μεγιστόπολι θύγατερ,
(3)βουλᾶν τε καὶ πολέμων
ἔχοισα κλαῖδας ὑπερτάτας
5 (4)Πυθιόνικον τιμὰν Ἀριστομένει δέκευ.

(1)Loving-minded Peace, (2)O daughter of Justice,
   maintainer of great cities,
(3)who hold the highest keys
   of counsels and wars,
5 (4)accept this honor due the Pythian victor Aristomenes.

After the announcement of the goddess' name (1), each element is increasingly specific. In the second element the name of her mother Δίκα and the epithet μεγιστόπολι define Hesychia's role as maintainer of that peace which derives from justice and makes cities great. The third turns to those activities of the polis which chiefly fall within her power, counsels and wars (cf. *Ol.* 12.4-5, of Tycha). Finally, the request opens at the beginning of its line with the ringing Πυθιόνικον (cf. Οὐλυμπιονίκαν at *Ol.* 4.8, quoted above) and introduces a specific individual by name. The climactic progression from a colorless verbal form (ἔχοι-

σα, 4) to an imperative (δέκευ, 5) parallels the examples at *Ol*. 2.12-14 (νέμων
... κόμισον) and at *Ol*. 4.6-9 (ἔχεις ... δέξαι).[20]

Catalogues

Many lists in Pindar are arranged climactically.[21] On three occasions he uses a rising tricolon to elaborate a form of πᾶς.

---

[20] *Nem*. 8 opens with increasing elements of greater specificity, as does *Pyth*. 2.1-2:

(1)Μεγαλοπόλιες ὦ Συράκοσαι, (2)βαθυπολέμου
τέμενος Ἄρεος, (3)ἀνδρῶν ἵππων τε σιδαροχαρ-
μᾶν δαιμόνιαι τροφοί ...

(1)O great city of Syracuse, (2)sanctuary for
Ares deep in war, (3)divine nourisher of men
and horses that delight in steel ...

Since (1) and (2) contain the same number of syllables, they cannot strictly be said to be of increasing length, but the sense of climax is evident in the much longer third element, which begins with the emphatic ἀνδρῶν and ends with the climactic δαιμόνιαι τροφοί. The invocation in *fr*. 122.1-8 contains five rising elements.

(1)Πολύξεναι νεάνιδες, (2)ἀμφίπολοι
Πειθοῦς ἐν ἀφνειῷ Κορίνθῳ,
(3)αἵ τε τᾶς χλωρᾶς λιβάνου ξανθὰ δάκρη
θυμιᾶτε, (4)πολλάκι ματέρ᾽ ἐρώτων
οὐρανίαν πτάμεναι
5   νοήματι πρὸς Ἀφροδίταν,
)—
(5)ὑμῖν ἄνευθ᾽ ἐπαγορίας ἔπορεν,
ὦ παῖδες, ἐρατειναῖς ⟨ἐν⟩ εὐναῖς
μαλθακᾶς ὥρας ἀπὸ καρπὸν δρέπεσθαι.

(1)Girls who welcome many guests, (2)attendants
of Persuasion in rich Korinth,
(3)you who burn the yellow tears of that fresh
frankincense, (4)often soaring in your thoughts
to the heavenly mother
5   of Loves, Aphrodite;
)—
(5)you, children, she permits to cull
without blame on couches of desire
the fruit of soft youth.

[21] In general, victory catalogues begin with the most important victories (usually the occasion for the ode) and do not build to a climax; rather, they attempt to display accumulative fullness. For that reason, they frequently end with an indication of abundance by means of such words as πᾶς and ὅσσος, after which the poet breaks off and changes to another topic. Cf. *Ol*. 7.80-87 (followed by ἀλλ᾽ ὦ Ζεῦ πάτερ, 87); 9.83-99 (followed by τὸ δὲ φυᾷ κράτιστον ἅπαν, 100); 13.29-46 (ὅσσα, 43); 98-114 (πᾶσαν, 112); *Pyth*. 5.109-117 (ὅσαι, 116); 9.79-103 (πᾶσιν, 102); *Nem*. 2.19-24 (μάσσον᾽ ἀριθμοῦ, 23); 10.2-20 (πάντ᾽... ὅσων, 19), 41-48 (μυρίον, 45); *Isth*. 1.52-63 (πάντα ... ὅσ᾽, 60); and 8.49-55 (ἄλλους τ᾽ ἀριστέας, 55). But

Climactic Elements in Pindar's Verse

Ol. 14.5-7:

5 σὺν γὰρ ὑμῖν τά ⟨τε⟩ τερπνὰ καί
   τὰ γλυκέ᾽ ἄνεται πάντα βροτοῖς,
   (1)εἰ σοφός, (2)εἰ καλός, (3)εἴ τις ἀγλαὸς ἀνήρ.

5 For through your agency *all* things pleasant
   and sweet are accomplished for mortals,
   (1)be he wise, (2)be he handsome, (3)be he an illustrious man.

Pyth. 1.41-42:

ἐκ θεῶν γὰρ μαχαναὶ **πᾶσαι** βροτέαις ἀρεταῖς,
(1)καὶ σοφοὶ (2)καὶ χερσὶ βιαταὶ (3)περίγλωσ-
   σοί τ᾽ ἔφυν.

For from the gods come *all* the means for human achievements:
(1)the wise (2)and strong of hand (3)and those
   who are naturally eloquent.

Pyth. 2.86-88:

ἐν **πάντα** δὲ νόμον εὐθύγλωσσος ἀνὴρ προφέρει,
(1)παρὰ τυραννίδι, (2)χὠπόταν ὁ λάβρος στρατός,
(3)χὤταν πόλιν οἱ σοφοὶ τηρέωντι.

Under *every* government the straight-talking man distinguishes himself,
(1)in a tyranny, (2)when the noisy people rule,
(3)and when the wise guard the city.

In all three cases the last category receives the rhetorical emphasis and is the most important in its context.[22] More complex is the "magnificat" at *Pyth.* 2.49-52.

   θεὸς ἅπαν ἐπὶ ἐλπίδεσσι τέκμαρ ἀνύεται,
50 θεός, (1)ὃ καὶ πτερόεντ᾽ αἰετὸν κίχε, (2)καὶ θαλασ-

Pindar is free to vary the pattern, as at *Isth.* 2.12-29, where, in a career catalogue for the deceased Xenokrates, after devoting 62 syllables to his Isthmian victory, he begins a new series with his Pythian victory (18 syllables), Panathenaic (56 syllables), and his brother's Olympic victory (96 syllables). Pindar allows the Panathenaic victory to break the ascending order of the games because the same charioteer, Nikomachos, drove for Xenokrates at Athens and Theron at Olympia. By ending with the Olympic victory, Pindar stresses the close relationship of the two brothers (Αἰνησιδάμου | παῖδες, 28-29), who share their charioteers and their victories (cf. κοιναὶ Χάριτες at *Ol.* 2.50).

[22] At *Pyth.* 6.46-54, Pindar elaborates ἅπασαν (46) with five elements, and although the last is slightly shorter than the preceding one, it preserves a sense of climax (cf. δέ, 52) and ends the ode.

> σαῖον παραμείβεται
> δελφῖνα, (3a)καὶ ὑψιφρόνων τιν' ἔκαμψε βροτῶν,
> (3b)ἑτέροισι δὲ κῦδος ἀγήραον παρέδωκ'· ἐμὲ δὲ χρεών . . .

> God accomplishes *every* purpose as soon as he wishes,
> 50   God, (1)who overtakes the winged eagle, (2)and surpasses the sea-going
> dolphin, (3a)and bows down one man among haughty mortals,
> (3b)while to others he gives ageless glory. But I must . . .

In the hymnal relative clause that elaborates ἅπαν (49), Pindar gives examples of Zeus' power in the traditional three spheres of air, sea, and land, further subdividing the last element concerning men (βροτῶν, 51) into two parts. The three elements are linked by καί and are of increasing length. Within the first two elements, the verb παραμείβεται ("surpass") intensifies the action of κίχε ("overtake"). The third element gains a sense of climax by moving from the realm of nature to that of human achievement, as Pindar specifies the effects of God's actions in human life. But even within the last member Pindar gives a further intensification and greater weight to the second half (3b) by moving from the harm that comes to a proud man ὑψιφρόνων τιν' (one thinks of Ixion, treated in the previous lines), to the fame that comes to others (viz. Hieron, shortly to be named). As often, the climactic element (3b) is introduced at the beginning of its line, here emphasized by an adversative δέ. The concluding phrase κῦδος ἀγήραον παρέδωκ' effects the shift from negative foil to positive example and permits the poet to intrude (ἐμὲ δέ, 52) and to redirect his program by putting aside his Archilochian blame of Ixion and turning to praise of Hieron.[23]

Lists of an individual's virtues or accomplishments are often arranged in climactic order. For example, the praise of Psaumis of Kamarina at *Ol.* 4.14-16 contains three rising elements:

> ἐπεί νιν αἰνέω, (1)μάλα μὲν τροφαῖς ἑτοῖμον ἵππων,
> 15   (2)χαίροντά τε ξενίαις πανδόκοις,
> (3)καὶ πρὸς Ἡσυχίαν φιλόπολιν καθαρᾷ
> γνώμᾳ τετραμμένον.

> For I praise him, (1)very earnest in his raising of horses,
> 15   (2)delighting in receiving guests from everywhere,
> (3)and devoted to city-loving Hesychia
> with a sincere mind.

The progression of the particles (μὲν . . . τε . . . καί) emphasizes the last as most important. There is some intensification from ἑτοῖμον in the first element to the

---
[23] For an analysis of this transitional passage, see below pages 72-73.

warmer χαίροντα in the second (strengthened by the word πανδόκοις). The third and longest element, emphatically introduced at the beginning of its line by καί, turns to Psaumis' habitual (τετραμμένον) and wholehearted (καθαρᾷ) devotion of mind (γνώμᾳ) to the cause of peace in his city (Ἡσυχίαν φιλόπολιν). This last quality is the most important: it completes the direct praise of Psaumis in this ode and serves as the basis for his praise in its companion ode, *Olympian* 5.[24]

At *Pyth.* 8.78-84 the poet leads up to Aristomenes' Pythian victory through a series of his minor successes:

>   (1)Μεγάροις δ' ἔχεις γέρας,
>   (2)μυχῷ τ' ἐν Μαραθῶνος, (3)"Ηρας τ' ἀγῶν' ἐπιχώριον
> 80 νίκαις τρισσαῖς, ὦ 'Αριστόμενες, δάμασσας ἔργῳ·

[24] This three-fold rising praise is noted by Gerber, "Pindar's *Olympian Four*" 19. There is a variation with four members in praise of a man at *Isth.* 2.37-42 (noted by Thummer, *Die Isthmischen Gedichte I* 149 and *II* 49):

>   (1)αἰδοῖος μὲν ἦν ἀστοῖς ὁμιλεῖν,
>   (2)ἱπποτροφίας τε νομίζων
>   ἐν Πανελλάνων νόμῳ·
>   (3)καὶ θεῶν δαῖτας προσέ-
>   πτυκτο πάσας· (4)οὐδέ ποτε ξενίαν
> 40 οὖρος ἐμπνεύσαις ὑπέστειλ' ἱστίον ἀμφὶ τράπεζαν·
>   ἀλλ' ἐπέρα ποτὶ μὲν Φᾶσιν θερείαις,
>   ἐν δὲ χειμῶνι πλέων Νείλου πρὸς ἀκτάν.

>   (1)He was esteemed in the company of his townsmen,
>   (2)he practiced horse-breeding
>   in the Panhellenic manner,
>   (3)and welcomed all the feasts
>   of the gods. (4)And never did a wind
> 40 cause him to furl the sails at his hospitable table,
>   but he would travel to Phasis in the summer
>   and in winter sail to the shore of the Nile.

Although the third member is slightly shorter than the preceding one, there is an intensification of particles (μὲν... τε... καὶ... δέ), with the widening progression from citizens to Panhellenic games, to festivals of the gods, and to the climactic depiction in three and one-half lines of the extent of Xenokrates' generosity to guests (ξενίαν, 39), which rises from negative (οὐδέ, 39) to positive (ἀλλ', 41) and ends the antistrophe. Cf. also the praise of the Western Lokrians at *Ol.* 11.17-19, where the climactic element switches to the positive:

>   (1)φυγόξεινον στρατόν
>   (2)μήτ' ἀπείρατον καλῶν
>   (3)ἀκρόσοφόν τε καὶ αἰχματὰν ἀφίξεσθαι.

>   [there you will meet no] (1)people who shun a guest
>   (2)or are inexperienced in noble things;
>   (3)they have great wisdom and martial strength.

)—
    (4)τέτρασι δ' ἔμπετες ὑψόθεν
    σωμάτεσσι κακὰ φρονέων,
    τοῖς οὔτε νόστος ὁμῶς
    ἔπαλπνος ἐν Πυθιάδι κρίθη . . .

                (1)At Megara you hold the prize,
    (2)and in the plain of Marathon, (3)and you dominated Hera's local contest
80   with three victories, Aristomenes, by your effort.
)—
    (4)And upon four boys' bodies you fell from above
    with hostile intent,
    for whom no homecoming as joyous as yours
    was decided at the Pythian festival . . .

The first location, Megara, is simply named; the second is designated by its main topographical feature (μυχῷ, 79); the third element proudly announces three victories and contains an address to the athlete; the fourth, introduced at the beginning of the triad, contains an elaborate account of his Pythian victory. The emphatic τέτρασι (81) neatly tops the τρισσαῖς (80) of the local entry, subtly implying that his one Pythian victory over four opponents outweighed his three local successes.

    At *Pyth.* 10.23-26, in praise of the victor's father, who had won two Olympic victories, Pindar declares that a man is happy and praiseworthy who fulfills the following conditions:

    (1)ὃς ἂν χερσὶν (2)ἢ ποδῶν ἀρετᾷ κρατήσαις
    (3)τὰ μέγιστ' ἀέθλων ἕλῃ τόλμᾳ τε καὶ σθένει,
25   (4)καὶ ζώων ἔτι νεαρόν
    κατ' αἶσαν υἱὸν ἴδῃ τυχόντα στεφάνων Πυθίων.

    (1)who with his hands (2)or with the might of his feet achieves victory
    (3)and wins the greatest of the contests with courage and strength,
25   (4)and while still living sees his son
    appropriately win Pythian crowns.

Although the first item, χερσίν, has some point in referring to a victor of the race in armor, the weightier ποδῶν ἀρετᾷ shifts the focus onto the more pertinent category. The third element alludes to the Olympic games, but without naming them, in order to avoid bathos when the Pythian games are named. The last element climactically introduces the most important condition at the beginning of the antistrophe (with emphatic καί), reserving the ringing στεφάνων Πυθίων for emphatic last position. The passage carefully builds toward the present victory of Hippokleas in the Pythian games while tactfully acknowledging the father's much more illustrious career; indeed, it implies that the crowning glory of the father's career was the Pythian victory of his son.²⁵

In a similar fashion, at *Ol.* 6.4-7, Pindar lists the conditions that necessitate praise of Hagesias.²⁶ But in this example Pindar faces a different tactical problem, for he does not wish to select just one item for praise. By considering this example, which departs slightly from the pattern we have been following, we can gain insight into the subtle stylistic emphases Pindar gives each passage:

>   (1)εἰ δ' εἴ-
> η μὲν Ὀλυμπιονίκας,
> 5 (2)βωμῷ τε μαντείῳ ταμίας Διὸς ἐν Πίσᾳ,
>   (3)συνοικιστήρ τε τᾶν κλεινᾶν Συρακοσ-
> σᾶν, τίνα κεν φύγοι ὕμνον
> κεῖνος ἀνήρ . . .

>   (1)If he should be
>   an Olympic victor,
> 5   (2)and steward of the altar of Zeus at Pisa,
>   (3)and co-founder of that famous city Syracuse,
>   what hymn of praise would he escape,
>   a man such as that . . .

The first element ends with the ringing Ὀλυμπιονίκας, which in other odes might be the climactic item; here, however, its brevity and the particle μέν indicate that even more important conditions will follow.²⁷ The second, introduced by τε, is longer and more specific (there are many Olympic victors, but few stewards of Zeus' altar at Pisa). At this point Pindar could have added a third, climactic element, perhaps introduced by an emphatic καί, as in two previous examples (*Ol.* 4.16 and *Pyth.* 10.25). But instead, he gives mixed signals. On the one hand, he introduces the third member with τε and gives it two fewer syllables than the second; on the other, it begins with the impressive συνοικιστήρ and ends with the ringing τᾶν κλεινᾶν Συρακοσσᾶν (no Seriphos this!). The reason for this delicate balance between Hagesias' priestly and civic accomplishments becomes clear in the rest of the ode, where both roles receive extended praise. As

---

[25] For variations on the form and content of this passage, see *Appendix 3* pages 189-192.
[26] The similarities of the two passages can be seen from the following paraphrases. At *Pyth.* 10.22 ff. Pindar says "that man deserves song who does x, y, and z" (**ὑμνητὸς οὗτος ἀνήρ** . . . ὃς ἄν . . .); at *Ol.* 6.4 ff. he says "if someone does x, y, and z, what song would that man escape" (εἰ δ' εἴη . . . τίνα κεν φύγοι **ὕμνον κεῖνος ἀνήρ**;).
[27] The fact that the mule race was the least prestigious of the equestrian events may have influenced Pindar to play down somewhat the victory in this ode, but he regularly emphasizes civic and military achievements when praising important men such as Hieron, Theron, and Chromios.

Gildersleeve has pointed out, the entire ode is balanced by pairs;[28] in the case of this versatile man Pindar is careful not to elevate one facet of his achievement at the expense of the other.

Pindar displays similar tact in the opening of *Isth.* 6, when he compares the victories of Lampon's sons to three rounds of drinking at a symposium (3-9):

>   ... (1)ἐν Νεμέᾳ μὲν πρῶτον, ὦ Ζεῦ,
>   τὶν ἄωτον δεξάμενοι στεφάνων,
> 5   (2)νῦν αὖτε Ἰσθμοῦ δεσπότᾳ
>   Νηρεΐδεσσί τε πεντήκοντα παίδων ὁπλοτάτου
>   Φυλακίδα νικῶντος. (3)εἴη δὲ τρίτον
>   σωτῆρι πορσαίνοντας Ὀ-
>   λυμπίῳ Αἴγιναν κάτα
>   — σπένδειν μελιφθόγγοις ἀοιδαῖς.

>   ... (1)First at Nemea, O Zeus,
>   by your favor they received the foremost crowns,
> 5   (2)and now again, by the grace of the Isthmos' lord
>   and the fifty Nereids, the youngest of the sons,
>   Phylakidas, is victorious. (3)May there be a third
>   bowl for us to prepare for Olympian Zeus the
>   Savior and pour a libation for Aigina
>   — consisting of honey-voiced songs.

The three elements move from the past (Pytheas' Nemean victory), to the present (Phylakidas' Isthmian victory), to the future (hopes for an Olympic victory). The earlier victory is mentioned briefly with no specification of victor (δεξάμενοι vaguely credits it to the family), while the second (the occasion of the present ode) is introduced at the beginning of its verse with the emphatic particles νῦν αὖτε and ends with the ringing Φυλακίδα νικῶντος. If the third member were given too much emphasis, it might detract from the present achievement of Phylakidas. Accordingly, three considerations keep it from being completely climactic: it is introduced at mid-line, it is shorter by one syllable than the second element, and it is hypothetical. On the other hand, several factors give it a sense of climax. First is the numerical progression, πρῶτον... αὖτε... τρίτον; second is the progression of particles, μὲν... νῦν αὖτε... δέ; third is the ascending order of the games themselves, Nemean, Isthmian, Olympian; fourth is the fact that the third element concludes the strophe and the whole development, appropriately beginning and ending with Zeus. Pindar is careful to balance the present achievement of Phylakidas against the strong hopes for an Olympic victory in the family without unduly undercutting the former or overly stressing the latter.

---

[28] Gildersleeve, *Pindar* 171-172.

At *Pyth.* 1.13-16 Pindar uses rising elements in a transition to single out a new subject:

> ὅσσα δὲ μὴ πεφίληκε Ζεύς, ἀτύζονται βοάν
> Πιερίδων ἀίοντα, (1)γᾶν τε (2)καὶ πόν-
>   τον κατ' ἀμαιμάκετον,
> 15 (3)ὅς τ' ἐν αἰνᾷ Ταρτάρῳ κεῖται, θεῶν πολέμιος,
>   Τυφὼς ἑκατοντακάρανος ...

> But those creatures without Zeus' love are terrified when they hear
> the shout of the Pierian Muses, (1)those on land (2)and
>   in the overpowering sea,
> 15 (3)and he who lies in dreadful Tartaros, enemy of the gods,
>   Typhos the hundred-headed ...

Just as rising elements specified the word ἅπαν at *Pyth.* 2.49 ff., these three elements elaborate the word ὅσσα by sketching the habitats of Zeus' enemies. There is progressive specification and intensification from the mere mention of γᾶν to the more imposing ἀμαιμάκετον qualifying the sea,[29] and finally, in climactic position at the beginning of its line, emphasized by the sudden shift to the masculine relative pronoun ὅς, we reach dread (αἰνᾷ) Tartaros and the specific monster, whose name is withheld until the beginning of the next verse and given the imposing epithet ἑκατοντακάρανος. The passage provides a transition from the quiet scene on Olympos depicted in the preceding strophe and antistrophe to the striking ekphrasis of Typhos that follows.

At the conclusion of his hymn to Kastor and Iolaos at *Isth.* 1.17-31, Pindar bids farewell to the two heroes and leads up to his new theme through a series of three subjects (32-35):[30]

> χαίρετ'. ἐγὼ δὲ (1)Ποσειδάωνι (2)Ἰσθμῷ τε ζαθέᾳ
> (3)Ὀγχηστίαισίν τ' ἀιόνεσσιν περιστέλλων ἀοιδάν
> (4)γαρύσομαι τοῦδ' ἀνδρὸς ἐν τιμαῖσιν ἀγακλέα τὰν
>   Ἀσωποδώρου πατρὸς αἶσαν
> 35 Ἐρχομενοῖό τε πατρῴαν ἄρουραν ...

> Farewell. But as I attire (1)Poseidon (2)and the sacred Isthmos
> (3)and Onchestos' shores in my song
> (4)I shall proclaim, while honoring this man, that illustrious

---

[29] The τε καί shifts the emphasis to the second member while setting them both apart from the third, introduced by τε. Cf. the progression τ'... καί ... τ' at *Nem.* 4.17-24, where the last element is elaborated in order to establish the ξενία between Pindar and Timasarchos.

[30] See Thummer, *Die Isthmischen Gedichte I* 128, 149 and *II* 20.

>— fortune of his father Asopodoros
35 and Orchomenos, his ancestral estate . . .

This rising series culminates in the Boiotian *sedes* of Poseidon at Onchestos (introduced at the beginning of the line), thus leading geographically to the forthcoming introduction of the father's estate at Orchomenos (35-37). As Bundy has shown, this transition is an adaptation of the rhapsodic closing formula in which the poet declares that he will keep the god in mind as he moves on to a new theme: χαῖρε ... αὐτὰρ ἐγὼ καὶ σεῖο καὶ ἄλλης μνήσομ' ἀοιδῆς.[31] Although Pindar says that he will include in his song Poseidon (the granter of the victory), the Isthmos (the site of the victory), and Onchestos (the Boiotian site of Poseidon's worship), in fact the participle περιστέλλων bypasses them so that Pindar can introduce Asopodoros, the recipient of Poseidon's favor, with the main verb γαρύσομαι (34), emphatically placed at the beginning of the verse, and complete the geographical relevance with the father's estate at Orchomenos, named at the beginning of the triad.

Occasionally Pindar will use a string of imperatives in progressive cola to end an ode, as at *Isth.* 5.62-63:[32]

(1)λάμβανέ οἱ στέφανον, (2)φέρε δ' εὔμαλλον μίτραν,
(3)καὶ πτερόεντα νέον σύμπεμψον ὕμνον.

---

[31] Cf. *h. Hom.* 2.495 *et saepe*; see Bundy, *Studia Pindarica* 46 note 34.
[32] See Thummer, *Die Isthmischen Gedichte I* 149 and *II* 97. More elaborate is the end of *Nem.* 5.50-54:

50   εἰ δὲ Θεμίστιον ἵκεις
      ὥστ' ἀείδειν, μηκέτι ῥίγει· (1)δίδοι
      φωνάν, (2)ἀνὰ δ' ἱστία τεῖνον
      πρὸς ζυγὸν καρχασίου,
      (3)πύκταν τέ νιν καὶ παγκρατίου
      φθέγξαι ἑλεῖν Ἐπιδαύρῳ διπλόαν
      νικῶντ' ἀρετάν, (4)προθύροισιν δ' Αἰακοῦ
      ἀνθέων ποιάεντα φέρε στεφανώ-
      ματα σὺν ξανθαῖς Χάρισσιν.

50   If it is Themistios you have come
      to sing, hold back no longer: (1)give forth
      your voice, (2)hoist the sails to the
      top of the mast,
   (3)proclaim that as a boxer and in the pankration
      he won at Epidauros a double
      victory, (4)and to the portals of Aiakos' temple
      bring the grassy crowns of flowers
      in the company of the Graces.

(1)take up a crown for him, (2)bring a fillet of fine wool,
(3)and send along this winged new song.

Although the second member has an equal number of syllables as the first, its series of long syllables and the epithet εὔμαλλον make it weightier. Once again the climactic member starts at the beginning of its verse, is introduced by an emphatic καί, is given the weight of more epithets, and reserves the most important word until the end, ὕμνον.

Before we turn to the complexities of longer catalogues, one brief example deserves attention, *Nem.* 4.33-35, where Pindar, who had begun to praise Aiginetan heroes by relating the deeds of Telamon, suddenly breaks off, and cites three reasons for discontinuing his catalogue:

τὰ μακρὰ δ' ἐξενέπειν ἐρύκει με (1)τεθμός
(2)ὧραί τ' ἐπειγόμεναι·
35 (3)ἴυγγι δ' ἕλκομαι ἦτορ νεομηνίᾳ θιγέμεν.

But I am prevented from telling the long account by (1)generic constraint (2)and the pressing hours;
35 (3)and by a love-charm I am drawn in my heart to celebrate the new-moon festival.

Each new member is longer and more intense than the preceding one. The first constraint, simply stated as the τεθμός (33), concerns the limitations imposed by the generic rules that govern an epinikion. Although the second reason, the lack of time, is linked only by τε, it is given greater weight and emphasis by its position at the beginning of the line and greater intensity by the adjective ἐπειγόμεναι ("pressing"). The third reason, the poet's own desire to celebrate the victory, is introduced by the more emphatic δ' (35), is in the first person, and is much more intensely felt, as the opening words, ἴυγγι δ' ἕλκομαι ἦτορ, indicate. There is also intensification from ἐρύκει με ("prevents me") to ἕλκομαι ἦτορ ("I am drawn in my heart"). As Miller has pointed out, "To these two external pressures (closely linked by τε) that arise from generic expectation and the conditions of performance, the poet then adds a third of a different order, internal and psychological: 'I am drawn as by a love-charm,' he says, 'to touch upon the new-moon festival'—in other words, to 'get down to business' with the particularities of the occasion."[33] Having built to this climax, Pindar forcefully rejects these considerations in the following lines (cf. ἔμπα, 36) before eventually resuming the catalogue.

We shall conclude with examples of longer and more complex catalogues. In each case it is necessary to determine whether the poet wishes to single out the

---

[33] Miller, "Digressive Leisure" 207-208.

last item for further elaboration or wishes merely to sketch the field without making any entry preeminent. The first, *Nem.* 3.53-58, approximates a priamel, by surveying Cheiron's pupils before arriving at the particular one of interest:

     βαθυμῆτα Χίρων τράφε λιθίνῳ
   (1)Ἰάσον᾽ ἔνδον τέγει, (2)καὶ ἔπειτεν Ἀσκλαπιόν,
55 τὸν φαρμάκων δίδαξε μαλακόχειρα νόμον·
   (3a)νύμφευσε δ᾽ αὖτις ἀγλαόκολπον
   Νηρέος θύγατρα, (3b)γόνον τέ οἱ φέρτατον
— ἀτίταλλεν ⟨ἐν⟩ ἁρμένοισι πᾶσι θυμὸν αὔξων,
   ὄφρα . . .

    Deep-devising Cheiron raised
  (1)Iason in his rocky cave (2)and then Asklepios,
55 whom he taught the gentle-handed province of medicine.
  (3a)And then he betrothed the splendid-breasted
  daughter of Nereus, (3b)and cherished her mighty offspring
— as he built up his spirit in all fitting pursuits,
  so that . . .

Although Iason's name is given prominence at the beginning of the line, nothing specific is mentioned about him. Asklepios' education, however, is elaborated in a relative clause. But since Cheiron played a key role in the marriage of Thetis as well as in the education of her son, the climactic member is divided into two parts. Although the marriage precedes in position (and in the natural order of things), and although Achilleus is modestly introduced at mid-line by τε, the greatest emphasis falls on him, for he is called φέρτατον and is said to have been brought up in all manner of fitting things (ἁρμένοισι πᾶσι), as opposed to Asklepios, who was only taught medicine.[34] Finally, the progression of verbs denoting rearing (τράφε . . . δίδαξε . . . ἀτίταλλεν) shows that Pindar reserved the rarer term for last place (emphatically introduced at the beginning of the line), and that it suggests more warmth ("cherish") than the others.[35] Having selected the true subject of interest, Pindar devotes the following epode (59-63) to Achilleus' career at Troy.[36]

---

[34] If πάντα θυμόν (the reading of the MSS) is accepted, then the point is that Cheiron schooled his *whole* spirit.
[35] There is also a slight suggestion that, since he "gave away" Thetis, Cheiron has greater attachment to her son. For the progression of τρέφω . . . ἀτιτάλλω, cf. *Il.* 16.191, 24.60, and *Od.* 19.354.
[36] Cf. the rising elements at *Isth.* 5.39-42 (noted by Thummer, *Die Isthmischen Gedichte I* 149) as Pindar leads up to praise of Aiginetan valor in war:

   λέγε, (1)τίνες Κύκνον, (2)τίνες Ἕκτορα πέφνον,
40 (3)καὶ στράταρχον Αἰθιόπων ἄφοβον

There is an example of four rising members at *Pyth.* 4.87-92, where the people of Iolkos, struck by the imposing figure of Iason, surmise who he might be:

> "Οὔ τί που οὗτος (1)'Ἀπόλλων,
>   (2)οὐδὲ μὰν χαλκάρματός ἐστι πόσις
> Ἀφροδίτας· (3)ἐν δὲ Νάξῳ φαντὶ θανεῖν λιπαρᾷ
> Ἰφιμεδείας παῖδας, Ὦτον καὶ σέ, τολ-
>   μάεις Ἐπιάλτα ἄναξ.
> 90 (4)καὶ μὰν Τιτυὸν βέλος Ἀρτέμιδος θήρευσε κραιπνόν,
> ἐξ ἀνικάτου φαρέτρας ὀρνύμενον,
> ὄφρα τις τᾶν ἐν δυνατῷ φιλοτά-
>   των ἐπιψαύειν ἔραται."

)—

> "He surely is not (1)Apollo,
>   (2)nor certainly is he the lord of the bronze chariot, the husband
> of Aphrodite; (3)and they say that in shining Naxos
> Iphimedeia's children died, Otos and you, bold
>   king Epialtas;
> 90 (4)and certainly Tityos was hunted down by Artemis' swift arrow,
> as it sped from her invincible quiver,
> to teach a person desire for attaining loves
>   within his power."

)—

In the epic-like context of *Pyth.* 4, the poet can indulge in this leisurely treatment of the impression Iason's appearance makes on people.[37] The progression from Apollo to Ares, to Otos and Epialtes, and finally to Tityos, climactically introduced by καὶ μάν (90) at the beginning of the verse and continuing to the end of the triad, shows that the folk of Iolkos come more and more to dread the potentially destructive power they sense in Iason. The technique of describing something by presenting the reactions of others, already conventional in Homer, is

---

> Μέμνονα χαλκοάραν· (4)τίς ἄρ' ἐσλὸν Τήλεφον
> τρῶσεν ἑῷ δορὶ Καΐκου παρ' ὄχθαις;

)—

> Tell, (1)who slew Kyknos, (2)who slew Hektor,
> 40 (3)and who slew the fearless general of the Aithiopians,
>   Memnon of the bronze arms? (4)Who then wounded good Telephos
>   with his own spear by the banks of the Kaïkos?

)—

The last element (note the shift from the plural τίνες at 39 to the singular τίς at 41) ends the epode, thus allowing the poet to introduce the name Aigina climactically at the beginning of the triad: τοῖσιν Αἴγιναν (43).

[37] Schroeder, *Pythien* 39-40 notes in passing the resemblance of Anchises' catalogue of goddesses at *h. Hom.* 5.93-99. It too exhibits increasing elements with increasing specificity.

used here with striking effect and creates a tension that is only relaxed by Iason's civilized words and behavior in the following scenes.

In the previous example a climactic arrangement was appropriate. Later in the poem, however, when Pindar catalogues the heroes who accompanied Iason on the Argo, the situation is different. He cannot single out any particular person, for that would detract from his hero, Iason.[38] On the other hand, the passage must have some sense of climax and closure (*Pyth.* 4.171-183):

    (1)τάχα δὲ Κρονίδαο
  Ζηνὸς υἱοὶ τρεῖς ἀκαμαντομάχαι
 ἦλθον Ἀλκμήνας θ᾽ ἑλικογλεφάρου Λή-
   δας τε, (2)δοιοὶ δ᾽ ὑψιχαῖται
 ἀνέρες, Ἐννοσίδα γένος, αἰδεσθέντες ἀλκάν,
 ἔκ τε Πύλου καὶ ἀπ᾽ ἄκρας Ταινάρου· τῶν μὲν κλέος
175 ἐσλὸν Εὐφάμου τ᾽ ἐκράνθη
  σόν τε, Περικλύμεν᾽ εὐρυβία.
 (3)ἐξ Ἀπόλλωνος δὲ φορμιγκτὰς ἀοιδᾶν πατήρ
— ἔμολεν, εὐαίνητος Ὀρφεύς.
 (4)πέμπε δ᾽ Ἑρμᾶς χρυσόραπις διδύμους υἱ-
   οὺς ἐπ᾽ ἄτρυτον πόνον,
 τὸν μὲν Ἐχίονα, κεχλά-
 δοντας ἥβᾳ, τὸν δ᾽ Ἔρυτον. (5)ταχέες {δ᾽}
180 ἀμφὶ Παγγαίου θεμέθλοις ναιετάοντες ἔβαν,
 καὶ γὰρ ἑκὼν θυμῷ γελανεῖ θᾶσσον ἔν-
  τυνεν βασιλεὺς ἀνέμων
 Ζήταν Κάλαΐν τε πατὴρ Βορέας, ἄνδρας πτεροῖσιν
 νῶτα πεφρίκοντας ἄμφω πορφυρέοις.

    (1)Swiftly came Kronian
  Zeus' three tireless warrior sons, born to
 round-eyed Alkmena and to Leda,
   (2)and the two high-plumed
 men, offspring of Poseidon, out of respect for their valor,
 from Pylos and steep Tainaros, who won
175 goodly glory, Euphamos
  and you, mighty Periklymenos.
 (3)And from Apollo came the father of songs,
— the famous minstrel Orpheus.
 (4)And Hermes of the golden wand sent two sons
   for the endless toil,
 Echion and Erytos, both
   burgeoning in their youth. (5)Swift

---

[38] Contrast the Homeric catalogue of ships, which culminates in the absent Achilleus.

180 to come were those dwelling at the base of Mt. Pangaion,
for with a cheerful heart their willing father Boreas,
king of the winds, swiftly outfitted
Zetas and Kalaïs, men whose backs both
bristled with wings of purple.

The five elements consist of 32, 54, 22, 35, and 66 syllables. Pride of place is given to Zeus' three sons (1), but Poseidon's two sons (2) are given greater specificity: Pindar provides their places of origin and their names and even addresses one of them in the second person.[39] Instead of continuing the climactic progression, however, the poet returns to a less imposing manner of treatment by switching to Orpheus (3), whom he depicts in few words, but to whom he still gives some emphasis by introducing him at the beginning of the line and by reserving his name until the very end of the antistrophe. As we shall see in the case of other long catalogues, this shorter member marks a low point from which the poet can build to another climax.[40] The next member, containing the sons of Hermes (4), although more impressive and introduced at the beginning of the epode, is nevertheless not very emphatic. The final entry, Boreas' sons (5), is the longest in the entire catalogue, but by introducing it at the end of the line without any fanfare Pindar avoids making it seem the most important. He does, however, end the description with the impressive details of the brothers' wings (cf. the emphatic ταχέες which introduced them): ἄνδρας πτεροῖσιν νῶτα πεφρίκοντας ἄμφω πορφυρέοις. By ending with this wondrous detail, Pindar provides a sense of climax and completion without singling out the final member.[41]

In contrast, when Teiresias predicts Herakles' career at *Nem.* 1.62-69, he relates the achievements in climactic order:

(1)ὅσσους μὲν ἐν χέρσῳ κτανών,
(2)ὅσσους δὲ πόντῳ θῆρας ἀιδροδίκας·
(3)καί τινα σὺν πλαγίῳ
65   ἀνδρῶν κόρῳ στείχοντα τὸν ἐχθρότατον
φᾶ ἑ δαώσειν μόρον.
(4)καὶ γὰρ ὅταν θεοὶ ἐν
πεδίῳ Φλέγρας Γιγάντεσσιν μάχαν

---

[39] In the previous example as well (*Pyth.* 4.89), Pindar gave variety to his list by directly addressing Epialtes in the middle of the catalogue.

[40] Cf. *Pyth.* 6.46-54, where σοφίαν δ' ἐν μυχοῖσι Πιερίδων (49) is at the middle of a five-element catalogue. Note the address to Poseidon (50-51), which adds warmth and variation to the penultimate item. Cf. also *Isth.* 5.30-35, where the third member (Περσεὺς δ' ἐν Ἄργει, 33) is the shortest. The climactic term is reserved for the beginning of the epode (ἀλλ' ἐν Οἰνώνᾳ, 34).

[41] Bundy, *Studia Pindarica* 2-3 points out the use of the θαῦμα motif to conclude a topic. For an example of the motif in an ekphrastic list, cf. the talking ram on Iason's δίπλαξ at Ap. Rh. *Arg.* 1.763-767.

ἀντιάζωσιν, βελέων ὑπὸ ῥι-
παῖσι κείνου φαιδίμαν γαίᾳ πεφύρσεσθαι κόμαν
ἔνεπεν· (5)αὐτὸν μὰν ἐν εἰρή-
νᾳ τὸν ἅπαντα χρόνον ⟨ἐν⟩ σχερῷ ...

(1)[he revealed] those he would slay on land,
(2)and those lawless beasts he would slay in the sea;
(3)and he said that there was one, the most hated of men,
65   who went about in crooked excess,
on whom he would bring doom.
(4)And furthermore, when the gods would engage the Giants
    in the Phlegran plain,
he said that, struck by his arrows, they would foul
    their bright hair
with earth. (5)But as for him, he would have continual
    peace for all time ...

Each successive member is longer, more specific, and more impressive than the preceding one, as is reflected in the progression of verbs: κτανών (62), δᾳώσειν μόρον (66), and γαίᾳ πεφύρσεσθαι κόμαν (68). The fourth element, introduced by καὶ γάρ ("and furthermore"), depicts in considerable detail the battle against the Giants, when Herakles will join forces with the Olympians themselves. At this point the catalogue is complete, but Pindar then proceeds to surpass it by adding an even longer and more impressive description (5) of Herakles' own fate (αὐτὸν μάν, 69), when he is admitted to the company of the gods on Olympos (69-72), a splendid portrayal of heavenly bliss which concludes the ode.

Another climactic catalogue occurs at *Nem.* 4.46-56, where a review of the realms of Aiakid rulers culminates in the deeds of Peleus:

(1)ἔνθα [sc. Κύπρῳ] Τεῦκρος ἀπάρχει
ὁ Τελαμωνιάδας· (2)ἀτάρ
Αἴας Σαλαμῖν' ἔχει πατρῴαν·
(3)ἐν δ' Εὐξείνῳ πελάγει φαενναν Ἀχιλεύς
50   νᾶσον· (4)Θέτις δὲ κρατεῖ
Φθίᾳ· (5)Νεοπτόλεμος δ' ἀπείρῳ διαπρυσίᾳ,
βουβόται τόθι πρῶνες ἔξοχοι κατάκεινται
Δωδώναθεν ἀρχόμενοι πρὸς Ἰόνιον πόρον.
(6)Παλίου δὲ πὰρ ποδὶ λατρίαν Ἰαολκόν
55   πολεμίᾳ χερὶ προστραπών
Πηλεὺς παρέδωκεν Αἱμόνεσσιν ...

(1)There [in Kypros] Teukros rules in exile,
    the son of Telamon, (2)whereas
    Aias holds ancestral Salamis;
(3)and in the Black Sea Achilleus holds the shining

50   island. (4)Thetis rules
     over Phthia, (5)Neoptolemos over the endless expanse,
     where cattle graze on jutting forelands that begin their descent
     from Dodona to the Adriatic coast.
     (6)But at the foot of Mount Pelion, after having subjected Iolkos
55   with the hand of war,
     Peleus handed it over to the Haimones ...

The first two elements are devoted to the sons of Telamon, who was praised at length earlier in the ode (25-32) before Pindar broke off the catalogue (see below page 52 note 15). Since Aias is a more important hero than Teukros, Pindar subtly shifts the balance in his favor. Although Teukros is given the impressive patronymic Τελαμωνιάδας, partly to connect him with the previous discussion of Telamon, the fact that he lives in exile (ἀπάρχει), whereas Aias holds the hereditary island of Salamis (Σαλαμῖν' ἔχει πατρῴαν), allows greater emphasis to fall on Aias. Three fine points reinforce this shift: the adversative ἀτάρ, the placement of Aias' name at the beginning of the line, and the emphasis the key word πατρῴαν receives at the end of the line and the strophe. Although Teukros has the patronymic, Aias holds the patrimonial estate.

The next strophe turns to the Peleids. Since Achilleus is mentioned at the beginning, he receives some emphasis, but Pindar provides little elaboration. Thetis is given even less attention. As in the case of Orpheus in the catalogue of Argonauts at *Pyth.* 4.176-177, her entry marks the low point; henceforth the movement will be climactic. The realm of Neoptolemos (5) is described in lavish detail.[42] So far the catalogue has consisted of the places where the heroes dwell, portrayed by means of static verbs. The climactic member (6), introduced at the beginning of its line, shifts to heroic action. In contrast to his five predecessors, Peleus claims no dwelling place, since he handed over Iolkos, which he had won, to the local inhabitants. Having singled out Peleus, Pindar goes on to devote the next fifteen lines (54-68) to his achievements.

We shall conclude this section with another long catalogue, *Isth.* 7.3-15:

        (1)ἥρα χαλκοκρότου πάρεδρον
        Δαμάτερος ἁνίκ' εὐρυχαίταν
5   ἄντειλας Διόνυσον, (2)ἢ χρυσῷ μεσονύκτιον
        νείφοντα δεξαμένα τὸν φέρτατον θεῶν,
        ὁπότ' Ἀμφιτρύωνος ἐν θυρέτροις
        σταθεὶς ἄλοχον μετῆλθεν Ἡρακλείοις γοναῖς;
        (3)ἢ {ὅτ'} ἀμφὶ πυκναῖς Τειρεσίαο βουλαῖς;
        (4)ἢ {ὅτ'} ἀμφ' Ἰόλαον ἱππόμητιν;

---

[42] For elaboration of the penultimate item in other catalogues, cf. *Pyth.* 1.77-78, 4.88-89, 178-179, 6.50-51; *Nem.* 3.54-55, 10.13-15; *Isth.* 2.19-22, and 7.10-12.

10   (5)ἢ Σπαρτῶν ἀκαμαντολογχᾶν; (6)ἢ ὅτε καρτερᾶς
     Ἄδραστον ἐξ ἀλαλᾶς ἄμπεμψας ὀρφανόν
     μυρίων ἑτάρων ἐς Ἄργος ἵππιον;
     (7)ἢ Δωρίδ᾽ ἀποικίαν οὕνεκεν ὀρθῷ
     ἔστασας ἐπὶ σφυρῷ
     Λακεδαιμονίων, ἕλον δ᾽ Ἀμύκλας
15   Αἰγεῖδαι σέθεν ἔκγονοι, μαντεύμασι Πυθίοις;

        (1)Was it when you raised up
    long-haired Dionysos as companion to
5   Demeter of the bronze cymbals? (2)or when, in a nighttime shower
        of gold, you received the greatest of the gods,
    when he stood at Amphitryon's gates
    and sought his wife to beget Herakles?
    (3)or because of Teiresias' wise counsels?
    (4)or for the skillful horseman, Iolaos?
10 (5)or for the Spartoi of the unwearied spears? (6)or when you sent back
        Adrastos from the fierce battle bereft
    of countless companions to Argos of the fine horses?
    (7)or because you established on firm
    footing the Doric colonization
    of the Lakedaimonians, and Amyklai fell
15 to the Aigeidai, your offspring, in accord with the Pythian oracles?

The movement of this catalogue is very similar to that of the catalogue of Argonauts at *Pyth.* 4.171-183. There Pindar avoided making any individual stand out; here he does not wish to single out any particular Theban accomplishment, but to survey highlights of the Theban tradition before adding to them the latest success of Strepsiadas. Therefore, he must eventually build to a climax, but without unduly narrowing the scope. The first member of 25 syllables recounts the birth of Dionysos, while the second of 46 elaborates that of Herakles. Items 3-5 are listed in staccato fashion and constitute the low point. Beginning with the Spartoi (5), the catalogue proceeds in climactic style.[43] First comes the defense of Thebes against the invasion of the Seven (6), described in 31 syllables and heightened by the second-person verb (ἄμπεμψας, 10). The final example (7), introduced at the beginning of its line, turns to the Theban offensive achievement, when the clan of the Aigeidai furthered Doric conquests by helping the Spartans take Amyklai. The greater length (45 syllables), the greater specificity, the two second-person references (ἔστασας, 13; σέθεν, 15), and the ringing reference at the end to Apollo's support (μαντεύμασι Πυθίοις, 15) all contribute to make this last item the most positive, without, however, elevating it above all the rest. The poet can then break in with the emphatic ἀλλά ... γάρ in the next verse (16) and turn to the newest

---

[43] The epithet ἀκαμαντολογχᾶν (10) sets the tone for the final two members dealing with Theban military exploits.

Theban accomplishment.[44] The point of emphasizing the last two entries, which sketch Theban military glory, becomes clear as Pindar deftly turns from the victor to his homonymous uncle, who died defending his fatherland (24-37).

Pyth. 3.61-76

We shall complete this survey with the carefully graded series of climactic elements in *Pyth.* 3.61-76, where Pindar completes his narrative of Asklepios with the famous words of self-exhortation and returns to the opening theme of the poem, his wish to provide a healer for Hieron:

  (1)μή, (2)φίλα ψυχά, (3)βίον ἀθάνατον
  σπεῦδε, (4)τὰν δ' ἔμπρακτον ἄντλει μαχανάν.
  (1)εἰ δὲ σώφρων ἄντρον ἔναι' ἔτι Χίρων, (2)καί τί οἱ
  φίλτρον ⟨ἐν⟩ θυμῷ μελιγάρυες ὕμνοι
65 ἁμέτεροι τίθεν, (3)ἰατῆρά τοί κέν νιν πίθον
  καί νυν ἐσλοῖσι παρασχεῖν ἀνδράσιν θερμᾶν νόσων
  ἤ τινα Λατοΐδα κεκλημένον ἢ πατέρος.
  (4)καί κεν ἐν ναυσὶν μόλον Ἰονίαν τάμνων θάλασσαν
  Ἀρέθοισαν ἐπὶ κράναν παρ' Αἰτναῖον ξένον,
70 ὃς Συρακόσσαισι νέμει βασιλεύς,
  (1)πραῢς ἀστοῖς, (2)οὐ φθονέων ἀγαθοῖς, (3)ξεί-
  νοις δὲ θαυμαστὸς πατήρ.
  (1)τῷ μὲν διδύμας χάριτας
  εἰ κατέβαν (2a)ὑγίειαν ἄγων χρυσέαν
  (2b)κῶμόν τ' ἀέθλων Πυθίων αἴγλαν στεφάνοις,
  τοὺς ἀριστεύων Φερένικος ἕλεν Κίρρᾳ ποτέ,
75 (3)ἀστέρος οὐρανίου
  φαμὶ τηλαυγέστερον κείνῳ φάος
  ἐξικόμαν κε βαθὺν πόντον περάσαις.

  (1)Do not, (2)my soul, (3)strive for the life
   of the immortals, (4)but exhaust the valid means at your disposal.
  (1)But if wise Cheiron were still living in his cave, (2)and if
   my honey-sounding hymns could put a charm
65 in his heart, (3)I could surely persuade him to provide a healer
   now as well to cure the feverish illnesses of good men,
   one called Asklepios or even Apollo.

---

[44] The long catalogue of Argive glories that opens *Nem.* 10 has a very similar structure, culminating in the two longest elements on Amphitryon and Herakles (13-18), after which Pindar breaks off further treatment and turns to the victor Theaios (24).

>——
70

(4)And I would have come, cleaving the Ionian sea in a ship,
   to the fountain of Arethousa and to my Aitnaian host,
   who rules as king in Syracuse,
   (1)kindly to townsmen, (2)not begrudging to the good, (3)and to guests
      a wondrous father.
(1)And if I could have come bringing him
   two joys, (2a)golden health
      (2b)and a celebration to grace the crowns from the Pythian games,
      which Pherenikos once won with his victory at Kirrha,
75 (3)I swear that my arrival would have been a light for him
   that outshone any heavenly star,
   once I had crossed the deep sea.

Altogether there are four consecutive climactic passages. The first climactic series, typical of the hymnal addresses we have seen, consists of increasingly longer elements. The forceful τὰν δ' (62) and the switch from the negative (μὴ ... σπεῦδε, 61-62) to the positive (ἄντλει, 62) mark the last element as climactic. With these words Pindar draws the "moral" from the stories he has just told of Koronis and Asklepios, but the lesson gained has evidently been unable to expel from his heart the desire to give relief to Hieron's sickness, which he had uttered at the opening of the poem ("Would that Cheiron were alive ..."),[45] for in the following lines (63-71) he gives full expression to that wishful thinking in a crescendo of contrary-to-fact conditions that complete the epode and continue in the following triad: (1)if ... (2)and if ... (3)then ... (4)and then. The fourth element, which begins with an emphatic καί (68), traces his journey with increasing specification as he travels across the Ionian sea to the spring of Arethousa and to his friend, reserving the important word ξένον (69) until the end of the period and the epode. He continues with a relative clause which begins the next triad and contains three-fold, rising praise of Hieron (71):

(1)πραῢς ἀστοῖς, (2)οὐ φθονέων ἀγαθοῖς, (3)ξεί-
νοις δὲ θαυμαστὸς πατήρ.

(1)kindly to townsmen, (2)not begrudging to the good, (3)and to guests
a wondrous father.

This one period, like a long Homeric hexameter, consists of a rising tricolon, which surveys Hieron's treatment of his fellow citizens, his equals, and finally his guests. While the word ἀγαθοῖς is a slight intensification from the more neutral and inclusive ἀστοῖς, the word θαυμαστός is very strong indeed.[46] The

---

[45] For an excellent analysis of the opening wish and its role in the argument of the poem, see H. Pelliccia, "Pindarus Homericus: *Pythian* 3.1-80," *HSCP* 91 (1987) 39-63.

[46] Cf. the similar effect of the climactic words δαιμόνιαι τροφοί at *Pyth.* 2.2 (discussed above note 20).

final word, πατήρ, expresses considerably more affection than πραΰς or οὐ φθονέων, and the switch from negative (οὐ φθονέων) to positive (πατήρ) also reinforces the sense of climax. Finally, the placement of ξείνοις at the head of its colon (reinforced by δέ and echoing ξένον, 69) marks the last item as the most important.[47]

In the fourth climactic element of the previous crescendo (68-71), Pindar imagines how he could have come (κεν ... μόλον, 68) to Syracuse and what kind of host he would have found (70-71). In the final crescendo he pictures what would happen if he could disembark (εἰ κατέβαν, 73), bringing Hieron two joys (διδύμας χάριτας, 72), which he then climactically specifies as (2a) golden health (2b) and victory celebrations like those Pherenikos used to win for him: (3) he would come to him as a light of deliverance more resplendent than any star. The asseverative φαμί and the image of the heavenly star (cf. the sun in the climactic element at Ol. 1.6) add intensity to the final member. That saving light would be, in essence, unending enjoyment of the repose of success, a state that is unattainable by mortals, as he had demonstrated in the very stories he told of Koronis and Asklepios and will confirm in the following lines (86-103). The second apodosis (ἐξικόμαν κε ... πόντον περάσαις, 76) completes the strophe by ringing back to the first apodosis (κεν μόλον ... τάμνων θάλασσαν, 69), thereby rounding off the poet's musings before the sudden break-off in verse 77: ἀλλ' ἐπεύξασθαι μὲν ἐγὼν ἐθέλω. This series of rising statements enacts the temporary ascendancy of emotion over reason as the speaker allows himself to elaborate upon the wishful thinking which opened the ode (Ἤθελον Χίρωνά κε ... ζώειν). If one fails to observe the crescendos of this passage, one misses the rhetorical *pathos* of the poet's devotion to Hieron and fails to appreciate the force of the opening words of the antistrophe, which return us to reality ("But for my part, I wish to pray ...," 77) and initiate the consolation Pindar offers Hieron in the face of his mortality.[48]

Conclusion

By close examination of these passages, I have tried to reconstruct some of the basic principles by which Pindar arranges his materials, from words to cola and from periods to strophes. I do not claim that every passage is constructed according to these principles—indeed many are not, and for good reason: ἔστι δὲ καὶ κόρος ἀνθρώπων βαρὺς ἀντιάσαι! Pindar frequently departs from any such scheme, but when he varies the pattern he does so for a purpose, and the diligent

---

[47] Cf. the climactic pair in praise of the house of the Oligaithidai at Ol. 13.2-3: ἥμερον ἀστοῖς, | ξένοισι δὲ θεράποντα.

[48] For a discussion of the poet's wishful thinking, his prayer, and the consolation in the ode, see Young, *Three Odes* 27-68 and Race, *Pindar* 53-62.

reader should notice the departure and attempt to understand its point.[49] I hope to have demonstrated how a careful reading of Pindar's verses reveals the minute care that this master craftsman took to give each item an emphasis κατὰ καιρόν and how aptly in *Nem.* 7.78-79, the passage cited at the beginning of the *Introduction*, he describes his Muse as one who:

> (1)κολλᾷ χρυσὸν (2)ἔν τε λευκὸν ἐλέφανθ' ἁμᾷ
> (3)καὶ λείριον ἄνθεμον ποντίας ὑφελοῖσ' ἐέρσας.

> (1)binds gold (2)together with white ivory
> (3)and the lily flower she takes from the dew of the sea.

---

[49] A good example (which I owe to Andrew Miller) of deliberate anticlimax occurs at *Ol.* 13.87-90:

> σὺν δὲ κείνῳ (1)καί ποτ' Ἀμαζονίδων
> αἰθέρος ψυχρῶν ἀπὸ κόλπων ἐρήμου
> τοξόταν βάλλων γυναικεῖον στρατόν
> 90 (2)καὶ Χίμαιραν πῦρ πνέοισαν (3)καὶ Σολύμους ἔπεφνεν.

> And on the back of Pegasos (1)he once fired
> from the cold recesses of the empty air upon
> the army of female archers, the Amazons,
> 90 (2)and he slew the fire-breathing Chimaira (3)and the Solymoi.

This diminuendo prepares for the *praeteritio* of the following line: διασωπάσομαί οἱ μόρον ἐγώ (91). Bakchylides has an example of decreasing elements at 5.176-182:

> λευκώλενε Καλλιόπα,
> στᾶσον εὐποίητον ἅρμα
> αὐτοῦ· (1)Δία τε Κρονίδαν
> ὕμνησον Ὀλύμπιον ἀρχαγὸν θεῶν,
> 180 (2)τόν τ' ἀκαμαντορόαν
> Ἀλφεόν, (3)Πέλοπός τε βίαν,
> (4)καὶ Πίσαν, ἔνθ'...

> White-armed Kalliope,
> halt your well-built chariot
> here. (1)Sing of Zeus, son of Kronos,
> the Olympian ruler of the gods,
> 180 (2)the ever-flowing
> Alpheos, (3)mighty Pelops,
> (4)and Pisa, where...

In contrast to Pindaric practice, Bakchylides here reduces each element (of 18, 10, 6, and 3 syllables respectively) by narrowing the qualifications until the last (and most relevant) stands alone. I have found no similar combination of increasing relevance with decreasing length in Pindar. Conversely, the only example of climactic elements I have found in Bakchylides is at 1.151-158.

Chapter 2

Elements of Style in Break-Offs

Pindar is notorious for suddenly intruding into a poem to break off a narrative. For example, in *Ol.* 1 he begins the account of the gods eating Pelops only to break in with "I cannot call any of the blessed gods a glutton; I stand back." Likewise, in *Pyth.* 11, after recounting Orestes' revenge on Klytaimestra and Aigisthos, he suddenly represents himself as being confused and off-course, and in *Ol.* 9 he breaks off his narrative of Herakles' fight against three gods by ordering his mouth to reject such talk—and there are many other examples. I shall not address the larger questions about the relevance of these passages to their entire odes nor about Pindar's adaptations of myths, but rather concentrate on the smaller points of language and style in such passages by posing these questions: Are there any stylistic indications that prepare the audience for such break-offs? What elements do they have in common? How are these seemingly spontaneous interruptions contrived? I have found that two important indicators signal the end of a section and prepare for the sudden appearance of the poet to redirect his song: (1) emphatically postponed words denoting death, suffering, or defeat and (2) divine epiphanies and actions. These two indicators (often combined) mark the high point of a narrative from which the poet turns abruptly (often in asyndeton) to other less elevated, but more positive, topics. He can introduce himself in two ways, either by an emphatic first personal pronoun (or verb), or by an imperative (or χρή) of self-exhortation.[1]

As in ring-compositional form, we shall begin and end with examples from *Pyth.* 1. At lines 27-31 Pindar completes his ekphrasis of Typhos' imprisonment under Mt. Aitna before announcing the poem's occasion, Hieron's Pythian chariot victory.

---

[1] For a thorough study of the first person in Pindar, see Lefkowitz, "First Person" 177-253, especially 179-182, where she demonstrates the use of first personal statements to conclude or introduce topics. For the distinction between an "indefinite" first personal statement (which enunciates a general principle) and an "encomiastic" first personal statement (which announces a poetic intention), see Miller, "Digressive Leisure" 208 note 25.

οἷον Αἴτνας ἐν μελαμφύλλοις δέδεται κορυφαῖς
καὶ πέδῳ, στρωμνὰ δὲ χαράσσοισ' ἅπαν νῶ-
τον ποτικεκλιμένον κεντεῖ.
εἴη, Ζεῦ, τὶν εἴη ἁνδάνειν,
30 ὃς τοῦτ' ἐφέπεις ὄρος, εὐκάρποιο γαί-
ας μέτωπον, τοῦ μὲν ἐπωνυμίαν
κλεινὸς οἰκιστὴρ ἐκύδανεν πόλιν...

    such is that creature confined between Aitna's dark-leaved peaks
    and the plain; and on that jagged bed the entire length
      of his outstretched back is *goaded*.
    Grant, O Zeus, grant that I may *please* you,
30   you who rule that mountain, the forehead of a
    fruitful land, whose neighboring city that bears
      its name was honored by its glorious founder...

A scholium (56 a) well expresses the rhetorical force of this passage: "After recounting Typhos' punishment, *as if affected by fear at the narrative* (ὥσπερ φόβῳ διατεθεὶς πρὸς τὰ διηγήματα), he prays for Zeus' favor." One of the ways in which Pindar maintains an oral, impromptu quality in his poetry is by appearing to react to his own statements, as if he were hearing them—like a listener—for the first time.[2] And in order to make Typhos' discomfort more vivid (and his own "fear" more verisimilar), he purposely reserves the main verb κεντεῖ ("goads") until the last word. By ending on this note of pain Pindar can suddenly interject a fervent prayer (in asyndeton) that he be pleasing to Zeus: εἴη, Ζεῦ, τὶν εἴη ἁνδάνειν. On a larger scale, the recoil from pain (κεντεῖ) to pleasure (ἁνδάνειν) underscores the transition from the negative exemplum (Typhos' frustrated opposition to Zeus) to the joyful occasion of Hieron's success (note the positive force of the epithet εὐκάρποιο in 30). Now this may seem to be a very small point and to put a great deal of weight on the word κεντεῖ, but when we compare other passages that accomplish similar transitions, we shall see the extent to which small points of style reinforce larger rhetorical movements in the odes.

In *Pyth*. 3 Pindar uses a similar procedure to effect the transition from a negative example to the positive program of the ode at lines 57-60, where he ends his narrative of Koronis and her son Asklepios by recounting how the latter dared to bring back a man from the dead. When Zeus became aware of his impiety, he blasted both men with a thunderbolt.

χερσὶ δ' ἄρα Κρονίων
ῥίψαις δι' ἀμφοῖν ἀμπνοὰν στέρνων κάθελεν

---

[2] Like the chorus in a drama, the lyric voice guides the reactions of the audience and at the same time displays the speaker's *ethos*.

>   ὠκέως, αἴθων δὲ κεραυνὸς ἐνέσκιμψεν μόρον.
>   χρὴ τὰ ἐοικότα πὰρ
>   δαιμόνων μαστευέμεν θναταῖς φρασίν
> 60 γνόντα τὸ πὰρ ποδός, οἵας εἰμὲν αἴσας.
> —   μή, φίλα ψυχά, βίον ἀθάνατον
>   σπεῦδε, τὰν δ' ἔμπρακτον ἄντλει μαχανάν.

>   And so a cast from Zeus' hands
>   took the breath from both men's breasts
>   in an instant; the flash of lightning *hurled down doom.*
>   *It is necessary* to seek what is proper from the gods
>   with our mortal minds,
> 60 by knowing what lies at our feet and what our human condition is.
> —   *Do not,* my soul, *strive* for the life
>   of the immortals, but exhaust the valid means at your disposal.

The sudden doom of Asklepios rapidly brings the narrative to a close[3] and gives earnestness to the gnome (59-60) and to the famous lines of self-exhortation (πρὸς ἑαυτόν, Σ 109) that encapsulate the παραίνεσις of the entire ode: μή, φίλα ψυχά ... σπεῦδε (61-62). By ending his narrative with the intervention of Zeus[4] and with the emphatic circumlocution for death, ἐνέσκιμψεν μόρον, the poet can display his ethical aversion by interjecting (in asyndeton) a gnomic

---

[3] For death as a natural theme for poetic closure, see Smith, *Poetic Closure* 118, 172-82.
[4] This divine intervention is related to what Bundy, *Studia Pindarica* 3 calls the θαῦμα motive. It often marks the high point of a narrative from which the poet can suddenly change to a less imposing subject. Another type of θαῦμα involves beholding and communing with the gods. Cf. *Nem.* 4.66-70, which terminates the long catalogue of Aiakid achievements with Peleus' vision of the divine assembly and the revelation of their gifts to him and his race.

>   εἶδεν δ' εὔκυκλον ἕδραν,
>   τὰν οὐρανοῦ βασιλῆες πόντου τ' ἐφεζόμενοι
>   δῶρα καὶ κράτος ἐξέφαναν ἐγγενὲς αὐτῷ.
>   Γαδείρων τὸ πρὸς ζόφον οὐ περατόν· ἀπότρεπε
> 70 αὖτις Εὐρώπαν ποτὶ χέρσον ἔντεα ναός.

>   He beheld the splendid circle of seats
>   on which the lords of the sky and sea sat
>   and revealed to him their gifts and his race's power.
>   The darkness beyond Gadeira is impassable; *turn back*
> 70 again the ship's tackle to the mainland of Europe.

Once again asyndeton (69) marks the break from the narrative and the return to the occasion of the ode by means of self-exhortation. Similar is the catalogue of Argive glories that opens *Nem.* 10 and ends with the apotheosis of Herakles and his marriage to Hebe. The final words of the catalogue (and the triad), καλλίστα θεῶν (18), help motivate the following break-off: βραχύ μοι στόμα πάντ' ἀναγήσασθ' (19).

imperative (χρή),[5] which turns abruptly from the negative exemplum toward the positive consolation of the poem.

In *Nem.* 9.24 ff. Pindar also completes the account of the disastrous campaign of the Seven against Thebes with the intervention of Zeus' thunderbolt, which splits open the ground and swallows up Amphiaraos before he can die a coward's death with a spear in his back (note the emphatically reserved αἰσχυνθῆμεν, 27).

```
              ὁ δ' Ἀμφιαρεῖ σχίσσεν κεραυνῷ παμβίᾳ
25         Ζεὺς τὰν βαθύστερνον χθόνα, κρύψεν δ' ἅμ' ἵπποις,
—          δουρὶ Περικλυμένου πρὶν νῶτα τυπέντα μαχατάν
           θυμὸν αἰσχυνθῆμεν. ἐν γὰρ δαιμονίοισι φόβοις
               φεύγοντι καὶ παῖδες θεῶν.
           εἰ δυνατόν, Κρονίων,
               πεῖραν μὲν ἀγάνορα Φοινικοστόλων
           ἐγχέων ταύταν θανάτου πέρι καὶ ζω-
               ᾶς ἀναβάλλομαι ὡς πόρσιστα, μοῖραν δ' εὔνομον
30         αἰτέω σε παισὶν δαρὸν Αἰτναίων ὀπάζειν,
—          Ζεῦ πάτερ, ἀγλαΐαισιν δ' ἀστυνόμοις ἐπιμεῖξαι
           λαόν.
```

```
           But for Amphiaraos' sake Zeus' almighty thunderbolt
25         sundered the deep-bosomed earth, and buried him and his team
—          before he could be smitten in the back by Periklymenos' spear
           and his warrior spirit be *disgraced*. For in *heaven-sent panics*
               even the gods' sons take flight.
           *If possible*, Son of Kronos, *I put off* as far as I can
               a lordly trial of life and death such as that
           against Phoenician spears; but grant to Aitna's sons,
30         *I beg* you, long hereafter the blessings of good rule,
—          Father Zeus, and public successes for the people
           to celebrate.
```

The gnome (27-28) rounds off the section by reiterating the themes of panic and defeat caused by divine intervention. At this point Pindar interjects an asyndetic prayer that leaps from the mythic exemplum to the present (note the connection implied by ταύταν, "such," 29), requesting Zeus to ward off further engagements with the Carthaginians; and as he completes the second part of the prayer

---

[5] Pindar is fond of stating the general case in a gnome (or gnomic exhortation) before applying it to the occasion at hand. Here the generalizing first person plural εἰμέν (60) prepares for the self-address in the following lines (61-62). In the example at *Nem.* 4.66-70 (see above note 4) the gnomic exhortation, Γαδείρων τὸ πρὸς ζόφον οὐ περατόν (69), sets up the nautical metaphor for the imperative ἀπότρεπε (69).

(note the μὲν...δέ, 28-29), he deftly turns from concern about war to requests for continued good government and civic achievements.[6]

In *Pyth.* 10, Pindar ends his account of Perseus' exploits with the petrification of his mother's captors on the island of Seriphos (46-52).

> ἔπεφνέν
> τε Γοργόνα, καὶ ποικίλον κάρα
> δρακόντων φόβαισιν ἤλυθε νασιώταις
> — λίθινον θάνατον φέρων. ἐμοὶ δὲ θαυμάσαι
> θεῶν τελεσάντων οὐδέν ποτε φαίνεται
> 50 ἔμμεν ἄπιστον.
> κώπαν σχάσον, ταχὺ δ' ἄγκυραν ἔρεισον χθονί
> πρώραθε, χοιράδος ἄλκαρ πέτρας.

> And he slew
> the Gorgon, and bearing her head embellished
> with locks of serpents he came to the islanders,
> — *bringing* them stony *death. As for me, in my wonderment*

[6] Cf. the break-off with the asyndetic prayer to Zeus at *Pyth.* 1.29 (above page 42). At *Nem.* 8.35 another asyndetic prayer to Zeus breaks off a negative exemplum and turns toward the positive program of the ode, but the recoil is not due to death (which is vividly described in lines 30-32) but to the baneful powers of falsifying speech (32-37), a subject close to the poet's heart:

> ἐχθρὰ δ' ἄρα πάρφασις ἦν καὶ πάλαι,
> αἱμύλων μύθων ὁμόφοι-
> τος, δολοφραδής, κακοποιὸν ὄνειδος·
> ἃ τὸ μὲν λαμπρὸν βιᾶται,
> τῶν δ' ἀφάντων κῦδος ἀντείνει σαθρόν.
>)—
> 35   εἴη μή ποτέ μοι τοιοῦτον ἦθος,
> Ζεῦ πάτερ, ἀλλὰ κελεύθοις
> ἁπλόαις ζωᾶς ἐφαπτοίμαν, θανὼν ὡς παισὶ κλέος
> μὴ τὸ δύσφαμον προσάψω.

> Indeed, even long ago hateful deception existed,
> companion of flattering tales, guileful
> contriver, evil-working disgrace,
> which represses the illustrious,
> and exalts for the obscure a fame that is *rotten*.
>)—
> 35 May *I* never have such a disposition,
> Father Zeus, but let me travel
> the straightforward paths of life, at death bequeathing
> my children no such disrepute.

The final word of the epode, σαθρόν ("rotten"), prompts the ethical (cf. ἦθος, 35) repugnance of the poet, who prays to be able to fulfill his true function as an encomiastic poet. As Carey, "Eighth Nemean Ode" 33 observes: "Pindar's closing word on the myth, σαθρόν, leaves us with a foul taste, a sense of corruption and decay...Pindar is using 'indignatio' to good effect."

nothing *the gods accomplish* ever seems
50   to be incredible.
Hold the oar, quickly *plant* the anchor in the ground
from the prow as a safeguard against the jagged reef.

Once again an emphatic periphrasis for killing (θάνατον φέρων) ends the section and motivates the first-personal interjection, which itself combines the θαῦμα motive with divine intervention: "As for me (ἐμοὶ δέ), in my wonderment (θαυμάσαι) nothing the gods accomplish (θεῶν τελεσάντων) ever seems to be incredible." The subsequent self-exhortation (in asyndeton) to hold the oar and to throw out the anchor turns the poem from the amazing and terrifying exploits of Perseus to the athletic accomplishments of Hippokleas.[7]

At *Ol*. 1.46 ff., Pindar reports that it was an envious neighbor who started the scandalous tale about Pelops being served as food to the gods.

> ὡς δ' ἄφαντος ἔπελες, οὐδὲ ματρὶ πολ-
>   λὰ μαιόμενοι φῶτες ἄγαγον,
> ἔννεπε κρυφᾷ τις αὐτίκα φθονερῶν γειτόνων,
> ὕδατος ὅτι τε πυρὶ ζέοισαν εἰς ἀκμάν
> μαχαίρᾳ τάμον κατὰ μέλη,
> 50   τραπέζαισί τ' ἀμφὶ δεύτατα κρεῶν
>   σέθεν διεδάσαντο καὶ **φάγον.**
> **ἐμοὶ δ'** ἄπορα γαστρίμαρ-
>   γον μακάρων τιν' εἰπεῖν· **ἀφίσταμαι.**

When you disappeared, and, try as they might, no
    searchers returned you to your mother,
some envious neighbor immediately whispered about
that into water boiling rapidly on the fire
they cut up your limbs with a knife
50   and for the main course distributed your flesh
    around the table *and ate it*.
But I cannot call any of the blessed gods
    a glutton. *I stand back.*

In order to make the narrative as gruesome as possible, Pindar carefully builds to a climax. The last word, φάγον, coming at the end of the antistrophe and introduced by καί ("*and ate* it") after the two previous verbs (τάμον . . . διεδάσαντο) coupled by τε, motivates the sudden intervention of the speaker at the beginning of the epode. "But I cannot call any of the blessed gods a glutton (γαστρίμαρ-

---

[7] Cf. *Pyth*. 3.57-62, where the climactic death of Asklepios is followed by a gnome and self-exhortation before Pindar returns to the program of the ode. Similar is *Nem*. 4.66-72 (see above note 4), which contains the climax of the narrative, a gnomic statement, and self-exhortation before it returns to the victorious family.

γον); I stand back." At this point, the poet can turn to his positive version of the tale, according to which Pelops was spirited away by Poseidon out of love.

A number of narratives end with emphatic references to killing. One of the clearest examples is in *Pyth.* 11, where Orestes returns to kill his mother and slaughter Aigisthos (36-41).

      ἀλλὰ χρονίῳ σὺν Ἄρει
—   **πέφνεν τε ματέρα θῆκέ τ' Αἴγισθον ἐν φοναῖς.**
  ἦρ', ὦ φίλοι, κατ' ἀμευσίπορον τρίοδον ἐδινάθην,
  ὀρθὰν κέλευθον ἰὼν
  τὸ πρίν· ἤ μέ τις ἄνεμος ἔξω πλόου
40 ἔβαλεν, ὡς ὅτ' ἄκατον ἐνναλίαν;
  Μοῖσα, τὸ δὲ τεόν ...

      But after a long-delayed fight
—   he *slew* his mother and laid Aigisthos *in gore.*
  Indeed, my friends, did I get confused where the way
  forked, when before I was on the straight road? Or did
  some wind throw *me*
40 off course, like a small boat at sea?
  Muse, it is your duty ...

The vivid periphrasis for death (θῆκε ... ἐν φοναῖς) ends the narrative section and gains added weight by coming at the end of the strophe.[8] The poet's distancing is particularly elaborate in this instance, because the exemplum is extremely negative and additional effort is required to prepare for the return to the victor and his father. "Indeed, my friends, did I get confused?"[9] Then follows, just as in the example from *Pyth.* 10 (above page 45), an address—here to his Muse—to return to the program of the ode.[10]

In several examples Pindar concludes narratives with an emphatic reference to the fighter's weapon. An elaborate break-off occurs at *Nem.* 6.50-57, where, after recounting Memnon's death at the hands of Achilleus (note the emphatic ἀκμᾷ | ἔγχεος ζακότοιο, 52-53), Pindar indicates his willingness to continue in this well-worn track of epic, but turns instead to his role as messenger (cf. ἄγγελος ἔβαν, 57b) of Alkimidas' athletic successes.

---

[8] It also closes a ring by echoing the prominent φονευομένου (17) at the beginning of the narrative; see Robbins, "Pindar's *Oresteia*" 3. For "a résumé of victims as terminal to a myth," see Young, *Three Odes of Pindar* 4 note 3.

[9] For a brief analysis of this passage and similar "confessions" of confusion, see Race, "Some Digressions" 1-8.

[10] The address to the Muse contains increasingly longer elements: (1)Μοῖσα, (2)τὸ δὲ τεόν, (3)εἰ μισθοῖο συνέθευ παρέχειν | φωνὰν ὑπάργυρον. ...

βαρὺ δέ σφιν
50b νεῖκος Ἀχιλεύς
— ἔμπεσε χαμαὶ καταβαὶς ἀφ' ἁρμάτων,
φαεννᾶς υἱὸν εὖτ' *ἐνάριξεν* Ἀόος **ἀκμᾷ**
ἔγχεος ζακότοιο. καὶ ταῦτα μὲν παλαιότεροι
ὁδὸν ἀμαξιτὸν εὗρον· *ἕπο-*
μαι δὲ καὶ αὐτὸς ἔχων μελέταν·
55 τὸ δὲ πὰρ ποδὶ ναὸς ἑλισσόμενον αἰεὶ κυμάτων
λέγεται παντὶ μάλιστα δονεῖν
θυμόν. ἑκόντι δ' ἐγὼ νώ-
τῳ μεθέπων δίδυμον ἄχθος
57b ἄγγελος ἔβαν ...

                          Grievous to them
50b was the strife Achilleus
— inflicted after dismounting from his chariot,
when he *slew* the son of shining Dawn *with the point*
of his raging spear. The older poets found in such deeds as those
a highway of song, *and*
I myself also follow diligently.
55 But whatever wave rolls in the path of the ship
is said to be every man's greatest
concern. On my willing back I accept
a double burden,
57b and have come as a messenger ...

In a very similar fashion at *Ol.* 9.76-83, Pindar breaks off his praise of Achilleus and Patroklos (note the emphatic δαμασιμβρότου αἰχμᾶς, 79)[11] with

---

[11] Emphatic references to weapons can also conclude topics of praise, as at *Ol.* 13.22-26:

ἐν δὲ Μοῖσ' ἁδύπνοος,
ἐν δ' Ἄρης ἀνθεῖ νέων οὐλίαις αἰχμαῖσιν ἀνδρῶν.
)— ὕπατ' εὐρὺ ἀνάσσων
25 Ὀλυμπίας, ἀφθόνητος ἔπεσσιν
γένοιο χρόνον ἅπαντα, Ζεῦ πάτερ ...

                     There flourishes the sweet-voiced Muse;
there thrives Ares in the *young men's deadly spears.*
)— Mightiest one, wide-ruling lord
25 of Olympia, *may you* never begrudge
my words of praise, Father Zeus ...

After ending climactically with the ringing νέων οὐλίαις αἰχμαῖσιν ἀνδρῶν (23), Pindar turns in the following triad to the athletic achievements of Xenophon by means of an asyndetic prayer (24-28). Cf. *Pyth.* 1.61-66, where the strophe dedicated to the advance of the Doric conquests ends with κλέος ἄνθησεν αἰχμᾶς (66). At the beginning of the antistrophe Pindar turns his

an asydetic prayer for inspiration (a variation of the conventional address to the Muses) as he turns to his role as vindicator (cf. ἦλθον | τιμάορος, 82-83) of his patron's athletic achievements.

> ἐξ οὗ Θέτιος †γόνος οὐλίῳ νιν ἐν Ἄρει
> παραγορεῖτο μή ποτε
> σφετέρας ἄτερθε ταξιοῦσθαι
> **δαμασιμβρότου αἰχμᾶς.**
> 80 εἴην εὑρησιεπὴς ἀναγεῖσθαι
> πρόσφορος ἐν Μοισᾶν δίφρῳ·
>   τόλμα δὲ καὶ ἀμφιλαφὴς δύναμις
> ἕσποιτο. προξενίᾳ δ' ἀρετᾷ τ' ἦλθον
> τιμάορος Ἰσθμίαισι Λαμπρομάχου μίτραις . . .

> From then on Thetis' child admonished him
> never in deadly warfare
> to take a stand away from his friend's own
> *man-slaying spear.*
> 80 *May I* find fluent speech as a
> fitting rider in the Muses' chariot,
>   and may courage and ample power
> attend me. Because of friendship and achievement I have
> come to vindicate the Isthmian crowns of Lampromachos . . .

Isth. 6 contains two versions of break-off. The first occurs in lines 31-36, where Pindar lists the deeds of Telamon and Herakles before turning to the particular episode of concern, the visit of Herakles to Telamon and his prediction of Aias' birth (37-54).

> εἷλε δὲ Περγαμίαν, **πέφνεν** δὲ σὺν κείνῳ Μερόπων
> ἔθνεα καὶ τὸν βουβόταν οὔρεϊ ἴσον
> Φλέγραισιν εὑρὼν Ἀλκυο-
>   νῆ, σφετέρας δ' οὐ φείσατο
> χερσὶν **βαρυφθόγγοιο νευρᾶς**
> 35 Ἡρακλέης. **ἀλλ'** Αἰακίδαν καλέων
> ἐς πλόον ⟨– –⟩ κύρησεν δαινυμένων.

> He took Troy and together with that man *slew* the tribes
> of Meropes, and when he encountered Alkyoneus,
> that herdsman as great as a mountain,
>   at Phlegrai, he did not withhold
> his hands from his *grievous-sounding bowstring,*

---

attention to the city of Aitna with a prayer to Zeus for their well-being: Ζεῦ τέλει' (67). Cf. also *Ol.* 7.19: Ἀργείᾳ σὺν αἰχμᾷ.

35   Herakles, that is. *But* when he came to summon Telamon
      to the voyage . . . he found them dining.

Since Pindar is here turning from one group of Herakles' deeds to another, he does not wish to make a strong break between them, as he will later in the poem (56-57), when he turns from ancient deeds to present victories. Therefore, he moderates the force of βαρυφθόγγοιο νευρᾶς (34) by using litotes (οὐ φείσατο, 33), and rather than introducing himself in the first person (as he does in the transition at 56-57), he uses ἀλλά (35) to turn to the specific incident of importance.[12] And, by enjambing the withheld name Ἡρακλέης (35), he keeps him as the center of attention while shifting from his martial deeds to his prophetic character (note the symposiastic setting of the prediction, once again indicating a transition from war to peace).

Later in the poem, however, Pindar must make a more emphatic break from the mythical narrative before turning to the occasion of the poem. At the climax of the narrative, Herakles prays that Telamon will father a brave son, and after Zeus sends an eagle (divine intervention) to confirm his prayer, Herakles names him Aias and predicts his career (52-57):

"'Ἔσσεταί τοι παῖς, ὃν αἰτεῖς, ὦ Τελαμών·
καί νιν ὄρνιχος φανέντος κέκλευ ἐπώνυμον εὐ-
    ρυβίαν Αἴαντα, λαῶν
ἐν πόνοις ἔκπαγλον Ἐνυαλίου."
55   ὣς ἆρα εἰπὼν αὐτίκα
ἕζετ'. ἐμοὶ δὲ μακρὸν πάσας ⟨ἀν⟩αγήσασθ' ἀρετάς·
Φυλακίδᾳ γὰρ ἦλθον, ὦ Μοῖσα, ταμίας . . .

"You will have the son you request, Telamon.
Take his name from the bird that appeared and call him
    mighty Aias, among men
formidable in the toils of Enyalios."
55   Having said that, he immediately
sat down. *But for me* it would take too long to recount all their deeds,
since I have come for Phylakidas' sake, Muse, as overseer . . .

The emphatic reference to deeds of war at the close of Herakles' speech helps motivate the break-off and effect the transition to the poet's role as master of ceremonies (ἦλθον . . . ταμίας, 57) for the celebrations of Phylakidas and his fami-

---

[12] The rhetorical movement of this passage is well expressed by Σ 47 e (noted by Slater, *Lexicon* s.v. ἀλλά, 1): "Now he begins to treat the particulars (τῶν ἐπὶ μέρους), after having accurately sketched the whole (τὸ ὅλον)." In fact, the ἀλλά resumes the incident introduced in 27-28: "[Telamon], whom [Herakles] took into bronze-loving war as a willing ally with his men from Tiryns."

ly.¹³ The words ἐν πόνοις ἔκπαγλον (54) are particularly appropriate in an ode celebrating pankratiasts, for whom Aias is the prototype.

Ol. 13.87-92 combines most of the topics we have seen:

    σὺν δὲ κείνῳ καί ποτ' Ἀμαζονίδων
    αἰθέρος ψυχρῶν ἀπὸ κόλπων ἐρήμου
    τοξόταν βάλλων γυναικεῖον στρατόν
90 καὶ Χίμαιραν πῦρ πνέοισαν καὶ Σολύμους **ἔπεφνεν.**
    διασωπάσομαί οἱ μόρον ἐγώ·
    τὸν δ' ἐν Οὐλύμπῳ φάτναι Ζηνὸς ἀρχαῖαι δέκονται.

)—

    ἐμὲ δ' εὐθὺν ἀκόντων
    ἱέντα ῥόμβον παρὰ σκοπὸν **οὐ χρή**
95 τὰ πολλὰ βέλεα καρτύνειν χεροῖν.
    Μοίσαις γὰρ ἀγλαοθρόνοις ἑκών
    Ὀλιγαιθίδαισίν τ' ἔβαν ἐπίκουρος.

    On the back of Pegasos from the cold recesses
    of the empty air he once fired upon the army
    of female archers, the Amazons, and by him
90 the fire-breathing Chimaira and Solymoi *were slain.*
    I shall say nothing about his own *doom,*
    but Pegasos is kept in the ancient stalls of Zeus on Olympos.

)—

    But as for me in casting whirling javelins on their straight
    path *I must not* hurl those many shafts
95 from my hands beside the mark.
    For I have willingly come to aid the splendidly-
    enthroned Muses and the Oligaithidai.

---

[13] Pindar also includes here the common break-off motif of "too much to tell." Similar is *Ol.* 2.81-85, where the prominence of death in the catalogue of heroes slain by Achilleus leads to the asyndetic break-off.

    ... ὃς Ἕκτορα **σφᾶλε,** Τροίας
    ἄμαχον ἀστραβῆ κίονα, Κύκνον τε **θανάτῳ πόρεν,**
    Ἀοῦς τε παῖδ' Αἰθίοπα. πολλά μοι ὑπ'
      ἀγκῶνος ὠκέα βέλη
    ἔνδον ἐντὶ φαρέτρας
85 φωνάεντα συνετοῖσιν.

    ... who *slew* Hektor, Troy's
    invincible tower of strength, and *gave to death* Kyknos
    and Dawn's Ethiopian son. *I have* many swift arrows
      under my arm
    in their quiver
85 that speak to the learned.

Here the emphatic ἔπεφνεν (90) concludes the list of Bellerophon's conquests, preparing for the asyndetic recoil by the poet (διασωπάσομαι ... ἐγώ, 91), the *praeteritio* of Bellerophon's own fate (μόρον, 91),[14] a brief concluding θαῦμα (Pegasos' translation to Olympos), self-exhortation (ἐμὲ δ'... οὐ χρή, 93-94), the topic of "too much to tell" (τὰ πολλά, 95), the presence of the Muses (96), and finally the introduction of the family's athletic successes by Pindar in his role as a "willing helper" (ἑκὼν ... ἔβαν ἐπίκουρος, 96-97).[15]

---

[14] Another example of turning from painful experience (in *praeteritio*) to success occurs at *Nem.* 5.14-20, which includes the presence of divinity (δαίμων, 16), the emphatic ἔλασεν (16), the asyndetic break-off (στάσομαι, 16), the gnomic justifications (16-18), and the preparation in lines 19-21 for the positive narrative of Peleus' winning of Thetis.

[15] Cf. κάρυξ ἑτοῖμος ἔβαν at *Nem.* 4.74, as the poet turns from the Aiakids' deeds to those of the Theandridai. A more complicated example is the interrupted catalogue of Aiakids at *Nem.* 4.25-35. After beginning with the example of Telamon, Pindar suddenly breaks off with a lengthy hesitative passage:

25 σὺν ᾧ [sc. Ἡρακλεῖ] ποτε Τροΐαν κραταιὸς Τελαμών
πόρθησε καὶ Μέροπας
καὶ τὸν μέγαν πολεμιστὰν ἔκπαγλον Ἀλκυονῆ,
οὐ τετραορίας γε πρὶν δυώδεκα πέτρῳ
ἥροάς τ' ἐπεμβεβαῶτας ἱπποδάμους ἕλεν
30 δὶς τόσους. ἀπειρομάχας ἐών κε φανείη
λόγον ὁ μὴ συνιείς· ἐπεί
ῥέζοντά τι καὶ **παθεῖν** ἔοικεν.

— τὰ μακρὰ δ' ἐξενέπειν ἐρύκει με τεθμός
ὧραί τ' ἐπειγόμεναι·
35 ἴυγγι δ' **ἕλκομαι** ἦτορ νεομηνίᾳ θιγέμεν.

25 with whom [sc. Herakles] once mighty Telamon
destroyed Troy and the Meropes
and that giant warrior, daunting Alkyoneus,
but not before he could smash twelve chariots with a boulder,
along with the horse-taming heroes riding in them—
30 two in each. One would have to be inexperienced
in battle to miss my point:
accomplishment usually involves *suffering* as well.

— But *I* am prevented from telling the long account by generic restraint
and the pressing hours;
35 and by a love-charm *I am drawn* in my heart to celebrate
the new-moon festival.

The mention of loss suffered in warfare (28-30) and in particular the word παθεῖν (32) prepare for the sudden interruption by the poet at the beginning of the strophe, as he deliberates whether or not to continue the exploits of the Aiakidai (which eventually he does in lines 44 ff.). For an analysis of this interrupted catalogue, see Miller, "Digressive Leisure" 202-212. In this poem Pindar uses both techniques for breaking off. In the above example (25-32), he ends the narrative with a reference to the loss and pain of battle, while at the end of the entire catalogue (69), he turns from the divine epiphany and the promise of greatness for Peleus' descendants to the occasion of the ode. See above note 4.

A complex example, which includes both death and divine intervention, occurs at *Isth.* 5.46-54, where Pindar praises Aigina for her bravery at the battle of Salamis.

>   πολλὰ μὲν ἀρτιεπής
>   γλῶσσά μοι τοξεύματ᾽ ἔχει περὶ κείνων
>   κελαδέσαι· καὶ νῦν ἐν Ἄρει μαρτυρῆσαι
>   κεν πόλις Αἴαντος ὀρθωθεῖσα ναύταις
>   ἐν πολυφθόρῳ Σαλαμὶς Διὸς ὄμβρῳ
> 50   ἀναρίθμων ἀνδρῶν **χαλαζάεντι φόνῳ**.
>   ἀλλ᾽ ὅμως καύχαμα κατάβρεχε σιγᾷ·
>   Ζεὺς τά τε καὶ τὰ νέμει,
>   Ζεὺς ὁ πάντων κύριος. ἐν δ᾽ ἐρατεινῷ
>   μέλιτι καὶ τοιαίδε τιμαὶ καλλίνικον χάρμ᾽ ἀγαπάζοντι.

>   My fluent tongue
>   has many arrows to sing
>   their praises, and recently Salamis, the island of Aias,
>   could testify to their martial prowess, since it was preserved
>   by their sailors during the devastating storm of Zeus,
> 50   when countless men perished in the *hailstorm of gore*.
>   *But nevertheless, drench* your vaunt in silence;
>   Zeus dispenses a variety of things,
>   Zeus the lord of all. And in poetry's delightful
>   honey such honors as these also welcome joyous victory song.

Since the rhetorical sense of this passage has been widely misunderstood, it is necessary to treat it in more detail, in order to see how Pindar has adapted the motif under discussion. Of crucial importance is the μέν in the first line: Pindar announces at the outset that he has many (πολλά, 46) arrows of praise, but the μέν (46) suggests that he will not use them all. What he in fact does is select one particular example to stand for the whole, namely the Aiginetans' glorious part in the victory at Salamis (cf. Hdt. 8.93, 122). Now the μέν still awaits an answer, but in the meantime the depiction of the battle of Salamis threatens to reach digressive proportions—Pindar has, as it were, let his enthusiasm carry him away. But by ending the account with the resounding "hailstorm of gore" (χαλαζάεντι φόνῳ, 50), he can suddenly turn from war to deeds of peace.[16] The μέν (46) is ultimately answered by the ἀλλ᾽ ὅμως (51), which rejects not only further treatment of the battle of Salamis, but also further examples of Aiginetan

---

[16] Cf. ἐν φοναῖς at *Pyth.* 11.37 (see above page 47). Note the presence of Zeus (Διός, 49). Cf. *Nem.* 1.62-69, where the catalogue of Herakles' deeds culminates in his fighting with the gods against the Giants and concludes with the vivid periphrasis for their death, φαιδίμαν γαίᾳ πεφύρσεσθαι κόμαν (68) "foul their bright hair with earth," from which Pindar turns suddenly to a depiction of Herakles' bliss on Olympos (αὐτὸν μάν, 69).

valor in war (ἐν Ἄρει, 48). "But nevertheless," (that is, in spite of the fact that I have many things to say about Aiginetan martial valor in general and about their recent performance at Salamis), "I must stop here" (and turn to their athletic achievements).

As Bundy pointed out, the expression τά τε καὶ τά in 52 does not refer to good and evil as almost everybody takes it, but designates the *variety* of Zeus' dispensations.[17] The point is that martial valor is but part of Aigina's blessings, which include as well her athletic successes, the subject of the coming lines. Most scholars have read these lines as fearful of boasting over victory lest it call forth envy from the gods,[18] but the importation of φθόνος into this passage has obscured its rhetorical point. The lines are indeed apologetic, but they apologize for turning from the glories of war to those of victory in athletics. Among the many good things that Zeus has given them are supremacy in war and athletics. By ending his account of the battle with the expression "hailstorm of gore," Pindar can praise the sailors' achievements and also give himself a valid reason for switching to less imposing accomplishments, but ones of the sort (cf. τοιαίδε, 54) that also (καί, 54) merit praise (cf. τιμαί, 54) and welcome victory song (καλλίνικον χάρμ' ἀγαπάζοντι, 54).

An especially striking example is the digression in *Ol.* 9, where, as Pindar begins to praise the Opountians, he states that "men become good and wise as divinity determines it" (28-29). He then illustrates this statement with the example of Herakles' combat against three gods.

                ἐπεὶ ἀντίον
30   πῶς ἂν τριόδοντος Ἡ-
      ρακλέης σκύταλον τίναξε χερσίν,
    (1)ἁνίκ' ἀμφὶ Πύλον σταθεὶς ἤρειδε Ποσειδάν,
    (2)ἤρειδεν δέ νιν ἀργυρέῳ τόξῳ πολεμίζων

---

[17] See Bundy, *Studia Pindarica* 74 note 100. For a discussion of the expression τά τε καὶ τά in this passage and others, see Bundy, "Quarrel" 80-81 and Race, "Two Pindaric Passages" 179-182 and "The End of *Olympia* 2" 257. A good formal parallel is *fr.* 141: θεὸς ὁ πάντα (= τά τε καὶ τά) τεύχων βροτοῖς | καὶ χάριν ἀοιδᾷ φυτεύει. Cf. also *Pa.* 6.132-134. The treatments of τά τε καὶ τά by Radt, *Pindars zweiter und sechster Paian* 178, Carey, *Five Odes* 114-115, and Hurst, "Observations" 131 all assume that at *Isth.* 5.52 it means "good and bad."

[18] The paraphrase by the lone scholiast on this passage refers to some vague source of envy: βρέχε ... τῇ σιωπῇ διὰ τὸν ἔξωθεν φθόνον. Some scholars follow Dissen, *Pindari Carmina* 2.570: *Tanta est laus vestra, ait, ut amplius gloriari nolim, ne deorum invidiam excitem. Iuppiter alio tempore etiam mala afferre potest* (e.g., Willcock, "The Fifth Isthmian" 40-45 and Most, "O. 2.83-90" 315). Others, following Wilamowitz, have sought an historical explanation (e.g., Hurst, "Observations" 131 and Bowra, *The Odes of Pindar* 50: "The command to keep silent is perhaps a caution against boasting too early before the Persians are finally driven out of Greece.") Introducing either "theology" or "history" into this passage distorts its straightforward encomiastic and rhetorical purposes. See Thummer, *Die Isthmischen Gedichte II* 94, who, however, misconstrues the meaning of τά τε καὶ τά and offers a reductively formalistic reading.

```
                Φοῖβος, (3)οὐδ' Ἀίδας ἀκινήταν ἔχε ῥάβδον,
                βρότεα σώμαθ' ᾇ κατάγει κοίλαν πρὸς ἄγυιαν
        35      θνᾳσκόντων; ἀπό μοι λόγον
                τοῦτον, στόμα, ῥῖψον·
                ἐπεὶ τό γε λοιδορῆσαι θεούς
        —       ἐχθρὰ σοφία, καὶ τὸ καυχᾶσθαι παρὰ καιρόν
                μανίαισιν ὑποκρέκει.
        40      μὴ νῦν λαλάγει τὰ τοι-
                    αῦτ'· ἔα πόλεμον μάχαν τε πᾶσαν
                χωρὶς ἀθανάτων· φέροις δὲ Πρωτογενείας
                ἄστει γλῶσσαν, ἵνα . . .
```

```
                            For how else
        30      could Herakles have brandished his club in his hands
                        against the trident,
                (1)when Poseidon took a stand before Pylos and pressed him hard,
                (2)and Phoibos pressed him in battle with his
                    silver bow, (3)nor did Hades keep still his staff,
                with which he leads down to his hollow abode the mortal bodies
        35      of the dying? Cast away from me
                    such a story, my mouth!
                For belittling the gods
        —       is a hateful skill and boasting out of place
                    sounds a note of madness.
        40      Stop babbling of such things now!
                        Keep war and all fighting
                clear of the immortals; apply your speech to the
                city of Protogeneia, where . . .
```

Pindar has carefully constructed this sequence in climactic order by giving each of the gods (Poseidon, Apollo, and Hades) increasingly longer treatments. In each case, the god appears with his characteristic weapon, and it is upon Hades' symbol of power, his ῥάβδος (33), that the emphasis falls. It is also evident that Pindar has reserved the somber word θνᾳσκόντων (35) until the very end and enjambed it. After this mention of death, Pindar can then reject this series of examples as inappropriate.[19] He continues in asyndeton, "Cast away from me such a story," and turns from this excursus on Herakles[20] to the local examples of

---

[19] For an analysis of the grammar and rhetoric of this passage, see Stinton, "Expressions of Disbelief" 67-68.

[20] Pindar is fond of digressing on his favorite hero before turning to the subject at hand. Cf. *Nem.* 3.22-28, on which see Race, "Pindaric Encomium" 151-152. At *Isth.* 1.12-14 the forceful φρῖξαν κύνες (13) prepares for the sudden appearance of the poet, who turns from this brief (but spirited) excursion on Herakles to praise of Herodotos' achievements (ἀλλ' ἐγὼ Ἡροδότῳ, 14). See Bundy, *Studia Pindarica* 43-44.

Pyrrha and Deukalion (and eventually to Patroklos) that provide a better measure of Epharmostos' achievements.[21]

The last example I wish to treat also builds to a climax, the famous roll call in *Pyth.* 1 of the battles that saved Greece from grievous slavery.

>   ἀρέομαι
> 75 (1)πὰρ μὲν Σαλαμῖνος Ἀθαναίων χάριν
>   μισθόν, (2)ἐν Σπάρτᾳ δ' ⟨ἀπὸ⟩ τᾶν πρὸ Κιθαιρῶ-
>   νος μαχᾶν,
>   ταῖσι Μήδειοι κάμον ἀγκυλότοξοι,
>   (3)παρ⟨ὰ⟩ δὲ τὰν εὔυδρον ἀκτὰν
>   Ἱμέρα παίδεσσιν ὕμνον Δεινομένεος τελέσαις,
> 80 τὸν ἐδέξαντ' ἀμφ' ἀρετᾷ, πολεμίων ἀνδρῶν **καμόντων**.
>)—
>   καιρὸν εἰ **φθέγξαιο**, πολλῶν πείρατα συντανύσαις . . .

> 75   I shall earn
>   (1)from telling of Salamis the Athenians' favor
>   as my reward, (2)and the Spartans' by telling of the battles
>   before Mt. Kithairon,
>   in which the curve-bowed Medes were beaten;
>   (3)but beside the well-watered bank of the Himeras
>   I shall pay to Deinomenes' sons the tribute of my hymn,
> 80   which they earned by their valor, when their enemies *were defeated*.
>)—
>   If *you would tell* the gist by combining the strands of many things . . .

By now it should come as no surprise that this rising series of battles concludes with a word such as καμόντων (80). In fact, Pindar has included the last three words, πολεμίων ἀνδρῶν καμόντων, for very specific reasons. For one thing, the word πολεμίων rings back to the earlier portion of the ode when Typhos was called πολέμιος (15) of the gods, thereby linking these two threats to human and divine civilization. But the phrase also serves as a summary seal to round off this section of the encomium on "deeds of war" before Pindar turns to Hieron's deeds of peace. And, by ending the passage—and the triad—with a verb indicating pain

---

[21] Bundy, *Studia Pindarica* 9 interpreted the exemplum as subjective: "The implication is that it would take the divine strength and daring of a Herakles to equal in praise the divine merits of the Opountians." Recently, however, Miller, in "Argumentation, Mimesis, and 'Myth' in the First *Olympian*," delivered at the CAMWS meeting in Tampa, April 1986, has suggested that these instances of Herakles holding his own against the gods may also serve as analogues for the victor, Epharmostos, who, Pindar tells us in the victory catalogue later in the poem (89-94), was as a boy forced to compete in the men's division at Marathon against πρεσβύτεροι (90) and won without losing a fall (ἀπτωτὶ δαμάσσαις, 92). If he is correct, then Pindar has purposefully let his enthusiasm for Epharmostos (and for his hero Herakles) carry him away to the point of impiety and seeming irrelevance.

and suffering, Pindar can then forcefully turn (in asyndetic self-exhortation) away from the tribulations of war to the concluding triad of the poem, in which he offers praise and counsel to Hieron concerning his domestic policies.²²

We have noted that each of these passages ends with a forceful word or phrase denoting death or suffering that prepares for the poet's sudden intrusion into his poem, whether it takes the form of an asyndetic prayer (e.g., εἴην, Ol. 9.80; εἴη, Pyth. 1.29, Nem. 8.35; εἰ δυνατόν, Nem. 9.28), an asyndetic question (e.g., ἦρ' ὦ φίλοι, Pyth. 11.38), an emphatic pronoun (e.g., ἐμοί, Ol. 1.52, Pyth. 10.48, Isth. 6.56; ἐγώ, Isth. 1.14), an asyndetic self-exhortation (e.g., ἀπό μοι... ῥῖψον, Ol. 9.35-36; οὐ χρή, Ol. 13.94; φθέγξαιο, Pyth. 1.81; μὴ σπεῦδε, Pyth. 3.61-62; σχάσον, Pyth. 10.51; κατάβρεχε, Isth. 5.51), or a first personal verb (e.g., ἀφίσταμαι, Ol. 1.52; διασωπάσομαι, Ol. 13.91; ἐδινάθην, Pyth. 11.38; στάσομαι, Nem. 5.16; ἕπομαι, Nem. 6.54; ἀναβάλλομαι, Nem. 9.29). In several instances divine presence provides a climactic sense of wonder (e.g., μακάρων, Ol. 1.52; Ποσειδᾶν... Φοῖβος... Ἀίδας, Ol. 9.31-33; Ζηνός, Ol. 13.92; Κρονίων, Pyth. 3.57; θεῶν, Pyth. 10.49; δαίμων, Nem. 5.16; δαιμονίοισι φόβοις, Nem. 9.27; Διός, Isth. 5.49). And, in returning to the positive program, Pindar often announces his encomiastic role (e.g., ἦλθον τιμάορος, Ol. 9.83-84; ἔβαν ἐπίκουρος, Ol. 13.97; ἄγγελος ἔβαν, Nem. 6.57b; ἦλθον... ταμίας, Isth. 6.57) and frequently invokes the authority of the Muses (e.g., Μοισᾶν, Ol. 9.81; Μοίσαις, Ol. 13.96; Μοῖσα, Pyth. 11.41; ὦ Μοῖσα, Isth. 6.57).

In every one of these examples, Pindar is turning from some painful aspect of existence to praise of positive achievement; each marks a major turning-point in its ode. Perhaps because all are so carefully crafted for their own poems, both thematically and formally, their many similarities have escaped the notice of commentators. Yet when they are all compared, they share so many features that they evoke a sense of wonder at Pindar's ability to give individual life to conventional topics: *ars est celare artem*.²³

---

²² Cf. the similar switch from deeds of war to those of peace at Ol. 2.81-83 (above note 13), Isth. 5.46-53 (above page 53), and Nem. 9.28-32 (above page 44).

²³ Pindar's technique was not lost on his great admirer (and frequent imitator), Horace. Cf. Carm. 3.3.65-72 and especially 2.1.33-40:

    qui gurges aut quae flumina lugubris
    ignara belli? quod mare Dauniae
     non decoloravere caedes?
35   quae caret ora *cruore nostro*?

    sed ne relictis, *Musa*, procax iocis
    Ceae *retractes* munera neniae;
     mecum Dionaeo sub antro
40   quaere modos leviore plectro.

CHAPTER 3
NEGATIVE EXPRESSIONS

Every reader of Pindar soon discovers that no small part of his stylistic artistry consists of expressing negatively ideas that in more straightforward speech would be expressed positively. A number of scholars have called attention to this phenomenon in passing,[1] but they have only scratched the surface of what constitutes one of the most important (and potentially confusing) stylistic and rhetorical techniques in Pindar's verse. There is not a single ode without at least one such negative expression, and most contain several instances. More important than mere number, however, is the fact that misunderstandings of particular passages have resulted from inadequate appreciation of Pindar's procedure. The purpose of this chapter is to survey the form, function, and vocabulary of negative expressions and to discuss a number of passages of importance; at the end we shall examine in detail a longer passage (*Pyth.* 9.70-103) that illustrates Pindar's effective use of this stylistic feature.

The Stylistic and Rhetorical Nature of Negative Expressions

The primary purpose of negative expressions in Pindar is to give variety (ποικιλία) to the vocabulary and discourse.[2] Since the basic thought behind every epinician ode is the rather simple "ἐσλὸν αἰνεῖν," the poet must either repeat himself endlessly or find new ways of expressing the same thought. In

---

[1] For example, Bury, *The Nemean Odes* 205 points out that μὴ κρύπτειν φάος ὀμμάτων (*Nem.* 10.40-41) is expressed positively at *Nem.* 7.66: ὄμματι δέρκομαι λαμπρόν, and Fränkel, *Early Greek Poetry* 448 note 18 has shown that σιγαλὸν ἀμαχανίαν ... φυγών (*Pyth.* 9.92) is equivalent to εὐμαχανίαν ... ἔφανας ... ὕμνῳ διώκειν (*Isth.* 4.2-3). More recently, Köhnken, "Litotes bei Pindar" 62-67 demonstrates that οὐκ ἀποδαμεῖ (*Pyth.* 10.37) is litotes for "ganz zu Hause" and discusses other instances in Pindar.

[2] Hermogenes notes that "negation" (ἀπόφασις) can be used to avoid repetition by varying the style: ὅταν δι' ἐγγύτητα τῆς λέξεως φεύγων τις τὴν ταυτότητα μεταβάλλῃ τὴν λέξιν (*Meth.* 37; 2.456.13-15, Sp.). For a survey of ancient views of litotes and related figures of speech, see Hoffmann, *Negatio Contrarii* 11-33.

much the same way that the oral epic poet can vary his use of formulae, so the written poetry of Pindar has at its disposal a large metaphorical vocabulary of positive and negative words and phrases that can be adapted to the meter and also express subtle nuances of sense and feeling. On the level of discourse, negative expressions often serve to provide variety in larger developments, particularly in catalogues and prayers, and to highlight a climactic, positive restatement.[3] Finally, in a number of cases, negative expressions have the additional effect of underscoring the ethical effort involved in successful action by depicting the adverse qualities that must be overcome. For example, the exhortation to Hieron at *Pyth.* 1.90, μὴ κάμνε λίαν δαπάναις, suggests by the verb κάμνειν the effort and pain that go into being generous.[4]

Perhaps the most succinct discussion of the stylistic and rhetorical background for the poetic use of negative expressions is in Aristotle's treatment of "stylistic impressiveness" (ὄγκος τῆς λέξεως) at *Rhet.* 3.1408a1 ff.:

> Antimachus' advice is also useful, namely to describe an object by the qualities it does not possess (ἐξ ὧν μὴ ἔχει), as he does in his description of Teumessus which begins: "There is a little wind-swept hill . . ." This kind of description can be prolonged indefinitely. This method of describing things negatively (ὅπως οὐκ ἔχει) can be used of good qualities or bad, whichever is useful at the time. Poets coin expressions of this kind, such as "stringless" and "lyreless" music, and they add epithets to describe qualities that are lacking (ἐκ τῶν στερήσεων). This is attractive in metaphors of proportion, as to say that the trumpet utters "a lyreless song." (G. M. A. Grube, trans.)

This procedure of describing things by the qualities which they do not have (ἐξ ὧν μὴ ἔχει, ὅπως οὐκ ἔχει, ἐκ τῶν στερήσεων) involves not only simple negatives, but also ἀ-privatives and metaphors of proportion, all of which abound in

---

[3] Among many examples, one might cite *Pyth.* 1.90: μὴ κάμνε λίαν δαπάναις followed by ἐξίει δ' ὥσπερ κυβερνάτας ἀνήρ | ἱστίον ἀνεμόεν (91-92); *Nem.* 5.50: μηκέτι ῥίγει followed by δίδοι | φωνάν (50-51); and *Nem.* 7.61: σκοτεινὸν ἀπέχων ψόγον followed by ὕδατος ὥτε ῥοὰς φίλον ἐς ἄνδρ' ἄγων | κλέος ἐτήτυμον αἰνέσω (62-63).

[4] Another example (among many) is at *Pyth.* 3.71, where Pindar says that Hieron is "not begrudging to the good" (οὐ φθονέων ἀγαθοῖς), meaning that he is "generous" to men of merit, but by casting it in the negative, the poet calls attention to Hieron's overcoming a natural fault of tyrants (cf. Hdt. 3.80.4: φθονέει . . . τοῖσι ἀρίστοισι). Aristotle labels this source of praise παρὰ τὸ προσῆκον "beyond expectations" at *Rhet.* 1.1367b14 and at 1368a13, and cites the example of Simonides' praise of Archedike, who in spite of being wife, sister, and mother of tyrants, οὐκ ἤρθη νοῦν ἐς ἀτασθαλίην. Likewise, at *Pyth.* 2.74, when Pindar says that Rhadamanthys' thought is "without blame" (ἀμώμητον) and that he "does not enjoy" (οὐδ' . . . τέρπεται) the deceptions of whisperers, he reminds us (and Hieron) how prone we are to their seductions. In general, by keeping before our eyes the contrasting terms of "failure," "oblivion," "blame," "selfishness," and "evil," Pindar never lets us forget that human existence is constantly poised between right and wrong choices, and that "success," "fame," "praise," "generosity," and "probity" are all the more remarkable and valuable for the many obstacles they must overcome.

Pindar's verse.[5] They can be used to deny a bad subject good qualities, such as ὅσσα δὲ μὴ πεφίληκε Ζεύς at *Pyth.* 1.13 (cf. *fr.* 81.2-3: τὸ δὲ μὴ Δί | φίλτερον, and *Pyth.* 2.42-43: ἄνευ Χαρίτων...| οὔτ'...γερασφόρον), or a good subject bad qualities, such as ἄδικον οὔθ' ὑπέροπλον ἥβαν δρέπων at *Pyth.* 6.48 (which, incidentally, reminds us of faults youth is prone to) and γλῶσσα δ' οὐκ ἔξω φρενῶν at *Isth.* 6.72. Let us begin with an example from *Pa.* 6.127-131:

> οὕνεκεν οὔ σε παιηόνων
> ἄδορπον εὐνάξομεν, ἀλλ' ἀοιδᾶν
> ῥόθια δεκομένα κατερεῖς,
> 130   πόθεν ἔλαβες ναυπρύτανιν
> δαίμονα καὶ τὰν θεμίξενον ἀρετ[άν.

> For we shall not put you to bed
> without a supper of paians, but rather
> receiving waves of songs you shall recount
> 130   where you came by your ship-ruling
> genius and that excellence for hospitality.

The first thing to note is that the οὐ (127) negates the verb εὐνάξομεν "we shall not put you to bed," and the concomitant idea is that of ἄδορπον "without supper." As a general rule in Pindar, an οὐ or μή is best taken primarily with the verb, although its force also applies to other ἀ-privatives and rejected words in the sentence.[6] Radt's comment is to the point: "Ein merkwürdiger Ausdruck für 'wir

---

[5] A quick survey of a lexicon reveals over a hundred different ἀ-privatives in Pindar. For the metaphor of "proportion" or "analogy," see Aristotle, *Poet.* 21.1457b22, where he gives the example of old age as "the evening of life." To take but one example of Pindar's metaphorical language, at *Pyth.* 4.283 he praises Damophilos with the statement, ὀρφανίζει μὲν κακὰν γλῶσσαν φαεννᾶς ὀπός. In straightforward (κυρίως) speech this means, approximately, "he suppresses backbiting." But Pindar has borrowed two metaphorical terms to give variety, subtlety, and depth to this statement. The first is the verb ὀρφανίζειν, "to bereave," one of a number of metaphorical terms expressing disapproval and avoidance (cf. κελαδεννᾶς τ' ὀρφανοί | ὕβριος at *Isth.* 4.8-9). The second term, φαεννός "bright," always (along with numerous other terms involving light discussed below) indicates conspicuousness. Likewise, the word ὄψ always has a positive connotation, usually indicating celebration. Thus, when Damophilos "deprives" slander of its "shiny" "voice," he (positively) puts it into obscurity (cf. Pindar's use of σκότος) and silence (cf. terms involving σιγά). To say, with Slater, *Lexicon* 525 that in this one instance the word φαεννός is "of the voice, *clear*" is to miss the bold metaphorical transfer from the visual realm to the auditory. In other words, Damophilos does not allow slander to possess the positive qualities of achievement and its celebration. Finally, the words κακὰν γλῶσσαν remind us that citizens are naturally inclined to backbite (cf. κακολόγοι δὲ πολῖται at *Pyth.* 11.28).

[6] The translation of Sandys, *Pindar* 543, "For we shall lay thee to rest, Aegina, not without banquet of paeans," slightly skews the meaning. The chorus wishes to assure Aegina that they do not intend to put her to bed without her fill of song. Granted, the difference may seem slight,

werden dich nicht unbesungen lassen.'"[7] As we shall see, εὐνάξομεν is one of a complex of metaphors describing the state of being without song in terms of sleep, death, forgetfulness, and silence.[8] There is also the notion of "dismissing" (as with χαῖρε in hymns). In sum, the hymnist assures Aigina that she will not be abandoned in silence, nor will she be without share of celebration. Here παιηόνων ἄδορπον nicely combines the ideas of feasting with song, the two components of proper *theoxenia* (cf. the positive εὐφώνοις θαλίαις at *Pyth.* 1.38). That this is the intended meaning is clear from what follows, for Pindar subsequently expresses himself positively: "but rather" (ἀλλ', 128).[9] This climactic assertion, carefully prepared by the negative statements, moves from στέρησις[10] (ἄδορπον) to ἕξις (δεκομένα), from deprivation (ἄδορπον) to abundance (ῥόθια), from silence (εὐνάξομεν) to speech (κατερεῖς).[11] By stating the negative first, Pindar not only produces striking metaphors, but by depicting what it is like not to have songs, he creates a tension that is relieved with the climactic assertion of Aigina's two claims to fame, her seamanship and hospitality.[12]

Achievement and its Celebration

If all the positive metaphorical terms associated with success (and by extension with its concomitant celebration) were categorized according to the senses and perception, they would be: *visual*, "bright"; *spatial*, "high, large, far reaching";

---

but important misunderstandings have resulted from overlooking this rule at *Nem.* 7.102 ff. See Slater, "Futures in Pindar" 93 with the objections of Cerri, "A proposito del futuro" 83-88.

[7] Radt, *Pindars zweiter und sechster Paian* 175.

[8] See below page 69. The positive verbs are ἀνάγω and (ἀν)εγείρω, which are almost always associated with song.

[9] Cf. ἀλλά at *Il.* 4.225 and *Od.* 6.44 (among many examples). Bundy, *Studia Pindarica* 22 note 50 and 36 note 3 points out the use of ἀλλά to reject foil and signal the climax, a very common phenomenon in Pindar, especially when shifting from negative to positive assertions, as here. Often there is also a shift of metaphorical terminology from the negative statement to the positive.

[10] The term στέρησις comes from Arist. *Rhet.* 3.1408a7 (quoted above), on which see the good discussion by Cope, *The Rhetoric of Aristotle* 68-70. Much of Pindar's alleged obscurity disappears when this technique of στέρησις → ἕξις is kept in mind.

[11] The word ῥόθια "breakers" gains its precise meaning from the preceding negative terms. In contrast to ἄδορπον it designates "fullness, abundance"; in contrast to εὐνάζειν it designates "activity" and "noise." At *Nem.* 7.62 the ῥοάς contrast with σκοτεινὸν ψόγον (61) and represent "free-flowing" praise, perhaps with a hint of "bright." At *Isth.* 7.19 the κλυταῖς ἐπέων ῥοαῖσιν are opposed to metaphors of sleep (εὕδει, 17) and forgetfulness (ἀμνάμονες, 17) and represent the "activity" and "sound" (cf. κλυταῖς ἐπέων) of song. In the passage from *Pa.* 6, note the urbane switch to the second person with κατερεῖς, indicating that not only will Aigina "stay awake," but she herself will declare her glories.

[12] Note the climactic arrangement of the two elements and the emphasis the second receives because of the emphatic τάν (131), its greater length, and the fact that it completes the period.

and *auditory*, "loud."[13] Victory—and its celebration—must be conspicuous: bright and bold so that it can be seen from afar, and loud enough for all to hear. The individual vocabulary is large.

Visual Display[14]

Light (χρονιώτατον φάος εὐρυσθενέων ἀρετᾶν, *Ol.* 4.10); radiance (ὑπέρτατον . . . φέγγος, *Pa.* 2.68); splendor (νικαφόρον ἀγλαΐαν, *Ol.* 13.14); illustrious (ἀγλααὶ νῖκαι, *Nem.* 11.20); shine (λάμπει δὲ σαφὴς ἀρετά, *Isth.* 1.22); blaze (φλέγεται δ' ἀρεταῖς, *Nem.* 10.2); evident (ἐπιφανέστερον, *Pyth.* 7.7); bright (λιπαρὸν κόσμον, *Ol.* 8.82-83); clear (ἐς φανερὰν ὁδόν, *Ol.* 6.73; σαφὴς ἀρετά, *Isth.* 1.22); φάει . . . ἐν καθαρῷ, *Pyth.* 6.14); apparent (πέφανται, *Nem.* 6.13b; πρόφαινεν, *Isth.* 8.56; πρόφατον, *Ol.* 8.16; ἀνέφανε, *Pyth.* 9.73; ἐπέδειξεν βίαν, *Nem.* 11.14).[15]

Spatial Display[16]

High, exalted (κλέος . . . ὑψηλόν, *Pyth.* 3.111; στέφανον ὕψιστον, *Pyth.* 1.100; ὑψοῦ . . . πατεῖν, *Ol.* 1.115; πτερύγεσσιν ἀερθέντ᾽ ἀγλααῖς, *Isth.* 1.64; πᾶσαν ὀρθώσαις ἀρετάν, *Isth.* 4.38; Μοῖρα πέμπῃ ἀνεκὰς ὄλβον ὑψηλόν, *Ol.* 2.21-22); distant (τηλαυγέσιν . . . στεφάνοις, *Pyth.* 2.6; τηλέφαντον ὄρσαι γέρας, *fr.* 5.2; περαίνει πρὸς ἔσχατον πλόον, *Pyth.* 10.28-29; τὸ δὲ κλέος τηλόθεν δέδορκε, *Ol.* 1.93-94); big, abundant (μέγα . . . κλέος, *Ol.* 8.10; ὁ πολύφατος ὕμνος, *Ol.* 1.8; εὐμαχανίαν . . . ἔφανας, *Isth.* 4.2); increase, flourish (ὕμνων ἄεξ᾽ . . . ἄνθος, *Ol.* 6.105; θάλλοισ᾽ ἀρετά, *Isth.* 5.17; εὐανθὴς ἅπας τέθαλεν ὄλβος, *Thren.* 7.7); movement, activity (ἀλλ᾽ . . . στεῖχ᾽, *Nem.* 5.2-3; ἀνάγει, *Isth.* 4.22).

---

[13] One could also include *taste*, "sweet" (cf. ἁδύς, γλυκύς, and μέλι) and *touch*, "soft" (cf. μαλ(θ)ακός, ἀγανός, and perhaps ἁβρός), but with the exception of τραχύς and one clear instance of πικρός there is no corresponding negative vocabulary. Steiner, *Crown of Song* frequently points out metaphors of light and dark, but does not mention the spatial and auditory metaphors.

[14] See the excellent chapter "Areta und Ruhm als 'Licht'" in Gundert, *Dichterberuf* 11-19. Opposing terms (which will be illustrated shortly) include σκότος, σκοτεινός, καλύπτω, κρύπτω, κρυφαῖος, and ἐπίκρυφος.

[15] Cf. ἐπιδείκνυμι at Bakch. 2.9, 3.93, Pindar *Pyth.* 4.253 and *fr.* 32. It is this term which ultimately came to designate the literary genre as ἐπιδεικτικός.

[16] Opposing terms include χαμαί, πίτνω, ἔνδον, ἐν μεγάρῳ, (κατα)φθίνω, δέω, ἐλινύω, κάθημαι, and various κατα-compounds. All of these designate downward motion, diminution, or confinement. For the nexus of ideas involving "increasing" and "flourishing" and their relationship to the epinician occasion, see Nisetich, *Poetry of Victory* 118 ff. and "Olympian 1.8-11" 62-65.

Auditory Display[17]

Sing out, celebrate (κελαδήσομεν, Ol. 2.2; εἰ δ' ἄεθλα γαρύεν ἔλδεαι, Ol. 1.3-4; Λοκρὶς παρθένος ἀπύει, Pyth. 2.19); announce (κάρυξ ἀνέειπέ νιν ἀγγέλλων, Pyth. 1.32; κλυτὰν φέροισ' ἀγγελίαν, Ol. 14.21; νίκαν... ἀπαγγελεῖ, Pyth. 6.18); proclaim (γεγωνητέον, Ol. 2.6; αὐτὸν... ὕπατον παίδων ἀνέειπεν, Pyth. 10.8-9; κάρυξε Θήβαν, Isth. 3.12); loud-sounding (ἀγαφθέγκτων ἀοιδᾶν, Ol. 6.91); boasting (κόμπον ἱείς, Nem. 8.49; ἐπέων καύχας ἀοιδά, Nem. 9.7); shouting (ὄρθιον ὤρυσαι, Ol. 9.109).

The list could easily be extended, but it is representative of the positive vocabulary of achievement and praise and must be kept in mind in order to understand Pindar's complex use of negative and antithetical expressions. In general, the successful athlete makes an open, public display of his excellence, he is proclaimed officially by the herald at the games, he brings glory to his city, and he himself is distinguished (cf. κριθείς at Nem. 7.7). Then the poet must cause that brightness, exaltation, and fame to be openly displayed in his poem. Thus, the same positive terms which apply to the victory also apply to the poet's attempt to match them in song.

At the end of *Isth.* 1, Pindar expresses the wish that his celebration of Herodotos might inspire the athlete to bring honor to Thebes with further victories at the Pythian and Olympic games. He describes Herodotos as "lifted up on the bright wings of the tuneful Pieridai" (εὐφώνων πτερύγεσσιν ἀερθέντ' ἀγλααῖς Πιερίδων, 64-65), which combines the positive qualities of sound (εὐφώνων), height (ἀερθέντ'), and brightness (ἀγλααῖς)—all aspects of conspicuousness. In contrast, Pindar concludes the ode with a gnome that portrays *ex contrario* what Herodotos cannot be if he wishes to further his athletic career: a miser who guards his "hidden" (κρυφαῖον, 67) wealth "inside" (ἔνδον, 67), who, instead of honoring his fellow men (cf. τιμὰν... τεύχοντ', 66-67), mocks them (ἐμπίπτων γελᾷ, 68),[18] who disregards the fact that he will die "without fame"

---

[17] Opposing terms include σιγάω, σιγά, σιγαλός, (δια)σωπάω, ἀκλεής, ἀγρυξία, λάθα, and ἀμνάμων.

[18] This derisive laughter which "attacks" (ἐμπίπτων, 68) others contrasts with the sweet laughter of victory which inspires *charis* as described at Pyth. 8.85-86: γέλως γλυκύς | ὦρσεν χάριν. Most, "Pindar I. 1.67-68," claims that ἐμπίπτω with dative "can only mean to attack someone physically in the serious attempt to inflict violent harm upon him" (102) and therefore construes the phrase ἄλλοισι δ' ἐμπίπτων γελᾷ to mean "if he encounters misfortune, laughs at it" (107). But in light of the parallels Bundy adduces (*Studia Pindarica* 88), it is much simpler to take ἐμπίπτων as a strong metaphor for κερτομεῖν.

(δόξας ἄνευθεν, 68). The contrasting terms are ἀγλααῖς—κρυφαῖον, πτερύγεσσιν ἀερθέντ'—ἔνδον, and εὐφώνων—δόξας ἄνευθεν.[19]

A similar contrast is developed in *Ol.* 12, where Ergoteles' racing fame would have "shed its leaves" (κατεφυλλορόησεν, 15)[20] and been "without fame" (ἀκλεής, 15), like a rooster that "fights within" (ἐνδομάχας, 14);[21] instead (νῦν δ', 17) he has been crowned at the great Panhellenic festivals, lives in companionship (ὁμιλέων, 19 contrasts with the στάσις of 16), and "exalts" (βαστάζεις, 19; cf. Σ 27 a: ἀντὶ τοῦ ἐπαίρεις καὶ αὔξεις) his new homeland.[22]

At *Nem.* 9.6-7 Pindar combines three important negative terms: ἔστι δέ τις λόγος ἀνθρώπων, τετελεσμένον ἐσλόν | μὴ χαμαὶ σιγᾷ καλύψαι. Here is an elaborate negative periphrasis of "ἐσλὸν αἰνεῖν" that contains our three aspects: spatial (χαμαί), auditory (σιγᾷ), and visual (καλύψαι). This is then contrasted (δ', 7) with the "fitting" (πρόσφορος, 7) song of "loud acclaim" (καύχας, 7) and the upward movement of ἀνὰ ... ἀνὰ ... ὄρσομεν (8). A close parallel is *Pyth.* 9.93-94 (discussed below page 84), where λόγον ... ἀλίοιο γέροντος (94) = λόγος ἀνθρώπων; (93) πεποναμένον εὖ (93) = τετελεσμένον ἐσλόν; and μὴ ... κρυπτέτω (94) = μὴ ... καλύψαι. Both are followed by vigorous affirmations of the need for praise.

There are two very similar passages in which Pindar highlights the joy, congratulations, and display of victory by portraying the opposite effect on the losers. The first is at *Ol.* 8.67-71:

ἐν τέτρασιν παίδων ἀπεθήκατο γυίοις
νόστον ἔχθιστον καὶ ἀτιμοτέραν γλῶσ-

---

[19] Cf. *Nem.* 1.31-32, where ἐν μεγάρῳ ... ἔχειν = ἔνδον νέμει; πλοῦτον κατακρύψαις = πλοῦτον κρυφαῖον; and φίλοις ἐξαρκέων contrasts with ἄλλοισι δ' ἐμπίπτων γελᾷ, while εὖ ... ἀκοῦσαι contrasts with δόξας ἄνευθεν. At *Isth.* 8.70 the expression ὑπὸ χειᾷ (or ὑπὸ κόλπου/ῳ; see Young, "Pindar Isthmian 8.70" and Papillon, "Isthmian 8.70") combines the ideas of concealment and confinement.

[20] This bold metaphor combines the idea of downward motion (κατα-) (cf. πίτνει χαμαί at *Pyth.* 8.93 and χαμαὶ πετοῖσαν at *Nem.* 4.41) with the notion of withering (cf. φθινοπωρὶς ... πνοά at *Pyth.* 5.120-121) and dying (cf. φθίνει at *Pyth.* 1.94). For examples of ἀρετά, κλέος, πλοῦτος, and ὕμνος combined with the idea of "flowering" and "flourishing," see Verdenius, *Commentaries I* 99 and Slater, *Lexicon* s.v. ἀνθέω and ἄνθος. Nisetich, "Leaves of Triumph and Mortality" 258-264 sees here a further allusion to *Il.* 6.146 ff., but κατεφυλλορόησεν can certainly be understood on its own terms within the context of Pindar's language.

[21] ἐνδο- (reinforced by συγγόνῳ παρ' ἑστίᾳ) is equivalent to ἔνδον and ἐν μεγάρῳ (discussed above note 19) and refers to the *obscurum* of the private realm, on which see H. Arendt, "The Public and the Private Realm" in *The Human Condition* 22-78 and esp. 71 note 78, where she notes that "the Greek and Latin words for the interior of the house, megaron [μέλαθρον ?] and atrium, have a strong connotation of darkness and blackness." κλέος can only be acquired in the public realm, while failure is consigned to the private. Cf. *fr.* 42, esp. προφαίνειν (1), ἐς μέσον χρὴ παντὶ λαῷ | δεικνύναι (4-5), and σκότει κρύπτειν (6).

[22] The meaning of βαστάζεις has been much disputed. I follow Verdenius, *Commentaries I* 101-102, who discusses other interpretations.

σαν καὶ ἐπίκρυφον οἶμον,
70 πατρὶ δὲ πατρὸς ἐνέπνευσεν μένος
γήραος ἀντίπαλον.

On four boys' bodies he put away from himself
a very hateful homecoming and speech with less honor
and an obscure path.
70 But into his grandfather he breathed courage
to wrestle against old age.

Each of the results of defeat that Alkimedon "put away from himself" (ἀπεθήκατο, a rejection-word similar to (ἀπο)φεύγω) has a corresponding positive expression in other odes. The opposite of the νόστος ἔχθιστος is the νόστος γλυκερός / γλυκύς (*Pyth.* 4.32 and *Nem.* 9.22-23); the opposite of the ἀτιμοτέρα γλῶσσα (cf. ἀκλεὴς τιμά at *Ol.* 12.15) is the εὐκλεὴς νόστος (*Nem.* 2.24); the opposite of the ἐπίκρυφος οἶμος is the φανερὰ ὁδός (*Ol.* 6.73) and καθαρὰ κέλευθος (*Isth.* 5.23). This series of negatives is then followed by a vigorous statement of what his victory did accomplish: instead (δέ, 70) it inspired courage in his grandfather. At *Pyth.* 8.81-87, with even more elaboration, Pindar mentions the same elements.

τέτρασι δ' ἔμπετες ὑψόθεν
σωμάτεσσι κακὰ φρονέων,
τοῖς οὔτε νόστος ὁμῶς
ἔπαλπνος ἐν Πυθιάδι κρίθη,
85 οὐδὲ μολόντων πὰρ ματέρ' ἀμφὶ γέλως γλυκύς
ὦρσεν χάριν· κατὰ λαύρας δ' ἐχθρῶν ἀπάοροι
πτώσσοντι, συμφορᾷ δεδαγμένοι.

And upon four boys' bodies you fell from above
with hostile intent,
for whom no homecoming as joyous as yours
was decided at the Pythian festival,
85 nor upon returning to their mother did sweet laughter
arouse joy all around; but to avoid their enemies
they shrink down alleyways, bitten by failure.

Aristomenes' opponents had a "homecoming" (νόστος) that was "not as joyous" (οὔτε... ὁμῶς ἔπαλπνος, litotes for unpleasant[23] and parallel to νόστον ἔχθιστον at *Ol.* 8.69), nor upon their return to their mother (parallel to the grandfather at *Ol.* 8.70) did sweet laughter "arouse χάρις all around" (parallel to ἀτιμοτέραν γλῶσσαν at *Ol.* 8.69), but they "shrink down alleyways" (κατὰ λαύρας is parallel to ἐπίκρυφον οἶμον at *Ol.* 8.69) "to avoid their enemies" (ἐχθρῶν is

---

[23] For another example of litotes with οὐχ ὁμῶς, cf. *Isth.* 3.6.

parallel to ἔχθιστον at *Ol.* 8.69). This negative portrayal is then contrasted (δέ, 88) with the victor, who is "flying" (πέταται, 90) on his "winged" (ὑποπτέροις, 91) manliness.[24] These two passages are also very similar rhetorically. Both celebrate the "manliness" (cf. ἀνορέας at *Ol.* 8.67 and ἀνορέαις at *Pyth.* 8.91) of boy wrestlers who have won in the most difficult fashion, by having to defeat four successive opponents, a feat sufficiently noteworthy to be found in inscriptions.[25] Having called attention to the large number of defeated boys, the poet can then dwell on details of their disappointed return to their families, not in order to sound a note of "savagely boyish exultation,"[26] but to emphasize by purposely exaggerated contrast the joys of hard-earned victory, in which there are many losers for each victor.[27]

In his paradigmatic choice at *Il.* 9.412-416, Achilleus wavers between a long, safe life at home without fame and an early, glorious death fighting before Troy. The heroic life requires risk (κίνδυνος) in the public realm of competition, for which the reward is fame. We have already seen at *Isth.* 1.64-68 the contrast between an anonymous τις who guards his hidden wealth inside and who dies without fame and the athlete who brings his city honor. At *Ol.* 6.9-11, Pindar contrasts deeds without risk with those entailing effort: ἀκίνδυνοι δ' ἀρεταί | οὔτε παρ' ἀνδράσιν οὔτ' ἐν ναυσὶ κοίλαις | τίμιαι· πολλοὶ δὲ μέμνανται, καλὸν εἴ τι ποναθῇ. Here the negative expression is brief and simple; at *Ol.* 1.81-84 occurs a remarkable series of negative ideas portraying the antithesis of heroic risk:

---

[24] The following lines in the poem contain a very impressive alternation of negative and positive observations, in the midst of which is the famous expression τί δέ τις; τί δ' οὔ τις; (95). It might be observed that the very subject of this chapter is "what a man is, and what a man is not."

[25] Σ 117 at *Pyth.* 8.81 gives the technical term for this achievement: ἄνευ κλήρου . . . νικήσαντος (= ἀνέφεδρος). For discussions see Moretti, *Iscrizioni Agonistiche Greche* 171-173, and Ebert, *Griechische Epigramme auf Sieger* 228-229. For individual inscriptions, cf. Ebert 32 (= Moretti 20), Ebert 55 (= Moretti 33), and Ebert 76 (= Moretti 64).

[26] Gildersleeve, *Pindar* 199. Pindar's portrayal is indeed vivid, especially in comparison with *Nem.* 11.26, where he simply predicts that Aristagoras would have enjoyed a better homecoming than his rivals: κάλλιον ἂν δηριώντων ἐνόστησ' ἀντιπάλων, but we are not meant to linger too long on the details, or to think that all those defeated in the great games had to sneak back into town, nor say with Gildersleeve of ἀτιμοτέραν γλῶσσαν that it "refers to the jibes and jeers of enemies in the gate" (199). We are meant to experience (metaphorically) the deprivation of defeat, so as to appreciate the glow of victory.

[27] Pindar has already prepared the reader for Aristomenes' hard work with the negative expression μὴ σὺν μακρῷ πόνῳ at *Pyth.* 8.73 and the positive δαμάσσας ἔργῳ at 80. The principle of going the extra mile to win making the victory more enjoyable is enunciated at *Nem.* 7.70-73, where Pindar (as eulogist/athlete) says that he has gone "all the way" in the pentathlon (significantly ending with wrestling), and as a result: εἰ πόνος ἦν, τὸ τερπνὸν πλέον πεδέρχεται (74). At *Pyth.* 5.45 ff. Karrhotos enjoys the fortune of being remembered with highest praise (λόγων φερτάτων μναμήι', 48-49) after his "great toil" (πεδὰ μέγαν κάματον, 47) because he won out of a field of forty contestants.

ὁ μέγας δὲ κίν-
δυνος ἄναλκιν οὐ φῶτα λαμβάνει.
θανεῖν δ' οἷσιν ἀνάγκα, τά κέ τις ἀνώνυμον
γῆρας ἐν σκότῳ καθήμενος ἕψοι μάταν,
ἁπάντων καλῶν ἄμμορος;

> A great risk
> does not captivate the man who is a coward.
> But since men must die, why would anyone sit in darkness
> and vainly stew a nameless old age,
> with no portion of all those noble deeds?

The position of οὐ creates a purposeful ambiguity. Although it may be taken with ἄναλκιν φῶτα ("Great danger | Calls to no coward's heart," Conway, *Odes of Pindar* 6), it is more natural to take it with λαμβάνει ("Great danger does not come upon the spineless man," Nisetich, *Pindar's Victory Songs*, 84). As often (cf. *Ol.* 6.9-11: ἀκίνδυνοι ... οὐ), Pindar employs a negative along with an ἀ-privative. Although the next sentence contains no overt negative, a rhetorical question with a τίς is equivalent to οὐδείς: "why would anyone?" means "no one would." Every word is carefully chosen. The prominent ἀνώνυμον (note the privative) corresponds to δόξας ἄνευθεν at *Isth.* 1.68 and ἀκλεής at *Ol.* 12.15; ἐν σκότῳ adds the visual dimension and contrasts with the extensive vocabulary of light and visibility that characterizes successful action in the public view, while καθήμενος portrays the stationary, spatially restricted life of the stay-at-home (cf. ἐνδομάχας at *Ol.* 12.14 and ἔνδον at *Isth.* 1.67). The verb ἕψοι corresponds to νέμει at *Isth.* 1.67 (and, as we shall see, with πέσσοντ' at *Pyth.* 4.186) and depicts an obsessive preoccupation with wealth and life that is ultimately "in vain" (μάταν), for it is deprived of (ἄμμορος; note the privative) all the noble aspects of human existence (ἁπάντων καλῶν). Not surprisingly, this extended negative characterization is immediately followed by an impressive positive description of Pelops' heroic attitude: ἀλλ' ἐμοὶ μὲν οὗτος ἄεθλος | ὑποκείσεται (84-85). In addition, Pindar goes on to state that from the games in Pelops' honor τὸ δὲ κλέος | τηλόθεν δέδορκε (93-94), an expression that compresses all three aspects under consideration: auditory (κλέος), spatial (τηλόθεν), and visual (δέδορκε).

At *Pyth.* 4.185-187, Hera inspires the heroes with a desire for sailing on the Argo:

185   ... μή τινα λειπόμενον
τὰν ἀκίνδυνον παρὰ ματρὶ μένειν αἰ-
ῶνα πέσσοντ', ἀλλ' ἐπὶ καὶ θανάτῳ
φάρμακον κάλλιστον ἑᾶς ἀρετᾶς ἅ-
λιξιν εὑρέσθαι σὺν ἄλλοις.

185   ... lest anyone be left behind
to remain with his mother and brood over a life
without risk, but rather, even if it meant death,
to gain the most noble remedy for his own valor
in the company of other age-mates.

Here, as the context demands, the emphasis is on going forth from the security of home to a life of risk in the public realm. λειπόμενον "left behind" indicates the privation of οὐ ... λαμβάνει at *Ol.* 1.81, while ἀκίνδυνον corresponds to κίνδυνος at *Ol.* 1.81; παρὰ ματρὶ μένειν denotes the "stay-at-home," which at *Ol.* 1.83 is portrayed by ἐν σκότῳ καθήμενος.[28] αἰῶνα corresponds to γῆρας at *Ol.* 1.83, the article τάν (which Gildersleeve, *Pindar* 296 correctly calls "contemptuous") reinforces the rejection made explicit by μάταν at *Ol.* 1.83, while πέσσοντ' (fittingly borrowed from the *Iliad* for this epic-like context), like ἕψοι at *Ol.* 1.83, stresses solicitous preoccupation. In both cases, the positive is forcefully introduced mid-line by ἀλλά.

Before concluding this section on achievement and its celebration, it is worthwhile to consider a few more examples of the negative side, namely of failure (or lack of participation) and its concomitant obscurity. *Fr.* 228 describes the state of "darkness" resulting from excusing oneself from participation: τιθεμένων ἀγώνων πρόφασις | ... ἀρετὰν ἐς αἰπὺν ἔβαλε σκότον. *Fr.* 229 describes the state of failure in terms of "silence": νικώμενοι γὰρ ἄνδρες ἀγρυξίᾳ δέδενται. Both aspects are combined (in the figure of synaesthesia, "black silence") at *Parth.* 1.9-10: ὁ δὲ μηδὲν ἔχων ὑπὸ σιγᾷ μελαίνᾳ κάρα κέκρυπται. At *Isth.* 8.70-71 Kleandros deserves praise "because he did not repress his youth in a hole" (ἥβαν γὰρ οὐκ ... ὑπὸ χειᾷ ... δάμασεν), that is, he "displayed it."[29] On the other hand, a successful deed may be described as "dead" if it is kept in silence (θνᾴσκει δὲ σιγαθὲν καλὸν ἔργον, *fr.* 121), or as "asleep" if it is "old" (ἐκ λεχέων ἀνάγει φάμαν **παλαιάν** | εὐκλέων ἔργων· ἐν ὕπνῳ | γὰρ πέσεν, *Isth.* 4.22-23), or as "forgotten," as at *Nem.* 6.20-21, where the victorious Praxidamas "stopped the forgetting of Sokleidas" (ἔπαυσε λάθαν | Σωκλείδα'), that is, "caused him to be remembered." All three ideas ("old," "sleeping," and "forgetting") are combined at *Isth.* 7.16 (ἀλλὰ **παλαιὰ** γάρ | εὕδει χάρις, **ἀμνάμονες** δὲ βροτοί) before the climactic assertion of song's celebratory role at the beginning of the next triad (18 ff.).[30] Finally, at *Nem.*

---

[28] It also parallels συγγόνῳ παρ' ἑστίᾳ at *Ol.* 12.14 and ἐν μεγάρῳ at *Nem.* 1.31. For a detailed analysis of *Pyth.* 4.186-187, see Race, "Pindar's Heroic Ideal" 350-356.

[29] See above note 19. The verb δάμασεν tactfully implies that it would have taken considerable effort to repress his youthful talents and its forcefulness, I believe, accords better with ὑπὸ χειᾷ than with the feeble expression ὑπὸ κόλπου/ῳ.

[30] The old fame must be "awakened"; cf. *Pyth.* 9.104-105: χρέος, αὖτις ἐγεῖραι | καὶ παλαιὰν δόξαν; *Ol.* 8.74: χρὴ μναμοσύναν ἀνεγείροντα φράσαι; and *Isth.* 4.22-23: ἐκ λεχέων ἀνάγει ... ἀνεγειρομένα. In two places, Pindar stresses the fact that his songs possess sound

7.12-13 Pindar equates lack of song with darkness: ταὶ μεγάλαι γὰρ ἀλκαί | σκότον πολὺν ὕμνων ἔχοντι δεόμεναι. "Those great deeds of courage (cf. μέγας... ἄναλκιν at *Ol.* 1.81) have great obscurity (cf. ἐν σκότῳ at *Ol.* 1.83) when they lack songs."

Praise and Blame[31]

Like the pairs of terms "light-dark," "sound-silence," "high-low," "moving-stationary" that we have been examining, where the one can be expressed as the negative of the other, so too praise is often defined as the negative of blame. Slater calls attention to two examples.[32] At *Nem.* 7.64 Pindar protests that if an Achaian is present "he will not blame me" (οὐ μέμψεταί μ'), and at *Isth.* 2.20 Xenokrates "did not blame" (οὐκ ἐμέμφθη) the driving of his charioteer. Both of these indicate (in litotes) *approval* for successful effort.

There are a number of less obvious examples. When Pindar prays to bequeath to his sons "fame without that (i.e., Odysseus') dishonor" (κλέος | μὴ τὸ δύσφαμον, *Nem.* 8.36-37), he is expressing negatively what elsewhere he puts in positive form (e.g., κλέος ἐτήτυμον at *Nem.* 7.63), while reminding us that "infamy" too is a form of κλέος. When, at *Ol.* 6.89-90, the poet will see if he can "escape the ancient reproach" (ἀρχαῖον ὄνειδος... εἰ φεύγομεν), he means that he expects approval for his tactful praise (with the urbane suggestion, "beyond what one would expect of a Boiotian"). At *Ol.* 1.35 the poet says that observing the propriety of saying good things about the gods entails "less blame" (μείων ... αἰτία), by which he also implies that it is more laudable. Similarly, at *Pyth.* 1.82 he says that if one is brief, then "less blame comes from men" (μείων ἕπεται μῶμος ἀνθρώπων), implying "more approval."[33]

At *Nem.* 7.61 Pindar declares that he is Thearion's guest-friend (ξεῖνός εἰμι), and says:

---

and activity by contrasting his art with that of the sculptor. The one occurs at the end of *Isth.* 2 (cf. οὐκ ἐλινύσοντας, 46), while the other opens *Nem.* 5: οὐκ ἀνδριαντοποιός εἰμι.

[31] For stimulating discussions of praise and blame in Pindar and archaic poetry, see G. Nagy, *The Best of the Achaeans* 222-252 and B. Gentili, *Poetry and its Public* 107-114.

[32] Slater, "Futures in Pindar" 93.

[33] In very similar passages (where silence or abbreviation is recommended), *Isth.* 1.63 gives the positive εὐθυμίαν μείζω φέρει, while οὐ σκαιότερον at *Ol.* 9.104 is litotes for "more appropriate," "better." Cf. Σ 156 d: οὐ σκαιότερον, ἀλλ' ἐκ τῶν ἐναντίων βέλτιον. Other scholl. gloss it as σοφώτερον (cf. σοφώτατον at *Nem.* 5.18 and ἀκοὰ σοφοῖς at *Pyth.* 9.78). Slater's "ill-omened" is wide of the mark. At *Nem.* 5.16 οὐ... κερδίων means "inappropriate," "worse." Behind all of these passages is the thought "it is impossible to please every kind of listener" (cf. Thouk. 2.35.2-3), and the negative expressions emphasize the difficulty of the poet's attempt to strike a proper balance.

> σκοτεινὸν ἀπέχων ψόγον,
> ὕδατος ὥτε ῥοὰς φίλον ἐς ἄνδρ' ἄγων
> κλέος ἐτήτυμον αἰνέσω.
>
> keeping away dark blame,
> like streams of water I shall bring to the man I love
> genuine fame as I praise him.

Since praise "mirrors" the brightness of success (cf. *Nem.* 7.14), it is not surprising that blame should be described as "dark." Here "keeping away dark blame" reinforces by contrast his intention to praise (αἰνέσω) by bestowing true fame, which he compares to streams of water (cf. ἀοιδᾶν ῥόθια at *Pa.* 6.128-129).[34]

To close this discussion of praise and blame, we shall examine two longer passages in detail, because the one from *Pyth.* 2 has caused considerable misunderstanding and comparison with the former clarifies its meaning. The first is at *Ol.* 1.52-53, when Pindar breaks off from the spiteful story told by one of the envious neighbors of how the gods ate Pelops' flesh:

> ἐμοὶ δ' ἄπορα γαστρίμαρ-
>   γον μακάρων τιν' εἰπεῖν· ἀφίσταμαι·
> ἀκέρδεια λέλογχεν θαμινὰ κακαγόρους.
>
> But I cannot call any
>   of the blessed gods a glutton. I stand back.
> Impoverishment is often the lot of those who speak evil.

As we know from line 35 (ἔστι δ' ἀνδρὶ φάμεν ἐοικὸς ἀμφὶ δαιμόνων καλά),[35] Pindar intends to reject the "slanderous" criticism of the gods and convert it into one of praise for them and for Pelops. To emphasize this shift, he tells what he is not going to do; not only is he unable to tell this particular story, but, as a general observation, impoverishment frequently results from defamation. As always, we must keep in mind the positive: namely, that praise is motivated by kindness expressed towards a friend and results in mutual χάρις. In contrast, blame is motivated by hatred and results in enmity. Its justified use is in conjunction with praise (cf. *Nem.* 8.39), but fault-finding for its own sake can become an alienating obsession, as Theophrastos shows in his depiction of κακολογία.[36] By eschewing the dangers of excessive blame, Pindar highlights his own version of the myth, which features instead the love of Poseidon for Pelops.

---

[34] Many have pointed out the close association in Pindar of water with praise, but Hubbard, *Pindaric Mind* 154 (following Finley, *Pindar and Aeschylus* 52-53) goes too far in calling it "a symbol for poetry."
[35] *Ol.* 9.37-38 provides a negative variation: τό γε λοιδορῆσαι θεούς | ἐχθρὰ σοφία.
[36] Thphr. *Char.* 28.1: ἔστι δὲ ἡ κακολογία ἀγωγὴ τῆς ψυχῆς εἰς τὸ χεῖρον ἐν λόγοις.

At *Pyth*. 2.52-56 Pindar effects a transition from his long ψόγος of Ixion (21-48) to the praise of Hieron:

>   ἐμὲ δὲ χρεών
>   φεύγειν δάκος ἀδινὸν κακαγοριᾶν.
>   εἶδον γὰρ ἑκὰς ἐὼν τὰ πόλλ' ἐν ἀμαχανίᾳ
> 55 ψογερὸν Ἀρχίλοχον βαρυλόγοις ἔχθεσιν
>   πιαινόμενον.

>   But I must
>   flee the persistent bite of reproaches,
>   for standing at a far remove I have seen
> 55 Archilochos the blamer often in straits as he fed on
>   dire words of hatred.

This passage is more elaborate than the one from *Ol*. 1, but it shares many common features, not least of which is the rhetorical function of switching from blame (one form of epideictic poetry) to praise (the other). In effect, the poet is saying, "I am finished presenting the negative side of life and intend to praise true accomplishment." At *Ol*. 1.52 he is unable to speak bad things; at *Pyth*. 2.52 he "must flee the persistent bite of reproaches."[37] At *Ol*. 1.52 he "stands back" from what the envious man (τις ... φθονερῶν, 47) had said of the gods; at *Pyth*. 2.54 he is "at a far remove" from Archilochos (the paradigmatic critic). At *Ol*. 1.53 he expresses the "poverty" of slander in a gnome; at *Pyth*. 2.54 he uses the concrete example of Archilochos, who was "often in straits." The following table will make clearer the close relationship of the vocabulary in these two passages.

Ol. 1.52-53	*Pyth*. 2.52-56
ἐμοὶ δ' (52)	ἐμὲ δέ (52)
ἄπορα ... εἰπεῖν (52)	χρεών φεύγειν δάκος (52-53)
ἀφίσταμαι (52)	ἑκὰς ἐών (54)
κακαγόρους (53)	κακαγοριᾶν (53)
θαμινά (53)	τὰ πόλλ' (54)
ἀκέρδεια (53)	ἐν ἀμαχανίᾳ (54)

---

[37] See Miller, "Pindar, Archilochus and Hieron" 138 note 13: "Since ἀδινόν means 'close,' 'thick,' 'crowded,' 'frequent' (not 'strong,' 'violent,' as Slater and others take it), Pindar may be implying that it is persistent ('relentless' G. Nagy, *The Best of the Achaeans* 225) censure, not censure *per se*, that must be avoided."

This elaborate eschewing of blame serves to highlight the following positive statement of the proper attitude: τὸ πλουτεῖν δὲ σὺν τύχᾳ πότμου σοφίας ἄριστον (56), which introduces lavish praise of Hieron.[38]

Kindness and Envy

Pindar uses a number of words to express the feeling of goodwill toward someone who has achieved success. The most important are φιλέω (φίλος, φίλιος) and χαίρω (χάρις, χάρμα), and they represent freely given, uninhibited joy, respect, and praise. Their most important contrasting term is φθονέω (φθόνος, φθονερός), which indicates feelings of ill-will expressing itself in a withholding of approval, a niggardliness, a resistance. The φθονερός is the stinter who begrudges others their fair share of joy, and is therefore illiberal; he expresses his meanness in criticism, disbelief, and refusal to participate in the spirit of the occasion. For example, at the beginning of his "Funeral Oration," Perikles portrays the great difference between the εὔνους ἀκροατής who is upset if the praise falls short (cf. ἐνδεεστέρως) and the listeners whose φθόνος is aroused at any exaggeration and who consequently withhold belief (ἀπιστοῦσιν) (Thouk. 2.35.2).

In order to express the concept of whole-hearted, generous recognition of the laudandus' worth (characteristic of one who is εὔνους), Pindar frequently employs negative expressions involving φθόνος. For example, at *Isth.* 5.22 ff. he says, "If someone has turned onto a clear road of god-given deeds,"[39]

    μὴ φθόνει κόμπον τὸν ἐοικότ' ἀοιδᾷ
25   κιρνάμεν ἀντὶ πόνων.

    do not begrudge to blend into your song
25   a fitting vaunt in return for hard work.

At *Isth.* 1.41 ff. occurs a very similar passage: "If someone devotes himself completely to excellence with expenses and hard work,"

    χρή νιν [sc. ἀρετὰν] εὑρόντεσσιν ἀγάνορα κόμπον
    μὴ φθονεραῖσι φέρειν
45   γνώμαις.

---

[38] For a survey of interpretations of this difficult sentence, see Gerber, "Pindar, *Pythian* 2.56." I have followed the interpretation of Miller, "Pindar, Archilochus and Hieron" 142: "It is wealth wielded in accordance with the dispensation of destiny that is the finest object of poetic skill."

[39] For a thorough discussion of this passage, see Bundy, *Studia Pindarica* 56-57. A good positive parallel is *Nem.* 8.48-49: χαίρω δὲ πρόσφορον | ... κόμπον ἱείς, which shows that μὴ φθόνει is the counterpart of χαίρω.

>   it is necessary to give those who achieve success a lordly vaunt
>   with no begrudging
> 45 thoughts.

At *Ol.* 6.6-7 the poet asks (rhetorically): "What song (τίνα... ὕμνον; = οὐδένα ... ὕμνον) would a man like that avoid," ἐπικύρσαις ἀφθόνων ἀστῶν ἐν ἱμερταῖς ἀοιδαῖς. The ἄφθονοι ἀστοί are those who, in positive terms, generously bestow praise out of delight (cf. ἱμερταῖς). In all three cases, negation of φθόνος expresses granting of high praise (as it does in very similar statements at Bakch. 3.67-68, 5.187-190, and 13.199-202).

The idea of generosity or bounty is also present in several other negative expressions. For example, at *Pyth.* 3.71 Hieron is "not begrudging to the good" (οὐ φθονέων ἀγαθοῖς), litotes for "munificent to."[40] Similarly, no one "more generous" (ἀφθονέστερον, *Ol.* 2.94) than Theron has appeared in a century. The sense of bounty is evident at *Nem.* 3.9, where Pindar prays to the Must to grant him "abundance" (ἀφθονίαν) of song. Likewise, at *Ol.* 11.7 he declares, "without stint (ἀφθόνητος) is such praise as this dedicated to Olympic victors"; ungrudged praise is lavish praise.[41]

With the previous passages in mind we can better understand a more difficult one, *Ol.* 6.74-76:

>   μῶμος ἐξ ἄλ-
>   λων κρέμαται φθονεόντων
> 75 τοῖς, οἷς ποτε πρώτοις περὶ δωδέκατον δρόμον
>   ἐλαυνόντεσσιν αἰδοία ποτιστά-
>   ξῃ Χάρις εὐκλέα μορφάν.

>   Blame which comes from
>   others who are envious hangs over
> 75 those, who have ever driven first around the twelve-lap
>   course and on whom venerable Charis sheds
>   glorious comeliness.

The rhetorical purpose of this statement is to lead up to the high praise of Hagesias' success (εὐτυχίαν, 81). Unless the passage differs radically from all other parallels, the meaning must be that praise and congratulations are due when "Charis sheds glorious comeliness" on victorious racers (the positive being reserved for climactic effect). The problem is that there is no explicit negative. The solution, however, lies in the words ἐξ ἄλλων. These "others" are (like the un-

---

[40] See above note 4 for further implications of this expression. See Carey, *Five Odes* 52-53 for detailed references to the traditional tyrant-type.

[41] For the connection of "without envy" (on the part of the poet) and "abundant" (with respect to the praise) in the word ἀφθόνητος, see Verdenius, *Commentaries II* 89.

specified τις in the examples from Bakchylides) φθονεροί who are alien to the spirit of *arete* and give blame, when what is called for is respect and praise (cf. εὐκλέα, 76).[42] The φθονεραὶ... ἐλπίδες at *Isth.* 2.43 are of the same stamp, and the ἄλλος ἀνήρ with stinting designs (φθονερὰ... βλέπων) at *Nem.* 4.39 provides a good parallel for ἐξ ἄλλων.[43] In all these instances, Pindar draws attention to the existence of φθόνος *in others* not only to show that it is inappropriate in the given circumstances, but also to remind us that generosity (whether with wealth or praise) entails suppressing natural tendencies of niggardliness.[44]

Various Expressions Denoting Association

One of the most remarkable manifestations of variety occurs in statements that concern association (or the lack of it). For example, at *Nem.* 6.31 noble deeds of the Bassidai are not lacking (οὐ σπανίζει). To say that someone has won crowns (cf. στεφάν[ων] ἐπίμοιρον at Bakch 1.158) can be expressed by οὐ νέοντ' ἄνευ στεφάνων (*Nem.* 4.77) or, as an injunction: μήτ' ἐν ὀρφανίᾳ πέσωμεν στεφάνων (*Isth.* 8.6a). With the same metaphor, the Kleonymidai are said to be ὀρφανοὶ ὕβριος (*Isth.* 4.8-9; cf. *Pa.* 6.8-9: ψόφον... ὀρφανὸν ἀνδρῶν), while Diagoras keeps straight down a path that is ὕβριος ἐχθράν (*Ol.* 7.90), and Damophilos has learned ὑβρίζοντα μισεῖν (*Pyth.* 4.284).

---

[42] Cf. Bakch. 13.199-205:

	ε]ἰ μή τινα θερσι[ε]πὴς
200	φθόνος βιᾶται,
	αἰνείτω σοφὸν ἄνδρα
	σὺν δίκᾳ. βροτῶν δὲ μῶμος
	πάντεσσι μέν ἐστιν ἐπ' ἔργοις·
	ἁ δ' ἀλαθεία φιλεῖ
205	νικᾶν.

	Unless someone is in the grip of
200	bold-speaking envy,
	let him praise the wise man
	with due justice. Men's blame
	is upon all deeds,
	but truth usually
205	prevails ...

As in the Pindaric passage, φθόνος and μῶμος are joined; the Pindaric μῶμος ἐξ ἄλλων is equivalent to Bakchylides' βροτῶν μῶμος.

[43] For an excellent discussion of this difficult passage, see Miller, "Digressive Leisure" 210-211. Lobel's emendation ἄλλος (= ἠλεός), adopted by S-M, is extremely improbable and otiose.

[44] For another example of eschewing φθόνος from an unspecified source in order to lead up to high praise, cf. *Ol.* 8.55 and the discussion below pages 154-156.

The attendance or help of a god (cf. σὺν θεῷ, *Isth.* 4.5) is subject to a number of negative variations such as οὐ θεῶν ἄτερ (*Pyth.* 5.76), οὐδὲ ... Χαρίτων ἄτερ (*Ol.* 14.8) (cf. the positive expressions σὺν ... Χάρισσιν at *Nem.* 5.54 and εὖ λαχὼν Χαρίτων at Bakch. 1.151), ἇς [viz. Artemis] οὐκ ἄτερ (*Pyth.* 2.7), ἄνευ σέθεν [viz. Eleithyia] οὐ (*Nem.* 7.2-3), and οὐκ ἄτερ Αἰακιδᾶν (*Isth.* 5.20).[45] At *Nem.* 2.12 Orion is "near" (μὴ τηλόθεν) the Pleiades, while Aigina is "near" the Graces (οὐ Χαρίτων ἑκάς, *Pyth.* 8.21); at *Pyth.* 4.5 Apollo is "on hand" (οὐκ ἀποδάμου Ἀπόλλωνος), and at *Pyth.* 10.37 the Muse is "present" (Μοῖσα δ' οὐκ ἀποδαμεῖ).[46] At *Ol.* 1.108 and *Pyth.* 9.90, the continued presence of the god is solicited with the expression μὴ λίποι, while at *Nem.* 3.76 Aristokleidas "has his share" of *aretai* (τῶν οὐκ ἄπεσσι; v.l. ἄπεστι). Three times Pindar stresses the fact that something is "one's own" with negative expressions: χάρμα δ' οὐκ ἀλλότριον (*Pyth.* 1.59), οὐ ξείναν ... γαῖαν ἄλλων (*Pyth.* 4.118), and ἀλλοτρίαις οὐ χερσί (*Isth.* 1.15).

A number of expressions involve "acquaintance." At *Ol.* 6.96-97 there is the positive statement that "music and song recognize Hieron" (ἀδύλογοι δέ νιν λύραι μολπαί τε γινώσκοντι).[47] At *Isth.* 2.30 the halls of Thrasyboulos' family are "not unfamiliar with" (οὐκ ἀγνῶτες) revels and songs, while at *Nem.* 1.23 Chromios' halls are "not unacquainted with" (οὐκ ἀπείρατοι) frequent foreign guests, and at *Isth.* 8.70 Kleandros' youth is "not without experience" (οὐκ ἄπειρον) of success. At *Ol.* 11.18 the Epizephyrian Lokrians are "not inexperienced in beautiful things" (μήτ' ἀπείρατον καλῶν),[48] and at *fr.* 198a.2 the poet describes himself as "not ignorant of the Muses" (οὐδ' ἀδαήμονα Μοισᾶν), while at *Pyth.* 9.58 Libya is "not unfamiliar with wild beasts" (οὔτ' ἀγνῶτα θηρῶν). All these instances of negation of an ἀ-privative are examples of litotes in vaunting statements.

Frequently the poet affirms his truthfulness by denying falsehood (cf. οὐ ψεύδεϊ τέγξω λόγον, *Ol.* 4.17-18; οὐ ψεύσομ' ἀμφὶ Κορίνθῳ, *Ol.* 13.52; πολλῶν ἐπέβαν καιρὸν οὐ ψεύδει βαλών, *Nem.* 1.18; οὐ ψεῦδις ὁ μάρτυς, *Nem.* 7.49), or his kindness by denying any hostility (cf. οὔτε δύσηρις ἐὼν οὔτ' ὦν φιλόνικος ἄγαν, *Ol.* 6.19; σκοτεινὸν ἀπέχων ψόγον, *Nem.* 7.61; οὐ τραχύς εἰμι, *Nem.* 7.76).

Finally, it should be noted that words such as φεύγω and λύω can serve as virtual negatives. For example, at *Ol.* 6.6 no man like Hagesias "could avoid" (κεν φύγοι) praise and at *Ol.* 11.17 the Epizephyrian Lokrians are described as

---

[45] Cf. *Pyth.* 12.28-29, ἄνευ καμάτου | οὐ; *Ol.* 9.77-78, μή ποτε | ... ἄτερθε (= "always beside"); and οὐκ ἄτερ (*Ol.* 8.45 and *Pyth.* 2.32).

[46] See Köhnken, "Litotes bei Pindar" 66-67.

[47] Kirkwood, *Selections* 94 approves of F. Johansen's taking Ortygia (92) as the antecedent of νιν, but that overlooks the fact that Ortygia is only mentioned in passing, while Hieron is praised in the preceding four lines (93-96). To refer vaguely to Ortygia at this point would ruin the carefully constructed climax that joins Hieron and Hagesias.

[48] Contrast the positive καλῶν ... ἴδριν of Hieron at *Ol.* 1.104.

not "shunning a guest" (φυγόξεινον). Frequently, these verbs are used to negate undesirable words. At *Pyth.* 9.92 the victor "has escaped the poverty of silence" (σιγαλὸν ἀμαχανίαν . . . φυγών), at *Pyth.* 2.52-53 Pindar "must flee the persistent bite of reproaches" (χρεών | φεύγειν δάκος), and at *Ol.* 6.89-90 the poet hopes to "escape the ancient reproach of 'Boiotian Swine'" (ὄνειδος . . . φεύγομεν), that is, to be praised for truthfulness and tact. At *Ol.* 4.21 the victory of Erginos "released him from the blame" (ἔλυσεν ἐξ ἀτιμίας) of the Lemnian women, that is, brought him their praise,[49] and at *Ol.* 2.51-52 success in the trial of the games "releases (one) from (the charge of) folly" (ἀφροσυνᾶν παραλύει), that is, gives one a name for intelligence.[50]

Litotes in Vaunts

Many examples (especially those with ἀ-privatives) which we have cited occur in sections of direct praise and may be called litotes (understatement which denies negative qualities). The phenomenon is too frequent to treat in detail, but a few observations are pertinent. There are two basic functions of this litotes; first, it attests to the ethical seriousness of the poet, who is careful to guard against exaggeration, and, secondly, it provides variation and a sense of climax in what might otherwise be a mere shopping-list of virtues. One example is the vaunt at *Ol.* 11.16-19:

> ἔνθα συγκωμάξατ'· ἐγγυάσομαι
> ὔμμιν, ὦ Μοῖσαι, φυγόξεινον στρατόν
> μήτ' ἀπείρατον καλῶν
> ἀκρόσοφόν τε καὶ αἰχματὰν ἀφίξεσθαι.

> Here join the celebration: I shall promise
> you, O Muses, that you will meet no people who shun a guest
> or are inexperienced in beautiful things;
> they have great wisdom and martial strength.

Here Pindar makes his praise of the Epizephyrian Lokrians convincing and interesting by artfully using litotes in the first two elements, but climactically switching to positive praise in the third (ἀκρόσοφόν τε καὶ αἰχματάν = the traditional

---

[49] Cf. οὐκ ἀτιμάσαντα at *Pyth.* 9.80. Behind the example of Erginos, as in the jibe of "Boiotian swine," is the figure παρὰ τὸ προσῆκον, for the negative expression implies that he gained the women's praise contrary to their earlier expectations.

[50] Cf. the positive statement at *Ol.* 5.16: εὖ δὲ τυχόντες [v.l. ἔχοντες] σοφοὶ καὶ πολίταις ἔδοξαν ἔμμεν. The negative expression also implies that this esteem is gained *despite* the commonsense view that it is simple folly to make great outlays of effort and expense when the results are so uncertain; cf. *Ol.* 5.15-16 and see Adkins, *Merit and Responsibility* 160.

doublet, *sapientia et fortitudo*).[51] The praise of Thrasyboulos at *Pyth.* 6.47-49 also exhibits this alternation:

> νόῳ δὲ πλοῦτον ἄγει,
> ἄδικον οὔθ' ὑπέροπλον ἥβαν δρέπων,
> σοφίαν δ' ἐν μυχοῖσι Πιερίδων.
>
> He uses his wealth with intelligence,
> he enjoys a youth without injustice or insolence,
> and culls wisdom in the haunts of the Pierian Muses.

Thrasyboulos makes intelligent use of his wealth, he enjoys a youth of justice and moderation, and he appreciates poetry. The litotes relieves the catalogue and gives a slight emphasis to the positive quality of σοφίαν (49). The word ὑπέροπλον (48) also reminds us of the "insolence" to which youth is all too often prone (cf. Arist. *Rhet.* 2.1389b7).

Litotes frequently occurs in vaunts which express the superiority of the subject. Instead of the positive statement "X is the greatest," Pindar resorts to the formula "no one is better than X." At *Nem.* 6.25 "no other house" (ἕτερον οὔ τινα οἶκον) possesses more boxing crowns; at *Ol.* 13.30-31 Xenophon's double victory achieved "what no mortal ever yet did before" (ἀνὴρ θνατὸς οὔπω τις πρότερον). At *Ol.* 1.104 the poet is confident that there is no host "more powerful" (μή τιν'... κυριώτερον) than Hieron, just as earlier in the poem he states that there is "no greater contest" than the Olympian (μηδ'... ἀγῶνα φέρτερον, 7); at *Ol.* 2.93-94 he swears that "no city has in a century given birth to a more generous man" (τεκεῖν μή τιν'... πόλιν... ἄνδρα μᾶλλον εὐεργέταν... ἀφθονέστερόν τε) than Theron; at *Pyth.* 1.49 he asserts that the Deinomenids have won such honor "as no other Greek enjoys" (οἵαν οὔτις Ἑλλάνων δρέπει); and, in the most comprehensive terms of all, at *Pyth.* 2.60 he declares that anyone who claims that "another is greater" (ἕτερόν τιν'... ὑπέρτερον) than Hieron "wrestles with an empty mind."[52]

Negative Expressions in Prayers

Since the language of prayers is naturally cautious and to a great extent apotropaic, negative expressions abound. Although a detailed examination of this phenomenon is beyond the scope of this chapter, what has already been said applies equally here: negatives provide abundant nuances of vocabulary and avoid the tedium of a list of positive requests. As a broad generalization, requests in

---

[51] For the climactic arrangement of this praise, see above page 23 note 24.
[52] Cf. the variations of οὐ κατελέγχειν at *Ol.* 8.19, *Pyth.* 8.36, *Nem.* 3.15, *Isth.* 3.14, and 8.65a. For further negative expressions in topics frequently found in vaunts, see *Appendix 3*.

prayers have two underlying hopes: (1) that the god be pleasantly disposed, and (2) that he give good things.⁵³ It is obvious that the second follows from the first and that either can just as easily be expressed in negative terms: (1) that the god not be displeased, and (2) that he not withhold (curtail, disrupt) good things. These two hopes are expressed positively at *Ol.* 2.13-14 (ἰανθεὶς ἀοιδαῖς | εὔφρων... κόμισον), while at *Ol.* 13.24-29 the first is negative (ἀφθόνητος ἔπεσσιν | γένοιο, 25-26) and the second is positive (νέμων... εὔθυνε... δέξαι, 27-29). At *Pyth.* 8.67-72 the first is positive: ἑκόντι... νόῳ | κατά τιν' ἁρμονίαν βλέπειν (67-68); the second is negative: θεῶν δ' ὄπιν | ἄφθονον αἰτέω... ὑμετέραις τύχαις (71-72). In both cases the privation of φθόνος is meant to convey bounteous approval.

There are numerous variations on the request that the gods not cease giving benefactions. For example, after praising Hieron at *Ol.* 6.92-97, Pindar prays that his prosperity may continue for a long time: μὴ θράσσοι χρόνος ὄλβον ἐφέρπων (97); more figuratively at *Pyth.* 5.120-121 he prays: μὴ φθινοπωρὶς ἀνέμων | χειμερία κατὰ πνοὰ δαμαλίζοι χρόνον. At *Ol.* 8.28-29 he prays: ὁ δ' ἐπαντέλλων χρόνος | τοῦτο πράσσων μὴ κάμοι; cf. Bakch. 5.36: εὖ ἔρδων δὲ μὴ κάμοι θεός.⁵⁴

At *Pyth.* 10.17-22 occurs a series of positive and negative requests:

}—

    ἕποιτο μοῖρα καὶ ὑστέραισιν
    ἐν ἀμέραις ἀγάνορα πλοῦτον ἀνθεῖν σφίσιν·
    τῶν δ' ἐν Ἑλλάδι τερπνῶν
20 λαχόντες οὐκ ὀλίγαν δόσιν, μὴ φθονεραῖς ἐκ θεῶν
    μετατροπίαις ἐπικύρσαιεν. θεὸς εἴη
    ἀπήμων κέαρ.

}—

    May fortune follow them as well in coming
    days to make their noble wealth blossom.
    And having been granted no small share
20 of pleasant successes in Hellas, may they encounter from the gods
    no invidious reversals. May divinity
    not be pained in heart.

First the request for continued benefits is put positively (ἕποιτο μοῖρα... ἀνθεῖν, 17-18); then, after mentioning their "no small share" of success, the poet switches to a negative, apotropaic expression (μὴ φθονεραῖς ἐκ θεῶν | μετατροπίαις ἐπικύρσαιεν, 20-21), that is, may the gods not cease their largesse.

---

⁵³ See Race, "Greek Hymns" 8-14.
⁵⁴ Similarly, at *Pyth.* 1.90 Pindar's advice to Hieron, μὴ κάμνε λίαν δαπάναις, means "keep on spending." For positive statements expressing the "joy" of spending, cf. *Ol.* 4.15: χαίροντά τε ξενίαις πανδόκοις, *Isth.* 4.29: δαπάνᾳ χαῖρον ἵππων, and *Isth.* 6.10: δαπάνᾳ τε χαρείς.

And, finally, concern for the god's good disposition comes last in litotes: ἀπήμων κέαρ = καρδίᾳ γελανεῖ at *Ol*. 5.2 (of a goddess) and means "with a glad heart."[55] The last request then leads to extended praise of the victorious father and son. In these examples from *Ol*. 2, *Pyth*. 8, and *Pyth*. 10, φθόνος has the same meaning when used of divinities as it does when referring to a human audience: withholding of pleasure or generosity.

Pyth. 9.70-103

We shall conclude this chapter by examining a longer passage in which the stylistic ποικιλία of negative expressions is especially impressive and has caused difficulties of interpretation.[56] At *Pyth*. 9.70 the poet ends his account of Kyrene's past by mentioning its fame in athletics: κλεινάν τ' [sc. πόλιν] ἀέθ-λοις. The last word (reserved for climactic effect) provides an easy transition to Telesikrates' Pythian victory (καί νυν, 71), which is amplified in positive terms in the following lines (71-75). Then, before beginning to catalogue the rest of Telesikrates' victories, Pindar pauses to explain how he will proceed (76-79):

> ἀρεταὶ δ' αἰεὶ μεγάλαι πολύμυθοι·
> βαιὰ δ' ἐν μακροῖσι ποικίλλειν
> ἀκοὰ σοφοῖς· ὁ δὲ καιρὸς ὁμοίως
> παντὸς ἔχει κορυφάν.
>
> There is always a great deal to say about mighty deeds,
> but elaboration of a few themes among longer ones
> is what wise men like to hear, for deft selection
> conveys the gist just as well.

There is a great deal that could be said about Pindar's literary theory as presented in these lines, but the most important word for our purposes is ποικίλλειν, for it suggests the *variatio* that is so apparent in the ensuing catalogue of verses 79-103.[57] And one of the ways in which this variety is apparent is through the use of negative expressions, of which there are five examples in a mere fifteen lines. The first occurs in lines 79-80:

---

[55] The full arguments for this interpretation are in Race, "Two Pindaric Passages" 182-188.

[56] Other possible choices include *Pyth*. 1.85-100, *Pyth*. 2.73-96, *Pyth*. 8.81-97, and *Nem*. 7.54-82.

[57] See Bundy, *Studia Pindarica* 17-18, who gives an excellent survey of the entire passage under discussion and concludes, "Here is a catalogue relieved of tedium by brevity (βαιά, line 80) and variety (ποικίλλειν, line 80)." See also the important analysis of verses 76-79 by Young, "Pindar, Aristotle, and Homer" 156-170.

> ἔγνον ποτὲ καὶ Ἰόλαον
> 80 οὐκ ἀτιμάσαντά νιν ἑπτάπυλοι Θῆβαι.

> Seven-gated Thebes formerly recognized
> 80 that Iolaos too did not dishonor him.

Until Bundy (and more recently Köhnken and Nash),[58] these lines were badly misunderstood because the almost formulaic nature of the negative expression οὐκ ἀτιμάσαντά νιν was not recognized. When the poet says that Iolaos—a personified, active force inherent in the games named in his honor—"did not dishonor him," he means "(the games of) Iolaos conferred honor on Telesikrates," i.e., Telesikrates won τιμή at the Iolaia.[59] It is all the more remarkable that this negative expression has caused so much difficulty, when every word has a formal equivalent in positive form just nine lines above (71-72):

> καί νυν ἐν Πυθῶνί νιν ἀγαθέᾳ Καρνειάδα
> υἱὸς εὐθαλεῖ συνέμειξε τύχᾳ.

> And now in holy Pytho the son of Karneiadas
> mingled her/it [Kyrene] with flourishing good fortune.

The following comparison of these two passages reveals how, in spite of their stylistic differences, they impart the same information.

	Pyth. 9.79-80	*Pyth.* 9.71-72
place of victory	Θῆβαι	ἐν Πυθῶνι ἀγαθέᾳ
giver of honor	Ἰόλαον	Καρνειάδα υἱός
recipient of honor	νιν [viz. Telesikrates]	νιν [viz. Kyrene]
giving of honor	οὐκ ἀτιμάσαντα	εὐθαλεῖ συνέμειξε τύχᾳ
time	ποτὲ καί	καί νυν

After brief mention of the highlights of Iolaos' career, the poet traces his lineage back to Amphitryon and tells of Alkmena's giving birth to two mighty sons: διδύμων κρατησίμαχον σθένος υἱῶν (86). Here again, the last word is the link with what follows. Pindar has purposely withheld the proper names of these

---

[58] See Köhnken, "Litotes bei Pindar" 63-66 and Nash, "The Theban Myth" 78 and 90. Also see Schroeder, *Pythien* 85-86 and Burton, *Pythian Odes* 48-49.

[59] Cf. the negative expressions, all in victory catalogues, at *Ol.* 13.34: Νεμεᾷ τ' οὐκ ἀντιξοεῖ; *Ol.* 7.86-87: ἐν Μεγάροισίν τ' οὐχ ἕτερον λιθίνα | ψᾶφος ἔχει λόγον; and *Nem.* 4.21: Καδμεῖοί νιν οὐκ ἀέκοντες ἄνθεσι μείγνυον. For the positive, cf. *Nem.* 6.39-41, where the Isthmos "honored Kreontidas (with victory)": Κρεοντίδαν | τίμασε and *Isth.* 2.18, where Apollo looked favorably upon Xenokrates "and gave him victory": πόρε τ' ἀγλαΐαν.

twins in order to present them climactically in the following lines ('Ηρακλεῖ ... Ἰφικλέα, 87-88) but since he has already recounted the deeds of Iolaos (80-82), a flat recital of their exploits might seem repetitious, however splendid they are. So, he resorts to a version of *praeteritio* cast in negative terms (87-88):

> κωφὸς ἀνήρ τις, ὃς Ἡρακλεῖ στόμα μὴ περιβάλλει,
> μηδὲ Διρκαίων ὑδάτων ἀὲ μέ-
> μναται, τά νιν θρέψαντο καὶ Ἰφικλέα.
>
> Dumb is any man who does not devote his speech to Herakles,
> and does not continually mention Dirka's waters,
>   which nourished him and Iphikles.

Whether κωφός is a "deaf-mute" and the sentence means "everyone talks about Herakles, etc." (= "objective" in Bundy's terms),[60] or means "dullard" and refers to poets "who are stupid not to talk about Herakles, etc." (= "subjective"), the rhetorical effect is the same: the subject is set beyond the need for detailed praise, because Herakles, Thebes, and Iphikles are treated fully (cf. στόμα περιβάλλει) and continually (ἀὲ μέμναται). By thus relieving himself of the need to say more about their exploits—the mere mention of their names being sufficient for everyone—he can conclude with "thanks" to them (a variation of the hymnal χαίρετε) for Telesikrates' victory: τοῖσι τέλειον ἐπ' εὐχᾷ κωμάσομαί τι παθὼν | ἐσλόν (89-89a).[61]

Now that the poet has completed his account of Telesikrates' Theban victories (in the Iolaia and the Herakleia), he pauses before passing on to others with a brief prayer, cast in negative terms, for continued inspiration, thus making a clean break between the Theban victories and those at Aigina and Megara, which are closer to the victor's homeland (89a-90):

>   Χαρίτων κελαδεννᾶν
> 90   μή με λίποι καθαρὸν φέγγος.
>
>   May the clear light
> 90   of the resounding Graces not leave me.

---

[60] Young, "Pindar's Style at *Pythian* 9.87f." and Nash, "The Theban Myth" 80-87 argue that the reference is "objective," but it could equally (given ἀὲ μέμναται, "continually mentions") refer to poets. See Bundy, "Quarrel" 75-76.

[61] Bundy, *Studia Pindarica* 70 note 86 shows how close the language of this "thank-you" is to Theogn. 341-342. The verb κωμάσομαι is an "encomiastic" future, which is fulfilled with its very utterance, (i.e., "I will [now] celebrate"). The τι παθὼν ἐσλόν is a nice variation (from the recipient's point of view) of οὐκ ἀτιμάσαντα (from the point of view of the games). Cf. also *Isth.* 2.24: παθόντες πού τι φιλόξενον ἔργον (of the Olympic heralds) and Bakch. 8.27-30: τελέσ[αις]... εὐχάς... [ὀ]πά[σσαι]s... ἄνδημ' ἐλαίας.

Negative Expressions

A positive form of this prayer is found at *Ol.* 9.82-83: τόλμα δὲ καὶ ἀμφιλαφὴς δύναμις | ἕσποιτο, which also introduces extended praise. μὴ λίποι is equivalent to ἕσποιτο and the καθαρὸν φέγγος is the clear light of praise (cf. κελαδεννᾶν) which illumines success and makes it apparent, "illustrious." And, finally, the Χαρίτων κελαδεννᾶν represent the beauty and χάρις (pleasure, goodwill) of celebratory poetry.

The following asseveration (cf. φαμί, 91) avers that a full three (δή, 91) times at Aigina and Megara Telesikrates has glorified "this city" (= Kyrene)[62] σιγαλὸν ἀμαχανίαν ἔργῳ φυγών (92), "by avoiding silent helplessness through his achievement," that is, by providing a ready subject for praise.[63] This is a variation of the positive declaration of his Pythian victory at 73-75: νικάσαις (73) = ἔργῳ (92), ἀνέφανε Κυράναν (73) = πόλιν τάνδ᾽ εὐκλεΐξας (91) and δόξαν ἱμερτὰν ἀγαγόντ᾽ (75) = σιγαλὸν ἀμαχανίαν . . . φυγών (92). It is important to note that in reporting these victories at Aigina and Megara, Pindar has reversed the usual order of a negative expression leading to a positive climax, which we have noted so often. Here he concludes with the negative statement (σιγαλὸν ἀμαχανίαν . . . φυγών, 92), so as not to detract from the public theme, the city of Kyrene (πόλιν τάνδ᾽ 91), while at the same time passing on to the victor, whose full praises he intends to sing, but not yet. In Bundy's terms, the negative expression provides a decrescendo before the final praise of the victor.

But before beginning the final catalogue of local victories (and here the words πόλιν τάνδ᾽ at 91 have neatly led us back to Kyrene), he prepares the way with an extended injunction to praise, this time to the people of Kyrene (ἀστοί always refer to local, fellow citizens):[64]

οὕνεκεν, εἰ φίλος ἀστῶν, εἴ τις ἀντά-
εις, τό γ᾽ ἐν ξυνῷ πεπομαμένον εὖ
μὴ λόγον βλάπτων ἁλίοιο γέροντος κρυπτέτω·
95 κεῖνος αἰνεῖν καὶ τὸν ἐχθρόν

---

[62] I am accepting Hermann's εὐκλεΐξας at 91. I find compelling the arguments of Burton, *Pythian Odes* 52-54. It can be stated as a law of convention that ἥδε πόλις always refers to the home of the victor (*pace* Péron, "La Victoire de Télésicrate" 70-71, approved by Verdenius, *Commentaries I* 60), and it is inconceivable that Pindar would have written three other odes for Telesikrates' victories at minor games. Finally, it is awkward for the poet to introduce himself before the οὕνεκεν (93), which says "for that reason" everyone should praise Telesikrates. οὕνεκεν must mean "because of his victories," not "because of my celebrations." See also the succinct but forceful comments of Kirkwood, "The Voice of Pindar" 19-21, who adds support to Burton's point that ἔργῳ (92) must denote athletic, not poetic, endeavor. Like Gerber, "Pindar and Bacchylides" 257, I find Hermann's εὐκλεΐξας more satisfactory than Bornemann's σε for τε, defended by Nash, "The Theban Myth" 98-99.

[63] Cf. the positive expression at *Isth.* 4.2-3: εὐμαχανίαν . . . ἔφανας . . . ὑμετέρας ἀρετὰς ὕμνῳ διώκειν. See above note 1.

[64] Note a similar concern for the reactions of the ἀστοί when Pindar is about to praise Hieron for his domestic policy at *Pyth.* 1.84 ff.; see below pages 166-167.

παντὶ θυμῷ σύν τε δίκᾳ καλὰ ῥέζοντ' ἔννεπεν.

> Therefore, let no one, whether a friendly citizen or one who is hostile,
>   put into obscurity a deed nobly done on behalf of all,
>   thereby doing harm to the command of the Old Man of the Sea,
> 95 who prescribed giving wholehearted and just praise
>   even to one's enemy when he performs well.

At line 73 the poet had said that Kyrene would receive Telesikrates graciously (νιν εὔφρων δέξεται). That promise is now fulfilled—Telesikrates has "returned" to his homeland—and the poet is, as it were, defining more precisely the word εὔφρων (and the negative expression, σιγαλὸν ἀμαχανίαν ... φυγών, 92): every fellow townsman in Kyrene—even some τις who may be hostile[65]— should openly proclaim (μὴ κρυπτέτω) this achievement (at least, γ') which all share (τό γ' ἐν ξυνῷ πεπον αμένον εὖ). And, by so doing, he will "not do harm to" (i.e., "heed") the command of the Old Man of the Sea. After these negative expressions, the poet can then assert the positive declaration: "he prescribed giving wholehearted and just praise even to one's enemy when he performs well."

Having ended on this climactic note with "let us all praise the victor," Pindar can boldly sum up the concluding items in the catalogue of successes, Telesikrates' local victories. Note the force of πλεῖστα νικάσαντά σε (97, in asyndeton), the silent (but heartfelt) testimony of the maidens (98-100), the climactic address, ὦ Τελεσίκρατες (100), and the open-ended ἔν τε καὶ πᾶσιν | ἐπιχωρίοις (102-103), re-emphasizing that we have arrived "home." It is not by accident that the additional account which then concludes the ode (103-125) is about a "local" ancestor of the victor.

In this catalogue we have seen a remarkable display of ποικιλία, of alternation between positive and negative statements, each carefully calculated to lead up to the next item. This is just one of the more obvious examples of Pindar's genius for craftsmanship that can be seen again and again throughout the odes. By paying close attention to Pindar's use of negatives one gains greater appreciation of his precise and artistic use of language, for he is just as likely to describe what things are *not* (ὅπως οὐκ ἔχει) as what they *are*.

---

[65] It is unnecessary to speculate, as does Burton, *Pythian Odes* 55, following H. J. Rose, that "Telesikrates had enemies in Cyrene who were loth to acclaim his successes." On the contrary, the implication of this conventional *omnibus celebrandus est* is that his success is shared by all (ἐν ξυνῷ, 93) and no one would be so mean as to deny him his praise (αἰνεῖν, 95).

CHAPTER 4

STYLE AND RHETORIC IN OPENING HYMNS

There are few Pindaric odes without hymns or prayers;[1] indeed, twenty-three of the forty-five epinicians open with addresses to deities. The ratio is even higher for Bakchylides' odes.[2] Although commentators have pointed out these hymnal features in passing, there has been no overall discussion of hymns in Pindar.[3] After briefly surveying the stylistic elements and rhetorical functions of hymns in general, we shall closely examine three exemplary *Olympian* odes. Then we shall distinguish the two basic forms of hymns, rhapsodic and cultic, whose features Pindar skillfully adapts and combines in his odes. Since it is impossible to examine in detail all his hymnal passages, I have restricted the discussion to poems with opening hymns, and even then I have selected only salient examples which illustrate his practice.[4]

Elements of Style

Before we look at the poems themselves, it is worthwhile to list the elements usually encountered in hymns, whether rhapsodic or cultic:

I. Invocation

    A. Basic Topics

        1. Name(s) (often an apostrophe)

        2. Attributes (epithets and titles)

---

[1] Only *Pyth.* 7, *Nem.* 2, *Isth.* 3, 8, and the fragmentary *Isth.* 9 have few or no formal hymnal elements.

[2] Of the thirteen preserved beginnings of Bakchylides' epinicians, nine open with addresses to deities. For an overview of Bakchylides' opening hymns, see *Appendix 2*.

[3] For treatments of various features of Greek hymns, see R. Wünsch, RE 9 (1916) 140-183 s.v. "Hymnos," Norden, *Agnostos Theos* 143-176, Keyssner, *Gottesvorstellung*, Meyer, *Hymnische Stilelemente*, Kleinknecht, *Gebetsparodie*, Klug, *Untersuchung zum Gebet*, E. von Severus, RAC 8 (1972) 1134-52 s.v. "Gebet," Kambylis, "Anredeformen," Race, "Greek Hymns," and *Pindar* 27-29. The observations of Bundy in *Studia Pindarica* 45-47, 77-81 *et passim*, and in "Quarrel" 49-77 *et passim*, still provide the best discussion of hymnal features in Pindar.

[4] I do not treat in detail the openings of *Ol.* 5, *Pyth.* 1, 8, 11, 12, *Nem.* 1, 8, or *Isth.* 1.

3. Genealogy
4. *Sedes* (abode, haunts, places of worship)
5. Powers (over areas, actions, individuals)
6. Deeds

B. Expansions
   1. Relative clauses (= Relativstil)
   2. Participial clauses (= Partizipialstil)
   3. Appositives (= Appositionstil)
   4. Repeated addresses
   5. Explanations
   6. Gnomes
   7. *Hypomneseis* ("reminders" of the god's past actions)
   8. *Ekphraseis* (of the god, his haunts, actions, etc.)
   9. Narratives
   10. Companion deities
   11. Amplification (superlatives, doublets, lists)

II. Request (imperative or optative)
   A. General summons (e.g., κλῦτε, ἄκουσον, ἵκεο, ἴτε)
   B. Specific petitions (e.g., δέξαι, πράσσετε, ὑμνεῖτε)
   C. Leave-taking (e.g., χαῖρε)

In spite of the conventionality of the form and language of hymns, there is considerable room for variation, since the hymnist is free to expand, emphasize, or omit any element listed above. As we shall see, Pindar carefully selects and arranges hymnal elements in order to integrate them into each poem. Since the occasion of every ode is celebratory, the import of every opening hymn is for the god to enjoy or join in the festivity, whether tacitly implied as in the odes to the Lyre (*Pyth.* 1.1-12) and Hora (*Nem.* 8.1-5), or expressed in such requests as ἵκεο (*Nem.* 3.3), ἄκουσον (*Nem.* 7.2), δέξαι (*Ol.* 8.10, *Pyth.* 12.5), κωμάσομεν (*Nem.* 9.1), or δεῦτ' ἐν χορόν (*fr.* 75.1).

The Rhetorical Functions of Hymns in Pindar

The τέλος of all hymns (and prayers) is to join god and man in synergistic endeavor.[5] The purpose of the invocation is to sketch the god's powers, to "remind" him of his abilities and actions, in order to draw upon them for the

---

[5] This cooperation is sometimes expressed as an alliance; cf. σύμμαχος ἔσσο at Sappho, *fr.* 1.28, γενοῦ δὲ σύμμαχος θέλων ἐμοί at Aisch. *Choe.* 19, and *te sociam studeo* at Lucretius, *De Rerum Nat.* 1.24.

particular occasion at hand, whether it be to join the celebration (and to enjoy the poem!) or to aid in some particular capacity.[6] As a result, every hymn displays a movement from general to particular,[7] from the vast and timeless powers of the god to the temporal needs of man, from past actions to present expectations, and, often, to hopes for the future. For that reason, the function of hymns is invariably prooimial. A sequential reading of any hymnal passage in Pindar reveals a process of continual specification, both of the god's powers and of the worshipper's relationship to him, until the two are joined in common effort on a specific project. In this way, hymns provide a broad background against which the ode's particular occasion stands out. Hence, the two principal functions of hymns may be defined as prooimial and contextual.[8] All hymns in Pindar perform these two functions (often simultaneously), as they do in other authors and genres.[9]

The hymn to Eleithyia that opens *Nem.* 7 can serve as a good introductory example.[10]

> Ἐλείθυια, πάρεδρε Μοιρᾶν βαθυφρόνων,
> παῖ μεγαλοσθενέος, ἄκου-
>   σον, Ἥρας, γενέτειρα τέκνων· ἄνευ σέθεν
> οὐ φάος, οὐ μέλαιναν δρακέντες εὐφρόναν
> τεὰν ἀδελφεὰν ἐλάχομεν ἀγλαόγυιον Ἥβαν.
> 5 ἀναπνέομεν δ' οὐχ ἅπαντες ἐπὶ ἶσα·
> εἴργει δὲ πότμῳ ζυγένθ' ἕτερον ἕτερα. σὺν δὲ τίν
> καὶ παῖς ὁ Θεαρίωνος ἀρετᾷ κριθείς
> εὔδοξος ἀείδεται Σωγένης μετὰ πενταέθλοις.

> Eleithyia, enthroned beside the deep-thinking Fates,
> daughter of mighty Hera, hear me,
>   giver of birth to children. Without you
> we behold neither light nor the darkness of night,

---

[6] A particularly transparent example of drawing upon vocabulary of the invocation for the request is *h. Hom.* 10, where the poet mentions Aphrodite's "charming face" (ἱμερτῷ προσώ-πῳ, 2) and "charming bloom" (ἱμερτὸν ἄνθος, 3) before requesting her help in producing a "charming song": δὸς δ' ἱμερόεσσαν ἀοιδήν (5). The tactic was not lost on Lucretius, who in his hymn to Venus mentions her "charm" (*lepore*, 15) in the description of her powers and then requests that she bestow "charm" (*leporem*, 28) on his verses.

[7] Cf. Quint. 3.7.7: *Verum in deis generaliter primum maiestatem ipsius eorum naturae venerabimur, deinde proprie vim cuiusque et inventa, quae utile aliquid hominibus attulerint.*

[8] Even rhapsodic hymns, whose main burden is a narration of the god's powers and deeds, were commonly known as προοίμια (cf. *Nem.* 2.1-3, Thouk. 3.104, and Plato, *Phaido* 60D).

[9] The hymns that open long poems such as Aratos' *Phainomena* and Lucretius' *De Rerum Natura* function primarily as *prooimia*, whereas dramatic choral hymns usually provide a background or context for the action, as, for example, the hymn to Eros at Soph. *Ant.* 781-801, which provides a context for the love between Haimon and Antigone; it also retains its prooimial function by leading up to τόδε νεῖκος (793).

[10] See the brief, good analysis of Carey, *Five Odes* 137-139.

nor do we come to have your sister of the splendid limbs, Youth.
5   Yet all of us do not exist for equal ends,
for the yoke of each man's destiny limits in different ways. But by your grace, Thearion's son, Sogenes, is famed in song
because he was distinguished for his excellence among pentathletes.

This invocation contains many of the stylistic elements listed above.

I. Invocation

  A. Basic Topics
    1. Name: Ἐλείθυια
    2. Attributes: βαθυφρόνων (of the Moirai), μεγαλοσθενέος (of Hera), ἀγλαόγυιον (of Heba)
    3. Genealogy: παῖ Ἥρας
    4. *Sedes*: πάρεδρε Μοιρᾶν
    5. Powers: γενέτειρα τέκνων
    6. Deeds: σὺν δὲ τίν ... εὔδοξος ἀείδεται Σωγένης

  B. Expansions
    1. Additive clauses: ἄνευ σέθεν, σὺν δὲ τίν
    2. Repeated addresses: σέθεν, τεάν, τίν
    3. Gnomes: ἀναπνέομεν ... ἕτερον ἕτερα
    4. Companion deities: Μοιρᾶν, Ἥβαν
    5. Amplification through doublets: φάος ... μέλαιναν εὐφρόναν; ἕτερον ἕτερα

II. Request: ἄκουσον

But more important than identifying the conventional features of this hymn is appreciating the economical way in which Pindar makes each element add important information. In the invocation he stresses two features of Eleithyia, her genealogy and her companion deities; both are very important for establishing her essence, for her close association with the "deep-thinking Fates" and with her "mighty" mother Hera (goddess of marriage) link her with both the older order represented by the Moirai and the newer dispensation of Zeus.[11] The epithets

---

[11] πάρεδρε Μοιρᾶν βαθυφρόνων (1) not only indicates her *sedes* (**πάρεδρε**; cf. ἕδραν at *Ol.* 14.2), but also indicates her companion deities (**πάρεδρε**; cf. πάρα at *Ol.* 14.10). For the close association of Eleithyia and the Fates, cf. *Ol.* 6.41-42, where Apollo sends them to effect the birth of Iamos, destined to become a *mantis*, and *Pa.* 12.17, where Eleithyia and Lachesis attend the birth of Apollo and Artemis. Most, *Measures of Praise* 137-139 argues in the face of hymnal conventions that πάρεδρος has a legal connotation here ("assessor") because he wishes to link it with other legal metaphors in the ode. The parallels he cites (*Ol.* 2.76 and 8.22) do not support his claim that "there can be no doubt that the word has a specifically legal significance" (138).

βαθυφρόνων and μεγαλοσθενέος point to the *wisdom* of the ancient Fates and the *power* of the new gods; together they form the potent combination of wisdom and strength characteristic of the reign of Zeus.[12]

As a result of Eleithyia's influence, a person is not born as a *tabula rasa*, but from the moment of birth has a certain destiny. Eleithyia not only provides the efficient cause of birth (γενέτειρα τέκνων, 2), but also helps determine the limits of each individual at birth. The first additive clause expresses in the negative (ἄνευ σέθεν, 2) what would happen without Eleithyia's work: we would never have existence or be conscious of the passage of time in the alternation of day and night, nor would we mature to youth, personified as Eleithyia's sister Heba. Even her epithet ἀγλαόγυιον, which appears only here in extant Greek literature, is carefully chosen; she represents the age of physical maturity able to compete in athletics (cf. γυῖον, 73), an age that is not only beautiful, but also capable of achieving ἀγλαΐα, that is, the splendor of athletic success (see below note 36). Fittingly, this is an ode to a boy pentathlete.[13]

The first additive clause (2-4) stresses the similarities of all men who are born and mature to youth. The two gnomes that follow (5-6) introduce the qualitative differences. The words οὐχ ἅπαντες ἐπὶ ἴσα (5) and ἕτερον ἕτερα (6) sketch the diversity of human aspiration (cf. ἀναπνέομεν... ἐπί, 5) and limitation (εἴργει δὲ πότμῳ ζυγένθ', 6).[14] As in the hymn that opens *Ol.* 12 (see below page 95), the description of the goddess' powers sketches a broad background of diverse experiences, the outlines, as it were, of many potential plots, one of which will be fulfilled by the experience of a specific individual. The second additive clause switches to the positive expression σὺν δὲ τίν (6), which marks an intensification over ἄνευ σέθεν (2). Whereas the first additive clause presented the general case (cf. ἐλάχομεν, 4), everything in the second becomes specific, beginning with the particularizing καί (7),[15] which applies the previous reflections to the case at hand: the victory of Sogenes, Thearion's son, in the pentathlon. Pindar has used the hymn to provide a serious meditation on the nature of existence and the possibilities for growth and success, thereby providing a context that imparts significance to the specific information of the ode.

---

[12] For more examples of the doublet in Pindar, see below note 31.

[13] See Köhnken, *Funktion* 43 note 35: "Die Wortstellung im ersten, verhältnismäßig langen, Satz (V. 1-4) ist auffallend. Ganz am Anfang steht die Gottheit Eleithyia, ganz am Ende ihre Schwester Heba: Eleithyia und Heba sind die bieden Pole, zwischen denen der noch sehr junge Sieger Sogenes steht. Die Form des Satzes (mit der ausdrücklichen Anrede γενέτειρα τέκνων für Eleithyia in der Mitte, V. 2) deutet die große Jugend des Siegers an: vgl. auch V. 91 f. (ἀταλὸν ἀμφέπων θυμόν) und 99 (Gebet für ἥβᾳ λιπαρῷ τε γήραϊ)."

[14] The word πότμῳ (6) recalls the fact that Eleithyia is a companion of the Fates, as does the verb ἐλάχομεν (4).

[15] Most, *Measures of Praise* 140 calls this an "exemplifying καί," but without further explanation. For other examples of καί which singles out a particular instance from other (stated or implied) possibilities, a usage not recognized in Denniston or in grammars, see below note 33.

Cultic Hymns in Three Olympian Odes

Pindar's creativity in adapting and integrating hymnal elements into his poems will become clearer if we examine three short *Olympian* odes composed largely of hymnal elements. First is *Ol.* 4.1-16, one of several poems that demonstrate why Pindar often refers to his epinicians as ὕμνοι.

       Ἐλατὴρ ὑπέρτατε βροντᾶς ἀκαμαντόποδος
          Ζεῦ· τεαὶ γὰρ Ὧραι
       ὑπὸ ποικιλοφόρμιγγος ἀοιδᾶς ἑλισσόμεναί μ' ἔπεμψαν
       ὑψηλοτάτων μάρτυρ' ἀέθλων·
       ξείνων δ' εὖ πρασσόντων
5   ἔσαναν αὐτίκ' ἀγγελίαν ποτὶ γλυκεῖαν ἐσλοί·
       ἀλλὰ Κρόνου παῖ, ὃς Αἴτναν ἔχεις
       ἶπον ἀνεμόεσσαν ἑκατογκεφάλα
          Τυφῶνος ὀβρίμου,
       Οὐλυμπιονίκαν
       δέξαι Χαρίτων θ' ἕκατι τόνδε κῶμον,
10   χρονιώτατον φάος εὐρυσθενέων ἀρετᾶν.
          Ψαύμιος γὰρ ἵκει
       ὀχέων, ὃς ἐλαίᾳ στεφανωθεὶς Πισάτιδι κῦδος ὄρσαι
       σπεύδει Καμαρίνᾳ. θεὸς εὔφρων
       εἴη λοιπαῖς εὐχαῖς·
       ἐπεί νιν αἰνέω, μάλα μὲν τροφαῖς ἑτοῖμον ἵππων,
15   χαίροντά τε ξενίαις πανδόκοις,
       καὶ πρὸς Ἡσυχίαν φιλόπολιν καθαρᾷ
          γνώμᾳ τετραμμένον.

       Driver most high of thunder with unwearied foot,
          Zeus. On you I call because your Horai
       in their circling round have sent me with song on varied lyre
       as a witness of the most lofty games.
       When guest-friends are successful,
5   good men are immediately cheered at the sweet news.
       And so, son of Kronos, you who rule Aitna,
       windy burden for hundred-headed
          Typhos the mighty,
       receive an Olympic victor
       and, for the sake of the Graces, this celebration,
10   longest-lasting light for achievements of great strength.
          For it comes with the chariot
       of Psaumis, who is crowned with olive from Pisa and is eager to arouse
       glory for Kamarina. May heaven look favorably
       on his future prayers,
       For I praise him, very earnest in his raising of horses,

15 delighting in receiving guests from everywhere,
and devoted to city-loving Hesychia
with a sincere mind.

Pindar has divided this hymn to Zeus into two parts. The opening invocation, Ἐλατὴρ ὑπέρτατε βροντᾶς ἀκαμαντόποδος Ζεῦ (1) is a type of summons, common in cultic hymns, that presupposes a request such as "hear me." The second part (ἀλλά ... τόνδε κῶμον, 6-9) contains a re-invocation and a specific request. Together, these two addresses manifest all the invocational elements listed above: name (Ζεῦ), attributes (ἐλατὴρ ὑπέρτατε), genealogy (Κρόνου παῖ), *sedes* (Αἴτναν), powers (βροντᾶς), and deeds (ἵπον Τυφῶνος ὀβρίμου). This passage well illustrates the typical movement of hymns from the general to the particular, from the god in all his powers to the specific occasion on which his help is requested, here δέξαι ... τόνδε κῶμον (9), "receive (i.e., welcome) this celebration." It is the function of the invocation to prepare for the request by defining those powers which the hymnist wishes to exploit. For example, Chryses invokes Apollo as ἀργυρότοξ᾽ at *Il.* 1.37 because he intends to ask for his arrows of plague (βέλεσσιν, 42). Here Pindar opens with the title ἐλατήρ "driver," whose relevance will become clear in the course of the poem. And, as Pindar disposes the god favorably for the request, he is concurrently preparing the listeners for the particulars of the occasion; in due time he will specify the nature of τόνδε κῶμον, thereby providing the details of the victory.

In order to appreciate Pindar's stylistic artistry, it is necessary to read his hymnal passages *sequentially*, carefully assessing what each new word and phrase adds, how much weight and emphasis is given to each element, and how the relationship between the god and the hymnist is being defined in light of the occasion. We have already noted the programmatic importance of the word ἐλατήρ. The epithet ὑπέρτατε (superlatives commonly amplify the stature of the god) and the qualifying genitives βροντᾶς ἀκαμαντόποδος prepare for the withheld name, Ζεῦ, for we know before its climactic pronouncement that the four previous words could only apply to him. This invocation also "reminds" Zeus of his interest in horsemen; after all, he is the best (ὑπέρτατε) driver and his thunder (presumably as it rumbles across the sky) has the attributes of horses (ἀκαμαντόποδος; cf. *Ol.* 3.3 and 5.3). As there is a hint of *hypomnesis* in the epithet ἐλατήρ, there is the suggestion of an *ekphrasis* in his driving his thundercloud across the sky.

By means of an explanatory clause, Pindar gives the reasons for his invocation of the god and defines his own role in the hymnal activity. As often, the γάρ (1) is shorthand for "(I call on you) because." The prominent τεαί makes Zeus the indirect cause of the hymnist's need: "since it was *your* Horai."[16] The phrase

---

[16] The τεαί is a variation of the relative pronoun which so often introduces justifications or additional information in hymns and here functions as a "reminder" of Zeus' interest in the cele-

ὑπὸ ποικιλοφόρμιγγος ἀοιδᾶς defines Pindar's sphere of activity, as does the word μάρτυρ'. The qualifying adjective ποικιλο- is not merely decorative, for it singles out what we have seen as one of the most important characteristics of Pindar's compositions, variety.

Significantly, the Horai are ἑλισσόμεναι. As the Seasons, they return in cyclical sequence; they too sketch a broad background of seasonal recurrence against which the present Olympiad and an individual's achievement will stand out.[17] The poet has been given a "mission" (cf. μ' ἔπεμψαν, 2), but it is not until the last word of the clause that we find out what has occasioned that calling. The anticipatory adjective ὑψηλοτάτων (3) amplifies its importance with slight suspense (as ὕπέρτατε did for Zeus in the first line), and it is only when we get to ἀέθλων (3), the last word of the period, that we know for certain that this is an epinician ode—or more specifically, an ode for an Olympic victory, since ὑψηλοτάτων ἀέθλων can only refer to the Olympic games (although once again Pindar reserves the specific name for climactic introduction). The opening address to Zeus now fits within a more specific framework. Zeus presides over the Olympic games through his custodians the Horai, who see to their orderly recurrence. Because of the prominent ἐλατήρ we anticipate that the ode will eventually concern an equestrian victory, but at this point we cannot be certain.

In the first four lines the poet describes his relationship to Zeus and the Horai as a duty ("they sent me"); in the two following lines (4-5) he defines his relationship to his human subject by means of a gnome: "when their hosts succeed, good men are immediately cheered at the pleasant news." Every word is programmatic: not only has the poet been "commissioned" as a witness; he is glad to announce the news of his guest-friend's success; his joy is spontaneous (αὐτίκ', 5) and the report is pleasant (γλυκεῖαν, 5). The first word ξείνων (4) strikingly effects the change of subject and emphasizes the close bond between the poet and his patron, while the last word, ἐσλοί (5), points to the nobility of their friendship and to the ethical propriety of celebrating successful action. The word μάρτυρ' (3) contains the idea of the poet's obligation, his χρέος; the word ἔσαναν ("joyously receive") characterizes the relationship of ξενία (elsewhere expressed as φιλία or χάρις) that marks the ἐσλοί. By casting this sentence in a gnome, Pindar not only states that he himself takes delight in his host's victory,

---

bration. The Horai fall under the topic of "companion deities," as do the Charites (9). Cf. Bakch. 12.4-7, where, in a γάρ-clause, Nika dispatches the poet to Aigina to celebrate a Nemean victory.

[17] Because of its proximity to ὑπὸ ποικιλοφόρμιγγος ἀοιδᾶς, many have seen a reference to dancing in ἑλισσόμεναι. Besides implying that the Horai were dancing to Pindar's music (an unprecedented notion), the image of dancing obscures the more important function of the Horai as goddesses of cyclical recurrence. Cf. Hes. *Th.* 58: περὶ δ' ἔτραπον ὧραι and Eur. *Alk.* 448-449: ἀνίκα Καρνείου περινίσσεται ὥρα. For a discussion see Gerber, "*Olympian* Four" 10-11, although he concedes (I believe unnecessarily): "a reference to dancing seems unavoidable, since no other explanation adequately accounts for the choice of participle."

but that in general all good men should. As a summoned witness he must tell the truth;[18] but the truth is sweet, for it announces his friend's success.[19]

After all this preparation, the poet can make his request of Zeus, but since it has been quite some time since the god was the subject, Pindar re-addresses him with an even fuller invocation. Like many re-invocations, this one is lengthier, more impressive, and provides details not mentioned in the initial invocation.[20] The ἀλλά (6), which regularly signals the request, strongly marks the coming imperative (δέξαι, 9),[21] while the eleven intervening words provide the god's genealogy (Κρόνου παῖ, 6) and *sedes*, Aitna, over which he holds sway. The name Aitna prepares for the fact that the victor is Sicilian, while the appositional phrase, "windy burden for hundred-headed Typhos the mighty" (7), provides a *hypomnesis*, a reminder of the triumph of Zeus over Typhos, whom he subdued with his thunderbolt (cf. κεραυνῷ at *Pyth.* 8.17 and βροντήν at Hes. *Th.* 854), thus giving additional point to the mention of βροντᾶς at the opening of the hymn. Even the word ἀνεμόεσσαν may provide an additional reminder, since Typhos was associated with winds (cf. Hes. *Th.* 869). Zeus is portrayed as a god who has himself experienced victory, so when the word Οὐλυμπιονίκαν comes (8),[22] it has particular appeal to him, whose own victory over Typhos is in a sense an archetypical Olympic victory.

The request itself consists of two petitions. In the first Pindar asks Zeus to "receive" (δέξαι, 9) the Olympic victor, that is, to "welcome," "take delight in" his achievement. The second petition, as often, concerns the song. It is introduced by the prepositional phrase Χαρίτων θ' ἕκατι (9) "and for the sake of the Graces," which provides the important χάρις, "joy," "pleasure," which the

---

[18] The poet's role as truthful messenger, as defined by the word μάρτυρ' (3), motivates his strong assertion of veracity after his high praise of Psaumis (οὐ ψεύδεϊ τέγξω | λόγον, 17-18), followed by the "proof" furnished by Erginos' example.

[19] Cf. Bakch. 9.4, where the poet is "ready" (εὔτυκος) to sing of the Nemean games. For other examples of the poet's eagerness to praise, see Maehler, *Bakchylides I*. ii 92.

[20] Cf. *Ol.* 8.9, where Olympia is re-invoked after an intervening account of divination: ἀλλ' ὦ Πίσας εὔδενδρον ἐπ' Ἀλφεῷ ἄλσος.

[21] Denniston, *Greek Particles* 14 cites R. Klotz' description of ἀλλά with the imperative as effecting "a transition from arguments for action to a statement of the action required," a function it performs in re-invocations, especially after intervening elaborations. Cf. *Ol.* 8.9 (after reflections on the activities in Olympia's precinct) and *Nem.* 11.9 (after a lengthy description of the devotion of Aristagoras' companions). In general, however, ἀλλά simply marks the request, as at *Ol.* 10.3, *Nem.* 9.3, and often.

[22] Note how this climactic title gains emphasis by coming first in its period and by occupying an entire colon. There are two readings, depending upon whether one accepts the θ' of the older MSS in line 9. Although support can be found for either reading (e.g., *Pyth.* 8.5: Πυθιόνικον τιμάν . . . δέκευ for taking Οὐλυμπιονίκαν with κώμον; or *Pyth.* 12.5-6: δέξαι στεφάνωμα τόδ'. . . αὐτόν τέ νιν for taking Οὐλυμπιονίκαν separately as a substantive), I prefer the latter (the reading of S-M and Turyn): "receive an Olympic victor and, for the sake of the Graces, this celebration."

hymnist seeks to instill in the occasion.[23] The deictic article τόνδε (9) finally indicates the specific occasion (κῶμον) "this celebration," but the reference remains vague as we still await the name of the victor and his city. The poet, however, is in no hurry, for he pauses to define the nature of this κῶμος in terms that make it clear that he is thinking chiefly of his song: "longest-lasting light for achievements of great strength" (10).[24] Coming as this does in the request, it is as much a description of poetry's ability to give permanence to deeds as it is a proleptic hope that Zeus' reception of it will insure that permanence.[25] The ringing words εὐρυσθενέων ἀρετᾶν (10), while applying strictly to Psaumis' deeds, also include, in a larger sense, Zeus' victory over Typhos, the subject of the *hypomnesis*.

As a general rule, explanatory clauses in hymns, besides persuading the god to be favorable, also perform the practical function of supplying details. The following γάρ-clause (10-12), strictly an explanation of why Zeus should approve this celebration, does just that. The emphatic first and last words give the name of the man and of his city, Ψαύμιος ... Καμαρίνᾳ; in between come the event and the game. We note that Psaumis is "eager to arouse glory" (11-12) for his city. Our first impression of him is of a man who is civic-minded.

In the direct praise of lines 14-15, formally an explanation (ἐπεί, 14) of the brief general prayer that divinity (θεός, 12) should be favorably disposed (εὔφρων, 12) to his future requests,[26] Pindar singles out three qualities in Psaumis: his earnest commitment to raising horses, his joy (χαίροντα, 15) at entertaining many visitors (ξενίαις πανδόκοις, 15), and his wholehearted devotion to the public weal (πρὸς Ἡσυχίαν φιλόπολιν καθαρᾷ γνώμᾳ τετραμμένον, 16). All three have been carefully prepared in the preceding lines. Zeus the ἐλατήρ would appreciate his horsemanship; the gnome (4-5) hinted at his hospitality (ξείνων, 4; ξενίαις, 15);[27] and his love for his city was evident in his eagerness (cf. σπεύδει, 12) to share his renown with it. There is also an ascending scale in the praise of Psaumis: from horses to guests to city.[28]

The first sixteen lines of the ode are part of, or extensions of, a hymn, the individual elements of which lead from Zeus to the Horai, to the poet, past Ty-

---

[23] See Race, "Greek Hymns" 8-10.

[24] For achievement (and its celebration) as "light," see Gundert, *Dichterberuf* 11-19.

[25] The ability of song to give permanence to deeds is expressed in similar terms at *Nem.* 4.6-8: ῥῆμα δ᾽ ἐργμάτων χρονιώτερον βιοτεύει, | ὅ τι κε σὺν Χαρίτων τύχᾳ | γλῶσσα φρενὸς ἐξέλοι βαθείας. Note the word χρονιώτερον and the assistance of the Charites.

[26] Bundy, *Studia Pindarica* 79 points out: "Subjective appeals to the future (prayers and wishes) may conclude any topic used to praise a currently existing entity and acquire, so used, a transitional function." Here the prayer θεὸς εὔφρων εἴη λοιπαῖς εὐχαῖς concludes praise of Psaumis' athletic successes (the εὐχαῖς refer to his hopes for further victories), and leads to the praise (cf. αἰνέω, 14) of his personal qualities.

[27] The qualification πανδόκοις indicates that his hospitality is on a grand (and perhaps Panhellenic) scale. It may also imply that he is generous to all classes of citizens, a quality of the φιλόπολις that Xenophon praises at *Ages.* 7.1-3. Both aspects are celebrated in *Ol.* 5.

[28] For an analysis of this climactic arrangement, see above pages 22-23.

phos, to the Graces, to Psaumis, and (if the capitalization is valid) to Hesychia. A succession of sentences, introduced by γάρ (1), δέ (4), ἀλλά (6), γάρ (10), and ἐπεί (14) articulate the parts. And within each sentence, careful placement gives precise emphasis to each word. The general invocation to Zeus in line 1 summons him to this event. The two subsequent requests complement each other. The first (6-10) asks for Zeus' approval of the present celebration and for the longevity of the song; the second (12-13) requests divine favor to continue into the future (λοιπαῖς, 13) on the grounds that (ἐπεί, 14) Psaumis shares his success with others.[29] Hymn, prayer, and eulogy are intricately combined to grace (cf. Χαρίτων, 9), illuminate (cf. φάος, 10) and give permanence (cf. χρονιώτατον, 10) to Psaumis' hard-earned achievements (cf. εὐρυσθενέων ἀρετᾶν, 10).[30]

The hymn to Tycha at the beginning of *Ol.* 12 is a good example of a hymn which provides a context for the celebratory occasion.

    Λίσσομαι, παῖ Ζηνὸς Ἐλευθερίου,
    Ἱμέραν εὐρυσθενέ᾽ ἀμφιπόλει, σώτειρα Τύχα.
    τὶν γὰρ ἐν πόντῳ κυβερνῶνται θοαί
    νᾶες, ἐν χέρσῳ τε λαιψηροὶ πόλεμοι
5   κἀγοραὶ βουλαφόροι. αἵ γε μὲν ἀνδρῶν
    πόλλ᾽ ἄνω, τὰ δ᾽ αὖ κάτω
6a ψεύδη μεταμώνια τάμνοισαι κυλίνδοντ᾽ ἐλπίδες·
—   σύμβολον δ᾽ οὔ πώ τις ἐπιχθονίων
    πιστὸν ἀμφὶ πράξιος ἐσσομένας εὗρεν θεόθεν,
    τῶν δὲ μελλόντων τετύφλωνται φραδαί·
10 πολλὰ δ᾽ ἀνθρώποις παρὰ γνώμαν ἔπεσεν,
    ἔμπαλιν μὲν τέρψιος, οἱ δ᾽ ἀνιαραῖς
    ἀντικύρσαντες ζάλαις
12a ἐσλὸν βαθὺ πήματος ἐν μικρῷ πεδάμειψαν χρόνῳ.
—   υἱὲ Φιλάνορος, ἤτοι καὶ τεά κεν
    ἐνδομάχας ἅτ᾽ ἀλέκτωρ συγγόνῳ παρ᾽ ἑστίᾳ . . .

---

[29] These others include fellow citizens (cf. φιλόπολιν, 16) and guest-friends (cf. ξενίαις, 15), a universalizing doublet frequently found in Pindar; see Bundy, *Studia Pindarica* 24-25, 67. The doublet citizen-stranger suggests the larger dimension of Panhellenism so dear to Pindar (cf. ξείνων, 4). See in general Herman, *Ritualised Friendship*.

[30] The companion ode, *Ol.* 5, is even more completely built of hymns and prayers. Each triad is devoted to a different deity, and the order is climactic: Kamarina, Athena, Zeus. Fittingly, the invocation of the last is by far the most elaborate. In many ways, the ode is an expansion of the word φιλόπολιν at *Ol.* 4.16, as the following words indicate: πόλιν (4), λαοτρόφον (4), νέοικον ἕδραν (8), πολιάοχε Παλλάς (10), στρατόν (12), δᾶμον ἀστῶν (14), πολίταις (16), and πόλιν (20). Commentators wrongly use similarities between the two odes to argue for the spuriousness of *Ol.* 5.

I entreat you, child of Zeus the Deliverer,
preserve the might of Himera, saving Fortune.
For on the sea it is you who guide the swift
ships, and on land the rapid battles
5 and assemblies for counsel. As for men,
their hopes often rise, while at other times they roll
6a down when they voyage across vain falsehoods.
— No human has yet obtained a sure
sign from the gods regarding an impending action;
their plans for future events lie hidden from view.
10 Many things happen to men unexpectedly:
some are unpleasant; but then some men who have
encountered grievous storms
12a exchange their pain for great good in a moment's time.
— Son of Philanor, truly would the fame of your feet,
like that of a local fighting cock by its native hearth . . .

Ergoteles' career represents a particular manifestation of Tycha's power as depicted in the hymn. The first two lines are an economical invocation and request. Of particular importance are the epithets: Zeus is Ἐλευθέριος and Tycha is σώτειρα. We would expect that the poem will eventually be concerned with these two qualities of fortune, while the locus of the action will be the city of Himera. By means of a clause introduced by γάρ (3), the poet devotes the rest of the strophe and antistrophe to a description of her powers. As is usual in such "doxologies," doublets abound. First comes Tycha's power on the sea (3-4); this is balanced by her influence on land, which is then subdivided into her control over wars and counsels.[31] The adversative γε μέν (5) introduces a description of how Fortune's power is experienced from the perspective of men in general (ἀνδρῶν, 5; ἐπιχθονίων, 7; ἀνθρώποις, 10), who cannot know how the future will turn out, but must act nonetheless, and in so doing suffer unexpected reversals. Although the description of Tycha's powers remains entirely on a generalized level, the fact that it opens with the theme of freedom and deliverance and concludes with ἐσλὸν βαθύ (12a), emphatically introduced at the beginning of its

---

[31] The last doublet λαιψηροὶ πόλεμοι | κἀγοραὶ βουλαφόροι (4-5) sketches chiastically the activities of war and peace, body and mind, ἔργον and λόγος, and what later became the commonplace, *fortitudo et sapientia*. The doublet also occurs in the list of Hekate's powers, at Hes. *Th.* 430-431: ἔν τ' ἀγορῇ . . . ἐς πόλεμον; cf. also *Il.* 1.490-491: εἰς ἀγορήν . . . ἐς πόλεμον and 3.150: πολέμοιο . . . ἀγορηταί. In Pindar, cf. *Pyth.* 8.3: βουλᾶν τε καὶ πολέμων (of Hesychia); *Pyth.* 2.63-65: θράσος δεινῶν πολέμων . . . βουλαὶ δὲ πρεσβύτεραι (of Hieron); and, for other expressions of the doublet, *Ol.* 4.25: χεῖρες δὲ καὶ ἦτορ (of Erginos); *Ol.* 6.17: μάντιν τ' ἀγαθὸν καὶ δουρὶ μάρνασθαι (of Amphiaraos); *Ol.* 11.19: ἀκρόσοφόν τε καὶ αἰχματάν (of the Western Lokrians); *Pyth.* 5.119: ἐπ' ἔργοισιν ἀμφί τε βουλαῖς (of Arkesilas); *Nem.* 8.8: χειρὶ καὶ βουλαῖς ἄριστος (of Aiakos); *Nem.* 9.39: χερσὶ καὶ ψυχᾷ δυνατοί (of the Aitnaians); *Nem.* 11.12: δέμας ἀτρεμίαν τε (of Arkesilas of Tenedos); and *Isth.* 5.61: χερσὶ δεξιόν, νόῳ ἀντίπαλον (of Pytheas).

verse, leads us to expect that the concrete example will illustrate the same movement.[32]

After all this preparation, the epode opens directly with an address to a specific man, the son of Philanor. The particles ἤτοι and καί, followed by τεά (13), turn from the generalities of the hymn to the person of the victor.[33] By first portraying the universal human condition in the hymn—essentially the Greek tragic view of life—Pindar makes the career of Ergoteles stand out as part of a greater order, for his experience is exemplary of the workings of Tycha: in particular, he has gone from ἀνιαραῖς ζάλαις (the *stasis* which made him an exile) to ἐσλὸν βαθύ (Panhellenic success in his new home). The dark background of failure and civil strife in the past makes the present celebration more significant.[34]

We shall conclude this section with *Ol.* 14, a poem which incorporates a complex array of hymnal elements.

> Καφισίων ὑδάτων
> λαχοῖσαι αἴτε ναίετε καλλίπωλον ἕδραν,
> ὦ λιπαρᾶς ἀοίδιμοι βασίλειαι
> Χάριτες Ἐρχομενοῦ, παλαιγόνων Μινυᾶν ἐπίσκοποι,
> 5 κλῦτ', ἐπεὶ εὔχομαι· σὺν γὰρ ὑμῖν τά ⟨τε⟩ τερπνὰ καὶ
> τὰ γλυκέ' ἄνεται πάντα βροτοῖς,
> εἰ σοφός, εἰ καλός, εἴ τις ἀγλαὸς ἀνήρ.
> οὐδὲ γὰρ θεοὶ σεμνᾶν Χαρίτων ἄτερ
> κοιρανέοντι χοροὺς
> 10 οὔτε δαῖτας· ἀλλὰ πάντων ταμίαι
> ἔργων ἐν οὐρανῷ, χρυσότοξον θέμεναι πάρα

---

[32] The emphasis on the change from bad to good fortune at the end of the antistrophe is unmistakable. Besides the contrast implied by μέν and δέ, the greater length, greater precision, the switch to personal agents (οἱ δ'), and the fact that the positive formulation completes the antistrophe all indicate a climactic statement.

[33] Bundy, *Studia Pindarica* 7 note 23 and 36 note 6 has pointed out that this hymn also contains elements of a summary priamel, particularly in the words πολλά (6, 10). All three words apply the generalizations of the hymn to the experience of Ergoteles with increasing specificity. The ἤτοι (on which see Köhnken, *Funktion* 123-124) marks the transition to a particular instance, while the καί points directly to the concrete example further specified by τεά. This use of καί, which might be called "particularizing" καί is quite common, especially before pronouns or proper names in climactic passages such as this, which single out a specific example. Cf. *Ol.* 13.84: ἤτοι καὶ ὁ . . . Βελλεροφόντας, which singles out Bellerophon as an example of god's helping power; *Ol.* 8.25: καὶ τάνδ'. . . χώραν; *Pyth.* 2.36: καὶ τόν (of Ixion); *Pyth.* 2.64: καὶ σέ (of Hieron); *Pyth.* 3.55: καὶ κεῖνον (of Asklepios); *Pyth.* 6.44: τῶν νῦν δὲ καὶ Θρασύβουλος; *Nem.* 7.7: καὶ παῖς ὁ Θεαρίωνος; *Nem.* 8.6: καὶ Διός; *Nem.* 8.18: καὶ Κινύραν; *Nem.* 8.23: καὶ Τελαμῶνος . . . υἱόν; *Isth.* 4.44: καὶ Μελίσσῳ; *Isth.* 5.59: αἰνέω καὶ Πυθέαν; and *Isth.* 7.21: καὶ Στρεψιάδᾳ. For a similar use of the Latin *et*, see Williams, *Aeneid* 267, ad Aen. 8.630.

[34] For an analysis of the plot of this ode, see Race, "Elements of Plot in Pindar's Twelfth Olympian" (forthcoming).

Πύθιον Ἀπόλλωνα θρόνους,
αἰέναον σέβοντι πατρὸς Ὀλυμπίοιο τιμάν.
⟨ὦ⟩ πότνι' Ἀγλαΐα
φιλησίμολπέ τ' Εὐφροσύνα, θεῶν κρατίστου
15 παῖδες, ἐπακοοῖτε νῦν, Θαλία τε
ἐρασίμολπε, ἰδοῖσα τόνδε κῶμον ἐπ' εὐμενεῖ τύχᾳ
κοῦφα βιβῶντα· Λυδῷ γὰρ Ἀσώπιχον ἐν τρόπῳ
ἐν μελέταις τ' ἀείδων ἔμολον,
οὕνεκ' Ὀλυμπιόνικος ἁ Μινύεια
20 σεῦ ἕκατι. μελαντειχέα νῦν δόμον
Φερσεφόνας ἔλθ', Ἀ-
χοῖ, πατρὶ κλυτὰν φέροισ' ἀγγελίαν,
Κλεόδαμον ὄφρ' ἰδοῖσ', υἱὸν εἴπῃς ὅτι οἱ νέαν
κόλποις παρ' εὐδόξοις Πίσας
ἐστεφάνωσε κυδίμων ἀέθλων πτεροῖσι χαίταν.

You to whom the waters of Kaphisos
belong, and who dwell in a land of fine horses,
O Graces, much-sung queens
of shining Orchomenos and guardians of the ancient Minyai,
5 listen to my prayer. For through your agency all things pleasant
and sweet come about for mortals,
be he wise, be he handsome, be he an illustrious man.
Yes, not even the gods arrange choruses or feasts
    without the august Graces, but stewards of all
10 works in heaven, they have their thrones beside
Pythian Apollo of the golden bow,
and worship the ever-flowing majesty of the father of Olympos.
O queenly Aglaia,
and Euphrosyna, lover of song, children of the mightiest
15 of the gods, hear me now—and may you, Thalia,
who crave song, look favorably on his celebration of fortune's kindness
as it steps lightly along. For I have come to sing of Asopichos
in Lydian mode as I practice my art,
because the land of the Minyai enjoys an Olympic victory
20 thanks to you. To the black-walled home
of Persephona go now,
    Echo, carrying the glorious news to his father,
Kleodamos, so that when you see him you can say that his son
has crowned his young hair at the famous vale of Pisa
with winged wreathes from the games that bring renown.

This ode contains most of the hymnal elements we have listed.

I. Invocation
  A. Basic Topics
    1. Names: Χάριτες, Ἀγλαΐα, Εὐφροσύνα, Θαλία, Ἀχοῖ
    2. Attributes: ἀοίδιμοι, πότνι', φιλησίμολπε, ἐρασίμολπε
    3. Genealogy: θεῶν κρατίστου παῖδες
    4. *Sedes*: ναίετε καλλίπωλον ἕδραν; Ἐρχομενοῦ;
          θέμεναι πάρα | Πύθιον Ἀπόλλωνα θρόνους
    5. Powers: βασίλειαι, ἐπίσκοποι, ταμίαι
    6. Deeds: σὺν γὰρ ὑμῖν... τὰ γλυκέ' ἄνεται πάντα; σέβοντι

  B. Expansions
    1. Additive clauses: αἴτε ναίετε, σὺν ὑμῖν,
    2. Participial clauses: λαχοῖσαι, θέμεναι
    3. Appositives: βασίλειαι, ἐπίσκοποι, ταμίαι
    4. Explanations γάρ (5, 8, 17)
    5. *Hypomneseis*: σὺν ὑμῖν...τὰ γλυκέ' ἄνεται πάντα; σέβοντι
    6. Companion deity: Ἀπόλλωνα
    7. Doublets: ὑδάτων... ἕδραν; τερπνὰ... γλυκέ';
          βροτοῖς... θεοί; χοροὺς... δαῖτας

II. Request
  A. General summons: κλῦτ', ἐπακοοῖτε
  B. Specific petition: ἔλθ' (of Echo)

As in the two previous examples, the names of the goddesses are reserved for the end of the period, thus creating suspense until the qualifying terms finally issue into a proper name. The epithet ἀοίδιμοι (3) is particularly important, for it "reminds" the Charites of their own fame in song, which is presently being renewed.[35] After a brief, perfunctory request, κλῦτ', ἐπεὶ εὔχομαι (5), Pindar sketches their powers in an explanatory clause (cf. γάρ, 5). All (πάντα, 6) pleasant and sweet things accrue to men from them, regardless of the field of excellence: εἰ σοφός, εἰ καλός, εἴ τις ἀγλαὸς ἀνήρ (7). The all-inclusive πάντα and βροτοῖς (6) are thus subdivided into constituent areas in which a man can find pleasure. The priamel motif is apparent: "one man achieves the pleasure the Graces bestow by being wise, another by his beauty, and another by success."

---

[35] Verdenius, *Commentaries I* 108 rightly insists on the word's passive sense here "much sung of," but it also looks forward to the Graces' close association with song in the rest of the ode as companion deities of Apollo (cf. 10-11) and "lovers of song" (cf. φιλησίμολπε ... ἐρασίμολπε, 14-16). For the active and passive senses of the adjective, see the discussion of Radt, *Pindars zweiter und sechster Paian* 107-108. Pindar frequently refers to the χάρις of his poetry, associates the Charites and the Muses, and even uses χάριτες to designate his poems; see Slater, *Lexicon* s.v. χάρις, 1.b.β.

But instead of turning immediately to the victor (the last category, ἀγλαός, would have been the most appropriate one),[36] Pindar switches to the role of the Charites among the gods, where they also oversee all (πάντων, 9) pleasant activities. These two panels, one of men's activities on earth and the other of the gods on Olympos, portray the Charites' range of powers as bestowers of joy on festive occasions. The scene in heaven (there is a hint of an *ekphrasis*) is paradigmatic of the present celebration on earth; it serves to "remind" the goddesses of their place in festive celebrations, especially when τιμά is called for (cf. τιμᾶν, 12).[37]

Having thus defined the Charites' role of gracing festivals, the poet could have proceeded directly in the second strophe to the present victory celebration, but instead, he begins a new movement by re-invoking them. As we have noted, re-invocations tend to be longer and more specific; here Pindar delineates each Grace's character in a series of rising elements (13-14):

(1)⟨ὦ⟩ πότνι' Ἀγλαΐα
(2)φιλησίμολπέ τ' Εὐφροσύνα, θεῶν κρατίστου
15 παῖδες, ἐπακοοῖτε νῦν, (3)Θαλία τε
ἐρασίμολπε, ἰδοῖσα τόνδε κῶμον ἐπ' εὐμενεῖ τύχᾳ
κοῦφα βιβῶντα.

(1)O queenly Aglaia,
(2)and Euphrosyna, lover of song, children of the mightiest
15 of the gods, hear me now—(3)and may you, Thalia,
who crave song, look favorably on his celebration of fortune's kindness
as it steps lightly along.

Ἀγλαΐα is simply described as πότνια; she rules over the celebration.[38] Εὐφροσύνα is φιλησίμολπε, an important specification of ἀοίδιμοι (3), for it singles out her love of dance and song that are at issue in the following lines (cf. κοῦφα βιβῶντα, 17; ἀείδων, 18). But Thalia's epithet ἐρασίμολπε is more intense than φιλησίμολπε (14).[39] The first two goddesses are provided a

---

[36] Miller, "*Thalia Erasimolpos*" 228 points out that in Pindar ἀγλαός is "a *vox propria* descriptive of agonistic success."

[37] For the divine festival as the counterpart of those on earth, cf. *h. Hom.* 3.182-203, at which the Charites dance while Apollo plays the lyre. The hymn to the Lyre at *Pyth.* 1.1-12 develops the topic into a vivid *ekphrasis*.

[38] For a discussion of the traits of these three goddesses, see Miller, "*Thalia Erasimolpos*" 225-231. As the hypostatization of success (cf. ἀγλαὸς ἀνήρ, 7), Aglaia is the necessary first cause of celebration, while her sisters, good cheer (Euphrosyna) and feasting (Thalia), follow to complete the joy.

[39] For an explanation of Thalia's prominence in this consolatory ode, see Miller, "*Thalia Erasimolpos*" 225-234, who points out (230): "If φιλησίμολπε means 'you who love [i.e., feel affection for] music,' then ἐρασίμολπε should be rendered 'you who *crave* [i.e., feel physical need for] music.'"

genealogy and asked to "pay heed now" (ἐπακοοῖτε νῦν, 17). Although the text and meaning of the verb are in doubt,[40] the verb and adverb of this re-invocation are more intense than the κλῦτ' (5), which initially summoned the goddesses. At this point the hymnal invocation seems complete, but suddenly the third Grace, Thalia, is not only added (τε), but is specially singled out from her sisters.[41] Pindar devotes more syllables to her than to either of the other Graces, and asks her, and her alone (cf. σεῦ ἕκατι, 20), to look with favor (ἰδοῖσα, 16)[42] upon this present celebration (τόνδε κῶμον, 16). The γάρ-clause (17-18) links the victor (whose name is finally given) with the singer's intention to praise him ('Ασώπιχον... ἀείδων ἔμολον), much as many Homeric hymns announce their themes, while the οὕνεκα-clause (19-20) immediately moves us to the larger scene of the komos, in which the city participates. Thalia thus represents the festivity of the whole city as it celebrates its Olympic status (οὕνεκ' 'Ολυμπιόνικος ἁ Μινύεια | σεῦ ἕκατι, 19-20). Her presence is made clearer by comparing Ol. 7.93-94, where the city of Rhodes is said to share in the victory of Diagoras' clan: Ἐρατιδᾶν τοι σὺν χαρίτεσσιν ἔχει | θαλίας καὶ πόλις.[43] Here the graces (the joyousness of the Eratidai in their victory) and the festivities (in which the entire city shares) are plural abstractions. Since the Charites (and Thalia) are resident goddesses of Orchomenos, they personally attend the celebration.

The depiction of the festivities has widened to include the city, whose designation, ἁ Μινύεια (19), echoes Μινυᾶν (4), thus providing a slight sense of closure before the totally unexpected address to the goddess Echo: "To the black-walled home of Persephona, go now, Echo" (20-24). The word μελαντειχέα

---

[40] The MSS give ἐπάκοοι and Bergk conjectured the present reading, which is adopted by most editors, although its derivation and meaning are very doubtful. The verb ἐπακούειν is normal in prayers; cf. Anakreon 357.8 PMG, Aristoph. Nub. 274, and the "Hymn to the Moirai," 1018b.3 PMG. For a discussion see Verdenius, Commentaries I 117, who reads ἐπακουοῖτε.

[41] See Miller, "Thalia Erasimolpos" 230. For additive τε, which singles out a specific or the most important item in a list, cf. Ol. 13.29, Pyth. 1.39, 4.3; Nem. 4.10, 19, 75; Isth. 5.7, Bakch 3.3, and 12.8, and see Verdenius, Commentaries I 34 and 118, who discusses other instances where τε means "and especially." See also Verdenius, Works and Days 4.

[42] As often, the participle forms part of the request. Verdenius, Commentaries I 119 takes it in its pregnant sense of "look with favor at," which well suits this context (he aptly cites fr. 75.7-8: Διόθεν τέ με σὺν ἀγλαΐᾳ | ἴδετε [sc. 'Ολύμπιοι] πορευθέντ' ἀοιδᾶν. Here ἰδεῖν is almost synonymous with δέξασθαι. The following ἰδοῖσα (22) used of Echo, however, surely carries more the sense of purpose "to see and tell Kleodamos" (pace Verdenius, 124; see now the review of D. E. Gerber, CR 38 [1988] 204). The scholia are divided on whether the ἰδοῖσα is singular or, by extension, plural in its force. The word order that separates Thalia from the other Graces and the fact that σεῦ ἕκατι (20) is singular unmistakably indicates that only Thalia is singled out. Miller, "Thalia Erasimolpos" 228-231 argues, following Gildersleeve, that her close connections with feasting make her especially appropriate for this komos.

[43] Cf. also Archil. 13.2 W: θαλίης τέρπεται... πόλις. As at Ol. 4.8 and Ol. 5.21, the adjective 'Ολυμπιόνικος is reserved for climactic presentation. In this ode it is neatly prefigured in the scene in heaven by Zeus' epithet 'Ολυμπίοιο (12).

(20), coming as it does in mid-line with no preparation, is as shocking as the sudden intrusion of *palida mors* at Horace, *Odes* 1.4.13. Every other sentence in the ode is logically connected by a particle. Here Pindar's notorious abruptness is especially effective. He has withheld one of the items of information about the victory, the father's name, until the end to counterbalance the joy of the rest of the ode. Up to this point, there has been no tension in the ode between joy and sorrow, for everything has been expressed in positive terms.[44] This last piece of information suddenly casts a shadow over the celebration: it transforms the poem from praise to consolation. A point of style underscores the poignancy of the situation with quiet dignity: the adjective νέαν (22), emphasized by its position at the beginning of its clause and isolated by eight words from its noun, the final word of the poem, χαίταν (24), informs us that Kleodamos died while his son was still a boy and never lived to see his triumph. The poem moves from Olympos (8-12), to earth (13-20), to Hades (20-24). The final scene in the underworld contrasts strikingly with that in heaven. Only the echo can travel there; there is no Thalia in Hades.[45]

Forms of Hymns

Pindar inherited a tradition consisting of two principal types of hymns, rhapsodic and cultic, and in order to understand fully the ways in which he adapted these types, it is necessary to distinguish their formal features.[46] The four opening hymns we have so far examined are all cultic.[47] Rhapsodic (or epic) hymns are

---

[44] In a similar fashion the festivities in *Ol.* 7 (quoted above) are undercut by the concluding sentence of the ode: ἐν δὲ μιᾷ μοίρᾳ χρόνου | ἄλλοτ' ἀλλοῖαι διαιθύσσοισιν αὗραι (94-95). The instability of fortune (and the consequent need to enjoy fully what good one has) is there stated in general terms; in *Ol.* 14 it becomes poignantly concrete.

[45] Dönt, "Zur 14. olympischen Ode" 126-135 provides some perceptive comments on the form of the hymn, but takes ἰδοῖσα (16), σεῦ (20), and even ἐστεφάνωσε (24) as plurals with all three Charites as subjects or antecedents. Besides flying in the face of Greek grammar and Pindaric practice, this interpretation involves the unprecedented notion of the Charites actually crowning the victor. See the criticisms of Verdenius, *Commentaries I* 119 and 125. Commentators have made too much of the fact that ἐστεφάνωσε is not middle. If in *Isth.* 1 Herodotos can wreathe his hand (φράξαι χεῖρα, 66) and in *Pyth.* 10 the Hyperboreans can wreathe their hair (κόμας ἀναδήσαντες, 40; cf. ἀνδησάμενος κόμαν with no difference in meaning at *Nem.* 11.28), then surely Asopichos can crown his hair (ἐστεφάνωσε . . . χαίταν). The full stop after ἐρασίμολπε (16) in S-M⁸ (1987) is surely a printing error.

[46] For a brief, lucid discussion of the characteristics of rhapsodic and cultic hymns, see Miller, *Hymn to Apollo* 1-5, and for a brief survey of rhapsodic elements in Pindar's opening hymns, see Schadewaldt, *Aufbau* 271-274.

[47] Other introductory cultic hymns include *Ol.* 5.1-8 (Kamarina), *Ol.* 8.1-11 (Olympia, on which see below pages 142-146), *Pyth.* 1.1-12 (Phorminx), *Pyth.* 8.1-18 (Hesychia), *Pyth.* 11.1-16 (Theban goddesses), *Pyth.* 12.1-6 (Akragas), *Nem.* 8.1-7 (Hora), *Nem.* 11.1-10 (Hestia, on which see Race, *Pindar* 28), *Isth.* 5.1-10 (Theia), *Pa.* 6.1-11 (Pytho), and *fr.* 75.1-12 (Olym-

represented chiefly by the collection of thirty-three Homeric Hymns and by the later imitations of Kallimachos and Theokritos.[48] The main intention of rhapsodic hymns is to sing *about* the god; they are characteristically more impersonal than cultic hymns, describe the god in the third person ("Er-Stil"), and are more concerned with relating the god's attributes and achievements than with obtaining any specific request. Typically, they open with the poet's announcement of his intention to sing about some divinity (always named in an objective case), proceed to describe the god's nature or narrate his exploits, and conclude with a leave-taking (usually marked by the imperative χαῖρε, as the hymnist switches to the second person) that solicits the god's approval of the song before the poet turns to another theme. They share a number of features with epic, including addresses to the Muse and aporetic questions. As we shall see, Pindar skillfully adapts rhapsodic elements for some of his opening hymns.[49]

Cultic hymns, in contrast, are decidedly more personal; they address the god in the second person ("Du-Stil"), often are concerned with a specific situation, and emphasize the request. Every element in a cultic hymn is part of a rhetorical strategy whose purpose is to dispose the god favorably toward the request, which often petitions the god's presence (cf. Sappho, *fr.* 1.25: ἔλθε μοι καὶ νῦν) and/or assistance (cf. Sappho, *fr.* 1.28: σύμμαχος ἔσσο). Cultic hymns play a much larger role than rhapsodic hymns in Pindar's poetry, as they do in Greek poetry generally. When cultic hymns are very brief and the request predominates, they become indistinguishable from prayers.[50]

---

pian gods). The name cultic designates *formal* characteristics and does not mean that such hymns were necessarily used in cultic practices; likewise, rhapsodic hymns were not necessarily sung by rhapsodes (or even in epic meter) and could be part of ritual celebrations.

[48] Not all the "Homeric" hymns are strictly rhapsodic; *h. Hom.* 8 (to Ares) and 24 and 29 (to Hestia) exhibit predominantly cultic features, as a comparison of *h. Hom.* 29 with *Ol.* 14 shows. A fine example of a late (third century B.C.) lyric rhapsodic hymn is Aristonous' "Hymn to Hestia" (Powell 164-165), which consists of two sentences: the first (lines 1-10) constitutes the invocation, the second (11-17) the envoi. Typically rhapsodic are the announcement of his intention to sing of the goddess (Ἑστίαν ὑμνήσομεν) and the envoi: Χαῖρε ... δίδου δ' ("be pleased and keep on granting").

[49] An example of a rhapsodic hymn within an ode is *Isth.* 1.15-32, where Pindar announces his intention to include the victor in a hymn to Kastor or Iolaos (ἐθέλω ἢ Καστορείῳ ἢ Ἰολάοι' ἐναρμόξαι νιν ὕμνῳ, 15-16). The *aporia* created by ἢ ... ἢ is immediately resolved, as Pindar chooses to hymn both of them (κεῖνοι, 17) and proceeds to relate their deeds (17-31), before taking leave of them (χαίρετ', 32) and turning to another theme. For a thorough analysis, see Bundy, *Studia Pindarica* 45-47, who points out that even the transitional statement of 32-34, ἐγὼ δὲ ... γαρύσομαι, is an adaptation of the rhapsodic formula, αὐτὰρ ἐγὼ ... μνήσομαι (e.g., *h. Hom.* 3.546); see also Schadewaldt, *Aufbau* 276 note 4.

[50] The distinction between cultic hymns and prayers mainly involves a question of emphasis. For example, a passage such as *Ol.* 2.12-15 contains many elements normally found in hymnal invocations (name, genealogy, *sedes*), but it is best to consider it a prayer, since the emphasis clearly falls on the request (ἀλλ' ... κόμισον). In contrast, cultic hymns have more elaborate invocations; indeed, sometimes there is not even a request (e.g., *Pyth.* 1.1-12 and *Nem.* 8.1-5). Prayers, however, consist mainly of requests, often to an unspecified divinity such as θεός (*Ol.*

Rhapsodic hymns generally begin with variations on two basic formulae. In the first type, *the poet announces in the first person his intention to sing* about a god. The phrase ἄρχομ' ἀείδειν occurs frequently in the Homeric Hymns (2, 11, 13, 16, 22, 26, and 28); closely related are the declarative ἀείδω (12, 18, and 27) and the intentional futures μνήσομαι (3 and 7) and ἀείσομαι (6, 10, 15, 23, and 30). In the second type, *the poet requests the Muse to sing*. A number of imperatives occur: ὕμνει (4, 9, and 14), ἔννεπε (5 and 19), ἀείσεο (17), ἀείδεο (20) and ἔσπετε (32 and 33). The close relation of these formulae to the opening of epics is apparent, if one compares *h. Hom.* 5.1 (Μοῦσά μοι ἔννεπε ἔργα) with the opening of the *Odyssey* (Ἄνδρα μοι ἔννεπε Μοῦσα).[51]

Implicit in the verbs ἄρχομαι and ἀείδειν are questions as to *where* to begin and *what* to sing about.[52] For that reason, aporetic questions are occasionally used to point up the difficulty of finding a suitable beginning or subject. The author of the *Hymn to Apollo* employs this prooimial technique twice: πῶς γάρ σ' ὑμνήσω πάντως εὔυμνον ἐόντα; (19, 207); it is found in epic as well: τίς τ' ἄρ' σφωε θεῶν ἔριδι ξυνέηκε μάχεσθαι; (*Il.* 1.8).[53] Pindar's first hymn (*fr.* 29) opens with a series of "rhapsodic" questions:

Ἰσμηνὸν ἢ χρυσαλάκατον Μελίαν
ἢ Κάδμον ἢ Σπαρτῶν ἱερὸν γένος ἀνδρῶν
ἢ τὰν κυανάμπυκα Θήβαν
   ἢ τὸ πάντολμον σθένος Ἡρακλέος
5 ἢ τὰν Διωνύσου πολυγαθέα τιμὰν
   ἢ γάμον λευκωλένου Ἁρμονίας
ὑμνήσομεν;

Shall it be Ismenos, or Melia of the golden spindle,
or Kadmos, or the holy race of the Spartoi,
or Theba of the dark veil,
   or the all-daring strength of Herakles,
5 or the wondrous honor of Dionysos,
   or the marriage of white-armed Harmonia
that we shall sing?

6.101) or χρόνος (*Pyth.* 1.46). Hymns regularly use imperatives (when a request is expressed), whereas prayers often employ optatives. But in practice the two forms merge. Indeed, to judge from Menander Rhetor, the Greeks themselves seemed to make no firm distinction between them, for he calls Chryses' prayer to Apollo at *Il.* 1.37-42 (cf. ἠρᾶθ' ὁ γεραιός, 35) a κλητικὸς ὕμνος (335.13, Sp.); see Meyer, *Hymnische Stilelemente* 7. In this chapter I have restricted myself to passages that are clearly hymnal.

[51] See van Groningen, *La composition littéraire* 63.

[52] For a discussion of the ἀρχή in Greek hymns, see Race, "Greek Hymns" 5-8 and "How Greek Poems Begin" (forthcoming).

[53] For a discussion of ἀπορία in the rhapsodic tradition, see Bundy, "Quarrel" 58-66; on page 78 he shows how "epic" questions can be answered at once or call forth a list. For an analysis of the aporetic passages in *h. Hom.* 3, see Miller, *Hymn to Apollo* 20-22 and 70-71.

These questions invert the intentional opening, "I shall sing of" (ἀείσομαι), by posing a question, "Of what shall I sing?" (ὑμνήσομεν). *Ol.* 2 also opens with a series of rhapsodic questions that seek the proper subjects of the poem:[54]

Ἀναξιφόρμιγγες ὕμνοι,
τίνα θεόν, τίν' ἥρωα, τίνα δ' ἄνδρα κελαδήσομεν;

Lyre-ruling hymns,
what god, what hero, and what man shall we celebrate?

In addition, rhapsodic hymns contain a formal leave-taking of their subjects (χαῖρε) before the singer announces his intention to turn to another subject of song (ἄλλης μνήσομ' ἀοιδῆς). The language of these conclusions (e.g., *h. Hom.* 2.494: ἀντ' ᾠδῆς; 9.7: καὶ μὲν οὕτω χαῖρε . . . ἀοιδῇ) shows that the primary concern of the rhapsodic hymnist is to offer the god a pleasing song, a dedication that will elicit his or her goodwill.[55]

Like the epic narrator, the poet of rhapsodic hymns remains anonymous; his interest centers on the god's powers and exploits and even when he ends the hymn with a request, it is generic.[56] For that reason scholars have labelled the rhapsodic hymn "objective." In contrast, the speaker of the cultic (or "subjective") hymn can emerge as an individual in specific historical circumstances, as do, for example, Sappho and Alkaios.

Although rhapsodic and cultic hymns have a number of elements in common, it is important to differentiate their overall characteristics. The following table provides a survey of their principal distinguishing features.

---

[54] Yet another variation of rhapsodic opening is illustrated by *fr.* 89a, the beginning of a hymn to Artemis, which poses the problem of where to begin (and where to end):

Τί κάλλιον ἀρχομένοισ[ιν] ἢ καταπαυομένοισιν
ἢ βαθύζωνόν τε Λατώ
καὶ θοᾶν ἵππων ἐλάτειραν ἀεῖσαι;

What is better for us as we begin or end
than to sing of deep-bosomed Lato
and the driver of swift horses?

The ἀρχομένοισ[ιν] is descended from the rhapsodic ἄρχομ' ἀείδειν. Cf. *Pyth.* 7.5-8 for a more distant relative: ἐπεὶ τίνα πάτραν, τίνα οἶκον ναίων ὀνυμάξεαι ἐπιφανέστερον Ἑλλάδι πυθέσθαι;

[55] For a detailed discussion of the epilogue of rhapsodic hymns, see Bundy, "Quarrel" 79-86.

[56] Even when the request appears to be for a specific place (τήνδε πόλιν, 13.3) or event (ἐν ἀγῶνι . . . τῷδε, 6.19-20), it still retains its generalized force, for it could be repeated in many different places and contests. Likewise, the ἡμᾶς (15) in Aristonous' rhapsodic hymn (see above note 48) is generalized by the word ἀεί (16) to include all future generations.

Function	Rhapsodic Hymns	Cultic Hymns
poetic intention	poet as composer ἄρχομ' ἀείδειν Μοῦσά μοι ἔννεπε[57]	poet as suppliant λίσσομαι εὔχομαι
divine subject	named in oblique case	directly addressed
treatment of subject	narrative (ὅs/ἥ . . .)	*hypomnesis* (εἴ ποτε)
selection of subject	rhapsodic questions (τίς; πῶς; ἤ . . . ἤ;)	*aporia* concerning an attribute[58]
leave-taking	salutation (χαῖρε, ἴληθι), request for a pleasing song, announcement of another song to follow	request (κλῦθι, ἐλθέ)

Opening Hymns with Rhapsodic Elements

Both Pindar and Bakchylides open odes with hymnal addresses that follow the tradition of rhapsodic hymns by asking some god (usually a Muse) to help them sing about a particular subject. By keeping in mind a simple rhapsodic opening such as that of *h. Hom.* 4.1 (Ἑρμῆν ὕμνει Μοῦσα), we can see precisely how Pindar expands the core. *Nem.* 10.1-2 is straightforwardly epic (cf. the opening of the cyclic *Thebaid*: Ἄργος ἄειδε θεά).

> Δαναοῦ πόλιν ἀγλαοθρό-
>   νων τε πεντήκοντα κορᾶν, Χάριτες,
> Ἄργος Ἥρας δῶμα θεοπρεπὲς ὑμνεῖτε . . .

> Of Danaos' city and that of his gloriously
>   enthroned fifty daughters,
> Argos, heaven-favored home of Hera, sing Graces . . .

---

[57] Since the request to the Muse is formally a prayer, it can be expanded with cultic features, as at *Il.* 2.484-485: Ἔσπετε νῦν μοι Μοῦσαι Ὀλύμπια δώματ' ἔχουσαι· | ὑμεῖς γὰρ θεαί ἐστε πάρεστέ τε ἴστέ τε πάντα. The lyric poets also expanded addresses to the Muses; cf. Alkman 3, 14, and 27 PMG; cf. also the invocation to Erato at Ap. Rh. *Arg.* 3.1-5 and Sokrates' parody of hymnic prooimia at *Phaidr.* 237A: ἄγετε δή, ὦ Μοῦσαι, εἴτε δι' ᾠδῆς εἶδος λίγειαι, εἴτε διὰ γένος μουσικὸν τὸ Λιγύων ταύτην ἔσχετε τὴν ἐπωνυμίαν.

[58] Rhapsodic hymns pose questions about which god to sing, which particular exploit to treat, or where to begin the narrative ("rhapsodic questions"); *aporia* in cultic hymns generally involves selecting the proper name, attribute, or epithet, as at Aisch. *Ag.* 160-161 and in Sokrates' parody quoted above note 57. For examples of *aporia* in cultic hymns, see Norden, *Agnostos Theos* 144-147.

Others, like the opening of *Pyth.* 4, can be much more complex.

> Σάμερον μὲν χρή σε παρ' ἀνδρὶ φίλῳ
> στᾶμεν, εὐίππου βασιλῆι Κυράνας,
> ὄφρα κωμάζοντι σὺν Ἀρκεσίλᾳ,
> Μοῖσα, Λατοίδαισιν ὀφειλόμενον Πυ-
> θῶνί τ' αὔξῃς οὖρον ὕμνων ...

> Today, Muse, you must stand at the side of a dear man,
> the king of Kyrana of the fine horses,
> so that during the celebrations of Arkesilas,
> you may swell the breeze of hymns
> owed to Lato's twins and to Pytho ...

The core of this invocation is the same as that of the rhapsodic hymn ("Muse, you must sing of Arkesilas"), but the simple imperative (ὕμνει) of the Homeric hymn becomes χρή σε ... στᾶμεν ... ὄφρα ... αὔξῃς οὖρον ὕμνων, while the subject is successively given as ἀνδρὶ φίλῳ ... βασιλῆι Κυράνας ... Ἀρκεσίλᾳ. It is fitting that *Pyth.* 4, the most "epic" of Pindar's odes, should have a rhapsodic opening.[59] The prominent word σάμερον accomplishes two things. First, it gives a sense of urgency to the request. Secondly, it indicates that the present celebration is but one of many others, past and future, at which the Muse must assist (παρ' ... στᾶμεν). Like a summary priamel, it suggests the other times and occasions which form a background for this specific event. Perhaps the translation, "on this special day," catches some of the tone of the word with its intensifying μέν.

Every additional word plays a role in the unfolding of the entire invocation. In particular, the word φίλῳ raises the mere duty of the word χρή to the level of

---

[59] See Braswell, *Fourth Pythian* 57-58. If the quantitative aspect of the word αὔξῃς is stressed, it might even refer to the unprecedented length of this ode. Other rhapsodic elements appear in this ode. One, for example, is the announcement of his intention to sing of Arkesilas and of the golden fleece at 67-68: ἀπὸ δ' αὐτὸν ἐγὼ Μοίσαισι δώσω | καὶ τὸ πάγχρυσον νάκος κριοῦ, where Μοίσαισι δώσω = ἀείσομαι. He also begins the narrative proper with rhapsodic questions (70-71):

> 70 τίς γὰρ ἀρχὰ δέξατο ναυτιλίας,
>   τίς δὲ κίνδυνος κρατεροῖς ἀδάμαντος
>   δῆσεν ἅλοις;

> 70 What beginning received them on their voyage,
>   and what danger bound them with strong nails
>   of adamant?

For the issue in rhapsodic hymns of finding the ἀρχή, see above page 104 and notes 52 and 54.

friendship and assures the Muse of a warm reception.⁶⁰ The epithet εὐίππου of Kyrana is naturally appropriate for a chariot-victory, while the word κωμάζοντι specifies the spirit of the occasion. The participle ὀφειλόμενον succinctly performs the function of a γάρ-clause by explaining why a song is necessary (χρή) today. In other words, on this day of celebration debts are being paid, but out of friendship. As we shall see (below pages 113-115), this nexus of themes also forms the basis for Pindar's elaborate apology in *Ol.* 10.⁶¹

Pyth. 9, another ode to a Kyrenean, also has a rhapsodic opening:

> Ἐθέλω χαλκάσπιδα Πυθιονίκαν
> σὺν βαθυζώνοισιν ἀγγέλλων
> Τελεσικράτη Χαρίτεσσι γεγωνεῖν
> ὄλβιον ἄνδρα διωξίππου στεφάνωμα Κυράνας·
> 5 τὰν ...

> I wish, as I announce that blessed man Telesikrates,
> a bronze-shielded Pythian victor,
> to proclaim with the aid of the deep-bosomed Graces
> a song to crown chariot-driving Kyrana.
> 5 whom ...

---

⁶⁰ The word φίλῳ also establishes from the very outset of the ode an atmosphere of friendship within which the counsel of the concluding lines can have their intended effect. Braswell, *Fourth Pythian* 60 claims that when Pindar uses the word φίλος it "need mean no more than that he has received a commission," but when he addresses such important men as Arkesilas and Hieron (*Pyth.* 1.92) as φίλοι and proceeds to give them advice, the word takes on greater significance.

⁶¹ *Nem.* 9.1-3 provides a variation of the opening of *Pyth.* 4.

> Κωμάσομεν παρ' Ἀπόλλωνος Σικυωνόθε, Μοῖσαι,
> τὰν νεοκτίσταν ἐς Αἴτναν, ἔνθ' ἀναπεπταμέναι
>   ξείνων νενίκανται θύραι,
> ὄλβιον ἐς Χρομίου
>   δῶμ'. ἀλλ' ἐπέων γλυκὺν ὕμνον πράσσετε.

> Let us go in celebration from Apollo's temple at Sikyon, Muses,
> to the newly-built city of Aitna, where the guests
>   overwhelm the wide-open gates to enter
> Chromios' blessed
>   home. And you must compose a sweet hymn of verses.

The prominent κωμάσομεν (1) corresponds to κωμάζοντι at *Pyth.* 4.2, while the reference to ξείνων (2) parallels the word φίλῳ at *Pyth.* 4.1 and assures the Muse of a kindly reception (see below note 73). ἐπέων γλυκὺν ὕμνον πράσσετε (3) is formally equivalent to ὄφρα ... αὔξῃς οὖρον ὕμνων at *Pyth.* 4.2-3, both of which are elaborations of the rhapsodic imperative, ὕμνει. These parallels provide additional support to the arguments of Gerber, "Short-Vowel Subjunctives" 86 that κωμάσομεν is a hortatory subjunctive.

The words ἐθέλω ... γεγωνεῖν are a variation of the intentional rhapsodic opening (cf. ἀείσομαι in the Homeric hymns).[62] Instead of the usual appeal to the Muse, the poet here states that he has the aid of the Charites (σὺν βαθυζώνοισιν ... Χαρίτεσσι). The extremely complex word order is at first confusing, but the syntax becomes clear when each verbal form is taken separately with its objects. The participle ἀγγέλλων governs the words Τελεσικράτη ... ὄλβιον ἄνδρα, while the main verb γεγωνεῖν takes the inner object διωξίππου στεφάνωμα Κυράνας: in the course of announcing the success of Telesikrates, Pindar will sing a crown of song for Kyrene.[63] The subordinate participle designates the human subject (ἄνδρα); the main verb introduces the mythical heroine.[64] By withholding her name until the very end of the period with the ringing phrase διωξίππου στεφάνωμα Κυράνας, Pindar can then proceed directly to tell her story with the hymnal relative (τάν, 5), so common in rhapsodic hymns to introduce accounts of the god. In fact, the following portrayal of Kyrene's career has many of the characteristics of rhapsodic narratives, including the heroine's genealogy, birth, upbringing, deeds, marriage, and offspring, along with dramatic dialogue which deepens the plot and portrays the character of the participants.[65]

Similar, but even more complex, is the rhapsodic opening of Ol. 3.1-5.

    Τυνδαρίδαις τε φιλοξείνοις ἀδεῖν
    καλλιπλοκάμῳ θ᾽ Ἑλένᾳ
    κλεινὰν Ἀκράγαντα γεραίρων εὔχομαι,
    Θήρωνος Ὀλυμπιονίκαν
    ὕμνον ὀρθώσαις, ἀκαμαντοπόδων
    ἵππων ἄωτον. Μοῖσα δ᾽ οὕτω ποι παρέ-
    στα μοι νεοσίγαλον εὑρόντι τρόπον
5   Δωρίῳ φωνὰν ἐναρμόξαι πεδίλῳ
    ἀγλαόκωμον.

I pray that I may please the hospitable Tyndaridai
and Helen of the beautiful locks,
as I pay honor to famous Akragas,

---

[62] See Slater, "Futures in Pindar" 86 and cf. Ol. 7.20-21: ἐθελήσω τοῖσιν ἐξ ἀρχᾶς ἀπὸ Τλαπολέμου | ξυνὸν ἀγγέλλων διορθῶσαι λόγον.

[63] See Bundy, Studia Pindarica 20-21: "[στεφάνωμα] is in truth the inner object of γεγωνεῖν; the song is a wreath to crown Kyrene," and Nisetich, "An Epinician Metaphor" 63.

[64] The rhapsodic hymn embedded in Isth. 1.14-34 provides good examples of Pindar's use of main verbs and dependent participles to dismiss and introduce subjects. In 14-16 the participle τεύχων (14) governs the man (Herodotos), while the main verb ἐθέλω ... ἐναρμόξαι (cf. ἐθέλω ... γεγωνεῖν at Pyth. 9.1-3) introduces the heroes Kastor and Iolaos. After taking leave of them, Pindar reverses the procedure: περιστέλλων ἀοιδάν (33) dismisses the divine subjects, while γαρύσομαι (34) introduces the human one (Asopodoros).

[65] For a survey and analysis of the narrative topics in the Homeric Hymns, see Miller, Hymn to Apollo 3, 6-8.

> when, for Theron, I raise up an Olympic
> victory hymn, the finest reward for his horses
> with unwearying feet. And for that reason, I believe, the Muse
> stood beside me as I found a newly shining way
> 5 to join to Dorian measure
> — my celebratory voice.

All the elements we saw in *Pyth.* 9 are here. The main verb εὔχομαι corresponds to ἐθέλω.[66] As in *Pyth.* 9, the infinitive (ἀδεῖν) governs the divine subject (the Tyndaridai), while the participles (γεραίρων and ὀρθώσαις) designate the lesser ones, Akragas and (climactically) Theron. Here, however, the order of subjects is reversed. Pride of place is given to the divinities, indicating that the Tyndaridai are the ἀρχή and τέλος of the ode (in 39 they reappear as guests of the Emmenidai). The infinitive ἀδεῖν reminds us that the ultimate purpose of a rhapsodic hymn is to please the god, its subject.[67] The first participial clause, κλεινὰν Ἀκράγαντα γεραίρων, corresponds to ἀγγέλλων Τελεσικράτη ... ὄλβιον ἄνδρα, while the second, Θήρωνος Ὀλυμπιονίκαν ὕμνον ὀρθώσαις, ἀκαμαντοπόδων ἵππων ἄωτον, corresponds to γεγωνεῖν ... διωξίππου στεφάνωμα Κυράνας, both *rhetorically*, since, coming last, it designates the subject that will shortly be elaborated, and *syntactically*, since it designates the song as the ἄωτον for Theron's victorious horses just as in *Pyth.* 9 the song was the στεφάνωμα for Kyrene.

In this one sentence Pindar has combined four distinct events and has arranged them, as Σ 1 b notes, in reverse chronological order (ἀντέστραπται δὲ ἡ τάξις). First came the victory of the horses (ἵππων, 4), in honor of which the poet will "raise up an Olympic victory hymn for Theron" (3), in the course of which he will praise Akragas (2), in the prayerful hope of pleasing the Tyndaridai (1). The one element so far lacking is mention of the Muse. Just as in *Pyth.* 9 he was accompanied by the Charites, in the following sentence he portrays the Muse as already having assisted him (4): Μοῖσα δ' οὕτω ποι παρέστα μοι ("And for that reason, I believe, the Muse stood beside me"). Since an appeal to the Muses rather than a declaration is expected in such a context, editors have naturally been tempted to emend the text, but no conjecture is convincing.[68] There is no reason why Pindar cannot claim that he has the Muse at his side, as in *Pyth.* 9 and at *Isth.* 5.21 he declares that the Graces are with him.[69] But most important is the word ποι, which turns an otherwise flat declaration into a respectful supposition.

---

[66] The choice of the more deferential εὔχομαι is no doubt determined by the fact that it is divinities (the Tyndaridai) whom he hopes to please.

[67] See above page 105 and Race, "Greek Hymns" 8-10. The verb ἁνδάνειν occurs nine times in Pindar; seven times it applies to gods.

[68] Mommsen's attempt to turn the statement into a request by emending the text to οὕτω μοι παρεστάκοι was accepted by Gildersleeve; for other attempts see Gerber, *Emendations* 37.

[69] Cf. Bakch. 5.9-10: ἦ σὺν Χαρίτεσσι βαθυζώνοις ὑφάνας | ὕμνον.

The Muse has already assisted the poet as he discovered a new style for the poem (νεοσίγαλον εὑρόντι τρόπον, 4).⁷⁰ A comparison of these rhapsodic openings reveals a firm basis of form underlying Pindar's adaptations and verbal ποικιλία, which, once grasped, elucidates the grammar that has puzzled so many commentators.

Combinations of Rhapsodic and Cultic Elements

One striking way in which Pindar displays his genius for inventiveness is in his combining rhapsodic and cultic hymnal elements. A good example is the opening of *Nem.* 3.⁷¹

>   Ὦ πότνια Μοῖσα, μᾶτερ ἁμετέρα, λίσσομαι,
>   τὰν πολυξέναν ἐν ἱερομηνίᾳ Νεμεάδι
>   ἵκεο Δωρίδα νᾶσον Αἴγιναν· ὕδατι γὰρ
>   μένοντ' ἐπ' Ἀσωπίῳ μελιγαρύων τέκτονες
>   5 κώμων νεανίαι, σέθεν ὄπα μαιόμενοι.
>   διψῇ δὲ πρᾶγος ἄλλο μὲν ἄλλου,
>   ἀεθλονικία δὲ μάλιστ' ἀοιδὰν φιλεῖ,
>   στεφάνων ἀρετᾶν τε δεξιωτάταν ὀπαδόν·
>   τᾶς ἀφθονίαν ὄπαζε μήτιος ἁμᾶς ἄπο·
> 10 ἄρχε δ' οὐρανοῦ πολυνεφέλα κρέοντι, θύγατερ,
>   δόκιμον ὕμνον· ἐγὼ δὲ κείνων τέ νιν ὀάροις
>   λύρᾳ τε κοινάσομαι. χαρίεντα δ' ἕξει πόνον
>   χώρας ἄγαλμα, Μυρμιδόνες ἵνα πρότεροι
>   ᾤκησαν, ὧν παλαίφατον ἀγορὰν
> 15 οὐκ ἐλεγχέεσσιν Ἀριστοκλείδας τεάν

---

[70] The terms εὑρόντι and ἐναρμόξαι adumbrate the rhetorical categories of *inventio* and *compositio*. The latter is restated below with the words ἐπέων θέσιν (8) and συμμεῖξαι πρεπόντως (9).

[71] Other openings that display mixtures of rhapsodic and cultic hymns are *Pyth.* 2.1-8 (to Syracuse), *Nem.* 1 (to Ortygia), and *Pa.* 2.1-5 (to Abderos). Radt, *Pindars zweiter und sechster Paian* 26, offers a very perceptive comparison of the openings of *Nem.* 1 and *Pa.* 2: "Auf die ausführliche Anrufung der Gottheit im Stil des Kulthymnus folgt beide Male mit σέθεν... ὕμνος ὁρμᾶται bzw. σέθεν... παιᾶνα διώξω ein typisches Element des epischen Hymnus, der sich vom Kulthymnus ja eben dadurch unterscheidet, dass an die Stelle des direkten Anrufs im Vokativ mit dazugehörigem κλῦθι, ἐλθέ, oder dgl. ein ankündigendes Verbum wie ἀείδω, ἀείσομαι, ἄρχομ' ἀείδειν tritt, von dem der Name der Gottheit grammatisch abhängig ist (Meyer 6 f. 20): Pindar, der sonst fast immer den prächtigeren und weihevolleren Stil des Kulthymnus vorzieht (Meyer 62. 67), hat hier beide in eigentümlicher Weise miteinander verbunden: statt einer Bitte, die man nach dem feierlich-nachdrücklichen Anruf erwartet, folgt eine nüchterne Programmankündigung." For examples of Bakchylides' mingling of hymnal forms, see *Appendix 2*.

> ἐμίανε κατ' αἶσαν ἐν περισθενεῖ μαλαχθείς
> παγκρατίου στόλῳ.

> O mistress Muse, my mother, I beg of you,
> come in the Nemean sacred month to this
> hospitable Dorian island of Aigina, for by the waters
> of Asopos are waiting the builders of honey-sounding
> 5   revels, young men who desire your voice.
> Various deeds thirst for different rewards,
> but victory in the games cherishes song most of all,
> the fittest companion for crowned achievements.
> Daughter of Zeus, grant from my skill no stint of such song,
> 10 and begin for your father who rules the cloud-covered sky
> a proper hymn; I shall impart it to the young men's voices
> and the lyre. A pleasant task will be its dedication
> to this land, where the Myrmidons of old
> dwelled, and whose long-famed assembly place
> 15 (by your grace) Aristokleidas did not stain with failure
> by weakening in the bouts of strength
> of the pankration.

We may isolate the rhapsodic features of this hymn by comparing the opening of *h. Hom.* 31: "Ἥλιον ὑμνεῖν αὖτε Διὸς τέκος ἄρχεο Μοῦσα.

h. Hom. 31	*Nem.* 3.1-11
Μοῦσα	Μοῖσα (1)
τέκος	θύγατερ (10)
Διός	οὐρανοῦ ... κρέοντι (10)
ἄρχεο	ἄρχε (10)
ὑμνεῖν	ὕμνον (11)

The opening of the Homeric hymn is very economical. The subject of the song (Helios) is directly stated, while the Muse, the offspring of Zeus, is told to begin to sing. Pindar eventually makes the same request, but embellishes the rhapsodic core with a lengthy cultic prayer to the Muse (1-9), which contains many of the features of cultic hymns: the verb of supplication (λίσσομαι, 1), the request to come (ἵκεο, 3), and the consistent "Du-Stil" (πότνια, 1; σέθεν, 5; ὄπαζε, 9), which establishes a close I-Thou relationship (cf. μᾶτερ ἀμετέρα, 1). The one element in the Homeric Hymn not directly accounted for is the αὖτε "on this occasion." It is present, however, in the overall dramatic situation,[72] because the ode is late (cf. ὀψέ, 80); the Muse's coming is urgent, for it is in the time of the Nemean festival and the young celebrants are eagerly awaiting (μαιόμενοι, 5) her voice. Pindar has invested the moment of performance with dramatic tension.

---

[72] Cf. σάμερον at *Pyth.* 4.1 (discussed above page 107).

Style and Rhetoric in Opening Hymns 113

The epithet πολύξέναν (2) of Aigina is meant to assure the goddess of a warm reception there.[73] Instead of proceeding directly with an explanation of why her presence is so necessary, Pindar uses a priamel (6-8) to highlight the fact that the occasion concerns athletic victory (ἀεθλονικία, 7) and to emphasize the pressing need for song (cf. διψῇ, 6; μάλιστ'... φιλεῖ, 7). The celebration cannot begin without her. As in the previous example, Pindar carefully portrays the cooperation of the Muse and himself. She must provide (ὄπαζε, 9)[74] a plentiful supply of song from his own wit; she must begin the hymn.[75] But after she prompts the song, the poet will entrust it (κοινάσομαι, 12) to the singers' voices and the lyre.[76] The verb κοινάσομαι corresponds to the intentional future in rhapsodic openings; he implies that it will take some work (πόνον, 12) on his part, but it will be pleasant (χαρίεντα, 12).[77] At this point the address to the Muse is complete, for with the pronouncement of the imperative ἄρχε, the hymn to Zeus has already begun, and Pindar is in fact imparting it (νιν, 11) to voices and instrumentation. As so often in hymnal passages, a relative clause (ὧν, 14) supplies the details of the occasion, here Aristokleidas' victory in the pankration.

In *Nem.* 3 Pindar enlivens the hymn (and the ode) by a sense of urgency because the ode is late. *Ol.* 10 provides a striking variation of the same topic.

Τὸν Ὀλυμπιονίκαν ἀνάγνωτέ μοι
Ἀρχεστράτου παῖδα, πόθι φρενός
ἐμᾶς γέγραπται· γλυκὺ γὰρ αὐτῷ μέλος ὀφείλων
ἐπιλέλαθ'· ὦ Μοῖσ', ἀλλὰ σὺ καὶ θυγάτηρ
Ἀλάθεια Διός, ὀρθᾷ χερί
5 ἐρύκετον ψευδέων
ἐνιπὰν ἀλιτόξενον.
ἕκαθεν γὰρ ἐπελθὼν ὁ μέλλων χρόνος
ἐμὸν κατᾴσχυνε βαθὺ χρέος.
ὅμως δὲ λῦσαι δυνατὸς ὀξεῖαν ἐπιμομφὰν

---

[73] Cf. *Ol.* 11.16-19, where he vouches for the hospitality ([μήτε] φυγόξεινον, 17) of the Western Lokrians and *Nem.* 9.1-3, where he informs the Muses of Chromios' many guests (ξείνων, 2). The prominent τάν (2) may imply that Aigina's great hospitality is well known. Cf. *Pa.* 6.131: καὶ τὰν θεμίξενον ἀρετ[άν. Pindar reserves the name Αἴγιναν (3) for emphatic last position in the period.

[74] The imperative ὄπαζε occurs frequently in the envois of rhapsodic hymns. Cf. *h. Hom.* 2.494, 24.5 (χάριν δ' ἅμ' ὄπασσον ἀοιδῇ), 30.18, 31.17.

[75] In rhapsodic hymns the god is often called the "beginning" of the hymn by virtue of being its opening subject (e.g., ἄρχομ' ἀείδειν and σεῦ δ' ἐγὼ ἀρξάμενος). But there is another sense in which the god himself "begins" or "directs" the hymn, as in *h. Hom.* 13.3: ἄρχε δ' ἀοιδῆς. See Race, "Greek Hymns" 5-8.

[76] Hubbard, "The Aeginetan Chorus" 1-9 takes κοινάσομαι as "communicate" and ὀάροις λύρᾳ τε as instrumental datives; see the objections of Carey, "Performance" 553 note 18.

[77] For the importance of the word *charis* in hymnal contexts, see above pages 93-94 with note 23. This is also an instance of the "Bereitwilligkeits-Motiv," on which see above note 19.

>   τόκος †θνατῶν· νῦν ψᾶφον ἑλισσομέναν
> 10   ὁπᾷ κῦμα κατακλύσσει ῥέον,
>   ὁπᾷ τε κοινὸν λόγον
>   φίλαν τείσομεν ἐς χάριν.

> Read me the Olympic victor's name,
> Archestratos' son, where it is written
> in my mind; for I owe him a sweet song
>   and have forgotten. O Muse, you and Truth,
>   the daughter of Zeus, with a correcting hand
> 5   absolve me from the charge of breaking a promise
>   and harming a guest-friend.
> For what was the future has come from afar
> and shamed my deep indebtedness.
> Nevertheless, interest on a debt can absolve one from
>   a bitter charge. Now just as the flowing wave
> 10 washes over the rolling pebble,
> so we shall pay back a theme of general concern
> in joyous friendship.

Here the request to the Muse and Truth[78] is embedded in "personal" difficulties that justify the urgency of his appeal. The fiction that he has forgotten[79] allows him to open the ode with a resounding declaration of Hagesidamos' Olympic victory, while at the same time preparing for the request. The explanatory clause that follows the request (γάρ, 7) amplifies the extent of his indebtedness (βαθὺ χρέος, 8). Here again he combines hymnal elements with "personal" concerns that enliven and extend inherited conventions. Underneath the elaborate details we can discern the adaptation of conventional elements, for *Ol.* 10.3-12 is essentially a topical elaboration of the rhapsodic framework of *Pyth.* 4.1-4.

Ol. 10.3-12	*Pyth.* 4.1-4
ὀφείλων (3)	ὀφειλόμενον (3)
Μοῖσ' (3)	Μοῖσα (3)
χρέος (8)	χρή (1)
φίλαν (12)	φίλῳ (1)

The opening imperative ἀνάγνωτέ μοι 'Αρχεστράτου παῖδα (1-2) is an adaptation of the rhapsodic formula ἄνδρα μοι ἔννεπε. Even the verb ἐπιλέλαθ' (3) is

---

[78] Gildersleeve, *Pindar* 213 takes "bystanders" as the subject of ἀνάγνωτε, but it is much simpler and more meaningful to take the Muse and Truth as its subject, thus providing a variation of the rhapsodic imperative "sing, Muse." Verdenius, *Commentaries II* 55 argues that it is used "absolutely," but that skirts the issue as to whom it is addressed.

[79] The "fiction" may have some basis in fact, for the year 476 (the first Olympiad celebrated after the Persian wars) must have been an extremely busy one for Pindar. See Race, *Pindar* 117.

reminiscent of the concern in rhapsodic hymns for remembering (and not forgetting) the god, as in the envoi of *h. Hom.* 1.18-19: οὐδέ πῃ ἔστι | σεῖ' ἐπιληθομένῳ ἱερῆς μεμνῆσθαι ἀοιδῆς.[80]

We shall conclude with the hymn to Thebes which opens *Isth.* 7, a hymn that combines many of the features we have been reviewing:[81]

      Τίνι τῶν πάρος, ὦ μάκαιρα Θήβα,
      καλῶν ἐπιχωρίων μάλιστα θυμὸν τεόν
      εὔφρανας; ἦρα χαλκοκρότου πάρεδρον
      Δαμάτερος ἁνίκ' εὐρυχαίταν
5   ἄντειλας Διόνυσον, ἢ χρυσῷ μεσονύκτιον
        νείφοντα δεξαμένα τὸν φέρτατον θεῶν,
      ὁπότ' Ἀμφιτρύωνος ἐν θυρέτροις
      σταθεὶς ἄλοχον μετῆλθεν Ἡρακλείοις γοναῖς;
      ἢ {ὅτ'} ἀμφὶ πυκναῖς Τειρεσίαο βουλαῖς;
      ἢ {ὅτ'} ἀμφ' Ἰόλαον ἱππόμητιν;
10 ἢ Σπαρτῶν ἀκαμαντολογχᾶν; ἢ ὅτε καρτερᾶς
        Ἄδραστον ἐξ ἀλαλᾶς ἄμπεμψας ὀρφανὸν
      μυρίων ἑτάρων ἐς Ἄργος ἵππιον;
      ἢ Δωρίδ' ἀποικίαν οὕνεκεν ὀρθῷ
      ἔστασας ἐπὶ σφυρῷ
      Λακεδαιμονίων, ἕλον δ' Ἀμύκλας
15 Αἰγεῖδαι σέθεν ἔκγονοι, μαντεύμασι Πυθίοις;
      ἀλλὰ παλαιὰ γάρ
      εὕδει χάρις, ἀμνάμονες δὲ βροτοί,
      ὅ τι μὴ σοφίας ἄωτον ἄκρον
      κλυταῖς ἐπέων ῥοαῖσιν ἐξίκηται ζυγέν·
20 κώμαζ' ἔπειτεν ἀδυμελεῖ σὺν ὕμνῳ
      καὶ Στρεψιάδᾳ.

      Which of your former native glories,
      O blessed Theba, most delighted
      your heart? Was it when you raised up
      long-haired Dionysos as companion to
5   Demeter of the bronze cymbals? or when, in a nighttime shower of

---

[80] Cf. *h. Hom.* 3.1: μνήσομαι οὐδὲ **λάθωμαι** and 7.58-59: οὐδὲ ... **ληθόμενον**; Theognis 1-2: οὔποτε σεῖο | **λήσομαι** ἀρχόμενος οὐδ' ἀποπαυόμενος; Kall. *h. Delos* 8: ὅστις Δήλοιο **λάθηται**; see Bundy, "Quarrel" 75 and Mineur, *Callimachus, Hymn to Delos* 58.

[81] See Bundy, *Studia Pindarica* 45 and "Quarrel" 65-67. The two long hymnal openings that contain catalogues of cities' glories, *Nem.* 10 (Argos) and *Isth.* 7 (Thebes), are both adaptations of rhapsodic techniques. *Nem.* 10 employs the direct opening ("sing Charites") and enlarges on the word θεοπρεπές (2) to list Argos' claims to fame. *Isth.* 7 poses a series of disjunctive questions in a fashion very similar to that of *h. Hom.* 3.207-215.

—	gold, you received the greatest of the gods,
	when he stood at Amphitryon's gates
	and sought his wife to beget Herakles?
	or because of Teiresias' wise counsels?
	or for the skillful horseman, Iolaos?
10	or for the Spartoi of the unwearied spears? or when you sent back
—	Adrastos from the fierce battle bereft
	of countless companions to Argos of the fine horses?
	or because you established on firm
	footing the Doric colonization
	of the Lakedaimonians, and Amyklai fell
15	to the Aigeidai, your offspring, in accord with the Pythian oracles?
	But ancient splendor
	sleeps; and mortals forget
)—	
	what does not attain wisdom's choice pinnacle
	by being yoked to glorious streams of verses.
20	Therefore celebrate in a sweetly sung hymn
	Strepsiadas.

This hymnal opening is one of the most impressive in the extant odes. Bundy has pointed out that besides containing an extended priamel, it also combines the disjunctive series of questions characteristic of the rhapsodic hymn (cf. *h. Hom.* 3.207-215) with the *hypomnesis* and request of a cultic hymn.[82] The general category which constitutes the foil consists of "former native glories" (τῶν πάρος καλῶν ἐπιχωρίων, 1-2); Thebes is asked to state which single one (τίνι, 1) pleased her *the most* (μάλιστ', 2). The epithet μάκαιρα (1) is especially important in this context because it suggests that Theba is "blessed" with many to choose from, thus allowing the poet to suggest a number of possibilities.[83] Of course, she will never be forced to choose; Pindar will tactfully select for celebration the latest glory on the basis of its newness.

The list that follows (3-15) is functionally a *hypomnesis* that reminds the goddess of her past (i.e., "if ever you were pleased by x, y, or z, so now welcome ... "), but it is also a "poetic epitome of Theban ancient history."[84] Beginning with the Σπαρτῶν ἀκαμαντολογχᾶν (10), the subject turns to Theban military strength. The last two events listed, the repulse of the "Seven against Thebes" (10-11) and the aid to the Lakedaimonians in taking Amyklai (12-15), sketch the full range of Thebes' martial prowess.[85] But the poet interrupts (ἀλλὰ ... γάρ, 16) any further movement to the present with a summarizing gnome

---

[82] For an analysis of the priamel, see Bundy, *Studia Pindarica* 6-7, and for the hymnal elements "Quarrel" 65-66.

[83] Cf. πολυώνυμε at *Isth.* 5.1 and θεοπρεπές at *Nem.* 10.2 (on which see above note 81).

[84] See Young, *Isthmian 7* 16-18, who provides a very perceptive analysis of this catalogue.

[85] For the climactic arrangement of the catalogue and the relevance of the military glory, see above pages 36-37.

(16-19) that marks all previous achievements as "ancient" (cf. παλαιά, 16).[86] At this point he can apply the logic of this lengthy preparation (ἔπειτεν, "therefore," 20) by leaping to the most recent example of Theban glory and requesting the goddess to join in the celebration (κώμαζ', 20) for the specific individual (καί, 21), Strepsiadas. The arrangement of the ensemble is essentially that of another rhapsodic opening, *Ol.* 2: god (Demeter, Dionysos), hero (Herakles, Teiresias, Iolaos), and man (Aigeidai, Strepsiadas).

Throughout this sketch of Pindar's opening hymns we have seen how he gives life to the hymnal tradition by constantly varying the expression of conventional rhapsodic and cultic elements, by adapting them to new uses, and by combining them with each other and with "personal concerns." But behind the striking innovations and the dazzling language remains a firm basis of conventional form. As in the case of all other poetic forms he inherited, Pindar pays the τόκος on his literary debt by realizing potentialities that previously remained latent.

---

[86] παλαιά (16) provides a summary and intensification of τῶν πάρος (1), which established the context of the priamel in the first place.

CHAPTER 5

FORMS AND FUNCTIONS OF PRAYERS

There are some sixty prayers in the epinicians. We have seen that they play an important role in opening hymnal passages, where various deities are petitioned to "accept" the poem or to aid in its composition. In this chapter, however, we shall concentrate on prayers that conclude odes and particularly on those which provide transitions from one topic of praise to another.[1]

Concluding Prayers

Three odes (*Pyth.* 5, *Isth.* 1 and 7) conclude with prayers that the victors may go on to win at more prestigious games, and five (*Ol.* 5, 7, 8, *Pyth.* 8, and *Nem.* 7) close with prayers for the future welfare of the athletes, their families, or their city. But a number of poems end with prayers modelled on the epilogues of Homeric Hymns, in which the rhapsodic poet typically bids farewell to the god and expresses the hope that he or she be pleased with the hymn and therefore provide for the worshippers' needs. An example is the end of *h. Hom.* 11.5:

Χαῖρε θεά, δὸς δ' ἄμμι τύχην εὐδαιμονίην τε.

As comparison with other examples shows, the word χαῖρε in this context means more than just farewell, for it expresses concern on the part of the poet that the god be pleased with the performance he has just heard.[2] And if he is pleased (that is, if his parting feeling is one of χάρις), then his goodwill will insure the sur-

---

[1] Kleinknecht, *Gebetsparodie* 1-9 provides a survey of early work on prayers. For a brief, but excellent account of prayers in Pindar, see Bundy, *Studia Pindarica* 77-83. After sketching the transitional function of prayers in terminating praise and leading to another topic (77-79), he concludes: "Indeed, the careful reader will find that there is no prayer in Pindar that does not follow these conventional rules" (79). For the distinction between prayers and hymns, see above page 103 note 50.

[2] See Race, "Greek Hymns" 8-10 and Miller, *Hymn to Apollo* 4, who observes that the demonstrative οὕτω in the formulaic expression οὕτω χαῖρε (cf. *h. Hom.* 1.20 *et saepe*) points to the present performance and means: be pleased with the song "as it now stands."

vival of the song and will dispose him to provide for the welfare of the worshippers. These two concerns, a favorable reception of the song and well-being of the worshippers, are neatly juxtaposed at the principal caesura in the closing prayer at h. Hom. 30.18: πρόφρων δ' ἀντ' ᾠδῆς | βίοτον θυμήρε' ὄπαζε.[3] The lyric poets readily adapted these closings, as the rhapsodic ending of Bakch. 17 demonstrates (130-132):

> 130 Δάλιε, χοροῖσι Κηίων
> φρένα ἰανθείς
> ὄπαζε θεόπομπον ἐσθλῶν τύχαν.

> 130 Delian Apollo, with your heart warmed
> by the Kean choruses,
> provide a heaven-sent attainment of blessings.

Here χοροῖσι ... φρένα ἰανθείς = πρόφρων ἀντ' ᾠδῆς; ὄπαζε = ὄπαζε; and θεόπομπον ἐσθλῶν τύχαν = βίοτον θυμήρε'.

Pindar draws upon this tradition to close several of his odes. Often the requests are in climactic order. The end of Ol. 1 provides a well-known example.[4]

> 115 (1)εἴη σέ τε τοῦτον ὑψοῦ χρόνον πατεῖν,
> 115b (2)ἐμέ τε τοσσάδε νικαφόροις
> ὁμιλεῖν πρόφαντον σοφίᾳ καθ' Ἑλ-
> λανας ἐόντα παντᾷ.

> 115 (1)May you walk on high for the rest of your time,
> 115b (2)and may I accompany victors whenever they win,
> and be foremost in wisdom among
> Greeks everywhere.

The first half of the prayer is for the continued well-being of Hieron, whose success in the games and high position in the state have been praised at length (100-114), while the second is for the poet and his poetry. There is no doubt which receives the greater emphasis by virtue of coming last, by being much longer, and by opening with the emphatic pronoun ἐμέ. The latter is nothing short of a declaration (couched in the more modest language of a prayer) of the author's

---

[3] Cf. also h. Hom. 2.494. At times the concern is for the song alone: καὶ σὺ μὲν οὕτω χαῖρε θεαί θ' ἅμα πᾶσαι ἀοιδῇ (h. Hom. 9.7; cf. 14.6).

[4] Wilamowitz, Pindaros 234 note 1 aptly remarks: "In dem Schlusse ist das Fortwirken der rhapsodischen Schlußgebete δίδου δ' ἀρετάν [sic] τε καὶ ὄλβον, δότε δ' ἱμερόεσσαν ἀοιδήν unverkennbar." See also Kranz, "Sphragis" 35.

determination to be the preeminent poet of praise in all Greece.⁵ The expression καθ' "Ελλανας... παντᾷ specifically heralds his Panhellenic preeminence in the epinician genre (cf. νικαφόροις, 115b) which extends, as in the present instance, even to Magna Graecia. This prayer is a form of σφραγίς, which binds together subject and poet in an affirmation of past glory and a hope for its continuance and repeated celebration in song.

A more elaborate version concludes *Ol.* 6, as Pindar envisions the voyage of Hagesias (along with the present ode) from Stymphalos to his second home in Syracuse (101-105):

                        (1)θεός
τῶνδε κείνων τε κλυτὰν αἶσαν παρέχοι φιλέων.
(2)δέσποτα ποντόμεδον, εὐθὺν δὲ πλόον καμάτων
ἐκτὸς ἐόντα δίδοι, (3)χρυσαλακάτοιο πόσις
105   'Αμφιτρίτας, ἐμῶν δ' ὕ-
μνων ἄεξ' εὐτερπὲς ἄνθος.

                        (1)May heaven
lovingly grant a glorious destiny for these and those people.
(2)Lordly ruler of the sea, vouchsafe a direct voyage
that is free from hardship, (3)and, husband of golden-spindled
105   Amphitrita, cause my hymns'
pleasing flower to burgeon.

Altogether, there are three requests. The first is to an undefined θεός (101) with an optative (παρέχοι, 102).⁶ The τῶνδε refers to the Stymphalians, in whose presence the ode is being performed, while the κείνων denotes the Syracusans, who will witness the ode's subsequent performance. As he did at *Ol.* 1.115, the

---

⁵ Gerber, *Olympian One* 177 (approved by Verdenius, *Commentaries II* 52) takes the participle ἐόντα (116) as "a statement of fact, not part of the prayer," in contrast to Gildersleeve, *Pindar* 139: "ἐόντα is part of the prayer, and not an assertion merely." Gerber and Verdenius offer no formal parallels; they only cite passages where Pindar asserts his preeminence in poetry. But if the participle is not part of the prayer, then it must give the circumstances or grounds for it: "since (or because) I am foremost," an exceedingly haughty assertion. *Isth.* 1.64-67 illustrates the distinction between the two types of participle: εἴη νιν... ἀερθέντ'... φράξαι χεῖρα τιμάν... Θήβαισι τεύχοντ'. The first participle (ἀερθέντ') is causative ("because he has been lifted up"), while the second (τεύχοντ') is part of the hope ("may he wreathe his hand *and bring honor* to Thebes"). The closing prayer at *Pyth.* 2.96 provides a close parallel of a subordinate participle which is part of the prayer: ἁδόντα δ' εἴη με τοῖς ἀγαθοῖς ὁμιλεῖν (on which see Most, *Measures of Praise* 120-121). Cf. also ἰανθείς, *Ol.* 2.13; ἄγων, *Ol.* 8.87; νέμων, *Ol.* 13.27; διδούς, *Pyth.* 1.57; ἁρμόσαις... ἐόντα, *Nem.* 7.98-100; and ἀκοντίζων, *Nem.* 9.55. For another example of ἐόντα as part of a prayer, cf. *Ol.* 6.104 and see below note 11.

⁶ Pindar usually uses the optative mood when addressing divinities in general (e.g., εἴη with no specified subject) or entities such as θεός, δαίμων, or χρόνος. See Hamilton, *Epinikion* 17-20 and 24 note 30.

poet prays first for the continued success of his addressees. The climactically withheld word φιλέων (102) points to a relationship based on χάρις,[7] while the words κλυτὰν αἶσαν (102) combine the two elements, essential to human happiness, that are frequently mentioned in closing prayers, success (αἶσαν = εὖ παθεῖν) and fame (κλυτάν = εὖ ἀκούειν).[8] The concluding prayer of Ol. 13 provides a variation:

> 115 Ζεῦ τέλει', (1)αἰδῶ δίδοι (2)καὶ τύχαν τερπνῶν γλυκεῖαν.

> 115 Zeus accomplisher, (1)grant them respect (2)and sweet attainment of pleasant things.

Here αἰδῶ is equivalent to εὖ ἀκούειν and denotes the respect that the Oligaithidai deserve for their achievements to date; τύχαν τερπνῶν γλυκεῖαν (cf. θεόπομπον ἐσθλῶν τύχαν at Bakch. 17.132) is equivalent to εὖ παθεῖν and refers to their future successes.[9]

The second request (103-104) also concerns physical well-being, namely a safe voyage for Hagesias,[10] while the third (104-105) concerns the fate of the song itself. The three prayers are arranged climactically and exhibit the same principles of increasing length, greater specification, and intensification we noted in hymns. The first request expresses a general concern for groups (τῶνδε κείνων τε, 102), the second is for a particular voyage (but without further specification), while the third, introduced by the prominent first personal pronoun ἐμῶν, specifically applies to the present ode. The imperative (δίδοι, 104) of the second request is more intense than the vaguer optative (παρέχοι, 102) of the first. The two addresses to Poseidon that introduce the second and third requests also increase in length: from δέσποτα ποντόμεδον (103) to χρυσαλακάτοιο πόσις | Ἀμφιτρίτας (104-105); in addition, the latter contains a proper name.

---

[7] φιλέων is one of many words (e.g., εὐμενής, πρόφρων, εὔφρων, and ἑκών), frequent in hymnal passages, that point to a relationship between god and man surpassing a crude *do ut des*. The same terms also elevate the poet's relationship to his patrons above mere contractual duty (χρέος). Cf. φίλῳ at *Pyth.* 4.1 (on which see above pages 107-108).

[8] The two elements are those mentioned at the end of *Pyth.* 1.99; cf. also *Nem.* 1.32: εὖ τε παθεῖν καὶ ἀκοῦσαι and *Isth.* 5.13: εὖ πάσχων λόγον ἐσλὸν ἀκούῃ. They are also implicit in the closing prayer of *Ol.* 1, where ὑψοῦ ... πατεῖν (115) = εὖ παθεῖν and σοφίᾳ (115b) = εὖ ἀκούειν. In general, see Bundy, *Studia Pindarica* 72 note 93.

[9] Bundy, *Studia Pindarica* 72 note 93 clears up once and for all the meaning of αἰδῶ, although some translators such as Bowra, *Pindar* 175 and Swanson, *Pindar's Odes* 56, and interpreters such as Hubbard, *Pindaric Mind* 142 continue to mistranslate it as "modesty."

[10] The scholia understand the voyage as a metaphor for Hagesias' life, a possible extension, but it refers primarily, as the address to Poseidon indicates, to Hagesias' imminent voyage to Syracuse. Pindar has already expressed hope that Hieron will gladly receive the performance of this ode in Syracuse (98-100); it is natural that he pray for a safe trip. For Poseidon as protector of ships, cf. *h. Hom.* 22.5-7.

And, within these two requests, the first is expressed in the negative (καμάτων | ἐκτὸς ἐόντα, 103-104),[11] whereas the second is climactically stated in the positive (ἄεξ', 105). The first asks for avoidance of pain or obstacles, the second for positive pleasure.[12]

Within the last two requests a subtle shift of emphasis is evident in the addresses to Poseidon. In the first, since he is called upon to protect voyagers, he is appropriately addressed as "ruler of the sea" (103). For the second request, however, he is addressed as "husband of golden-spindled Amphitrita" (103-104). No one, to my knowledge, has noticed that Poseidon is here being invoked under two different aspects. As lord of the waves, he would have little concern with poetry, but as a husband (πόσις, 104) he would be at leisure to enjoy it.[13] As in *Ol.* 1.115b, where the prominent ἐμέ turned climactically to the poet's wishes for the song, so here ἐμῶν δ' (105) concludes with the poet's hopes that his song will enjoy another performance in Syracuse, where it will bloom even more (cf. ἄεξ', 105) and bring pleasure (cf. εὐτερπές, 105). The two petitions, balanced by δέ (103, 105) turn from physical well-being (εὖ παθεῖν) to celebration in song (εὖ ἀκούειν), from the dangers of the active life to the pleasurable celebration of success.

In evoking the image of a poetic ἀγών, the prayer that concludes *Nem.* 9 is reminiscent of the rhapsodic envoi that requests success of the song in the contest: δὸς δ' ἐν ἀγῶνι | νίκην τῷδε φέρεσθαι (*h. Hom.* 6.19-20).[14]

            Ζεῦ πάτερ,
εὔχομαι (1)ταύταν ἀρετὰν κελαδῆσαι
   σὺν Χαρίτεσσιν, (2)ὑπὲρ πολλῶν τε τιμαλφεῖν λόγοις
55 νίκαν, ἀκοντίζων σκοποῖ' ἄγχιστα Μοισᾶν.

            Father Zeus,
I pray that I may (1)celebrate his achievement
   with the Graces' aid, (2)and surpass many in honoring with words
55 his victory, by casting my javelin nearest the goal of Muses.

---

[11] The ἐόντα (104) here provides added support that the ἐόντα at *Ol.* 1.116 is part of the wish, although most translations obscure the fact. See above note 5.

[12] For the sense of climax in switching from negative to positive, see *Chapter 3 passim*.

[13] Alkinoos provides a good analogy. As king of the Phaiakians, he is first of all concerned with the welfare of the stranger, but with his wife Arete in the leisure of the banquet, he appreciates the poetic skills of Odysseus. The epithet χρυσαλακάτοιο emphasizes Amphitrita's domestic qualities; for a portrayal of her courtly conduct in Poseidon's palace, cf. Bakch. 17.109-116. The two prayers sketch the god's powers in the active realm and his enjoyment of contemplative leisure, a doublet effectively used by the author of *h. Hom.* 3; see Miller, *Hymn to Apollo* 13-17.

[14] See Lefkowitz, "First Person" 181-182.

The two requests in this prayer concern the two constituents of success: εὖ παθεῖν and εὖ ἀκούειν. The first asks that the poet's celebration (κελαδῆσαι, 54 = εὖ ἀκούειν) of Chromios' overall achievement (ταύταν ἀρετάν, 54 = εὖ παθεῖν) possess grace (σὺν Χαρίτεσσιν, 54); the second asks that he surpass others (ὑπὲρ πολλῶν, 54) in bestowing honor (τιμαλφεῖν λόγοις, 54 = εὖ ἀκούειν) on Chromios' victory (νίκαν, 55 = εὖ παθεῖν).

These two requests also adumbrate an important dichotomy in poetic theory and practice between a poem's ability to charm and its truthfulness (cf. *dulce* and *utile* in the Latin tradition). Although it is introduced by τε, the weight is clearly on the second request, in which Pindar emphasizes the content (λόγοις, 54) of his poetry, and through the metaphor of throwing the javelin nearest the target he expresses the hope that he offer an accurate presentation of his subject's success.[15] Of great importance is the fact that the first request involves the Charites, the second the Muses. As Bundy has pointed out, the Charites in general represent the persuasive charm of poetry, while the Muses represent its truth.[16] In short, Pindar hopes that his celebration of Chromios' achievement will be pleasing, and, even more importantly, as reliably accurate (σκοποῖ' ἄγχιστα, 55) as any poet could make it, however many (cf. πολλῶν, 54) might try.[17]

The last terminal prayers we shall examine occur at the end of *Ol.* 7, where Pindar concludes his catalogue of Diagoras' victories with a prayer for Zeus' favor. Because the ending of the ode has been consistently misinterpreted, it is necessary to treat it in some detail.

ἀλλ' ὦ
Ζεῦ πάτερ, νώτοισιν Ἀταβυρίου
μεδέων, τίμα μὲν ὕμνου τεθμὸν Ὀλυμπιονίκαν,
ἄνδρα τε πὺξ ἀρετὰν εὑ-

---

[15] Cf. *Ol.* 2.89-100, 13.93-100, *Nem.* 6.26-28, and especially *Pyth.* 1.42-45, where Pindar fears that his enthusiasm (cf. μενοινῶν, 43) might cause him to exaggerate (cf. βαλεῖν ἔξω, 44) and prays that he may do full credit to Hieron's great merit (μακρὰ ῥίψαις, 45) and thereby surpass his rivals (ἀμεύσασθ' ἀντίους). See Lefkowitz, "The Poet as Athlete" 18-24.

[16] See Bundy, "Quarrel" 79 note 95: "The Muses guarantee profit and the Charites pleasure: the Muses are the professors of truth and the Charites its rhetoricians. Working together, they produce understanding in a balance between instruction and delight." See also Mullen, *Choreia* 83: "The Muses have more to do with the ode's truth and its powers of enduring in the memory of men, the Graces more to do with the ode's beauty and its powers of persuading the heart by ravishing the senses." Pindar warns of the dangers of χάρις devoid of truth at *Ol.* 1.30-34 and of truth devoid of appropriateness at *Nem.* 5.16-17: οὔ τοι ἅπασα κερδίων | φαίνοισα πρόσωπον ἀλάθει' ἀτρεκές. Pindar carefully distinguishes "beauty" from "truth," unlike Keats, who sought to fuse them into one in his "Ode On a Grecian Urn." Cf. also Bakch. 9.1-6 and see below page 185 with note 8.

[17] Pindar twice elsewhere uses πολλοί of rivals to emphasize the uniqueness of his poetic program; cf. *Ol.* 13.44-45: δηρίομαι πολέσιν | περὶ πλήθει καλῶν and *Pyth.* 4.248: πολλοῖσι δ' ἄγημαι σοφίας ἑτέροις.

ρόντα. δίδοι τέ οἱ αἰδοίαν χάριν
90 καὶ ποτ' ἀστῶν καὶ ποτὶ ξεί-
νων. ἐπεὶ ὕβριος ἐχθρὰν ὁδὸν
εὐθυπορεῖ, σάφα δαεὶς ἅ τε οἱ πατέρων
ὀρθαὶ φρένες ἐξ ἀγαθῶν
ἔχρεον. μὴ κρύπτε κοινόν
σπέρμ' ἀπὸ Καλλιάνακτος·
Ἐρατιδᾶν τοι σὺν χαρίτεσσιν ἔχει
θαλίας καὶ πόλις· ἐν δὲ μιᾷ μοίρᾳ χρόνου
95 ἄλλοτ' ἀλλοῖαι διαιθύσσοισιν αὖραι.

But, O
father Zeus, you who rule Atabyrion's
slopes, honor this hymn's due praise of an Olympic victor
and the man who has won achievement at boxing.
Grant him respectful joy
90 from both townsmen and outsiders,
for he travels a straight road
that hates insolence, because he has clearly learned
from his noble forebears what things true minds
prophesy. Keep not in obscurity the public
lineage of Kallianax,
for when the Eratidai celebrate
the city too holds festivals. But in one portion of time
95 different winds rapidly shift at various times.

The ἀλλ' (87), as often, signals the request,[18] which is here divided into concern for the well-being of his song and for its subject: τίμα μὲν ὕμνου τεθμὸν... ἄνδρα τε πὺξ ἀρετὰν εὑρόντα. In the prayers we examined that conclude Ol. 1 and 6, Pindar prays first for the well-being of Hieron and Hagesias and then for his song. Here he reverses the order, with the result that the victorious boxer becomes the center of attention.[19] Now that Diagoras is singled out, Pindar adds a further petition (τε, 89) that the divine τιμή requested in the previous lines be extended to include "respectful joy" (αἰδοίαν χάριν, 89) from Diagoras' own citizens and foreign friends (καὶ ποτ' ἀστῶν καὶ ποτὶ ξείνων, 90). The following sentence explains (cf. ἐπεί, 90) why Diagoras deserves friendly respect: his way is inimical to *hybris*, thanks to the wisdom he has gained from his forefathers.[20]

---

[18] As Bundy, *Studia Pindarica* 22 note 50 and 36 note 3 has pointed out, ἀλλά is a very important transitional word in Pindar, for it breaks with what has preceded and emphasizes what follows. This double function is particularly evident when ἀλλά introduces a prayer.

[19] For the climactic arrangement of this prayer, see above page 19.

[20] All commentators to my knowledge take the aorist participle δαείς as copulative, but I think a stronger case could be made out for its being causal. He shuns ὕβρις *because* he has clearly learned correct (ὀρθαί) attitudes from his family.

So far the prayer has been straightforward, but the imperative μὴ κρύπτε (92) poses a problem of interpretation. To whom is it addressed? Is it still to Zeus, as most have taken it? Heyne, *Pindari Carmina* 101, for example, glossed it as *serva, ne sine perire*, and Boeckh, *Pindari Opera* 177-179 saw in it a reference to contemporary Rhodian politics. Farnell, *Pindar* 57 took it as a continuation of τίμα μέν (88) and Verdenius, *Commentaries I* 85-86 applies it to Zeus (taking the following τοι as both directive and explanatory of why Zeus' protection is needed). Or is it self-exhortation, as the scholia understood it? In this case, I believe that the scholia are correct (although some of them begin the self-address with δαείς). The main difficulty in taking Zeus as the subject is that no satisfactory sense can be made of κρύπτε. What does it mean for Zeus not to "hide" the seed? Young, *Three Odes* 94-96 insists on the floral image of seed and understands it as a prayer for the "continuance of Diagoras' family" (94). He adduces *h. Hom.* 2.307, 353 and Hes. *Op.* 138 and takes κρύπτε to mean "keep buried," "make perish." But where does Pindar (or any other archaic poet) pray for Zeus not to extinguish (i.e., continue to let live) any people? If μὴ κρύπτε is litotes for "let live" or even "long live," the thought is unparalleled. But when one considers that μὴ κρύπτειν and μὴ καλύπτειν are almost technical terms in Pindar for "celebrate," then the scholiast's gloss of ὕμνει (170 c) is very compelling, especially in light of close parallels, τό γ' ἐν ξυνῷ πεποναμένον εὖ | μὴ ... κρυπτέτω (*Pyth.* 9.93-94) and τετελεσμένον ἐσλόν | μὴ ... **καλύψαι** (*Nem.* 9.6-7), which support the meaning of "keep concealed" or "not celebrate." Of particular importance is the qualification ἐν ξυνῷ at *Pyth.* 9.93, which strengthens the meaning of κοινόν at *Ol.* 7.92 as "in which the city shares."[21]

If this interpretation is correct, then the prayer to Zeus is formally complete at 92 with the reference to what Diagoras has learned from his ancestors (πατέρων, 91). Now that they have become the center of attention, Pindar makes a final declaration of the need to praise them: μὴ κρύπτε κοινόν | σπέρμ' ἀπὸ Καλλιάνακτος (92-93). The following sentence explains (cf. τοι, 93) why one should celebrate the race of Kallianax. The Eratidai are φιλοπόλεις; their joyous successes (χαρίτεσσιν, 93; cf. χάριν, 89) are a matter of public concern, since their celebrations are shared by the city as well (cf. ἔχει | θαλίας **καὶ πόλις**, 93-94), including performance of the present ode, most of which, not incidentally, is devoted to the glorious history of Rhodes.[22] The final gnome, which suddenly

---

[21] Cf. ξυνὸν λόγον (21), which designates the forthcoming narrative as of common interest to Diagoras, his family, and Rhodes. See van Groningen, *La composition littéraire* 354.

[22] See the paraphrase of van Groningen, *La composition littéraire* 357 note 1: "ce qui fait le charme de la vie des Ératides, fait en même temps la joie de la ville entière." The word κοινόν (92), emphasized by its prominent position in the command, is not a mere metaphor for "famous" (ἔνδοξον, Σ 170 b), nor a vague reference to "the unity of the family maintained throughout its history" (Verdenius, *Commentaries I* 86), but has the sense of "in which others share," the normal meaning that κοινός has in Pindar and which is explained precisely in the

introduces the theme of changing fortune,[23] is not addressed to Zeus, but to the celebrants, reminding them to enjoy the present occasion to its fullest.[24]

Medial Prayers

We have seen that prayers are effective means for beginning and ending odes. In this section we shall look at those which occur in the middle of odes, where they can conclude a development, begin another one, or perform both functions simultaneously.

In a number of instances, prayers are used to make a sharp break with preceding material that is negative. For example, as we have seen (above page 42), the long description of Typhos' agony under Mt. Aitna (*Pyth.* 1.15-28) is terminated by the asyndetic prayer εἴη, Ζεῦ, τὶν εἴη ἀνδάνειν (29), which turns the ode to its positive task of announcing Hieron's victory. Likewise, in *Pyth.* 2, after excoriating the "crooked citizen" in lines 81-82, Pindar gives the discussion a positive turn with οὔ οἱ μετέχω θράσεος. φίλον εἴη φιλεῖν (83).[25] In *Nem.* 8, after portraying the envy and misrepresentation involved in the contest over

---

following sentence: Ἐρατιδᾶν τοι σὺν χαρίτεσσιν ἔχει θαλίας καὶ πόλις. The race of Kallianax is common to the city inasmuch as Rhodes too (καί) shares in the celebration of their achievements. Cf. *Ol.* 10.11-12: κοινὸν λόγον | φίλαν τείσομεν ἐς χάριν, where Σ 13 m correctly paraphrases it as τὸν κοινὸν τοῦ παντὸς γένους καὶ πάσης τῆς πόλεως ἔπαινον προσφιλῶς καὶ κεχαρισμένως ἀποτίσωμεν. As in *Ol.* 7, the word κοινόν is immediately followed by an explanation that refers to the city's interest in the matter: νέμει γὰρ Ἀτρέκεια πόλιν Λοκρῶν Ζεφυρίων (13).

[23] For a formal parallel, cf. *Isth.* 1.64-68, where the concluding prayer that Herodotos may cap his career with Pythian and Olympian victories is sealed with a gnomic justification. For a thorough study of the theme of change in Pindar, see Krause, *Schicksalswechsels* 91-138.

[24] Other final prayers include *Ol.* 8.84-88 (see below pages 161-163), *Pyth.* 2.96 (see Bell, "Second Pythian" 29-30), *Pyth.* 5.117-124, *Pyth.* 8.98-100, *Nem.* 7.89-101 (see Rusten, "Pindar's Prayer to Heracles"), *Isth.* 1.64 (see Bundy, *Studia Pindarica* 80-83), and *Isth.* 7.49-51 (see Young, *Isthmian 7* 32-33).

[25] The request at *Parth.* 1.11-14 performs a similar function:

φιλέων δ' ἂν εὐχοίμαν
Κρονίδαις ἐπ' Αἰολάδᾳ {τε}
καὶ γένει εὐτυχίαν τετάσθαι
ὁμαλὸν χρόνον.

Gladly would I pray
  that the children of Kronos ordain happiness
for Aioladas and his race
for time unbroken.

The word φιλέων gets its point by contrasting with the preceding gnomes (8-10) that portray the omnipresence of envy (παντὶ δ' ἐπὶ φθόνος ἀνδρὶ κεῖται | ἀρετᾶς) and the plight of the obscure (ὁ δὲ μηδὲν ἔχων ὑπὸ σι- | γᾷ μελαίνᾳ κάρα κέκρυπται).

Achilleus' arms, the poet suddenly abjures any such intentions in his own character, εἴη μή ποτέ μοι τοιοῦτον ἦθος (35), before proceeding to his positive program.[26]

More complex is the prayer at *Nem.* 9.28-33.

>   εἰ δυνατόν, Κρονίων,
>   πεῖραν μὲν ἀγάνορα Φοινικοστόλων
>   ἐγχέων ταύταν θανάτου πέρι καὶ ζω-
>   ᾶς ἀναβάλλομαι ὡς πόρσιστα, μοῖραν δ' εὔνομον
> 30   αἰτέω σε παισὶν δαρὸν Αἰτναίων ὀπάζειν,
>
>   Ζεῦ πάτερ, ἀγλαΐαισιν δ' ἀστυνόμοις ἐπιμεῖξαι
>   λαόν. ἐντί τοι φίλιπποί τ' αὐτόθι καὶ κτεάνων
>   ψυχὰς ἔχοντες κρέσσονας
>   ἄνδρες.

>   If possible, son of Kronos,
>   I put off as far as I can a lordly trial
>   of life and death such as that
>   against Phoenician spears; but grant the blessings of good rule,
> 30   I beg you, long hereafter to Aitna's sons,
>
>   Father Zeus, and public successes for the people
>   to celebrate. For they are lovers of horses there
>   and men whose souls are masters of their
>   possessions.

We have seen (above page 44) that this prayer follows immediately upon the exemplum of the disastrous campaign of the "Seven" (16-27) and the mention of "heaven-sent routs" (δαιμονίοισι φόβοις, 27). As in the previous examples, the prayer recoils from what preceded and is asyndetic. It has two main parts, delineated by μέν (28) and δέ (29) and reinforced by two addresses to Zeus (Κρονίων, 28 and Ζεῦ πάτερ, 31). The first part deprecates war, the second is a positive request for the benefits of peace.

As ταύταν (29) shows, the first request refers directly to the preceding narrative.[27] Pindar prays that he personally may be far from having to chronicle any such fight for survival as that disastrous war of the "Seven." The adjective Φοινικοστόλων (28), whether capitalized or not, undoubtedly refers to the presence

---

[26] See above page 45 note 6. In order to contrast his own attitude with that of the φθονεροί (90), who are jealous of any success, Pindar ends *Pyth.* 2 with a prayer that he may "be pleasing" to the good men: ἀδόντα δ' εἴη με τοῖς ἀγαθοῖς ὁμιλεῖν. Unlike the other prayers treated above, this one is not asyndetic because it caps a gnomic passage (93-96) that has already made a clean break from the portrayal of the φθονεροί.

[27] ταύταν is equivalent to τοιαύταν "such as that"; see Slater, *Lexicon* s.v. οὗτος, 1. b.

of aggressive Carthaginians.²⁸ There is an implicit comparison between the Carthaginians and the Argives; their attack on any territory under Aitna's influence would be as presumptuous and as futile as that abortive attack on Thebes. And in the background is their defender, Chromios, who at 39 is compared to Hektor.

In contrast, the poet prays for good governance at home (μοῖραν δ' εὔνομον, 29). The formulation αἰτέω σε (30) is more intense than the mere εἰ δυνατόν of the first request, and in light of the word παισίν (30), the address to Ζεῦ πάτερ has additional point.²⁹ After praying for peaceful good government, he adds a further request that the people may have cause for victory celebrations (ἀγλαΐαισιν δ' ἀστυνόμοις ἐπιμεῖξαι, 31). This positive request is then justified (τοι, 32) by depicting the devotion of Aitnaians to athletics (φίλιπποι, 32) and their willingness to spend their wealth on it (κτεάνων ψυχὰς ἔχοντες κρέσσονας, 32).³⁰

Another function of prayers is to punctuate praise before passing on to another topic. Many of them are brief and often they are expressed in the negative. For example, at Ol. 8.28-29, in the midst of extravagant praise of Aigina the poet suddenly interjects the hope that the island's favored status will continue: ὁ δ' ἐπαντέλλων χρόνος | τοῦτο πράσσων μὴ κάμοι. The demonstrative τοῦτο marks the preceding praise as the subject of concern. One naturally prays for continued blessings only after a forceful presentation of what they are. It is in this sense that all such brief prayers are concluding. Likewise the sudden prayer at Nem. 7.67-68: ὁ δὲ λοιπὸς εὔφρων | ποτὶ χρόνος ἕρποι brings to an end Pindar's high praise of Thearion and his affirmation of his own truthfulness.³¹ At Ol. 6.97, Pindar marks the end of his praise of Hieron's good governance, piety, and fame with the prayer, μὴ θράσσοι χρόνος ὄλβον ἐφέρπων, before

---

²⁸ The ending -στολος indicates an active incursion of Phoenician arms (ἐγχέων, 29). Many commentators have denied any direct reference to the Carthaginians in this compound, but it is difficult not to think of them in the context of an ode celebrating Sicilian martial prowess.

²⁹ At any rate, Ζεῦ πάτερ is a much more familiar and warmer appellation than Κρονίων, since it establishes a close I-Thou relationship between the worshipper and the god (cf. pater noster). An examination of the passages in the odes where the appellation Κρονίων appears shows that it stresses his martial and prophetic side as god of the thunderbolt. For example, at line 19 of the same ode, Zeus Kronion warns Adrastos not to set out on his expedition: Κρονίων ἀστεροπὰν ἐλελίξαις. At Pyth. 3.57 he blasts Asklepios: χερσὶ δ' ἄρα Κρονίων ῥίψαις; and at Nem. 1.16-17 he provides Sicilian prowess in war: ὤπασε δὲ Κρονίων πολέμου μναστῆρά οἱ χαλκεντέος | λαὸν ἵππαιχμον. In two places in the odes he is not associated with war, but in both instances the title πατήρ also occurs: at Pyth. 4.23: αἴτιαν δ' ἐπί οἱ Κρονίων Ζεὺς πατὴρ ἔκλαγξε βροντάν, and at Nem. 10.76, when Polydeukes addresses his prayer to πάτερ Κρονίων. The final example of Κρονίων in a martial context (Pyth. 1.71) is treated below page 140.

³⁰ A narrowing of focus is discernible from all the citizens in the city (παισὶν . . . Αἰτναίων, 30; λαόν, 32) to the wealthy citizens (φίλιπποι . . . ἄνδρες, 33) who are devoted to athletic glory, and eventually to the model individual, Chromios (Χρομίῳ, 34), climactically introduced at the beginning of the sentence.

³¹ See Bundy, "Quarrel" 82 note 99.

requesting that Hieron graciously receive the celebration of Hagesias that comes from Stymphalos.[32] Although the preceding lines are lost, the prayer for continued stability at *Pa.* 2.26-27 follows praise of the Thrakian homeland as fertile (γαῖαν ἀμπελόεσσάν τε καί | εὔκαρπον, 25-26): μή μοι μέγας ἕρπων | κάμοι ἐξοπίσω χρόνος ἔμπεδος.[33]

Transitional prayers, however, can often be more elaborate. For example, in *Ol.* 2, after declaring that the Emmenidai of Akragas "were the cynosure of Sicily" (Σικελίας τ' ἔσαν | ὀφθαλμός, 9-10) and praising them for their wealth and excellence, the poet concludes his praise with the following prayer (12-15):

    (1)ἀλλ' ὦ Κρόνιε παῖ 'Ρέας, (2)ἕδος Ὀλύμπου νέμων
      ἀέθλων τε κορυφὰν πόρον τ' Ἀλφεοῦ,
        (3)ἰανθεὶς ἀοιδαῖς
      εὔφρων ἄρουραν ἔτι πατρίαν σφίσιν κόμισον
15   λοιπῷ γένει.

    (1)But, O son of Kronos and Rhea, (2)ruling over your abode on Olympos
      and over the pinnacle of contests and over the ford of Alpheos,
        (3)cheered by my songs
      willingly preserve their native land for their
15   offspring yet to come.

This prayer is formally very regular. It begins with the god's genealogy (cf. παῖ, 12) and then proceeds to his sedes (ἕδος, 12) before making the request.[34] Surprisingly, however, the Olympic games are only mentioned in passing (ἀέθλων τε κορυφάν, 13). In accord with the principle of increasing relevance, the emphasis falls instead on the location (πόρον τ' Ἀλφεοῦ, 13). One wonders why Pindar concludes with the location rather than with the festival. I think that if Pindar had ended with the games, then he would have aroused the expectation that the contest would be the main topic of the prayer. Instead, by ending with the geographical feature, he prepares for the fact that the request involves a *place* (ἄρουραν, 14). The prominence of the two *sedes* in the invocation, Zeus' heavenly abode (Ὀλύμπου, 12) and his earthly one (πόρον τ' Ἀλφεοῦ, 13) may be explained by the fact that the prayer is for the protection of the abode (cf. οἴκημα ποταμοῦ, 9) of the Emmenidai, their ἄρουραν... πατρίαν (13). By thus stressing Zeus' own parentage (cf. παῖ, 12) and his sense of place (cf. ἕδος, 12), the poet reminds him of his own lineage and favored spots and thereby tries to dis-

---

[32] By putting a comma after ἐφέρπων, S-M obscures its concluding function. Better Turyn, who places a period after it.

[33] For the formulaic language of these prayers, see Young, *Three Odes* 93 note 3.

[34] This is one of the rare examples where both parents of the god are provided, and the variation is pleasing, since one is given adjectivally (Κρόνιε), the other as a genitive ('Ρέας). For a discussion of the increasing elements, see above page 17.

pose him favorably toward protecting the land (ἄρουραν, 14) of the Emmenidai for their offspring (λοιπῷ γένει, 15).

After praising the Korinthians at great length at *Ol.* 13.6-23, Pindar utters a similar prayer (24-30):

>   (1)ὕπατ' εὐρὺ ἀνάσσων
> 25   Ὀλυμπίας, (2)ἀφθόνητος ἔπεσσιν
>   γένοιο χρόνον ἅπαντα, Ζεῦ πάτερ,
>   (3)καὶ τόνδε λαὸν ἀβλαβῆ νέμων
>   Ξενοφῶντος εὔθυνε δαίμονος οὖρον·
>   (4)δέξαι τέ οἱ στεφάνων ἐγκώμιον
>   τεθμόν, τὸν ἄγει πεδίων ἐκ Πίσας,
> 30   πενταέθλῳ ἅμα σταδίου
>   νικῶν δρόμου.

>   (1)Most exalted, wide-ruling lord
> 25   of Olympia, (2)may you not begrudge my words
>   for all time to come, Father Zeus,
>   (3)and, as you guide this people free from harm,
>   direct the wind of Xenophon's fortune;
>   (4)and receive as tribute for his crowns this celebratory
>   rite, which he brings forth from the plains of Pisa,
> 30   by winning in both the pentathlon
>   and the stadion race.

I have marked the four increasingly longer elements of this prayer. The point of the reference to Olympia is obvious in this ode that begins with the word Τρισολυμπιονίκαν, while the adverb εὐρύ reminds the god of his wide dominion. As in the case of hymns, there is a continuous specification until the poet arrives at the details of the occasion. The first request is expressed in the negative: ἀφθόνητος ... γένοιο (25-26), "may you be without envy." The ἔπεσσιν (25) refer to Pindar's words of praise for Korinthos in the preceding lines (4-23), which will be elaborated upon later in the ode (52-60).[35] Being "without envy" is litotes for being "gracious."[36]

We have seen several other examples of requests for the effectiveness of the song coupled with requests for the well-being of the people. The two are separated by the appellation Ζεῦ πάτερ (26), which the poet has purposely withheld for climactic effect, for it shows a greater warmth than the opening address which stressed Zeus' wide-ranging power (ὕπατ' εὐρὺ ἀνάσσων, 24). There is a subtle movement toward specificity in the third element: the first part (τόνδε λαὸν ἀβλαβῆ νέμων, 27) employs a dependent participle and the negative expression

---

[35] See Bundy, "Quarrel" 56.
[36] See Race, "Greek Hymns" 12-14.

(ἀβλαβῆ); this is followed by a positive statement: Ξενοφῶντος εὔθυνε δαίμονος οὖρον (28). The name, prominently placed at the beginning of the colon, and the positive imperative (in contrast to the preceding negative expression, ἀφθόνητος γένοιο, 25-26) make this a more specific and forceful request. It is followed by a final request, introduced by a climactic τε, that Zeus accept (that is, be pleased with) the present celebration of Xenophon's triumph at Olympia: δέξαι τέ οἱ στεφάνων ἐγκώμιον τεθμόν (29). In a relative clause describing the song (τόν, 29), Pindar finally announces the long-withheld events that occasioned the poem, πενταέθλῳ ἅμα σταδίου νικῶν δρόμον (30). The prayer continually narrows its focus, from Zeus' wide rule, to the people of Korinthos, to her successful citizen, Xenophon, and to his unprecedented double Olympic victory.

In *Pyth*. 10.12-16 Pindar recounts the remarkable achievements of young Hippokleas' father: twice victor at Olympia of the race in armor and winner at the Pythian games as well. His name is withheld until the last word, Φρικίαν (16), and the poet follows this extraordinary career with an asyndetic prayer (17-22):

)—

20

ἕποιτο μοῖρα καὶ ὑστέραισιν
ἐν ἀμέραις ἀγάνορα πλοῦτον ἀνθεῖν σφίσιν·
τῶν δ' ἐν Ἑλλάδι τερπνῶν
λαχόντες οὐκ ὀλίγαν δόσιν, μὴ φθονεραῖς ἐκ θεῶν
μετατροπίαις ἐπικύρσαιεν. θεὸς εἴη
ἀπήμων κέαρ· εὐδαίμων δὲ καὶ ὑμνητὸς οὗτος ἀνὴρ γίνεται σοφοῖς ...

)—

20

May destiny follow them as well
in days to come, to make their lordly wealth flourish.

And having been granted no small share
of pleasant successes in Hellas, may they encounter from the gods
no invidious reversals. May divinity
not be pained in heart; happy and a subject for songs
is such a man in the eyes of the wise ...

The first two prayers concern the future. The first requests that the family's (σφίσιν, 18) wealth will continue to bloom; the second that they (specifically the father and son) may continue to add to their illustrious athletic record. The third seeks assurance that divinity (θεός, 21) will have no resentment at their present success, for the father has reached the limits of human happiness (22-29).[37]

At *Isth*. 7.37 ff., after expressing his own sense of relief at the present victory (cf. νῦν, 37) and the joy of its celebration (ἀείσομαι χαίταν στεφάνοισιν

---

[37] The arguments for regarding θεὸς εἴη ἀπήμων κέαρ as a prayer and the following δέ (22) as explanatory are given in Race, "Two Pindaric Passages" 182-188.

ἁρμόζων, 39), Pindar cautiously adds a prayer that the gods not disrupt his (or the victor's) peaceful pursuit of success on a day-by-day basis (39-42):

>
> 40
>
> ὁ δ' ἀθανάτων μὴ θρασσέτω φθόνος,
> ὅτι τερπνὸν ἐφάμερον διώκων
> ἔκαλος ἔπειμι γῆρας ἔς τε τὸν μόρσιμον
> αἰῶνα.

>
> 40
>
> May the envy of the immortals not cause disruption
> because in seeking the pleasure that comes day by day
> I shall calmly approach old age and my fated
> lifetime.

The "envy" of the gods here, as always in Pindar, implies a disruption (cf. θρασσέτω, 39) of a long succession of good fortune.[38] The "I" in this passage is not just personal to Pindar, but also expresses the hopes of Strepsiadas and of Thebes as well. The word ἔκαλος (41) indicates unhampered, free pursuit of daily pleasures and advancement into old age and the future that the gods hold in store.[39] As Young points out, this is an expression of the classical carpe-diem philosophy, which stems from Homer and finds frequent expression in Pindar.[40] Here the poet looks to the future with confident hopes that he (and Strepsiadas) will pursue obtainable goals within their limitations. After all this preparation, Pindar can finally voice his prayer that Apollo grant "us" (ἄμμι, 49)[41] a Pythian crown.

We shall conclude this discussion with a complex and difficult transitional prayer. At *Pyth.* 8.56-60, after a farewell to Alkman and thanks for predicting the victory of Aristomenes, Pindar begins a transition to the athlete's other victories by means of a prayer to Apollo (61-72):

> (1)τὺ δ', (2)'Εκαταβόλε, (3)πάνδοκον
> ναὸν εὐκλέα διανέμων
> Πυθῶνος ἐν γυάλοις,

---

[38] As many have noted, the words ἀθανάτων μὴ θρασσέτω φθόνος are similar to the words attributed to Solon at Herodotos 1.32: τὸ θεῖον πᾶν ἐὸν φθονερόν τε καὶ ταραχῶδες. In both cases the issue is the continuance of good fortune. By giving men a mixture of good and evil (cf. *Il.* 24.525-548) and never an unbroken sequence of happiness, the gods appear to begrudge man what they themselves possess. In that sense they are "stingy." For a good discussion of φθόνος in Pindar, see Kirkwood, "Blame and Envy" 169-183.

[39] The expression τὸν μόρσιμον αἰῶνα "my fated life" includes death, which is the concern of the following gnomes.

[40] See Young, *Isthmian 7* 31.

[41] The plural ἄμμι has its full force here, for the victory is shared by the entire polis. It follows four first-person singular expressions (ἔτλαν, 37; μοι, 37; ἀείσομαι, 39; ἔπειμι, 41), which Young, *Isthmian 7* 30 has argued are "first person indefinites"; such an interpretation somewhat obscures their personal warmth in this poem for a fellow Theban.

(4a)τὸ μὲν μέγιστον τόθι χαρμάτων
65 ὤπασας, (4b)οἴκοι δὲ πρόσθεν ἁρπαλέαν δόσιν
πενταεθλίου σὺν ἑορταῖς ὑμαῖς ἐπάγαγες·
— ὦναξ, ἑκόντι δ' εὔχομαι νόῳ
κατά τιν' ἁρμονίαν βλέπειν
ἀμφ' ἕκαστον, ὅσα νέομαι.
70 κώμῳ μὲν ἀδυμελεῖ
Δίκα παρέστακε· θεῶν δ' ὄπιν
ἄφθονον αἰτέω, Ξέναρκες, ὑμετέραις τύχαις.
εἰ γάρ τις ἐσλὰ πέπαται μὴ σὺν μακρῷ πόνῳ . . .

(1)And you, (2)far-shooter, (3)who govern
the all-welcoming famous temple
in the vales of Pytho,
(4a)there you granted the greatest
65 of joys, (4b)and earlier at home you bestowed the sought-after gift
of the pentathlon in your sister's and your festival.
— O king, I pray that with a willing mind
you look with harmonious favor
on each step that I take.
70 Beside the sweetly singing revel
Justice has taken her stand, and I ask for the gods'
ungrudging regard, Xenarkes, on your family's good fortune,
for if someone tries to gain good things without extensive effort . . .

The increasing length of the opening elements is apparent.[42] The first word of the third element (the *sedes*), πάνδοκον (61), emphasizes the Panhellenic stature of the Pythian shrine in order to lend weight to Aristomenes' victory there, and the additional epithet, εὐκλέα (62), suggests the renown that also attaches to a victory there. The participle διανέμων (62), has the metaphorical sense (only here and at *Pyth.* 4.261) of "govern," but it must retain a measure of its usual denotation of "distribute," which is appropriate to the god who "gave" (ὤπασας; cf. δόσιν . . . ἐπάγαγες, 65-66) victory to Aristomenes. The invocation has stressed the *sedes*, which serves as the basis for the following clauses that contrast (cf. μὲν . . . δέ) the location of the contests: τόθι . . . οἴκοι (64-65). The fact that the Pythian victory alluded to in the μέν clause is his most important one (cf. μέγιστον, 64) is offset by the greater length of the δέ clause, although it concerns a victory in local Aiginetan games dedicated to Apollo and Artemis (cf. ὑμαῖς, 66). It is noteworthy, however, that this victory is in the pentathlon (given some emphasis at the beginning of the line), whereas his Pythian crown is for wrestling.[43]

---

[42] See Kambylis, "Anredeformen" 177 note 2.

[43] This fact gives more meaning to the initial announcement of the present victory as νεώτατον καλῶν (33), which is followed by the emphatic παλαισμάτεσσι γάρ (35) at the beginning

As Bundy has pointed out, this section is part of a much larger development that, little by little, catalogues the victories of Aristomenes and his immediate family.[44] The first, initially introduced at 19 (the place of victory and his patronymic are given) and then specified as in wrestling at 35, is his current Pythian victory. The fact that he comes from a naturally athletic family prompts the illustrative digression in lines 39-60 on inherited determination (φυᾷ τὸ γενναῖον ἐπιπρέπει | ἐκ πατέρων παισὶ λῆμα, 44-45).[45] The prayer to Apollo that begins in verse 61 returns to the Pythian victory (μέν, 64), but bypasses it (δέ, 65) in order to review Aristomenes' earlier victories in local games in honor of Apollo and Artemis. Having thus used Apollo as a bridge between Aristomenes' victories at Delphi and Aigina, the poet can use him to call attention to his own role as poet, by requesting that Apollo continue to look favorably on his poetic efforts.[46] We have seen (above page 123) in the prayer at *Ol.* 6.103-105 that Poseidon was invoked under two different aspects. Here Apollo is reinvoked as ἄναξ, a title connoting a closer personal connection than Ἑκαταβόλε at 61 (cf. *Pyth.* 9.44, where Cheiron calls Apollo ὦ ἄνα).

Pindar follows this prayer with a new movement, returning to the present celebration (κώμῳ ἀδυμελεῖ, 70) and affirming that it has been justly earned (Δίκα παρέστακε, 71). The μέν ... δέ construction, however, shows that once again the reference to the present Pythian victory is a spring-board to a another victory, this time future successes for Xenarkes' family (cf. ὑμετέραις τύχαις, 72). The θεῶν ὄπιν ἄφθονον (71-72) is litotes for a "favorable and beneficent regard" and the τύχαις refer to the family's future success (cf. τύχαν at *Ol.* 13.115 and Bakch. 17.132). This prayer is then justified by an extensive explanation (γάρ, 73) that stresses the need for hard work (μακρῷ πόνῳ, 73) and divine assistance in order to be victorious. Both elements have been present in Aristomenes' career and have accounted for his victories at Megara, Marathon, and at the Aiginetan Heraia, thus supporting the likelihood of his future success.[47] The theme of hard work (cf. δάμασσας ἔργῳ, 80) then serves as a lead-in for a final, extended account of his Pythian victory, as the poet stresses the fact that he won it the hard way, by having to defeat four successive opponents (81-84).[48]

---

of the epode. Aristomenes is obviously a well-rounded athlete, but has come to follow the example of his maternal uncles, who were both accomplished wrestlers.

[44] Bundy, *Studia Pindarica* 70 note 84.

[45] There is a strong suggestion in the narrative that Amphiaraos and Alkman are models for Xenarkes and Aristomenes. Both sons possess their father's native gifts and are successful, whereas their fathers were not.

[46] Burton, *Pythian Odes* 184 compares this prayer with that at *Pyth.* 9.89a-90 and says of both: "The poet seeks a special inspiration at a crucial moment in his poem."

[47] Cf. *Nem.* 10.30-36, where Theaios' hard work (cf. οὐδ' ἀμόχθῳ καρδίᾳ, 30) and his numerous victories in minor games lend support to his hopes for an Olympic victory.

[48] For the climactic arrangement of this final victory catalogue, see above pages 23-24. For a brief discussion of winning ἄνευ κλήρου, see above page 67.

Pythian 1

We shall conclude this chapter by examining in some detail the middle three triads of *Pyth.* 1, in which the argument of the poem is articulated by seven prayers, the highest concentration in any ode. We have already discussed (above page 42) how the first prayer at 29, εἴη, Ζεῦ, τὶν εἴη ἁνδάνειν, dramatically turns the ode from the agony of Typhos to the announcement of Hieron's achievements (30-33). In the following lines, Pindar expresses his expectation that the new city of Aitna will have a more splendid future (cf. φερτέρου, 35) and continue from this auspicious beginning to be famous for additional triumphal celebrations (35-38). He seals this ringing prediction with a prayer to Apollo (39-40):[49]

> Λύκιε καὶ Δάλοι' ἀνάσσων
> Φοῖβε Παρνασσοῦ τε κράναν Κασταλίαν φιλέων,
> 40 ἐθελήσαις ταῦτα νόῳ τιθέμεν εὔανδρόν τε χώραν.

> Lord of Lykia, and you who rule over Delos,
> O Phoibos, and who love Parnassos' Kastalian spring,
> 40 willingly take these things to heart and make this a land of brave men.

The ταῦτα (40) sums up the preceding hopes Pindar had entertained for the city of Aitna, while the phrase **εὔανδρον** χώραν points forward to the introduction (after an explanatory clause crediting the gods with all human success) of "that man" (**ἄνδρα** κεῖνον, 42), an embodiment of the εὐανδρία for which he prays.

Immediately after announcing his eagerness to praise (αἰνῆσαι μενοινῶν, 43) "that man" in terms that betoken the greatness of his subject ("may I not cast the javelin outside the lists, but surpass my rivals with a long throw," 44-45), Pindar prays that Hieron's happiness may continue (46):

> εἰ γὰρ ὁ πᾶς χρόνος ὄλβον μὲν οὕτω
> καὶ κτεάνων δόσιν εὐθύ-
> νοι, καμάτων δ' ἐπίλασιν παράσχοι.

> May all time continue to grant him
> such happiness and prosperity,
> and make him forget his hardships.

The fact that this prayer for continued prosperity precedes the actual praise of Hieron—this is the only place in the odes where this occurs—points to the great-

---

[49] For an analysis of the rising elements in this prayer, see above page 17. The use of τίθημι in two different senses in a prayer is paralleled at Alkm. 27.2-3 PMG: ἐπὶ δ' ἵμερον | ὕμνῳ καὶ χαρίεντα τίθη χορόν.

ness of Hieron: in anticipating his praise (42-45), Pindar feels called upon to knock on wood, as it were. The οὕτω, which in other prayers refers specifically to preceding praise (cf. 56), here more generally applies to the past: "as heretofore."[50] The prayer actually announces the grounds for praise; the μέν and δέ articulate the two aspects of his happiness: the first concerns wealth (ὄλβον, κτεάνων δόσιν), while the second indirectly alludes to successful action. Although the last-mentioned part receives the emphasis and proves to be the one that is elaborated in the following lines, in which Pindar praises Hieron's (and his family's) prowess in war (47-51), one is struck by the fact that Pindar has chosen to emphasize Hieron's suffering by using the negative expression "forgetfulness of toils" (καμάτων ἐπίλασιν) rather than the positive "recollection of success." As so often, the negative expression is followed by a forceful positive restatement, here given additional emphasis by coming at the beginning of the antistrophe (ἦ κεν ἀμνάσειεν..., 47), but the words τλάμονι ψυχᾷ παρέμειν' (48) continue to insist on the hardships he endured. The sudden shift to the plural verb εὑρίσκοντο (48) indicates that the generalized phrase ἐν πολέμοισι μάχαις (47) refers to the battle of Himera (whose glory Hieron shared with his older brother Gelon, who was actually in command). The concluding phrase πλούτου στεφάνωμ' ἀγέρωχον (50) brings us full circle to the first part of the prayer for continued wealth (κτεάνων δόσιν, 46). This reprise rounds off this portion concerning Himera before turning to the battle of Kyma, for which Hieron took full credit. He now holds the spotlight alone (50-55):

50   νῦν γε μὰν
        τὰν Φιλοκτήταο δίκαν ἐφέπων
        ἐστρατεύθη· σὺν δ' ἀνάγκᾳ νιν φίλον
        καί τις ἐὼν μεγαλάνωρ ἔσανεν.
            φαντὶ δὲ Λαμνόθεν ἕλκει
—   τειρόμενον μεταβάσοντας ἐλθεῖν
        ἥροας ἀντιθέους Ποίαντος υἱὸν τοξόταν·
        ὃς Πριάμοιο πόλιν πέρσεν, τελεύτα-
        σέν τε πόνους Δαναοῖς,
55   ἀσθενεῖ μὲν χρωτὶ βαίνων, ἀλλὰ μοιρίδιον ἦν.

50   But now
        like another Philoktetes,
        he has taken to the field, and even the proud man
        was compelled to seek his friendship. They say
            that the god-like heroes came to fetch him
—   from Lemnos, wasting from his wound,

---

[50] See Gildersleeve, *Pindar* 246. The expression ὁ πᾶς χρόνος (46) is equivalent to τοῦτον χρόνον at *Ol.* 1.115 and designates the time remaining in his life.

> Poias' archer son,
> who destroyed Priam's city and ended
> the Greeks' toils.
> 55 He walked on weak flesh, but he fulfilled his destiny.

The emphatic νῦν γε μάν (50) and the elaborate comparison with Philoktetes give much greater emphasis to this campaign than to Himera. The choice of Philoktetes also explains why Pindar had emphasized Hieron's suffering (cf. καμάτων, 46). The scholia (supposedly on the authority of Aristotle) claim that Hieron was suffering from kidney stones. We shall probably never know for certain what was actually the case, for Pindar has omitted any details, lest they trivialize the general point he wishes to make: ῥέζοντά τι καὶ παθεῖν ἔοικεν. Hieron is the man of the hour for the Greeks; he has won hard-earned victories. We expect some elaboration, but must wait until these two battles are eventually named and given fuller treatment, in chiastic order, in lines 72-75 (Kyma) and 79-80 (Himera).[51]

After this heroic comparison, Pindar seals his praise with yet another prayer (56-57):

> οὕτω δ' Ἱέρωνι θεὸς ὀρθωτὴρ πέλοι
> τὸν προσέρποντα χρόνον, ὧν ἔραται και-
> ρὸν διδούς.

> In like fashion may god sustain Hieron
> in time to come, and give him due measure
> of his desires.

Here the οὕτω (in contrast to οὕτω at 46) refers directly to the preceding material, and requests that Hieron continue to be given divine guidance as Philoktetes had been (cf. μοιρίδιον ἦν, 55). This prayer, so similar to that in 46, serves to round off this section devoted to Hieron's military exploits.[52] The most distinctive feature of the second prayer is the prominence of the name Ἱέρωνι (56), referred to at the beginning of the section merely as ἄνδρα κεῖνον (42).

At this point, Pindar has completed the section on Hieron's martial efforts (although leaving many things unspecified until later in the poem). In order to make a new beginning, he invokes the Muse (58-60):

---

[51] I am following the excellent analysis of Carey, "Pindarica" 21-27, who convincingly argues that in lines 47-55 Pindar is sketching the same battles that he later names and is not referring to the affair involving Western Lokroi (which he treats in *Pyth.* 2).

[52] Besides the repetition of οὕτω (46, 56), the expression τὸν προσέρποντα χρόνον (57) echoes ὁ πᾶς χρόνος (46), while ὀρθωτὴρ πέλοι (56) is equivalent to εὐθύνοι (46) and διδούς (57) recalls δόσιν (46).

> Μοῖσα, καὶ πὰρ Δεινομένει κελαδῆσαι
> πίθεό μοι ποινὰν τεθρίππων·
> χάρμα δ' οὐκ ἀλλότριον νικαφορία πατέρος.
> 60   ἄγ' ἔπειτ' Αἴτνας βασιλεῖ φίλιον ἐξεύρωμεν ὕμνον.
>
> Muse, I beg you to join with Deinomenes too as you sing
> the reward for the chariot,
>   because the joy of his father's victory is no stranger to him.
> 60   Come, then, let us compose a loving hymn for Aitna's king.

We must remember that Hieron's "deeds of war" only reflected upon his position in Syracuse and had nothing directly to do with the city of Aitna. In order to reintroduce that city and the event that occasioned the ode, Pindar bids his Muse to include Hieron's son Deinomenes in the celebration on the grounds that his father's victory is "no alien joy."[53] The following lines constitute the "loving hymn," which details the Doric institutions on which the city was founded (61-66); it is duly concluded with yet another prayer (67-70):

> Ζεῦ τέλει', αἰεὶ δὲ τοιαύταν 'Αμένα παρ' ὕδωρ
> αἶσαν ἀστοῖς καὶ βασιλεῦσιν διακρί-
>   νειν ἔτυμον λόγον ἀνθρώπων.
> σύν τοι τίν κεν ἀγητὴρ ἀνήρ,
> 70   υἱῷ τ' ἐπιτελλόμενος, δᾶμον γεραί-
>   ρων τράποι σύμφωνον ἐς ἡσυχίαν.
>
> Zeus accomplisher, may men's true report
> always ascribe such good fortune as this to the citizens and their
>   kings by the waters of the Amenas.
> For with your help, a ruler may,
> 70   with his son as viceroy, honor his people and turn them
>   to harmonious peace.

The word τοιαύταν (67) refers back to Pindar's praise of the city's institutions. The burden of the prayer is the harmonious relationship between the kings (Hieron and Deinomenes) and their people that will promote domestic peace. The explanatory clause (τοι, 69) adds the hope that with Zeus' guidance (σὺν . . . τιν, 69) they will achieve that concord (σύμφωνον ἡσυχίαν, 70). The reference to father and son completes the ring and marks the end of the "loving hymn."

---

[53] For rhapsodic elements in this new beginning, see Schadewaldt, *Aufbau* 271 note 3. Köhnken, "Hieron und Deinomenes" provides an excellent analysis of the end of this ode and proves conclusively that after this brief introduction of Deinomenes Hieron again becomes the addressee of the poem.

The hymn ends with the reassuring words σύμφωνον ἐς ἡσυχίαν, which create a sense of repose before a new direction is suddenly introduced by the following asyndetic prayer for security from external enemies (71-73):

> λίσσομαι νεῦσον, Κρονίων, ἥμερον
> ὄφρα κατ' οἶκον ὁ Φοίνιξ ὁ Τυρσα-
> νῶν τ' ἀλαλατὸς ἔχῃ, ναυ-
> σίστονον ὕβριν ἰδὼν τὰν πρὸ Κύμας,
> οἷα Συρακοσίων ἀρχῷ δαμασθέντες πάθον . . .

> I beseech you, son of Kronos, make the
> Phoenicians and Etruscans keep their war cry
> quietly at home, now that they have seen their aggression
> bring woe to their fleet before Kyma,
> such defeat did they suffer at the hands of the Syracusans' chief . . .

Here, as in *Nem.* 9.27, Zeus' patronymic Κρονίων (71) is used in a prayer concerned with the aggression of foreign enemies. The tone of supplication in the fervent introductory words λίσσομαι νεῦσον (71) contrasts markedly with the quite mood of the preceding prayer, and is explained by the fact that the ones offering the prayer (the Greeks) really have no control over what the Carthaginians and Etruscans decide to do. They can only react and hope to discourage them. The participial clause (ἰδών, 72) really functions as an explanatory clause: "Please convince them to stay at home, since they have seen how self-destructive their aggression (ὕβριν, 72) was at Kyma." The previous prayer was grounded in the rational behavior of the citizens acting under divine leadership (cf. σύν τοι τίν κεν, 69); this last one is a fervent appeal to Zeus to force the bellicose enemies to keep their war-cry at home.[54] And, as if in order to add further evidence to persuade them, Pindar lists the three major battles by name (Salamis, Plataia, and Himera) that repelled foreign aggression in the east and west (75-80). This roll call ends the fourth triad, and after an elaborate transitional passage (81-84), the poet devotes the remainder of the last triad to praise (embedded in counsel) of Hieron's domestic policies, which, if followed, may lead to that ideal of σύμφωνος ἡσυχία. *Pythian* 1, a poem so rich in all the stylistic and rhetorical features treated in this study, also proves to be an excellent model for Pindar's use of prayers to articulate his odes.

---

[54] There is no hope in the prayer that the Carthaginians and Etruscans will ever enjoy ἡσυχία as the Greeks can; the best that can be expected is that they will confine their bellicose nature (cf. ἀλαλατός, 72) at home, where it will not be bothersome (ἥμερον, 71). In this respect, they resemble Typhos, who retains his fierce nature, but is restrained by the power of Zeus.

CHAPTER 6

AN ANALYSIS OF *OLYMPIAN* 8

Any approach to poetry ultimately proves its worth by its usefulness in illuminating the features of individual poems. The following analysis of *Olympian* 8 applies the principles of style and rhetoric discussed in the previous pages to an entire ode. The poem itself, the only one celebrating an Olympic victory won by an Aiginetan, has received very little attention as a complete work.[1] What criticism exists tends to be negative. For example, Fennell faults it for a "lack of unity," while Farnell detects "manifold signs of haste" and calls the poem an "improvisation." We shall see, however, that their adverse judgments actually arise from misconceptions concerning the performance of this poem and from the importation of irrelevant historical speculation, which together have caused serious misunderstanding of the sense and rhetorical tone in key passages. I do not claim that it is a great poem, for there are a number of far greater Pindaric odes, but it is a finely crafted work which touches on important themes and (most importantly for our purposes) it exhibits *all* the traits of Pindaric style and rhetoric which we have observed in the preceding chapters, and which, if properly understood, disprove many of the criticisms levelled against it. If the following analysis raises the estimation of this poem to any degree, then I shall consider that it has rendered a service.

The poem begins with a hymn and ends with a prayer, it introduces several topics by means of climactic statements that utilize the principles we have explored, it effectively alternates positive and negative expressions to highlight topics, and exhibits numerous fine points of style throughout. Furthermore, it contains one of the most misunderstood rhetorical maneuvers in the odes, Pindar's introduction of the trainer Melesias. It treats many of the themes that occur throughout the odes: the relationship between man and god, between foreknowledge and fulfillment, between destiny and individual effort, between natural talent and training, and between success and failure. Since, however, a full-scale treatment of these topics is beyond the scope of this study, we shall concentrate mainly on stylistic matters and problems of interpretation.

---

[1] A survey of the bibliographies of Gerber, Rico, and Thummer reveals not a single article devoted to an overall study of *Ol.* 8.

Let us begin with the opening hymn, one of the most difficult in the odes.

> Μᾶτερ ὦ χρυσοστεφάνων ἀέθλων, Οὐλυμπία,
> δέσποιν' ἀλαθείας, ἵνα μάντιες ἄνδρες
> ἐμπύροις τεκμαιρόμενοι παραπειρῶν-
>   ται Διὸς ἀργικεραύνου,
> εἴ τιν' ἔχει λόγον ἀνθρώπων πέρι
> 5 μαιομένων μεγάλαν
> ἀρετὰν θυμῷ λαβεῖν,
> — τῶν δὲ μόχθων ἀμπνοάν.
> ἄνεται δὲ πρὸς χάριν εὐσεβίας ἀνδρῶν λιταῖς·
> ἀλλ' ὦ Πίσας εὔδενδρον ἐπ' Ἀλφεῷ ἄλσος,
> 10 τόνδε κῶμον καὶ στεφαναφορίαν δέ-
>   ξαι. μέγα τοι κλέος αἰεί,
> ᾧτινι σὸν γέρας ἕσπετ' ἀγλαόν.

> O mother of the golden-crowned games, Olympia,
> mistress of truth, in whose precinct men who are seers
> examine burnt offerings to test
>   Zeus of the bright thunderbolt,
> to see if he has any word concerning men
> 5 who are striving in their heart
> to win a great victory
> — and gain a respite from their toils.
> But accomplishment is accorded to men's supplications
>   in return for piety.
> And so, Pisa with your grove of beautiful trees on the Alpheos,
> 10 receive this celebration and its wearing of the victory crown,
>   for great and everlasting fame is his
> who receives your illustrious prize.

By calling her the "Mother of golden-crowned games," Pindar implies that is both the "most famous" (cf. Σ 1. g., πρωτεύειν τῇ δόξῃ) as wells as the "originator" (cf. Σ 1. h., τὴν πρώτην) of the great athletic contests. Her most striking attribute is that she is the "queen of truth" (δέσποιν' ἀλαθείας, 2). The rest of the hymn will clarify in what sense she can be so called.

The subordinate clause introduced by the adverb ἵνα (2), which substitutes for the more common relative pronoun, does not elaborate on the goddess' powers as is customary in hymnal invocations, but rather describes the activities of two groups of men in her precinct. First are the seers (μάντιες ἄνδρες, 2), who, by inspecting burnt offerings, try to determine before the event what the outcome will be for the contestants. Second are the athletes themselves, who eagerly desire to win (ἀνθρώπων μαιομένων, 4). In employing the generalized plurals Pindar is being deliberately vague. He does not tell us that these seers are the Iamidai (as the scholia duly inform us), nor does he say that Alkimedon received a favorable oracle (as most moderns assume). All he says is that unspecified seers try to determine if Zeus has any word (εἴ τιν' ἔχει λόγον) about the contestants. In fact, the verb παραπειρῶνται suggests tentativeness or indirection (i.e., through the medium of burning sacrifices). Furthermore, the movement of the sentence decidedly shifts the emphasis in the last three lines (5-7) to the second group of men, the desirous athletes. These small indications of style are important for establishing the force of the much misunderstood gnome that opens the antistrophe: "But accomplishment (ἄνεται δέ) is accorded to men's supplications (ἀνδρῶν λιταῖς) in return for piety (πρὸς χάριν εὐσεβίας)."

Whose supplications are these? The seers' or the athletes'? The scholia choose the former, claiming that pious seers (the Iamidai are mentioned as especially pious) receive more favorable oracles. Boeckh, *Pindari Opera* 180 followed them: *preces vatum pro certantibus, ut deus fausto illis oraculo benignus sit*, but that interpretation supposes much more than the mere act of divination described by the phrase ἐμπύροις τεκμαιρόμενοι παραπειρῶνται, for it implies partisan praying on behalf of favored contestants (*pro certantibus*). Dissen, *Pindari Carmina* 95 realized the problems in Boeckh's interpretation: [*preces*] *non vatum, opinor, a quorum piis precibus si res penderet, omnes vincerent, sed τῶν μαιομένων ἀρετὰν λαβεῖν. Hi enim, opinor, adhibito popa sacrificant et adstant precantes victoriam omenque bonum. Vates autem non ipsum sacrificium peragit, sed hostias cremantes inspicit et oraculum edit.*[2] Pindar is not praising the piety of μάντιες ἄνδρες, but that of athletes who desire (cf. μαιομένων, 5) a favorable result from their labors. The activities of the seers are foil for the real subject of interest, successful effort.

By following Dissen's argument, much better sense results if the gnome expresses a *contrast*[3] between, on the one hand, the activities before the contest of the seers who attempt to find a sign (τεκμαιρόμενοι παραπειρῶνται) and of the athletes who desire (μαιομένων) to win, and, on the other hand, what actually comes to be. Whether or not Zeus has some word to impart to the seers, regardless of how eagerly the athletes wish to win, the truth will be decided and success will be awarded by the help of a god (in this instance Zeus) in return for men's pious devotion. *Ol.* 6.77-81 provides an excellent gloss on this passage. There

---

[2] See also Mezger, *Siegeslieder* 378: "ἀνδρῶν: nicht der Seher (schol.), sondern der μαιόμενοι." Dissen aptly cites *Il.* 2.305 ff., where Kalchas attends the sacrifice and reads the omen. There are two good parallels in Pindar. At *Pyth.* 4.193-196 Iason prays for a safe journey; lightning flashes from the sky (197-198); Mopsos the seer encourages them to set out (201-202). At *Isth.* 6.42-49 Herakles prays (cf. λίσσομαι, 45) for Telamon to have a brave son; Zeus sends an omen (49-50); Herakles himself reads the omen "like a seer" (ἄτε μάντις ἀνήρ, 51) and predicts Aias' martial prowess. The word μαιομένων is virtually equivalent to λισσομένων.

[3] Many translators simply ignore the δέ (8) (Lattimore, *The Odes of Pindar* 23; Bowra, *Pindar* 210), treat it as explanatory (Fennell, *The Olympian and Pythian Odes* 86; Sandys, *Pindar* 85; Conway, *The Odes of Pindar* 48), or make it additive (Puech, *Olympiques* 106).

Pindar assures us that Hagesias' Stymphalian relatives are such successful athletes because they have regaled Hermes "with so many prayerful sacrifices" (λιταῖς θυσίαις | πολλὰ δὴ πολλαῖσιν, 78-79) "in pious fashion" (εὐσεβέως, 79) and therefore "he accomplishes their success" (κραίνει . . . εὐτυχίαν, 81) "with his deep-thundering father" (σὺν βαρυδούπῳ πατρί, 81). The following table reveals the resemblances between the two passages:

Ol. 8.3-8	*Ol.* 6.77-81
ἄνεται (8)	κραίνει (81)
εὐσεβίας (8)	εὐσεβέως (79)
λιταῖς (8)	λιταῖς (78)
Διὸς ἀργικεραύνου (3)	σὺν βαρυδούπῳ πατρί (81)

Also, at *Ol.* 3.38-41 the poet states that Theron and the Emmenidai have gained such fame in horse racing thanks to the Tyndaridai because they welcome them at so many feasts and piously (εὐσεβεῖ γνώμᾳ, 41) keep their rites.[4]

As mother of the crown games, Olympia is the "queen of truth" not just because oracles in her precinct may come true, but because she decides the greatest athletic events in accordance with the will of Zeus (Διὸς ἀργικεραύνου, 3).[5] This ἀλάθεια denotes "how something actually turns out to be," a sense it *always* has in Pindar.[6] By deciding the issue of athletics at the highest level (cf. **Μᾶτερ χρυσοστεφάνων ἀέθλων**, 1), Olympia makes manifest "true" or actual performance. At the founding of the Olympic games as described at *Ol.* 10.53-55, Time was present to reveal the actual truth: ὅ τ' ἐξελέγχων μόνος ἀλάθειαν ἐτήτυμον Χρόνος; that is, time and the Olympic games prove by testing what actually is the case (ἀλάθεια).

At this point in the poem, since the intervening lines of description (2-8) have led quite a ways from his initial invocation of Olympia, Pindar re-invokes her, much as he does Zeus in *Ol.* 4 after intervening observations (see above page

---

[4] Cf. *Nem.* 10.49-54, where Kastor and Polydeukes assure the athletic success of Theaios' clan in return for their hospitality (ξενίαν, 49) and sense of justice (δικαίων, 54). Cf. also Bakch. 1.156-157, where Zeus makes Argeios an Isthmian victor in return for generosity: 'Ισ[θ]μιόνικον | θῆκεν ἀντ' [εὐε]ργεσιᾶν.

[5] Cf. βαρυγδούπου Διός at 44. In both cases Zeus is identified by his lightning and thunder because they are one of his principal means of communicating omens. Cf. *Pyth.* 4.194, where Iason calls upon ἐγχεικέραυνον Ζῆνα, who responds with lightning (στεροπᾶς, 198), and Bakch. 17.66, where Minos calls for an omen of lightning from Zeus ἀναξιβρέντας. His other chief omen is the eagle (cf. *Isth.* 6.50)—both appear frequently in Homer; at *Pyth.* 1.5-10 they are the two symbols of his power.

[6] Cf. *Ol.* 7.68-69: τελεύταθεν δὲ λόγων κορυφαί | ἐν ἀλαθείᾳ πετοῖσαι; *Ol.* 10.54, *Pyth.* 3.103, *Nem.* 5.17, 7.25, and *Isth.* 2.10. At *Ol.* 10.4 he invokes the aid of Alatheia as representative of what he actually accomplishes in the poem. She vouches for the delivery of the ode; Atrekeia assesses its value. See Verdenius, *Commentaries I* 78 and *II* 125.

93), with a resumptive ἀλλά (9), asking the Olympian precinct to receive (δέξαι, 10) this victory celebration (τόνδε κῶμον, 10) and the wearing of a victory crown (στεφαναφορίαν, 10). But before proceeding with our analysis, we must address the problem created by the word στεφαναφορίαν. The term simply means "the wearing of a crown," but those who maintain the mistaken idea that the ode was performed at Olympia have invented a new meaning for it: "a procession to dedicates a crown in a sanctuary." The misunderstanding begins with Boeckh, *Pindari Opera* 179: *oda Olympiae cantata est, quum instituta comissatio esset et pompa, qua corona in Altin deferebatur; quae est* στεφανηφορία. Most scholars have perpetuated this fiction.[7]

Two problems arise as a result: one of fact (where was the ode performed? what is a στεφαναφορία?), the other of judgment. As we shall see, in two places later in the ode it becomes certain that the ode was performed in Aigina. The στεφαναφορία turns out to be descriptive of the celebratory *komos* (κῶμον καὶ στεφαναφορίαν is essentially hendiadys for "victory celebration").[8] The problem of judgment arises as a corollary, once one assumes that the ode was performed at Olympia, for if that were true, then it would have to have been written quickly. Thus, Fennell, *Olympian and Pythian Odes* 83-84, who believes that the ode "was sung in the στεφαναφορία directly after the victory, when the kômos attended the victor to the altar of Zeus in the Altis," and therefore concludes, "unless the poet trusted the diviners sufficiently to prepare the ode beforehand, the composition must have been very rapid," not surprisingly finds "a lack of unity in the construction of this ode." And yet, in his commentary he never produces a single instance to support this claim. But Farnell, elaborating on this negative assessment, produced the following fanciful criticism (*Pindar* 59):

> The manifold signs of haste discernible in this ode may be explained by the fact that it was to be sung at Olympia immediately after the games, which would necessarily hurry the composition . . . Composed then against time—unless indeed Pindar had some preternatural foresight that Alkimedon would win—the

---

[7] See Dissen, *Pindari Carmina* 92, Donaldson, *Pindar's Odes* 52, Mezger, *Pindars Siegeslieder* 375, Gildersleeve, *Pindar* 192, Fennell, *Olympian and Pythian Odes* 84, Sandys, *Pindar* 82, Werner, *Siegesgesänge* 61, and Nisetich, *Pindar's Victory Songs* 117. Farnell, *Pindar* 60 recognizes the basic meaning of the word, but, because he is so committed to his belief that the ode was performed at Olympia (note how it intrudes in the parenthesis), he is forced to create a special meaning: "Naturally [στεφαναφορίαν] would signify 'the wearing of the crown' by the victor (who goes with the komos to the altar of Zeus); but this does not make an appropriate phrase with δέξαι. It is true that the kindred words στεφανηφόρος, στεφανηφορεῖν refer to the wearing of crowns by the official or by the participants in a rite; but Pindar may here intend a different sense for the word, 'the bearing the garland in the procession to lay on the altar.'"

[8] See Galiano, *Olímpicas II* 32 and Puech, *Olympiques* 106: "cette procession triomphale." Cf. *Pyth.* 8.19-20, where Apollo "received" Xenarkes' son: Ξενάρκειον ἔδεκτο Κίρραθεν ἐστεφανωμένον | υἱὸν ποίᾳ Παρνασσίδι Δωριεῖ τε κώμῳ and *Pyth.* 3.73: κῶμον . . . στεφάνοις. For other examples of hendiadys with στέφανος, see below page 166 with note 3.

146   Style and Rhetoric in Pindar's Odes

ode has the interest of being the longest and most elaborate of Pindar's "improvisations."

The circularity of Farnell's underlying logic is obvious: if it was performed on the spot, then it had to be composed quickly; therefore it is a hastily composed, inferior poem.[9] The request to Olympia to "receive" the celebration does not require the celebrants to be in Olympia any more than in *Pa.* 6 (performed in Delos) the chorus had to be in Aigina to say to her that she will "receive" their song: ἀλλ' ἀοιδᾶν | ῥόθια δεκομένα κατερεῖς (128-129).[10]

Returning to the hymn, we see that it, like the other opening hymns we have surveyed, exhibits a continual movement toward specification. The generalizing plurals used of seers and athletes (ἄνδρες, 2; ἀνθρώπων, 4; ἀνδρῶν, 8) yield to this one victory celebration. The attempts to predict the future (τεκμαιρόμενοι παραπειρῶνται, 3) and the hopes of striving athletes yield to the actual result (ἄνεται δέ, 8; στεφαναφορίαν, 10). And, like the other re-invocations we have examined, this one is longer and more precise: "Pisa's grove of beautiful trees on the Alpheos River" (9). The repetition in στεφαναφορίαν (10) of χρυσοστεφάνων (1) in the invocation is a particularly pleasing touch that provides a sense of closure to the hymn.[11]

The process of specification continues after the hymn, for the ᾧτινι (11) in the gnome which follows gives the first indication of an individual victor (implied in the abstract noun στεφαναφορίαν, 10), who, after a summary priamel (12-14), will turn out to be Alkimedon (17).

>
> (1)ἄλλα δ' ἐπ' ἄλλον ἔβαν
> ἀγαθῶν, (2)πολλαὶ δ' ὁδοί
> σὺν θεοῖς εὐπραγίας.
> 15 (3a)Τιμόσθενες, ὔμμε δ' ἐκλάρωσεν πότμος
> Ζηνὶ γενεθλίῳ· ὅς σὲ μὲν Νεμέᾳ πρόφατον,
> (3b)Ἀλκιμέδοντα δὲ πὰρ Κρόνου λόφῳ
> θῆκεν Ὀλυμπιονίκαν.
>
> (1)Different good things happen
> to each man, (2)and many are the paths
> to god-given success.
> 15 (3a)Timosthenes, destiny allotted your family

---

[9] Unlike Fennell, Farnell eagerly points out what he claims to be signs of hasty composition (at verses 12-14, 21-22, 42-45, 47, 53, and 68-69) and tendentiously makes any incongruity he discovers (or invents) support his assumption.

[10] See Thummer, *Die Isthmischen Gedichte I* 32 note 11. The word δέξαι is a general hymnic term that means "accept this offering," whether it is the *komos* or the song, and by itself gives no indication as to place. In the example from *Pyth.* 8.19-20, quoted above note 8, Apollo receives the crowned victor *from* Kirrha in an ode performed at Aigina (cf. τόθι, 64).

[11] Cf. the more elaborate repetition that concludes the opening hymn of *Pyth.* 1.1-12.

to Zeus, its progenitor, who made you distinguished at Nemea,
(3b)and made Alkimedon, by the Hill of Kronos,
an Olympic victor.

As we have often seen, the two members of the foil are joined in mid-line. The first stresses variety, the second quantity, two factors commonly present in the foil of priamels. The second, longer by one syllable, is slightly more specific: the first member mentions only the good things that happen (ἔβαν) to men; the second involves men's divinely assisted accomplishments.[12] Pindar has reserved the ringing phrase σὺν θεοῖς εὐπραγίας for emphatic final position at the end of the antistrophe. When he opens the epode with the proper name Timosthenes, the direct address, the specification of σὺν θεοῖς by Ζηνί (16) and of εὐπραγίας by Νεμέᾳ πρόφατον (16), all signs point to the arrival at the climactic element. But by immediately introducing the plural ὔμμε (15), Pindar can then cap Timosthenes' victory at Nemea with Alkimedon's at Olympia. Of the many roads to success Timosthenes' has led to Nemea, Alkimedon's to Olympia. The rather brief σὲ μὲν Νεμέᾳ πρόφατον (16)[13] is outdone in weight, intensity, and specificity by Ἀλκιμέδοντα δὲ πὰρ Κρόνου λόφῳ | θῆκεν Ὀλυμπιονίκαν (17-18), also introduced at the beginning of the verse, which reserves the ringing word Ὀλυμπιονίκαν for final position.

Now that Alkimedon holds center stage, he is praised briefly in transition (19-20):

(1)ἦν δ' ἐσορᾶν καλός, (2)ἔργῳ τ' οὐ κατὰ εἶδος ἐλέγχων
20 (3)ἐξένεπε κρατέων
        πάλᾳ δολιχήρετμον Αἴγιναν πάτραν·
    ἔνθα . . .

    (1)He was beautiful to behold, (2)and in action not discrediting his looks,
20 (3)by winning in the wrestling-match
        he had long-oared Aigina proclaimed as his fatherland,
    where . . .

This climactic triplet of increasingly longer cola (given variety by the negative expression in the second element) follows the stages of the actual contest, passing from Alkimedon's beauty to his performance, to his victory and the public proclamation of his city. It has often been noted that Pindar does not supply

---

[12] For the movement from natural, divine, or merely external considerations to successful human action in climactic passages, see above page 13 note 11.

[13] For other examples of addressing a penultimate item in the second person, cf. *Ol.* 9.17, *Pyth.* 4.88-89, and 6.50-51. Carey, "Prosopographica Pindarica" 1-6 presents very good reasons for identifying Timosthenes as the grandfather mentioned in 70.

detailed information about the events themselves.[14] He does, however, accurately sketch the overall contest. Anyone who has attended a school wrestling-match can fill in the details: the initial appearance of the wrestler ("He looks good, but is he?"), his performance that confirms the initial impression, the resulting victory, and the pride of the school that shares his glory when its name is announced and enshrined in record. The last item of essential information, his fatherland, is held in the limelight by the relative adverb ἔνθα, which initiates extended praise of the island (21-30):

)—

ἔνθα σώτειρα Διὸς ξενίου
πάρεδρος ἀσκεῖται Θέμις

ἔξοχ᾽ ἀνθρώπων. ὅ τι γὰρ πολὺ καὶ πολλᾷ ῥέπῃ,
ὀρθᾷ διακρῖναι φρενὶ μὴ παρὰ καιρὸν
25   δυσπαλές· τεθμὸς δέ τις ἀθανάτων καὶ
    τάνδ᾽ ἁλιερκέα χώραν
παντοδαποῖσιν ὑπέστασε ξένοις
κίονα δαιμονίαν—
ὁ δ᾽ ἐπαντέλλων χρόνος
τοῦτο πράσσων μὴ κάμοι—
30   Δωριεῖ λαῷ ταμιευομέναν ἐξ Αἰακοῦ·
τὸν ...

)—

where Themis, the saving goddess, enthroned
beside Zeus, god of hospitality, is respected in practice

more than by any other people, because where much hangs in the
    balance for many parties,
adjudicating with correct judgment without offending propriety
25   is a difficult problem to wrestle with. But some ordinance of the gods
    has set up this island state
for visitants from all places
as a divine pillar—
and may coming time not tire
of maintaining that position—
30   a land held in trust by the Dorian people from the time of Aiakos,
    whom ...

These lines sound praises of Aigina's ξενία (cf. Διὸς ξενίου, 21; ξένοις, 26), a constant theme in the eleven odes to Aiginetans (and even in the remains of *Isth* 9; cf. οὐ θέμιν ... ξείνων ὑπερβαίνοντες, 5-6). It is instructive to compare a very similar passage in praise of the island of Tenedos at *Nem.* 11.8-9, containing almost identical vocabulary: καὶ ξενίου Διὸς ἀσκεῖται θέμις αἰενάοις | ἐν τρα-

---

[14] He is, however, reserving one striking detail of Alkimedon's victory for climactic introduction after he returns to him at line 65; see below page 159.

πέζαις. The major difference between them is underlined by a point of style in *Ol.* 8, the triadic enjambment of ἔξοχ' ἀνθρώπων (26). These powerful words call forth an explanation: the Aiginetans are the most fervent devotees of that θέμις, which like the Romans' *ius gentium*, protects relationships between alien states and individuals, because (γάρ, 23) Aigina is a great trading state where important issues are decided that require fine judgment (ὀρθᾷ διακρῖναι φρενί) lest they miss the just mark (μὴ παρὰ καιρόν).[15] The negative expression μὴ παρὰ καιρόν (24) is followed by a ringing affirmation of Aigina's divinely-ordained status among the Greek states. It is important to realize how lavishly Pindar praises Aigina in this section: he calls her the most ardent worshipper of Themis among all Greeks and claims that an "ordinance of the gods" (τεθμός; cf. Θέμις, 22) has made "this particular island state" (καὶ τάνδ' ἁλιερκέα χώραν)[16] a "divine pillar" for visitors from everywhere. He has purposely ended this praise with the ringing expression κίονα δαιμονίαν, which calls forth an apotropaic prayer:

ὁ δ' ἐπαντέλλων χρόνος
τοῦτο πράσσων μὴ κάμοι—

The rhetorical effect of this abruptly inserted prayer is to underscore the great extent of the preceding praise, as if Pindar checks himself after having been carried away to the point of excess. If one compares this conventional prayer with those surveyed above pages 79-80 and 130-140, it will be seen that all have the same rhetorical function: to temper praise by calling attention to the blessings that have been granted to the recipient by the grace of the gods and to ask for their continuance. And yet, since the early nineteenth century this prayer has been understood to have sinister implications. Boeckh, *Pindari Opera* 181 duly notes the similarity of this prayer to that of *Ol.* 6.97, but adds: *Ac sane tum de Aeginetis iam potuit aliquis sollicitus esse ingravescente indies Atheniensium superbia*. In discussing the prayer at the end of the ode, he glosses the word πόλιν (88) with *Aeginetarum civitatem, quam triennio post depressit Nemesis* (186). Dissen, *Pindari Carmina* 98 combines these two remarks in his gloss on the prayer at 28-29: *Sunt verba poetae solliciti. Insula triennio post ab Atheniensibus capta.* The persistence of this tradition is apparent in the following comments of Podlecki, *Early Greek Poets* 224-225 in his analysis of the prayers at 28-29 and at the end of the ode:

---

[15] The emphatic enjambment of δυσπαλές (25) supports Gildersleeve's observation, *Pindar* 195: "More or less pointed allusion to the πάλη of the victor."

[16] The καί is best taken as an example of a particularizing καί (see above page 97 note 33). In spite of attempts such as that by Farnell, *Pindar* 62 to explain it away as meaning "this land of our hearts," the deictic τάνδ' proves that the ode was performed in Aigina. See above page 83 note 62.

Then *a tone of concern creeps in*: "may time in its rise not tire of accomplishing this." The poem closes with a prayer that "Zeus send no contentious spirit of revenge, but may give them a life without woes and make them and their city flourish" (vv. 86-88). The last phrases *seem to strike once again a note of apprehension*. Within a few years of the performance of this ode, in the summer of 458 B.C., there occurred the "great naval battle" between Athens and Aegina. (my emphasis).

Besides reading specific details into a conventional, generalized prayer (the italicized words reveal how subjective such criticism is), this analysis makes Pindar a veritable political prophet. We shall see that ramifications of such subjective historicizing have also obscured the rhetoric of Pindar's praise of Melesias.

To return to the text, we see that by being cast in the negative the prayer (which ends the strophe) provides a contrast for the positive movement at the beginning of the antistrophe, where Pindar stresses the local tradition that has given the island its continuous stability within the Panhellenic community. The prayer also puts a seal on the divine dispensation and permits the poet to turn to the historical tradition of the Aiginetans.[17] The first and last words in line 30 are proper nouns that proudly announce their race (Δωριεῖ) and their progenitor (Αἰακοῦ); the word ταμιευομέναν "held in trust" hints at Aigina's business acumen as wells as expresses their proud maintenance of both the Achaian and the Doric traditions. The temporal value of ἐξ Αἰακοῦ neatly puts us back into the time of the myth, introduced by the usual relative (31-46).

>   τὸν παῖς ὁ Λατοῦς εὐρυμέδων τε Ποσειδᾶν,
>   Ἰλίῳ μέλλοντες ἐπὶ στέφανον τεῦ-
>   ξαι, καλέσαντο συνεργόν
>   τείχεος, ἦν ὅτι νιν πεπρωμένον
>   ὀρνυμένων πολέμων
> 35 πτολιπόρθοις ἐν μάχαις
>   λάβρον ἀμπνεῦσαι καπνόν.
>   γλαυκοὶ δὲ δράκοντες, ἐπεὶ κτίσθη νέον,
>   πύργον ἐσαλλόμενοι τρεῖς, οἱ δύο μὲν κάπετον,
>   αὖθι δ' ἀτυζόμενοι ψυχὰς βάλον,
> 40 εἷς δ' ἐνόρουσε βοάσαις.
>   ἔννεπε δ' ἀντίον ὁρμαίνων τέρας εὐθὺς Ἀπόλλων·
>   "Πέργαμος ἀμφὶ τεαῖς,
>   ἥρως, χερὸς ἐργασίαις ἁλίσκεται·
>   ὡς ἐμοὶ φάσμα λέγει Κρονίδα
>   πεμφθὲν βαρυδούπου Διός·

---

[17] Although the intercalated prayer may appear to be spontaneous, the careful artistry of this praise of Aigina provides little evidence of "haste" or "improvisation."

45   οὐκ ἄτερ παίδων σέθεν, ἀλλ' ἅμα πρώτοις ἄρξεται
     καὶ τετράτοις."

whom Leto's son and wide-ruling Poseidon,
as they were preparing to crown Ilion with battlements,
   summoned to help build
the wall, because the city was destined,
   once wars had begun
35 with battles that sack cities,
   to breathe forth ravening smoke.
And when the wall was freshly built, three grey snakes
tried to jump upon the rampart: two fell down
   stunned witless and gave up their lives,
40 but one leapt up with a shout of triumph.
As he considered the adverse omen, Apollo immediately declared:
"Pergamos is captured,
   hero, at the site of your handiwork;
this information is sent me by a vision
   from deep-thundering Zeus, son of Kronos —
45 not without your children; rather it will commence with the first ones
   and also with the fourth."

This myth brings together the major themes of this ode: cooperation between god and man, the role of destiny in shaping a family's successes and failures, prophecy, and accomplishment delayed for generations.[18] The major interpretative difficulty is created by the word τετράτοις (46) in Apollo's prophecy, when he says that Troy will fall to the first and fourth children of Aiakos. Several explanations have been offered,[19] but I find the most satisfactory to be that the first generation (after Aiakos by *exclusive* reckoning) refers to Telamon's sack of Troy in the time of Laomedon, while the fourth (this time counting Aiakos by *inclusive* reckoning) refers to Neoptolemos' defeat of Priam.[20] In all, four

---

[18] See Robbins, "The Broken Wall," 320-321 and Hubbard, "Aeacus in Pindar" 21-22. Carey, who identifies Timosthenes as the victor's grandfather, makes good comparisons between the myth and the victor's family ("Prosopographica Pindarica" 6): "In the victor's family Pindar sees a fateful connection (πότμος 15) with Zeus. The connection is begun by the grandfather's victory at Nemea, but it is only completed (and perceived) when his grandson wins at Olympia. Thus we have a destiny which takes generations to come to fulfilment. The myth too tells of a fated sequence of events (πεπρωμένον 33). The destiny of Troy is begun by Aiakos, but for its completion it must wait for Aiakos' descendant Neoptolemos, who will take the city."

[19] From the scholia on there have been various attempts to explain the precise meaning of Apollo's prediction. For a review of interpretations see Robbins, "The Broken Wall" 317-321 and Hubbard, "The Myth of Aeacus" 17-20. I agree with Robbins that τετράτοις should stand. Rather than emending (against all MSS) to τερτάτοις (an Aeolic form unattested elsewhere), I prefer the explanation Hubbard offers (but rejects) in note 35: "It may be that Pindar... omitted Aeacus from the counting of generations in πρώτοις but included him with τετράτοις." See Cookesley, *Pindari Carmina* 148 and Puech, *Olympiques* 108.

[20] Robbins, "The Broken Wall" 319 lists other examples of inclusive reckoning in Pindar.

generations of Aiakids are directly involved in the Trojan cycle, from the construction of Troy's walls to their destruction, and the enjambed last words of Apollo's prophecy, καὶ τετράτοις, imply them all.

This brief synopsis of Troy's history, from its beginning to its end, is projected through prophecy, a device frequently used to complete a narrative. The clause ὣς ἦρα ... εἴπαις (46), a conventional tag borrowed from epic narrative, marks the end of Apollo's prediction and initiates a rapid shift to a new topic.[21]

                 ὣς ἦρα θεὸς σάφα εἴπαις
(1)Ξάνθον ἤπειγεν καὶ Ἀμαζόνας εὐίπ-
    πους καὶ ἐς Ἴστρον ἐλαύνων.
(2)Ὀρσοτρίαινα δ' ἐπ' Ἰσθμῷ ποντίᾳ
    ἅρμα θοὸν τάννεν,
50   ἀποπέμπων Αἰακόν
—   δεῦρ' ἀν' ἵπποις χρυσέαις
    καὶ Κορίνθου δειράδ' ἐποψόμενος δαιτικλυτάν.

                After the god had spoken these clear words,
(1)he sped his team to Xanthos, to the Amazons of the fine
    horses, and to the Ister.
(2)But the god of the trident drove his swift chariot
    to the Isthmos on the sea,
50   as he escorted Aiakos
—   here with his golden team
    on his way to visit the ridge of Korinthos famed for festivals.

The depiction of the two gods' journeys (46-52) accomplishes the transition to the new topic. The emphasis shifts to Poseidon, who is climactically introduced at the beginning of the line ('Ὀρσοτρίαινα δ', 48), given a much longer treatment, and described in more specific terms. Although Apollo has played a much more important role in the narrative, Pindar reserves the longer treatment for Poseidon, who conveys Aiakos back to Aigina; and by heading on to Korinth, he not only brings us to the scene of the celebration (δεῦρ'),[22] but also subtly brings the topic

---

[21] Cf. Pyth. 4.13-56, followed by ἦ ῥα Μηδείας ἐπέων στίχες (57); Pyth. 8. 44-55, followed by τοιαῦτα μέν | ἐφθέγξατ' Ἀμφιάρηος (55-56); Pyth. 9.51-65, followed by ὣς ἄρ' εἰπὼν ἔντυεν τερπνὰν γάμου κραίνειν τελευτάν (66; on which see Bundy, Studia Pindarica 2-3); Nem. 1.61-72 (cf. ἔνεπεν, 69), which ends the ode; Isth. 6.52-54, followed by ὣς ἦρα εἰπὼν αὐτίκα | ἕζετ' (55-56); Isth. 8.35a-45, followed by ὣς φάτο Κρονίδαις | ἐννέποισα θεά (45-45a).

[22] The δεῦρ' here and τάνδ' at 25 together provide sufficient proof to dispel the notion that the ode was performed at Olympia. Boeckh, Pindari Opera 183 (followed by Dissen, Pindari Carmina 102 and Fennell, Olympian and Pythian Odes 89) claims that δεῦρο means "to the place about which we are talking." His only example, Plato, Phaido 58B, provides no convincing parallel because Phaido is there quoting the Athenian law (see Burnet, Plato's Phaedo 58). See Carey, "Two Transitions" 287 note 3.

back to athletics and celebrations by very effectively reserving the epithet "famed for its festival" (δαιτικλυτάν, 52) until the end of the long period.[23] While Apollo goes to places on rivers increasingly remote from men (the Ister implies the Hyperboreans), Poseidon comes to the mainland (ἐπ' Ἰσθμῷ ποντίᾳ) to visit his festival there. As often in such transitional passages, speed is emphasized: Apollo "hurried" (ἤπειγεν) and Poseidon rode in his "swift" (θοόν) chariot.[24]

At this point in the ode we might well expect the reintroduction of the victor and further praise of his athletic achievements. The gnome that follows could serve to introduce most any topic (53):

τερπνὸν δ' ἐν ἀνθρώποις ἴσον ἔσσεται οὐδέν.

Nothing will be equally pleasing among men.

Pindar could also have expanded this statement into a priamel, "one man will find pleasure in one thing, another in another, but as for me . . . ,"[25] but without further delay, he emphatically introduces Melesias,[26] incidentally providing the first indication in the ode that the victor is a boy (54-64):

    εἰ δ' ἐγὼ Μελησία ἐξ ἀγενείων
      κῦδος ἀνέδραμον ὕμνῳ,
55 μὴ βαλέτω με λίθῳ τραχεῖ φθόνος·
    καὶ Νεμέᾳ γὰρ ὁμῶς
    ἐρέω ταύταν χάριν,
    τὰν δ' ἔπειτ' ἀνδρῶν μάχας
    ἐκ παγκρατίου. τὸ διδάξασθαι δέ τοι
60 εἰδότι ῥᾴτερον· ἄγνωμον δὲ τὸ μὴ προμαθεῖν·
    κουφότεραι γὰρ ἀπειράτων φρένες.

---

[23] See Dissen, *Pindari Carmina* 103: "*reducimur igitur sensim ad gymnicorum certaminum cogitationem*," and Cookesley, *Pindari Carmina* 149: "This incidental allusion to games seems to bring Pindar back to his more immediate subject."

[24] Cf. *Pyth.* 3.43, where speech is followed by immediate action: ὡς φάτο· βάματι δ' ἐν πρώτῳ, and *Pyth.* 9.67-68: ὠκεῖα δ' ἐπειγομένων ἤδη θεῶν | πρᾶξις ὁδοί τε βραχεῖαι (with the comments of Bundy, *Studia Pindarica* 2-3).

[25] Σ 70 c aptly cites the priamel at *Od.* 14.228: ἄλλος γάρ τ' ἄλλοισιν ἀνὴρ ἐπιτέρπεται ἔργοις. Another (70 d) tries his hand at composing one: οὐχ ὁμοίως ἐπὶ τοῖς αὐτοῖς τέρπονται ἅπαντες· ἄλλος γὰρ ἄλλο προκρίνει. οὐδὲν δὲ τοῦ νικᾶν τερπνότερον παρὰ τοῖς ἀνθρώποις. Bundy, "Quarrel" 80 paraphrases it: "Different themes give pleasure to different people; I trust that in turning from Aiakos to Melesias I shall give offense to no one." I would alter this slightly to follow the scholia by saying "in turning to Melesias *instead of* to Alkimedon."

[26] The juxtaposition of the poet (by means of a first personal pronoun or verb) and his subject (εἰ δ' ἐγὼ Μελησία) at the head of the period is a conventional motif descended from rhapsodic hymns (e.g., αὐτὰρ ἐγώ σε, *h. Hom.* 9.8; Ἑρμῆν ἀείδω, 18.1; σεῦ δ' ἐγὼ ἀρξάμενος, 18.11). Cf. ἀλλ' ἐγὼ Ἡροδότῳ at *Isth.* 1.14 with the remarks of Bundy, *Studia Pindarica* 45.

κεῖνα δὲ κεῖνος ἂν εἴποι
ἔργα περαίτερον ἄλλων, τίς τρόπος ἄνδρα προβάσει
ἐξ ἱερῶν ἀέθλων
μέλλοντα ποθεινοτάταν δόξαν φέρειν.

  But if I have recounted in my hymn Melesias' glory
   gained from beardless youths,
55 let no ill will cast a rough stone at me,
  because I can likewise declare at Nemea too
  a victory of this sort,
— and subsequently another gained in the bouts of the men's
  pankration. The ability to teach is clearly easier
60 for one who knows, whereas it is foolish not to have foreknowledge,
  for flighty are the minds of men without experience.
  But he, more than all others, could tell
  of such accomplishments and what maneuver would advance a man,
  who from the sacred games
   would win his greatest desire, glory.

We have seen (above pages 73-75) that Pindar and Bakchylides often use negative expressions in claiming to ward off φθόνος (whether from the gods or from unspecified men) when they are bestowing praise, not because they are afraid of specific individuals, but in order to highlight the generous spirit in which they intend their eulogy to be received. Pindar is about to deliver the most extensive tribute to a trainer in the extant odes; by giving the appearance of hesitation through his use of negative expressions (cf. οὐδέν, 53; μή, 55), he is creating a tension that will be released with a triumphant vindication of his praise. But the rhetoric of this passage has long been misunderstood, for historicistic commentators from the beginning of the nineteenth century have tried to fabricate a web of anti-Athenian sentiment behind the poet's seemingly apologetic attitude,[27] but not even the scholiasts so much as hint at such nonsense. In fact, the introduction of purported Athenian-Aiginetan relations into *any* of the Aiginetan odes (and this is particularly true of *Pyth.* 8) is without basis. With respect to *Ol.* 8 several considerations militate against reading politics into the praise of Melesias. For one thing, Pindar has just praised Aigina to the skies for her treatment of foreigners

---

[27] Dissen, *Pindari Carmina* 103 noted that Melesias was an Athenian and added *idem vero invidia flagrabat apud Aeginetas*. Donaldson, *Pindar's Odes* 57 suggested that there was ill will against Melesias "because the Athenians and Aeginetans were never on good terms." From these humble seeds a thickening jungle of speculation grew, in recent years promoted by Wade-Gery, "Thucydides the Son of Melesias" 247-248 and especially by Bowra, *The Odes of Pindar* 214: "Melesias . . . is being attacked as an Athenian, and his employers almost for co-operating with the national enemy"; see his *Pindar* 151 for further details. Hints of this spicy fabrication can be found in Jebb, "Pindar" 160, Gildersleeve, *Pindar* 197-198; Fennell, *The Olympian and Pythian Odes* 90; Puech, *Pindare: Olympiques* 108; Lattimore, *The Odes of Pindar* 152; Woloch, "Athenian Trainers" 103-104; Werner, *Pindar* 514; Conway, *The Odes of Pindar* 50; and Nisetich, *Pindar's Victory Songs* 118.

(21-29); can we now suppose that Melesias constitutes a glaring exception? For another, we are not even certain that Melesias was an Athenian. The scholia to *Ol.* 8 consider him an *Aiginetan* (cf. inscr. a); only at the end of another ode, *Nem.* 4, does a scholium mention in passing ἐστὶ τὸ γένος Ἀθηναῖος (155 a).[28] Second, the dating in the scholia, even of the Olympian odes, is far from certain when not confirmed by reliable evidence, particularly by *P. Oxy.* 222.[29] Furthermore, even if the date of 460 is correct for *Ol.* 8, the decisive battles against Athens lie more than a year in the future. We have no idea what the status of Melesias or of Aiginetan affairs was in 460, a period in which all the Greek poleis were constantly adjusting relationships.[30] Finally, the passage makes sense in the context of the ode itself and can be understood on its own terms. The scholia are totally ignorant of a Pindar caught in a web of political embarrassment, but they are keenly aware of the rhetoric of the passage and offer cogent explanations. I cite one example (71 b.):

> εἰ δὲ ἐγώ, φησι, τὸ γενόμενον τῷ Μελησίᾳ ἐκ τῶν ἀγενείων κῦδος ἀνέδραμον τῷ ὕμνῳ, τοῦ Ἀλκιμέδοντος ἀφέμενος· οἷον, παρεκβὰς ἦλθον ἐπ' αὐτόν... μηδεὶς [δέ] με μεμψάσθω. Ὅμηρος· ὁ ξεῖνος εἴπερ μάλα μηνίει.

> But if, Pindar says, I have recounted the fame belonging to Melesias from beardless youths, having left off from Alkimedon; that is, I have digressed to turn to him . . . let no one blame me. As Homer says: "Even if the stranger is very angry [too bad for him]."

Far from being a cringing apology, this scholiast regarded the passage as defiantly assertive, quoting Telemachos' words to Eumaios (*Od.* 17.14-15): "Even if the stranger is very angry, it will be so much the worse for him, for (γάρ) truly I love to speak the truth."[31] Likewise, Pindar's feigned regard for the objections of any in his audience who might find extended praise of a trainer out of place is swept away by his explanation (cf. γάρ, 56).

Although it is more elaborate, the opening of *Isth.* 1 provides a close rhetorical parallel. There Pindar pretends that Delos might resent his turning to Thebes as his theme (μή μοι κραναὰ νεμεσάσαι Δᾶλος = μὴ βαλέτω με λίθῳ τραχεῖ

---

[28] See Wilamowitz, *Pindaros* 398.

[29] The scholia offer no date for *Ol.* 6, conflicting dates for *Ol.* 2, 4, 5, 9, and 10, and an incorrect date for *Ol.* 14. See the discussion by Grenfell and Hunt of *P. Oxy.* 222 in *Oxyrhynchus Papyri* 2.90-95.

[30] As we have seen, scholars cite the naval battle between Athens and Aigina in 458 as if Pindar knew more than a year in advance that it would take place and that Aigina would lose.

[31] Σ 70 a conveys an even more defiant tone: πράξω δὲ ὅμως τὸ τοιοῦτον [i.e., digress to praise Melesias], εἰ καὶ μὴ πᾶσι χαρίζομαι. "Nevertheless, I shall do it, even if I do not please everybody." Cf. also Σ 70 c: εἰ γὰρ ἀηδὲς τοῦτο τοῖς ἄλλοις δοκεῖ, ἀλλ' οὖν ἐμοὶ προσφιλές.

φθόνος), but explains that he will, through divine assistance, complete both their songs (ἀμφοτερᾶν τοι χαρίτων σὺν θεοῖς ζεύξω τέλος, 6). In *Ol.* 8 he envisions that those who want to hear about Alkimedon's Olympic victory might be irritated by his putting the trainer first.[32] This allows him to justify his putting the trainer on the level of the athlete *because* (γάρ) *he too* (καί) *likewise* (ὁμῶς) won a *similar* (ταύταν) distinction at Nemea: the praises of the trainer are praises of the athlete and vice versa (cf. αὐτῷ γέρας Ἀλκιμέδων, 65).[33] The concern is unwarranted; the poet's tact is vindicated. Why has he gone to such trouble? Any answer is complex, but one can say that this pretense has enlivened what might otherwise be a matter-of-fact recitation. Furthermore, it has revealed the poet's character as one who, like Telemachos in the passage quoted by the scholiast, is willing to speak freely whatever anyone else may think.[34] In addition, by concentrating the audience's attention on Melesias, it introduces one of the major themes of the poem: (fore)knowledge.

But first, let us attend to a detail of Pindar's style. After announcing that Melesias too had won a crown game as a boy, he continues with a brief account of his career as a man:

---

[32] A word needs to be said about the tense of the word ἀνέδραμον (54). Logically, a future is required, as Σ 71 b points out (cf. also Semonid. *fr.* 10 W, which the scholiast at Eur. *Phoin.* 207 glosses as ἐπιδραμεῖν μέλλω), but by using the aorist the poet presents his case as if it were a *fait accompli*: "If I have (now) . . . ," which I think contributes to the assured tone the scholiasts catch in their paraphrases.

[33] The ambiguity of ἐξ ἀγενείων κῦδος (54)—whether it refers to honors Melesias won "from beardless (competitors)" or "from beardless (trainees)"—is exploited in the following lines (55-66): it means both. For a different view, see Carey, "Two Transitions" 287-290, who deduces an Isthmian victory from the word δαιτικλυτάν (52).

[34] The topic itself eventually became a stereotype, as in this late (fourth-century A. D.) eulogy for a deceased professor (LP 556, Page):

> ἐὰν δὲ δόξω τῷ πάθει νικώμενος
> π]ολλαῖς ἐπαίνων ἐμπεσεῖν ὑπερβολαῖς
> τι]μῶν τὸν ἄνδρα, μηδὲ εἷς βασκαινέτω.
> φ]θόνος γὰρ οὐδείς, φησί που Δημοσθένης
> 25 ἐκ] τοῦ παλαιοῦ συγγραφέως ἀποσπάσας,
> πρὸς τ]οὺς θανόντας τοῖς ἔτι ζῶσι τέως.

> If, overcome with emotion, I appear
> to fall into great excess of praise
> as I honor the man, let no one disparage me,
> because "there is no envy," says Demosthenes
> 25 (quoting the ancient writer),
> "felt for the dead by those still living."

Although the topic arises from similar concerns, the resolution differs greatly: in this late example, a mere citation of a classical authority (here Demosthenes; cf. *de Cor.* 315) suffices to clear away all objections.

τὰν δ' ἔπειτ' ἀνδρῶν μάχας
ἐκ παγκρατίου. τὸ διδάξασθαι δέ τοι ...

The ringing ἀνδρῶν μάχας (v. l. μάχαν), followed by ἐκ παγκρατίου, enjambed at the beginning of the epode,[35] underscores Melesias' wide experience in athletics: he was victorious as an adult in the heaviest contest. The choice of the word μάχας deliberately stresses the experiential element.[36] The words τὸ διδάξασθαι turn from his career as an athlete to that of an ἀλείπτης. The following lines are full of words expressing nuances of knowledge. One who really knows (εἰδότι) his art teaches more easily. As often, Pindar then switches to negative expressions to show what it would be like *not to have* the knowledge of a Melesias: "It is foolish (ἄγνωμον) not to have foreknowledge (τὸ μὴ προμαθεῖν), for flighty are the minds (φρένες) of those without experience (ἀπειράτων)." These reflections are then followed by the climactic statement (in the positive) of what a trainer like Melesias (κεῖνος) can accomplish in preparing a man to win his heart's desire, a victory in the crown games.[37] We can reconstruct from these lines the following sequence: πεῖρα (actual experience; cf. ἀπειράτων), leading to knowledge (εἰδότι) and to προμάθεια (foreknowledge; cf. προμαθεῖν), which enable one to instruct (διδάξασθαι) others.[38]

At this point comes the climactic reintroduction of the victor:

65 νῦν μὲν αὐτῷ γέρας 'Αλκιμέδων
    νίκαν τριακοστὰν ἑλών.
)—

65 At this point his glory is Alkimedon,
    who has won his thirtieth victory.
)—

---

[35] Pindar frequently employs strophic enjambment for the contest; cf. *Nem.* 3.17: παγκρατίου στόλῳ; *Pyth.* 1.33: ἅρμασι; *Isth.* 2.17: εὐάρματον; *Isth.* 2.38: ἱπποτροφίας; *Isth.* 3.13: ἱπποδρομίᾳ; and *Ol.* 1.110: σὺν ἅρματι. See Nierhaus, *Strophe und Inhalt* 93 note 53.

[36] Cf. μάχας at Bakch. 1.144 and 2.4 (both for Argeios of Keos). The parallel with the Pindaric passage and the reference to his feet ποσσί[ν τ' ἐλα]φρό[ς] at 1.145 together suggest that Argeios' victory was in the pankration rather than in boxing.

[37] Note the emphasis that ἐξ ἱερῶν ἀέθλων receives at the head of its period. I take the prepositional phrase with φέρειν ("win fame [gained] from the games") rather than with προβάσει, which means "advance to the line" (cf. προβάς at *Nem.* 7.71). Cf. ἐξ ἀγενείων κῦδος at 54: "fame (gained) from beardless youths" and χάριν ... ἐκ παγκρατίου at 57-59: "joyous victory (gained) from the pankration."

[38] Carey, "Prosopographica Pindarica" 6 calls Melesias' foreknowledge a secular form of prophecy, which parallels Apollo's prophecy and the efforts of the *manteis*. In particular, the expression μέλλοντα ποθεινοτάταν δόξαν φέρειν (64) echoes μαιομένων μεγάλαν ἀρετὰν θυμῷ λαβεῖν (5-6); the desirous athlete needs both piety and training to win.

The grammar of this verbless sentence has occasioned a variety of interpretations, from the scholia onwards,[39] but the most meaningful reading results from supplying an ἐστίν after γέρας: "At this point (νῦν μέν) his glory [is] Alkimedon." The μέν does not simply emphasize the adverb νῦν (*contra* Slater, *Lexicon* s.v. μέν 1.b); it indicates that there are (or may be) other occasions besides the present. Like σάμερον μὲν χρή at the beginning of *Pyth.* 4 (see above page 107), it suggests that this is one of a series of such events that began in the past and may well continue into the future. Pindar is careful not to close off the possibility of more victories for Melesias. This sentence is packed with subtle grammatical interrelationships. The αὐτῷ functions as a possessive, ἀπὸ κοινοῦ, with γέρας (Alkimedon is *his* glory) and with νίκαν (it is *his* thirtieth victory), and even serves as the indirect object of ἑλών (Alkimedon won it *for him*). The triad ends with trainer and athlete sharing the limelight, but the movement of the two lines decidedly shifts the emphasis to the athlete, who is named and whose action ends the epode (ἑλών).

The final triad opens with the long-awaited praise of the athlete himself. So far he has shared his praise with Timosthenes (15), with Ζεὺς γενέθλιος (16), with his city (21-30), with his ancestor Aiakos (31-52), and with his trainer (54-66); at last he is alone on the stage (67-69):[40]

>   (1)ὃς τύχᾳ μὲν δαίμονος, (2)ἀνορέας δ' οὐκ ἀμπλακών
>   (3)ἐν τέτρασιν παίδων ἀπεθήκατο γυίοις
>   νόστον ἔχθιστον καὶ ἀτιμοτέραν γλῶσ-
>   σαν καὶ ἐπίκρυφον οἶμον,
> 70   πατρὶ δὲ πατρὸς ἐνέπνευσεν μένος
>   γήραος ἀντίπαλον.

>   (1)who, by divine destiny, (2)but also by not failing his manhood,
>   (3)on four boys' bodies put away from himself
>   a very hateful homecoming and speech with less honor
>   and an obscure path.
> 70   But into his grandfather he breathed courage
>   to wrestle against old age.

---

[39] One (86 a), followed by Gildersleeve, *Pindar* 198 and Fennell, *The Olympian and Pythian Odes* 91 suggests that the participle ἑλών stands in place of the infinitive ἑλεῖν. Two scholia supply either ἤνεγκεν or περιεποίησεν (86 a, d). I follow Σ 86 c: ἐπὶ τοίνυν τοῦ παρόντος δόξα αὐτῷ ἐστιν ὁ Ἀλκιμέδων. See Lonicerus, *Pindari Opera* 103, the earliest Latin translator (1535): *Nunc enim ipsi honos praestò est, Alcimedon trigesimam victoriam nactus* and Schmid, Πινδάρου Περίοδος 217, followed by Benedictus Πινδάρου Περίοδος 156: *Nunc quidem ipsi decus est Alcimedon victoriam tricesimam adeptus*.

[40] For an appreciation of the movement of these lines, see Schürch, *Zur Wortresponsion* 96.

In their movement these lines recall those that originally introduced Alkimedon (19-20):

> (1)ἦν δ' ἐσορᾶν καλός, (2)ἔργῳ τ' οὐ κατὰ εἶδος ἐλέγχων
> 20 (3)ἐξένεπε κρατέων
> πάλᾳ δολιχήρετμον Αἴγιναν πάτραν·
> ἔνθα ...

Each of the three elements is longer than the preceding one; the first two are joined mid-line, while the third, containing the main verb, is climactically introduced at the beginning of its line. In each case the first element concerns natural and divine endowments, while the second (stated in negative terms) shifts the emphasis to action. In the earlier passage, a τε connects the first two elements; in the latter one, the contrast is much stronger: although he had the blessing of good fortune (τύχᾳ μὲν δαίμονος) he did not fall short in manly courage (ἀνορέας δ' οὐκ ἀμπλακών). This emphasis on his manliness is explained in the third element: "on *four* children's limbs . . . ." This is the most detail Pindar gives of Alkimedon's victory: he won the hard way, by having to defeat four successive opponents.[41]

In both passages the third element introduces the *effect* of the victory on others. In the first, the victory causes his fatherland to be proclaimed; in the second, because Pindar wishes to dwell a bit longer on the triumph in order to savor its enjoyment, he depicts its disheartening effect on the four defeated boys so that he can, in contrast, describe the encouragement it brought the boy's grandfather (πατρὶ δὲ πατρός). As in the first example, the boy takes a brief bow, while the glory of his triumph radiates to others.

The introduction of the paternal grandfather comes as a surprise, for it bypasses the father, who would normally be given precedence. The following lines are ominous (72-73):

> 70 πατρὶ δὲ πατρὸς ἐνέπνευσεν μένος
> γήραος ἀντίπαλον·
> Ἀίδα τοι λάθεται
> — ἄρμενα πράξαις ἀνήρ.

> 70 But into his grandfather he breathed courage
> to wrestle against old age.
> Hades is forgotten, you know,
> — by a man who has done fitting things.

---

[41] For the topic of "winning the hard way" and a discussion of this passage in connection with *Pyth.* 8.81-87, see above pages 65-67. The word παίδων confirms the classification of his victory and neatly contrasts with his "manliness" (ἀνορέας) in the preceding line.

The word ἀντίπαλον recalls the earlier pun with the word δυσπαλές (25). Initially the gnome seems to mean that the aged grandfather, through his participation in his grandchild's victory (he undoubtedly oversaw the youth's training), is rejuvenated and forgets about his own death ('Αίδα λάθεται), but as we shall soon see, he and Alkimedon have other deaths to be consoled for. Pindar, however, leaves the matter to rest here and turns to wider concerns.

In the next strophe Pindar broadens the topic still further by turning to the *effect* of the victory on the clan.

> ἀλλ' ἐμὲ χρὴ μναμοσύναν ἀνεγείροντα φράσαι
> 75 χειρῶν ἄωτον Βλεψιάδαις ἐπίνικον,
> ἕκτος οἷς ἤδη στέφανος περίκειται
> φυλλοφόρων ἀπ' ἀγώνων.

> But I must awaken memory to announce
> 75 the foremost victories won by the hands of the Blepsiadai,
> whose sixth crown now wreathes them
> from the leaf-bearing games.

The word μναμοσύναν purposefully contrasts with the preceding λάθεται;[42] in contrast to the grandfather's forgetting Hades, Pindar returns to his obligation of awakening the memory of achievement, specifically the chief victories gained by the hands of the Blepsiadai.[43] The word ἕκτος receives emphasis from two stylistic points: it comes first in its verse and it precedes the relative pronoun.[44] The ἤδη ("now") has the additional sense of "thus far," "up to this point" and, like νῦν μέν (65), leaves open the future to additional victories.[45]

The following lines return to the theme of death and reveal why the father was never mentioned (77-84):

> ἔστι δὲ καί τι θανόντεσσιν μέρος
> κὰν νόμον ἐρδομένων·
> κατακρύπτει δ' οὐ κόνις

---

[42] For other examples of the contrast, cf. Hes. *Th.* 102-103: αἶψ' ὅ γε δυσφροσυνέων ἐπιλήθεται οὐδέ τι κηδέων | μέμνηται, and see above page 115 note 80. The expression ἐμὲ χρὴ μναμοσύναν ἀνεγείροντα φράσαι (74) is an elaboration of the hymnic verb μνήσομαι (e.g., *h. Hom.* 3.1, 7.2, and often in epilogues, where it announces a change of theme).

[43] The words ἄωτον Βλεψιάδαις ἐπίνικον (75) imply a summary treatment of their *chief* victories (cf. στεφάνων ἄωτοι at *Ol.* 9.19), soon specified as six wins in the major games: φυλλοφόρων ἀπ' ἀγώνων (76), a phrase which echoes χρυσοστεφάνων ἀέθλων (1) and ἐξ ἱερῶν ἀέθλων (64). Appropriately, the ode is full of references to crowns.

[44] Pindar frequently emphasizes a word by placing it before the relative pronoun which introduces its clause. See the list of examples at Slater, *Lexicon* s.v. ὁ A.5 (to which add *Ol.* 13.31, *Nem.* 7.90, and *Isth.* 4.35b).

[45] Cf. ἤδη at *Ol.* 13.102 and *Nem.* 2.22.

```
80      συγγόνων κεδνὰν χάριν.
        Ἑρμᾶ δὲ θυγατρὸς ἀκούσαις Ἰφίων
        Ἀγγελίας, ἐνέποι κεν Καλλιμάχῳ λιπαρὸν
        κόσμον Ὀλυμπίᾳ, ὅν σφι Ζεὺς γένει
        ὤπασεν.
```

But for those who have died there is also a share
in ritual observances,
since the dust does not bury
80   the dear joy of relatives.
   — When Iphion hears the report from Hermes' daughter
Angelia, he could tell Kallimachos about the shining
adornment at Olympia, which Zeus granted
to their family.

The word θανόντεσσιν (77) comes with great weight; the dead are now included in the celebration, for they too share in rituals. The following words specify the dead even further: they are relatives (συγγόνων) for whom the achievements of the living are dear (κεδνὰν χάριν).[46] We await the names. The point of the elaborate fiction in lines 81-84 is that the herald (under Hermes' aegis) at the games proclaimed the victory of Alkimedon, Iphion's son. The poet envisions this news (personified as Angelia, Hermes' daughter) reaching Iphion, who would then announce (ἐνέποι, 82) it to Kallimachos (presumably his brother and Alkimedon's uncle).[47] We are not told how the boy's father and uncle died, but in light of the closing prayer there is every reason to believe that they died of disease.[48]

```
        ἐσλὰ δ' ἐπ' ἐσλοῖς
85      ἔργα θέλοι δόμεν, ὀξείας δὲ νόσους ἀπαλάλκοι.
        εὔχομαι ἀμφὶ καλῶν
            μοίρᾳ νέμεσιν διχόβουλον μὴ θέμεν·
        ἀλλ' ἀπήμαντον ἄγων βίοτον
        αὐτούς τ' ἀέξοι καὶ πόλιν.
```

[46] Note the effective hypallage of συγγόνων κεδνὰν χάριν (contrast e.g., κεδνῶν τοκέων at Isth. 1.5). Dornseiff, Pindars Stil 39 calls attention to two other instances of hypallage in Ol. 8: τεαῖς χερὸς ἐργασίαις (42) and ἐν τέτρασιν παίδων ἀπεθήκατο γυίοις (68).

[47] Dissen, Pindari Carmina 107 credits K. O. Müller with the discovery of this conceit. Carey, "Prosopographica Pindarica" 6 proposes that Kallimachos is the victor's father because "it is surprising that the father should be treated as an intermediary in this way rather than, as at the close of O. 14, as the recipient of the news of the son's victory." But the point of the conceit is precisely that Iphion would have heard his own name announced by the herald (just as Kleodamos does in Ol. 14) and would thus be in a position to inform the other relative, Kallimachos.

[48] When relatives are killed in battle, Pindar makes note of the fact (cf. Isth. 4.16-17b and Isth. 7.25 ff.).

>   May he [Zeus] willingly give
> 85   good works upon good works, and ward off painful diseases.
>   I pray that when it comes to their portion of blessings he not bear
>   resentment with its wavering counsel,
>   but rather grant them a lifetime free from pain,
>   and make them and their city burgeon.

The prayer is addressed to Zeus, who has dominated the poem in many roles: as overseer of the games at Olympia and at Nemea, at which Alkimedon and Timosthenes have won (cf. 3, 16-18), as the patron of the clan (cf. Ζηνὶ γενεθ-λίῳ, 16), as the *paredros* of Themis (Διὸς ξενίου, 21) revered by the city of Aigina, and in the myth as the sender of the omen to Apollo (cf. Κρονίδα... βαρυγδούπου Διός, 43-44). In order to lead into the prayer, Pindar neatly reserves the name of Zeus (the fifth time he is mentioned by name in the ode)[49] until the end of the section depicting the news of the victory traveling to Hades: ὅν σφι Ζεὺς γένει | ὤπασεν (83-84). These words define the aspect upon which the prayer will draw: his role as guardian of the genos (cf. Ζηνὶ γενεθλίῳ, 16).

The prayer consists of five petitions. The first leads naturally from the preceding words, Ζεὺς γένει | ὤπασεν (83-84), for θέλοι δόμεν asks for a continuance of past benefits depicted by the verb ὤπασεν, namely that the efforts (cf. ἔργα, 85) of Alkimedon and his family meet with additional (ἐπ', 84) successes.[50] Since the second petition is the only one in the epinician odes that requests freedom from diseases (νόσους ἀπαλάλκοι, 85), it is difficult to avoid the conclusion that Alkimedon's family had suffered from them.[51] The third petition, introduced by εὔχομαι in asyndeton, is the longest and contains three parts. The first two provide variations of the first two petitions. The one (86) requests Zeus not to waver in his counsel and be annoyed at their successes.[52] The

---

[49] The artistic variations on Zeus' names and powers throughout the ode are worthy of note; Pindar reserves the nominative form until the last to provide a smooth transition to the prayer. In one sense, this ode is an extended hymn to Zeus.

[50] For other odes that conclude with prayers for further victories, cf. in particular *Pyth.* 5.124 (note ἔπι and γένει) and *Isth.* 7.49-51; see also Bundy, *Studia Pindarica* 77-78.

[51] The qualification ὀξείας (85) may indicate that they suffered from especially painful ones.

[52] This is a very difficult passage. Many personify Nemesis (e.g., Gildersleeve, *Pindar* 200; Sandys, *Pindar* 93; Bowra, *Pindar* 213; Conway, *The Odes of Pindar* 51; Swanson, *Pindar's Odes* 36), but with no warrant from the text or the scholia. Besides, it is most irregular to conceive of Zeus making Nemesis do anything, for she is above him. Slater, *Lexicon* s.v. νέμεσις gives its meaning as "apportionment," which makes good sense, but I cannot find any parallel. I take the phrase νέμεσιν... μὴ θέμεν (86) as equivalent to μὴ... νεμεσάσαι (*Isth.* 1.3) on the analogy of *Pyth.* 4.276: θέμεν σπουδάν (= σπεύδειν); cf. Σ 113 a: μὴ φθονηθῆναι. The qualification διχόβουλον (86), however, presents a problem. A very similar expression occurs at *Nem.* 10.89, when Polydeukes "did not make his counsel double" (οὐ διπλόαν θέτο βουλάν), meaning that he unhesitatingly chose life for Kastor. The phrase νέμεσιν διχόβουλον, however, is difficult to construe. I would translate it, "when it comes to their portion of blessings, may he not bear resentment with its wavering counsel," that is, may he wholeheartedly and unhesitatingly be pleased with the successes of the family and continue to grant

other (87) is similar to the request in 85 about warding off diseases, but more general: it asks for a life free of pain. There is considerable artistry in the use of negative expressions in this series of requests. The first is positive ("Continue to grant"), the next three are negative ("Ward off diseases," "Do not be resentful," "Give a life free of pain"), and the last is positive ("Make them and their city burgeon"). The gradation is very subtle: Pindar uses a verb of avoidance (ἀπαλάλκοι, 85), a prohibition (μὴ θέμεν, 86), an ἀ-privative (ἀπήμαντον, 87), and finally a positive verb (ἀέξοι, 88). The ἀλλά (87) sets off the last two requests as they lead from avoidance of pain, subordinated by the participle ἄγων (87), to the climactically positive verb (ἀέξοι, 88). The last word, πόλιν (88), recalls the high praise of Aigina earlier in the ode and serves as a reminder (like καὶ πόλις at *Ol*. 7.94) that the city shares in the success of its citizens.

Conclusion

In the context of Pindar's victory odes, three elements are necessary for successful performance (i.e., ἀρετά, ἔργα): divine dispensation (e.g., πότμος, αἶσα, τύχα, θεός, δαίμων), natural ability (e.g., φυά, μορφά), and training (e.g., διδασκαλία, (προ)μανθάνειν, μελέτα).[53] There are numerous other factors, such as wealth (πλοῦτος), determination (τόλμα), and ambition (μέριμνα), but the above three categories have proved to be the most important in the subsequent tradition. *Ol*. 8 explores the interrelationship of these three elements. First is divine dispensation, depicted in the opening hymn to Olympia, where seers attempt to learn of Zeus' will. This aspect is the central point of the myth where Troy is destined (cf. πεπρωμένον, 33) to fall at the hands of Aiakos' descendants. Alkimedon's own career has been blessed with all three factors. Destiny has made Zeus the patron of his family (ὔμμε δ' ἐκλάρωσεν πότμος | Ζηνὶ γενεθλίῳ, 15-16) and he won by divine dispensation (τύχᾳ δαίμονος, 67). He possessed ability (cf. καλός ... εἶδος, 19; ἀνορέας, 67) and was well trained by Melesias, whose practical knowledge (cf. εἰδότι, 60) facilitates his teaching (τὸ διδάξασθαι, 59). His instruction carries with it the test of experience (contrast ἀπειράτων, 61) and his kind of foreknowledge (cf. προμαθεῖν, 60) provides the best means for being victorious.

---

additional ones. This makes it similar to such prayers for continued favor as at *Pyth*. 10.20-21: μὴ φθονεραῖς ἐκ θεῶν μετατροπίαις ἐπικύρσαιεν. The scholia, however, understand διχόβουλον to mean "of opposing counsel" and gloss it with ἐναντίαν, but once again I cannot find a clear parallel. Although the general meaning of the prayer is not in doubt, its precise sense is.

[53] The Sophists distinguished three requirements (ability, instruction, and practice), thereby eliminating from consideration divine assistance (or subsuming it under natural gifts). In turn, they distinguished carefully between instruction and practice, which are not differentiated by Pindar. For an overview of these terms, see Shorey, "Φύσις, Μελέτη, Ἐπιστήμη" 185-201.

I cannot see how Fennell supposed that the ode lacked unity. Every section is logically connected and takes its place in the overall scheme of the ode, which praises the achievement of Alkimedon within a universe ruled by Zeus, and as part of an ethnic tradition extending from Aiakos, through a clan (the Blepsiadai), and to a family with its own joys and sorrows. From beginning to end it provides a meditation on the nature of success—how its foundations are laid by gods, furthered by family predecessors who may not live to share directly in the victories of their offspring (Aiakos, Iphion, Kallimachos), aided by expert teaching, and finally realized in deed (cf. ἔργον at 19, 63, and 85). All of these factors and considerations lie behind this boy's victory at Olympia, the queen of truth.

APPENDIX 1

CLIMACTIC PAIRS

In *Chapter 1* we concentrated on climactic passages containing three or more members. Here we shall examine a number of pairs, where the second is longer and receives more emphasis. In each case we shall try to determine why Pindar chooses to emphasize the second and what rhetorical purpose it serves in its ode. We shall start with four examples from *Pyth.* 1, beginning with one of the best-known passages in antiquity, the ἔκφρασις of Aitna's eruption at *Pyth.* 1.22-24:

(1)ποταμοὶ δ' ἀμέραισιν
μὲν προχέοντι ῥόον καπνοῦ
αἴθων'· (2)ἀλλ' ἐν ὄρφναισιν πέτρας
φοίνισσα κυλινδομένα φλὸξ ἐς βαθεῖ-
αν φέρει πόντου πλάκα σὺν πατάγῳ.

(1)during the days rivers of lava
pour forth a tawny stream
of smoke, (2)but in times of darkness
a rolling red flame carries rocks into the deep
expanse of the sea with a crash.

The second half of the description is longer, more intense, and much more impressive. Portents are generally more terrifying at night (cf. *Nem.* 1.48-58). In the daytime the smoke is the most visible feature of the erupting volcano, whereas at night the red flame stands out (cf. *Ol.* 1.1-2: αἰθόμενον πῦρ ... διαπρέπει νυκτί) and sounds are amplified.[1] By thus building to a climax (cf. μὲν ...

---

[1] Macrobius (5.17.11) comments on the accuracy of Pindar's daytime and nighttime descriptions. As commentators are wont to point out, the second element even mimics the sound of the crashing boulders. The emphasis also shifts from sight to sound in the following pair of clauses (26): τέρας μὲν θαυμάσιον προσιδέσθαι, θαῦμα δὲ καὶ παρεόντων ἀκοῦσαι, lending support to interpreters from Dissen to Kirkwood who interpret παρεόντων as a genitive absolute ("when people are present").

ἀλλά), Pindar ends the period and this description on a note of wonder (cf. τέρας ... θαῦμα, 26) before completing his treatment of Typhos (27-28).[2]

After quoting the proverb "good outing, better return" at 33-35, Pindar predicts that Aitna's successes will continue into the future or, given φερτέρου (35), perhaps even improve (35-38):

> ὁ δὲ λόγος
> ταύταις ἐπὶ συντυχίαις δόξαν φέρει
> λοιπὸν ἔσσεσθαι (1)στεφάνοισί ν⟨ιν⟩ ἵπποις τε κλυτάν
> (2)καὶ σὺν εὐφώνοις θαλίαις ὀνυμαστάν.

> And this saying,
> given this present success, inspires the expectation that the city
> hereafter will be (1)renowned for its crowns and horses,
> (2)and have its name proclaimed amid tuneful festivities.

The two parts of this prediction contain the two elements necessary for happiness. The doublet στεφάνοισι ἵπποις τε, hendiadys for "victorious horses,"[3] constitutes success (εὖ παθεῖν). It is followed by celebration in song (εὖ ἀκούειν).[4] The emphasis, as usual in Pindar, falls on the latter: it is longer, it begins its verse with an emphatic καί, and it completes the period.

As the poet turns to final praise of Hieron in lines 81 ff., he exhorts himself to be brief, explaining that thereby he will lessen criticism (μῶμος ἀνθρώπων, 82). In the following lines he gives two reasons for such censure (82-84):

> (1)ἀπὸ γὰρ κόρος ἀμβλύνει
> αἰανὴς ταχείας ἐλπίδας,
> (2)ἀστῶν δ' ἀκοὰ κρύφιον θυμὸν βαρύ-
> νει μάλιστ' ἐσλοῖσιν ἐπ' ἀλλοτρίοις.

> (1)for nagging tedium
> dulls keen expectations,
> (2)and citizens can be grieved in their secret hearts
> especially when they hear of others' successes.

We might term the first reason aesthetic, since it shows concern for the tedium produced by a speaker's prolixity that dulls listeners as they begin to anticipate the

---

[2] He uses what Bundy, *Studia Pindarica* 3-14 has called the θαῦμα motive to end his painterly description. For other examples of the motif of wonder used to punctuate descriptions, see Race, *Classical Genres* 56-67.

[3] Cf. στεφάνων ἀρετᾶν τε ("crowned achievements") at *Nem.* 3.8.

[4] For many more examples of this "double crown," see above pages 122-125 and below pages 192-194.

next topic. Everyone has experienced that moment when an audience says to itself, "That's enough of that, let's get on with it." The second reason is ethical, for it concerns the relationship between the audience and the person being praised, specifically between Hieron and his fellow citizens (note the emphatic ἀστῶν, 84), not all of whom in the intense political environment of a major Greek polis will be delighted to see him successful. The length of the second reason and its position at the beginning of the line (reinforced by δέ) lead one to expect that it is the more important of the two, and in fact the following lines bear this out, for Pindar rejects it strongly (ἀλλ' ὅμως, κρέσσον γὰρ οἰκτιρμοῦ φθόνος, | μὴ παρίει καλά, 85-86) and continues in the rest of the ode to counsel Hieron on the proper treatment of his fellow citizens (by which, of course, he will minimize their envy).

And as he completes his exhortation to Hieron, he offers two examples of rulers for consideration in lines 94-98:

(1)οὐ φθίνει Κροί-
σου φιλόφρων ἀρετά.
95 (2)τὸν δὲ ταύρῳ χαλκέῳ καυτῆρα νηλέα νόον
ἐχθρὰ Φάλαριν κατέχει παντᾷ φάτις,
οὐδέ νιν φόρμιγγες ὑπωρόφιαι κοινανίαν
μαλθακὰν παίδων ὀάροισι δέκονται.

(1)The loving-minded excellence
of Kroisos does not perish,
95 (2)but that man of pitiless spirit, Phalaris, who burned others
in his bronze bull, is overwhelmed by universal execration,
and no lyres in banquet halls welcome him
into gentle fellowship with boys' voices.

Of course it is Kroisos' "loving-minded *areta*" that embodies the true model for Hieron, but Pindar chooses instead to emphasize the negative example. It begins its line with the emphatic τὸν δέ (95), is much longer, and is much more intense. There are good reasons for Pindar to end with it. First of all, it provides a realistic warning: all too often Sicilian tyrants abused their power. Secondly, Pindar avoids both the flattery that would attach to his comparing Hieron directly to Kroisos and the subsequent envy it might arouse in others.[5] Finally, this vivid warning emphasizes the seriousness of his role as advisor to the king (cf. ὦ φίλε, 92). He has chosen his words carefully: the name of Kroisos survives

---

[5] Because of his lavish dedications at Delphi, it was only natural that eulogists should recognize Hieron as a modern-day Kroisos, as does Bakchylides in his third ode. But Pindar has already compared Hieron in lines 50-55 to Philoktetes (in the section on Hieron's "deeds of war"), and perhaps for that reason (along with his stated concern for avoiding envy) he softens the obvious comparison in this section.

because it is his *areta* that continues to live; Phalaris' name also continues to be spoken, but only as invective in the mouths of everyone (ἐχθρὰ παντᾷ φάτις, 96);[6] he is no fitting subject for encomia such as the present song. Pindar has skillfully ended the negative portrayal by actually depicting the positive celebration (ὅπως οὐκ ἔχει), thereby ringing back to the opening of the ode. In sum, the flattery implicit in the comparison with Kroisos is mitigated by the warning presented in the depiction of Phalaris.

In a number of places where Pindar mentions two gods, the emphasis falls on the second. At *Ol.* 7.49-51 Pindar reports the blessings showered on Rhodes by Zeus and Athena:

(1)κεί-
νοις ὁ μὲν [sc. Ζεὺς] ξανθὰν ἀγαγὼν νεφέλαν
50 πολὺν ὗσε χρυσόν· (2)αὐτὰ δέ σφισιν ὤπασε τέχναν
— πᾶσαν ἐπιχθονίων Γλαυκ-
ῶπις ἀριστοπόνοις χερσὶ κρατεῖν.

(1)Zeus
brought a yellow cloud and upon them
50 rained gold in abundance; (2)but the grey-eyed goddess herself gave
— them every kind of skill to surpass mortals
with their superlative handiwork.

In this passage Pindar bypasses (cf. μέν, 49) the wealth that Zeus has showered upon Rhodes,[7] in order to concentrate on the technical skills that Athena herself (αὐτά, 50) provided them and which are praised in the following lines (52-53) as the source of their great fame (κλέος βαθύ, 53).

At *Nem.* 3.50 Pindar notes that two goddesses marvelled at Achilleus' youthful prowess in hunting; he gives slight emphasis to Athena, who was his great champion throughout his career: τὸν ἐθάμβεον (1)Ἄρτεμίς τε (2)καὶ θρασεῖ' Ἀθάνα. As goddess of the hunt, Artemis naturally admires Achilleus' ability; Athena's epithet "bold" indicates the aspect of his character that she particularly admired. At *Isth.* 1.30-32 Pindar completes his rhapsodic hymn to Iolaos and Kastor by bidding the heroes farewell:

---

[6] Contrast *Pyth.* 3.112, where Nestor and Sarpedon are "spoken of by everyone" (ἀνθρώπων φάτις) because of their renown in epic poetry.

[7] The detail of Zeus' shower of gold elaborates the notice in the Homeric catalogue about Tlepolemos' Rhodes (*Il.* 2.670): καί σφιν θεσπέσιον πλοῦτον κατέχευε Κρονίων. See Young, *Three Pindaric Odes* 82-85. Pindar foreshadows this emphasis on Athena at line 43, when Helios tells his children that they would gladden with sacrifices the heart of the father and of his spear-thundering daughter: (1)πατρί τε θυμὸν ἰάναιεν (2)κόρᾳ τ' ἐγχειβρόμῳ.

30 (1)Ἰφικλέος μὲν παῖς ὁμόδαμος ἐὼν Σπαρτῶν γένει,
   (2)Τυνδαρίδας δ' ἐν Ἀχαιοῖς
       ὑψίπεδον Θεράπνας οἰκέων ἕδος.
   χαίρετ'.

30 (1)Iphikles' son belonging to the race of the Spartoi,
   (2)and the son of Tyndareus dwelling among the Achaians
       on his highland abode of Therapna.
   Farewell.

The climactic presentation of the two heroes preserves their intrinsic importance (Kastor is semi-divine) before their dismissal (χαίρετ', 32), in spite of the fact that Iphikles is the more pertinent model for the Theban victor, Herodotos.[8]

In order to emphasize the bond that unites Thebes and Aigina in the wake of the Persian War, Pindar recounts the favor of Zeus for their eponymous nymphs at *Isth.* 8.19-23:

     ὃ (1)τὰν μὲν παρὰ καλλιρόῳ
20   Δίρκᾳ φιλαρμάτου πόλι-
       ος ᾤκισσεν ἀγεμόνα·
)—
     (2)σὲ δ' ἐς νᾶσον Οἰνοπίαν
       ἐνεγκὼν κοιμᾶτο, δῖον ἔνθα τέκες
     Αἰακὸν βαρυσφαράγῳ πατρὶ κεδνότατον
     ἐπιχθονίων· ὃ καί ...

     Zeus (1)established Theba beside the beautiful streams
20   of Dirka to dwell as mistress
        of a chariot-loving city;
)—
     (2)but you he brought to the island of Aigina
        and slept with you, and there you bore divine
     Aiakos, dearest of mortals to his father
     of the deep-rumbling thunder. And Aiakos ...

There is no doubt about the emphasis to the second example receives by its greater length, its placement at the beginning of the triad, and its direct address; it also leads into the main narrative.

One and the same pair of elements can appear in either order, depending on the demands of the particular rhetorical circumstances. For example, at *Ol.* 6.58-59 Iamos steps into the middle of the Alpheios river to pray to his two divine progenitors for the gift of "people-nourishing honor":

---

[8] Cf. the similar procedure at *Pyth.* 11. 59-64; see Race, "Six Crowns" 37.

> ἐκάλεσσε (1)Ποσειδᾶν' εὐρυβίαν,
> ὃν πρόγονον, (2)καὶ τοξοφόρον Δά-
> λου θεοδμάτας σκοπόν ...
>
> he called upon (1)widely-ruling Poseidon,
> his grandfather, (2)and the bow-wielding watcher
> over divinely-built Dalos ...

Poseidon (his maternal grandfather) is designated by the general epithet "widely-ruling," whereas Apollo is specifically called the watcher over his sacred *sedes* at Delos. Throughout the narrative, his father Apollo has played the more important role, and in the following lines (61 ff.) it is he who directly answers Iamos' prayer and bestows upon him the gift of prophecy. In contrast, at *Ol.* 8.46-52 (see above pages 152-153) the order is reversed as Apollo yields to Poseidon, who conveys Aiakos to Aigina and returns the topic to athletics.

At *Isth.* 4.19-20, the poet cites two of Poseidon's cultic centers:

> ὁ κινητὴρ δὲ γᾶς (1)'Ογχηστὸν οἰκέων
> 20 (2)καὶ γέφυραν ποντιάδα πρὸ Κορίνθου τειχέων ...
>
> The shaker of the earth (1)dwelling at Onchestos
> 20 (2)and at the sea-flanked bridge before the walls of Korinthos ...

The emphasis appropriately falls on the second element because the poet is proceeding from the Boiotian cultic center near the Theban athlete to the Isthmos, where he won his victory. At *Isth.* 1.32-34, another ode to a Theban, he reverses the order:

> ἐγὼ δὲ (1)Ποσειδάωνι (2)'Ισθμῷ τε ζαθέᾳ
> (3)'Ογχηστίαισίν τ' ἀιόνεσσιν περιστέλλων ἀοιδάν
> γαρύσομαι τοῦδ' ἀνδρὸς ἐν τιμαῖσιν ἀγακλέα τὰν
> 'Ασωποδώρου πατρὸς αἶσαν.
>
> But as I attire (1)Poseidon (2)and the sacred Isthmos
> (3)and Onchestos' shores in my song
> I shall proclaim in this man's praises the famous fortune
> of his father Asopodoros.

In this case he has already announced the victory and therefore leads from the game site to the local Boiotian cultic center, in order to introduce the topic of the victor's father whose estate is in the neighboring city of Orchomenos.[9]

---

[9] For a more detailed analysis of this passage, see above pages 27-28. A subtle example of reversal occurs in a pair of stock phrases at *Isth.* 4.10: (1)φθιμένων (2)ζωῶν τε φωτῶν and at

Pindar twice uses examples of foxes and lions to discuss the qualities of those he is praising. One is the gnome that concludes *Ol.* 11.19-20:

τὸ γὰρ ἐμφυὲς (1)οὔτ' αἴθων ἀλώπηξ
20   (2)οὔτ' ἐρίβρομοι λέοντες διαλλάξαιντο ἦθος.

For (1)neither ruddy fox
20   (2)nor roaring lions would exchange their inborn character.

There is no doubt that greater emphasis is placed on the second example: it begins its line, it is longer, and the epithet ἐρίβρομοι is more impressive than the mere αἴθων, as lions are more impressive than foxes. The switch to the plural also helps to give greater weight to the lions. In part because of this climactic emphasis Bundy was led to interpret the gnome as "subjective" and argued that the lions stood for the poet of natural talent as opposed to the fox, who represented a merely artful versifier. Although his interpretation gave some point to the epithet ἐρίβρομοι, it was ultimately untenable, as many critics of his *Studia Pindarica* were quick to point out.[10] But the climactic order also makes excellent sense if the gnome applies to the inborn characteristics of the Western Lokrians, who were just praised for wisdom and martial courage ἀκρόσοφόν τε καὶ αἰχματάν (19). Surely the fox represents the first quality, while the lions embody their prowess in war, another instance of the doublet *sapientia et fortitudo*.

At *Isth.* 4.45-47 in praise of the pankratiast Melissos, Pindar reverses the two comparisons:

45   (1)τόλμᾳ γὰρ εἰκώς
θυμὸν ἐριβρεμετᾶν θηρῶν λεόντων
ἐν πόνῳ, (2)μῆτιν δ' ἀλώπηξ,
αἰετοῦ ἅ τ' ἀναπιτναμένα ῥόμβον ἴσχει.

45   (1)He resembles the courage
of loudly-roaring lions in his heart
during the struggle, (2)but in skill he is a fox,
which rolls on its back to check the swoop of the eagle.

Isth. 7.30: (1)ζώων τ' (2)ἀπὸ καὶ θανών. In the first instance, Pindar emphasizes the living men because he wishes to stress the continuity of athletic prowess that has distinguished Melissos' family and still continues with its living representative. In the latter, he emphasizes death because he is praising the victor's uncle who fell in battle. For a brief account of the topic of *heros mortuus/vivens*, see Young, *Isthmian 7* 20-23.

[10] When I first met Bundy in spring 1973, I asked him if there was anything in *Studia Pindarica* that he would change after ten years. Without hesitation he answered that it would be his analysis of the ending of *Ol.* 11. He said that he had originally interpreted it as "objective," but that in writing it up he came to see that a case could also be made for its referring to the poet. He said that he decided to present the weaker case just to arouse some debate!

Why does the fox hold the climactic position here? Pindar lavishes praise on the athlete's courage in the actual trial (ἐν πόνῳ), but his skill is his more remarkable quality, because, as we are informed in the following lines, he was smaller than his opponents and had to compensate with skill for what he was denied by nature (cf. φύσιν, 49).[11]

At *Nem.* 1.26-30 Pindar again employs the doublet of wisdom and strength, this time in praise of Chromios:

> (1)πράσσει γὰρ ἔργῳ μὲν σθένος,
> (2)βουλαῖσι δὲ φρήν, ἐσσόμενον προϊδεῖν
> συγγενὲς οἷς ἕπεται.
> (3)'Αγησιδάμου παῖ, σέο δ' ἀμφὶ τρόπῳ
> 30 τῶν τε καὶ τῶν χρήσιες.

> (1)For strength achieves its result in action,
> (2)but wisdom in counsels, for those who are
> naturally endowed to foresee what will happen.
> (3)But, Son of Hagesidamos, in your manner
> 30 there are uses for both.

Here the emphasis falls on intelligent counsel (cf. μὲν ... δέ), but Pindar then caps the climactic pair with the vaunt that Chromios possesses the use of both.[12]

At *Pyth.* 8.6-12 occurs the only instance in the epinicians of an anaphoric address in a hymn, when Pindar lists the two powers of Hesychia:

> (1)τὺ γὰρ τὸ μαλθακὸν ἔρξαι τε καὶ παθεῖν ὁμῶς
> ἐπίστασαι καιρῷ σὺν ἀτρεκεῖ·
> (2)τὺ δ' ὁπόταν τις ἀμείλιχον
> καρδίᾳ κότον ἐνελάσῃ,
> 10 τραχεῖα δυσμενέων
> ὑπαντιάξαισα κράτει τιθεῖς
> ὕβριν ἐν ἄντλῳ ...

> (1)For you know how to produce gentleness and equally
> to enjoy it with accurate propriety;
> (2)and you, whenever someone fixes implacable

---

[11] For a discussion of this topic, see below page 191.

[12] In this respect he resembles his leader Hieron, who possesses martial valor and wise counsel; cf. *Pyth.* 2.63-65: νεότατι μὲν ἀρήγει θράσος ... βουλαὶ δὲ πρεσβύτεραι. For other examples of two terms being surpassed by a third which unites them both with a form of ἀμφότερος, cf. *Pyth.* 1.99, 10.2, *Nem.* 6.2, and *Isth.* 1.6; see Bundy, *Studia Pindarica* 37-39. Cf. also *Pyth.* 11.43-45, where τῶν (45) unites both father and son. Carey, *Five Odes* 114-116 argues that three separate terms (σθένος, φρήν, and μαντεία) form a priamel, but the μὲν ... δέ construction proves that ἐσσόμενον ... ἕπεται qualifies βουλαῖσι δὲ φρήν.

Appendix 1

            hatred in his heart,
10   roughly oppose the
            aggression of enemies by putting
            it in the bilge ...

Like the lyre at the beginning of *Pyth.* 1, Hesychia has a dual nature (cf. μαλθακὸν ... τραχεῖα, 6-10); she not only produces pleasure for good men, but also overwhelms enemies.[13] In both cases, Pindar emphasizes the latter ability; he then expands upon the last trait with the examples of Porphyrion and Typhos.

At *Ol.* 1.87 Poseidon honors Pelops' prayer by giving him his chariot and team to race against Oinomaos.

86b   τὸν μὲν ἀγάλλων θεός
         ἔδωκεν (1)δίφρον τε χρύσεον (2)πτεροῖ-
)—   σίν τ' ἀκάμαντας ἵππους.

86b   The god honored him
         with the gift of (1)a golden chariot (2)and winged
)—   horses that never tire.

The golden chariot is surpassed by the winged horses, which are the real wonder of his divine gift to Pelops. There is no Myrtilos here; in Pindar's version Pelops wins because his team is divine. The mention of the tireless horses ends the epode. The first word of the final triad is ἕλεν (88); there is no appreciable interval between the giving of the gift and the successful trial.

In *Nem.* 9, Pindar uses a climactic doublet to compare Chromios to Hektor (39-42):

                          (1)λέγεται μὰν
               "Εκτορι μὲν κλέος ἀνθῆσαι Σκαμάνδρου χεύμασιν
40   ἀγχοῦ, (2)βαθυκρήμνοισι δ' ἀμφ' ἀκταῖς Ἑλώρου,
—   ἔνθ' Ἀρείας πόρον ἄνθρωποι καλέοισι, δέδορκεν
              παιδὶ τοῦθ' Ἁγησιδάμου φέγγος ἐν ἁλικίᾳ πρώτᾳ.

                        (1)Truly they say
             that Hektor's fame blossomed by Skamandros'
40   streams, (2)but by the craggy banks of the Heloros,
—   at the place men call Areia's Ford, such a beacon shone forth
            for the son of Hagesidamos in his earliest youth.

---

[13] Cf. the same elements in the climactic pair that ends *Nem.* 4.95-96: **μαλακὰ** μὲν φρονέων ἐσλοῖς, | **τραχὺς** δὲ παλιγκότοις ἔφεδρος. For a detailed analysis of Hesychia's powers, see Bundy, *Hesychia in Pindar*.

The μὲν... δέ construction and the supplementary details noticeably shift the emphasis to Chromios' first victory,[14] while the elaborate chiastic structure ("Εκτορι | κλέος ἀνθῆσαι | Σκαμάνδρου χεύμασιν → ἀκταῖς Ἑλώρου | δέδορκεν φέγγος | παιδὶ Ἁγησιδάμου) demarcates the comparison as a unit.

At the end of the same ode Pindar uses two climactic pairs to depict the celebration of Chromios' equestrian victory (48-53):

> (1)ἡσυχία δὲ φιλεῖ
> μὲν συμπόσιον· (2)νεοθαλὴς δ' αὔξεται
> μαλθακᾷ νικαφορία σὺν ἀοιδᾷ·
> θαρσαλέα δὲ παρὰ κρατῆρα φωνὰ γίνεται.
> 50 (1)ἐγκιρνάτω τίς νιν, γλυκὺν κώμου προφάταν,
> —   (2)ἀργυρέαισι δὲ νωμάτω φιάλαισι βιατάν
> ἀμπέλου παῖδ', ἅς ποθ' ἵπποι...

> (1)Peace loves
> the symposium, (2)but the victory flourishes
> with new bloom to the strains of soft song,
> and the voice waxes confident beside the wine-bowl.
> 50 (1)Let someone mix the bowl, the sweet prophet of the revel,
> —   (2)and let him serve the powerful child of the vine
> in the silver cups, which his horses once...

The first pair, as Bundy pointed out, contrasts (cf. μὲν... δ') the relaxation after toil (ἡσυχία), which loves the symposium, with the song's ability to make the victory blossom again.[15] A climactic pair of imperatives then follows to move attention from the mixing bowl to the silver cups, which commemorate his victory at Sikyon and symbolize the sharing of the victory among fellow citizens.

In *Nem.* 11 Pindar reviews two reasons for failure (29-32):

> ἀλλὰ βροτῶν (1)τὸν μὲν κενεόφρονες αὖχαι
> 30 ἐξ ἀγαθῶν ἔβαλον· (2)τὸν δ' αὖ καταμεμφθέντ' ἄγαν
> ἰσχὺν οἰκείων παρέσφαλεν καλῶν
> χειρὸς ἕλκων ὀπίσσω θυμὸς ἄτολμος ἐών.

> But of mortals (1)empty-minded confidence expels
> 30 one man from good achievements, (2)while a timid spirit,
> holding back by the hand another man who overly slights

---

[14] Cf. a similar emphasis on the location in the climactic introduction of the battle of Himera at *Pyth.* 1.79: παρὰ δὲ τὰν εὔυδρον ἀκτὰν Ἱμέρα.

[15] See Bundy, *Studia Pindarica* 23. In note 51 he recommends putting a full stop after ἀοιδᾷ (49), arguing that the following sentence begins a new movement depicting the singing and drinking at the celebration. I think rather that it elaborates on the preceding sentence.

his own strength, deprives him of distinctions that belong to him.

Much greater emphasis is given to the second element, because in this ode Aristagoras' parents curtailed his athletic career before he could compete in the Pythian and Olympian games.

At *Pyth.* 2.67-71 Pindar makes a major shift in the ode, as he turns from praise of Hieron, whom he dismisses with a hymnal farewell (χαῖρε, 67), to the remainder of the ode.

   χαῖρε· (1)τόδε μὲν κατὰ Φοίνισσαν ἐμπολάν
   μέλος ὑπὲρ πολιᾶς ἁλὸς πέμπεται·
   (2)τὸ Καστόρειον δ' ἐν Αἰολίδεσσι χορδαῖς θέλων
70 ἄθρησον χάριν ἑπτακτύπου
   φόρμιγγος ἀντόμενος.

    Farewell. (1)This song is being sent like Phoenician
  merchandise over the grey sea;
  (2)but as for this Kastoreion song in Aiolic strains, may you gladly
70 receive this gift of the seven-stringed
  lyre and look favorably upon it.

In (1) he describes the preceding portion of the song as having been sent on a Phoenician merchant vessel. Presumably he is stressing its lavish praise and its contractual nature. In contrast (μέν ... δ'), the part of the ode that remains is described as a Kastoreion song (i.e., for a chariot victory) sung in Aeolic melody. That the second receives the emphasis is clear from its position at the beginning the line, its greater length, and the direct address to Hieron. Of particular importance is the fact that he is here addressed as if he were a god, thus continuing the hymnal style apparent in the farewell χαῖρε. In fact, the whole passage is a reworking of the rhapsodic closing in which the poet bids the god farewell, asks him to be pleased with the song, and informs him that he will proceed to another subject. Here Hieron is asked to come forward and look favorably (θέλων, 69) on this song, which Pindar describes as a χάριν (70). Whereas the preceding lines have been composed to fulfill a contractual obligation (cf. ἐμπολάν, 67), the coming lines are composed in a spirit of friendly counsel.[16] The purpose of this transitional passage is to prepare for the remarkable addendum to the ode that offers counsel (couched in first-personal recommendations) instead of praise, much as the last triad of *Pyth.* 1 turns from praise to counsel.[17]

---

[16] For the contrast between the poetic obligation and the freely given song, cf. *Ol.* 10.7-12: χρέος ... χάριν.

[17] Kirkwood, *Selections* 154 and Most, *Measures of Praise* 96-101 rightly reject any reference in τὸ Καστόρειον to another poem, but they see in the μέν ... δέ antithesis a contrast between two qualities in the whole poem rather than between two parts of the poem. See Bundy,

Pindar often presents pairs of victories in climactic order. At the end of *Isth.* 1 he prays that his praise may inspire Herodotos to go on to win in more prestigious games (65-67):

> 65   ... ἔτι καὶ (1)Πυ-
> θῶθεν (2)'Ολυμπιάδων τ' ἐξαιρέτοις
> 'Αλφεοῦ ἔρνεσι φράξαι χεῖρα τιμὰν ἑπταπύλοις
> Θήβαισι τεύχοντ'.

> 65   ... that also (1)from
> Pytho (2)and from the Olympics he may wreathe
> his hand with the choicest garlands from the Alpheos, as he
> brings honor to Thebes.

The simple Πυθῶθεν is topped by the lavish description of the "choice" Olympic crown. Likewise, in *Isth.* 3 Melissos' previous Isthmian victory in the pankration is eclipsed by his Nemean victory in the chariot race (11-13):

> (1)ἐν βάσσαισιν 'Ισθμοῦ
> δεξαμένῳ στεφάνους, (2)τὰ δὲ κοίλᾳ λέοντος
> — ἐν βαθυστέρνου νάπᾳ κάρυξε Θήβαν
> ἱπποδρομίᾳ κρατέων.

> (1)winning crowns in the Isthmian
> glens, (2)and then in the hollow valley
> — of the deep-chested lion he had Thebes proclaimed
> when he won the chariot race.

Once again the more impressive victory is given much more detailed treatment and in this case the event's impressiveness is enhanced by its enjambment at the beginning of the epode.

At *Nem.* 11.24-26 Pindar avows that had Aristagoras competed in the greatest games he would have been victorious. The emphasis is on an Olympic victory:

> ἐμὰν δόξαν (1)παρὰ Κασταλίᾳ
> 25 (2)καὶ παρ' εὐδένδρῳ μολὼν ὄχθῳ Κρόνου
> κάλλιον ἂν δηριώντων ἐνόστησ' ἀντιπάλων.

"Quarrel" 84 note 103. For a formal parallel, cf. *Nem.* 4.44-45: ἐξύφαινε... καὶ τόδ'... Λυδίᾳ σὺν ἁρμονίᾳ μέλος πεφιλημένον, which introduces the forthcoming portion of the poem. Note that the word πεφιλημένον, like χάριν at *Pyth.* 2.70 (cf. φίλιον at *Pyth.* 1.60 and φίλαν ἐς χάριν at *Ol.* 10.12), indicates that the forthcoming song is motivated by generosity and friendship.

>   In my opinion, had he gone to compete (1)at Kastalia
> 25   (2)and at the well-wooded hill of Kronos,
>   he would have had a better homecoming than his wrestling opponents.

At *Nem.* 10.27-28 Pindar catalogues the Isthmian and Nemean victories of Theaios in climactic order:

> (1)τρὶς μὲν ἐν πόντοιο πύλαισι λαχών,
> (2)τρὶς δὲ καὶ σεμνοῖς δαπέδοις ἐν Ἀδραστείῳ νόμῳ.

> (1)three times having won at the gates to the sea,
> (2)and three times as well on the hallowed ground in the tradition established by Adrastos.

The second element receives considerable emphasis: it is longer, more impressive, has the proper name Adrastos, and ends its period (before the striking address to Zeus that follows at 29: Ζεῦ πάτερ). Most important of all is the weight imparted by the particles μὲν ... δὲ καί. Generally, Pindar tends to emphasize Isthmian over Nemean victories. Here, presumably, he wishes to connect Nemea closely to Argos, the victor's home, through Adrastos, the Argive hero.

In two instances Pindar presents two possibilities as an either-or choice in which the latter is clearly the intended one, even though he never expressly says so. In his appeal to Arkesilas to repatriate the exiled Damophilos, Pindar tells the riddle of Oidipous about the oak tree, which, in spite of having been felled and stripped, still remains useful (266-269):

> (1)εἴ ποτε χειμέριον πῦρ ἐξίκηται λοίσθιον,
> (2)ἢ σὺν ὀρθαῖς κιόνεσσιν
>   δεσποσύναισιν ἐρειδομένα
> μόχθον ἄλλοις ἀμφέπει δύστανον ἐν τείχεσιν,
> ἐὸν ἐρημώσαισα χῶρον.

> (1)if eventually it ends up in a winter's fire,
> (2)or if, pressed into service
>   with upright columns,
>   it performs a wretched labor in alien walls,
>   having left its own place desolate.

The greater relevance of the second analogy to the exiled Damophilos is patent—in spite of many fanciful interpretations—especially in the three concluding words "having left its own place (or land) desolate." The point is that the native worth of Damophilos is still a valuable asset in spite of his having been shorn of his position and outwardly disgraced (cf. αἰσχύνοι δέ οἱ θαητὸν εἶδος, 264). And if Arkesilas does not realize this potential, Damophilos will be put into service in another city (ἄλλοις... ἐν τείχεσιν, 268). Indeed the very last words of the poem, Θήβᾳ ξενωθείς (299), inform Arkesilas that Damophilos has already found a warm welcome in Thebes. But by the choice of the words μόχθον... δύστανον he indicates that Damophilos cannot be happy serving another master. What remains is for Arkesilas to be certain of the good intentions of the exile; Pindar supplies that reassurance in lines 279-299. While there is some worth in Damophilos' serving as fuel, how much better would it be for him to be a supporting beam in the government at Kyrene.[18]

At *Pyth.* 11.22-28 Pindar poses two reasons for Klytaimestra's murder of Agamemnon:

>   (1)πότερόν νιν ἄρ' Ἰφιγένει' ἐπ' Εὐρίπῳ
> σφαχθεῖσα τῆλε πάτρας
>   ἔκνισεν βαρυπάλαμον ὄρσαι χόλον;
> (2)ἦ ἑτέρῳ λέχεϊ δαμαζομέναν
> 25 ἔννυχοι πάραγον κοῖται; τὸ δὲ νέαις ἀλόχοις
> — ἔχθιστον ἀμπλάκιον καλύψαι τ' ἀμάχανον
> ἀλλοτρίαισι γλώσσαις·
> κακόλογοι δὲ πολῖται.

>   (1)Was it the sacrificial slaughter of Iphigeneia
>   at the Euripos far from her homeland
>   that provoked her to kindle her heavy-handed anger?
>   (2)Or did sleeping at night in subjection to another's bed
> 25   cause her to stray? That sin
> — is most hateful in young wives and impossible to conceal
>   because of others' tongues,
>   since townsmen are scandalmongers.

---

[18] A few lines later in his appeal to Arkesilas to heal the rifts in the city, Pindar contrasts how easily disruptions can occur with the difficulty of restoring proper order (272-274):

> (1)ῥᾴδιον μὲν γὰρ πόλιν σεῖσαι καὶ ἀφαυροτέροις·
> (2)ἀλλ' ἐπὶ χώρας αὖτις ἕσσαι δυσπαλὲς
>   δὴ γίνεται, ἐξαπίνας
> εἰ μὴ θεὸς ἁγεμόνεσσι κυβερνατὴρ γένηται.

> (1)For easily can even weaklings disrupt a city;
> (2)but to set her back in place again is a difficult
>   task indeed, unless a god suddenly
>   comes to guide the leaders.

Pindar had just said that Arkesilas has the cure for his city's ills and that Paian Apollo supports him. Here he reassures him of that divine help which can facilitate the difficult task of rebuilding after a political crisis. Thus the passage moves from the disruption of order at the lowest levels (cf. ἀφαυροτέροις, 272) to the divine guidance that enables leaders to bring secure rest to the city.

The first reason entails what was done to her, and because she was the passive victim we may feel some sympathy for her χόλος. But the second is her own doing and Pindar describes it as a "most hateful sin" (ἔχθιστον ἀμπλάκιον, 26). Although Pindar never answers the question—indeed, both play an important part in the estrangement from Agamemnon that turned her into a "pitiless woman" (νηλὴς γυνά, 22)—the emphasis falls on the second reason. We are left with the impression of an unfaithful wife hounded by scandalous rumors.[19]

We shall end with the most elaborate series of climactic pairs in the odes, as Pindar rings changes on the doublet *sapientia et fortitudo* in praise of Korinthos' ancient renown for wisdom and courage in battle at *Ol.* 13.49-60:

    ἐγὼ δὲ ἴδιος ἐν κοινῷ σταλείς
50 (1)μῆτίν τε γαρύων παλαιγόνων
  (2)πόλεμόν τ' ἐν ἡρωίαις ἀρεταῖσιν
   οὐ ψεύσομ' ἀμφὶ Κορίνθῳ, (1a)Σίσυφον
   μὲν πυκνότατον παλάμαις ὡς θεόν,
  (1b)καὶ τὰν πατρὸς ἀντία Μή-
   δειαν θεμέναν γάμον αὐτᾷ,
   ναῒ σώτειραν Ἀργοῖ καὶ προπόλοις·
55 (2a)τὰ δὲ καί ποτ' ἐν ἀλκᾷ
   πρὸ Δαρδάνου τειχέων ἐδόκησαν
   ἐπ' ἀμφότερα μαχᾶν τάμνειν τέλος,
  (2a1)τοὶ μὲν γένει φίλῳ σὺν Ἀτρέος
   Ἑλέναν κομίζοντες, (2a2)οἱ δ' ἀπὸ πάμπαν
60 εἴργοντες· ἐκ Λυκίας δὲ Γλαῦκον ἐλ-
   θόντα τρόμεον Δαναοί. τοῖσι μέν . . .

  But I, as an individual embarked upon a public theme,
50 (1)in proclaiming the intelligence of their ancestors
  (2)and warfare amidst their heroic achievements,
   shall tell no lies about Korinthos, by citing (1a)Sisyphos,
   like a god in his very shrewd skillfulness,
  (1b)and Medea who defied her father
   to make her own marriage
   and to become the savior of the Argo and her crew;
55 (2a)and formerly as well in their might
   before the walls of Dardanos they came to be considered

---

[19] See van Groningen, *La composition* 359: "Des deux explications qu'il nous donne de son crime c'est sans doute la seconde qui prévaut à ses yeux." The emphasis on her adultery also prepares for the concluding words of the narrative: θῆκέ τ' Αἴγισθον ἐν φοναῖς (37). Pindar's climactic presentation accords well with the observation of Herington, "Pindar's Eleventh *Pythian*" 141-143, that a similar shift of emphasis occurs in the course of Aischylos' *Agamemnon*. For an opposing view of the relationship between Pindar and Aischylos, see Robbins, "Pindar's *Oresteia*."

>   on both sides decisive in determining the outcome of the battles,
>   (2a1)whether they came with the dear son of Atreus in an effort
>   to recover Helen, (2a2)or at every turn were trying to
> 60   prevent them: for the Danaans trembled before Glaukos
>   who came from Lydia, and to them he boasted . . .

Pindar first sketches the two qualities of the Korinthians in an order which emphasizes their prowess in war. Unless there is some compelling reason for a reversal, we would expect them to be elaborated in the same order and with a similar emphasis, and so they are, but they are very skillfully subdivided.[20] The first two examples, in climactic order, are (1a) Sisyphos and (1b) Medea. The latter example opens with an emphatic καὶ τάν (53) at the beginning of its line and continues to the end of the strophe. The antistrophe is devoted to the heroic exploits in the Trojan war, where Korinthians fought on both sides (2a). These are then subdivided into those (τοὶ μέν, 58) who fought on the Greek side (2a1), and those (οἱ δ', 59) who were allies of the Trojans (2a2). By ending with Glaukos, Pindar can follow Homer's lead (cf. *Il.* 6.152-211) and introduce the narrative of his ancestor Bellerophon (63-92). In the manner of a priamel, these lines sketch Korinthian glories before arriving at the one crowning example, Bellerophon, who combines both traits of the Korinthians: inventiveness and martial prowess.[21]

---

[20] On the analogy of τοῦδ' ἀνδρὸς ἐν τιμαῖσιν at *Isth.* 1.34 and ἐν κορυφαῖς ἀρετᾶν μεγάλαις at *Nem.* 1.34, Bundy, *Studia Pindarica* 52 note 45 maintained that the phrase ἐν ἡρωίαις ἀρεταῖσιν applies to the present-day heroic exploits of Korinthos' athletes, but it is awkward to reintroduce them at this point, especially when the phrase aptly describes the forthcoming exploits of the Korinthians in epic.

[21] See Carey, "Three Myths" 162 note 74.

APPENDIX 2

BAKCHYLIDES' OPENING HYMNS

Bakchylides inherited the same hymnal conventions as Pindar, but his opening hymns differ from Pindar's in several important respects. For one thing, they are much shorter: the longest is a mere fourteen short lines. In none are there "personal concerns" as in *Nem.* 3 or *Isth.* 1, impressive catalogues as in *Isth.* 7, vivid scenes as in *Pyth.* 1, or dynamic goddesses such as Hesychia (*Pyth.* 8), Eleithyia (*Nem.* 7), Hora (*Nem.* 8) or Theia (*Isth.* 5). Indeed, it is fair to say that none has that memorable grandeur which Pindar imparts to every one of his opening hymns.[1]

Cultic Hymns

The differences between the two poets' styles will become clearer by comparing an opening cultic hymn by each. First, Pindar's hymn to Eleithyia (*Nem.* 7.1-8):

    Ἐλείθυια, πάρεδρε Μοιρᾶν βαθυφρόνων,
    παῖ μεγαλοσθενέος, ἄκου-
        σον, Ἥρας, γενέτειρα τέκνων· ἄνευ σέθεν
    οὐ φάος, οὐ μέλαιναν δρακέντες εὐφρόναν
    τεὰν ἀδελφεὰν ἐλάχομεν ἀγλαόγυιον Ἥβαν.
5   ἀναπνέομεν δ' οὐχ ἅπαντες ἐπὶ ἴσα·
    εἴργει δὲ πότμῳ ζυγένθ' ἕτερον ἕτερα. σὺν δὲ τίν
    καὶ παῖς ὁ Θεαρίωνος ἀρετᾷ κριθείς
    εὔδοξος ἀείδεται Σωγένης μετὰ πενταέθλοις.

We have already analyzed this hymn in some detail (above pages 87-89) and have seen that the depiction of the goddess' powers and their effects on men in general provides a serious meditation on the relationship between one's natural endow-

---

[1] For a general comparison and assessment of Pindar's and Bakchylides' opening hymns, see Schadewaldt, *Aufbau* 276 and Carey, "Bakchylides' Experiments" 15-16.

ments at birth and the success he achieves as he matures. Bakchylides' hymn to Nika at 11.1-14, his longest (and perhaps most impressive) opening hymn, provides a good basis for comparison:

      Νίκα γλυκύδωρε· [⏑ – γὰρ
      σοὶ πατ[ὴρ – – ⏑ – –
      ὑψίζυ[γος – ⏑ ⏑ –
      ἐν πολυχρύσωι ⟨τ'⟩ Ὀλύμπωι
5   Ζηνὶ παρισταμένα
      κρίνεις τέλος ἀθανάτοι-
      σίν τε καὶ θνατοῖς ἀρετᾶς·
      ἔλλαθι, [βαθυ]πλοκάμου
      κούρα Σ[τυγὸς ὀρ]θοδίκου· σέθεν δ' ἕκατι
10   καὶ νῦ[ν Μετ]απόντιον εὐ-
      γυίων κ[ατέ]χουσι νέων
      κῶμοί τε καὶ εὐφροσύναι θεότιμον ἄστυ·
      ὑμνεῦσι δὲ Πυθιόνικον
      παῖδα θαητ[ὸ]ν Φαΐσκου.

      Victory of the sweet gift,
      . . . . . .
      and in golden Olympos,
5   standing at Zeus' side,
      you decide the outcome
      of achievement for immortals and mortals,
    look favorably, daughter of thick-haired
      Styx of straight judgment, for thanks to you
10   revelry and good cheer
      of strong-limbed youths
    now possess the divinely-honored town of Metapontion,
    as they sing of the Pythian victor,
      the glorious son of Phaïskos.

The following table reveals the remarkable verbal similarities of these two hymns.

Bakch. 11.1-14	*Nem.* 7.1-8
Ζηνὶ παρισταμένα (5)	πάρεδρε Μοιρᾶν (1)
κρίνεις (6)	κριθείς (7)
ἀρετᾶς (7)	ἀρετᾷ (7)
ἔλλαθι (8)	ἄκουσον (2)
κούρα Σ[τυγὸς ὀρ]θοδίκου (9)	παῖ μεγαλοσθενέος Ἥρας (2)
σέθεν δ' ἕκατι (9)	σὺν δὲ τίν (6)
καὶ νῦ[ν (10)	καί (7)

εὐγυίων (10-11) ἀγλαόγυιον (4)
ὑμνεῦσι (13) ἀείδεται (8)
παῖδα Φαΐσκου (14) παῖς Θεαρίωνος (7)

In spite of the close resemblances of vocabulary, form, and function,[2] the two hymns differ in one important respect. In the analysis of Pindar's hymn to Eleithyia, we saw how economically he uses epithets to define the characteristics and powers of the goddesses, and noted that even the seemingly ornamental epithet ἀγλαόγυιον may point to a function of Heba that deepens her significance in the hymn. In contrast, the adjective εὐγυίων (10-11), used of the young revelers in Bakchylides' hymn, is scarcely more than decorative, and the same is true of ὑψίζυ[γος (3), πολυχρύσωι (5), and [βαθυ]πλοκάμου (8). Only γλυκύδωρε (1) and ὀρθοδίκου (9) assume any importance by suggesting that victory is a gift of the gods awarded according to venerable principles of justice.[3] Rarely does one sense that Pindar chooses a word merely for its decorative appeal, and each rereading of a Pindaric hymn reveals hidden depths of insight. In contrast, to a great extent because of the profusion of epithets, Bakchylides' hymns tend to glitter on the surface and rarely reveal any deeper significance.[4]

---

[2] For example, both hymns reserve the most specific information until the last sentence: σὺν δὲ τίν | καὶ παῖς ὁ Θεαρίωνος ... ἀείδεται (Nem. 7.6-8) = σέθεν δ' ἕκατι | καὶ νῦ[ν] ... ὑμνεῦσι ... παῖδα θαητ[ὸ]ν Φαΐσκου (Bakch. 11.9-14).

[3] Since, however, the epithet γλυκύδωρος occurs in two other opening hymns, at 3.3 (modifying Kleio) and at 5.4 (modifying the ἄγαλμα of the Muses), it appears to be little more than ornamental; ὀρθόδικος also occurs at 14.23 (modifying Kleoptolemos of Thessaly).

[4] A comparison of Bakchylides' hymn to Hestia (14B) with the hymn to Hestia that opens Nem. 11 reveals similar differences between the poets' styles. The hymn (probably to Day) that opens Bakch. 7, provides a representative sample of Bakchylides' inefficient verbiage, particularly in lines 6-10, where he uses vocabulary very similar to that we have seen in his hymn to Nika (11.1-14) and in Pindar's hymn to Eleithyia (Nem. 7):

    ... κρίνειν τα[χυτᾶτά τε] λαιψηρῶν ποδῶν
    Ἕλλασι καὶ γυί[ων ἀ]ριστάλκες σθένος·
    ὦι δὲ σὺ πρεσβύ[τατο]ν νείμηις γέρας
    νίκας, ἐπ' ἀνθρ[ώπ]οισιν εὔδοξος κέκλη-
10   ται καὶ πολυζή[λωτ]ος ...

    ... to judge the swiftness of fleet feet
    for Greeks and the limbs' overpowering strength;
    and he whom you grant your foremost award
    of victory, is called famous among men
10   and greatly envied ...

For one thing the adjective λαιψηρῶν merely repeats what is implicit in τα[χυτᾶτα, but even more revealing is his use of six words (ἐπ' ἀνθρ[ώπ]οισιν εὔδοξος κέκληται καὶ πολυζή[λωτ]ος) to convey the thought that Pindar expresses in two at Nem. 7.8: εὔδοξος ἀείδεται. For an opposite assessment of Bakchylides' use of epithets in narrative, see Segal, "Bacchylides

Perhaps the most remarkable of all Bakchylides' openings is the hymnal address to Hieron in Ode 5:

> Εὔμοιρε [Σ]υρακ[οσίω]ν
> ἱπποδινήτων στρατα[γ]έ,
> γνώσηι μὲν [ἰ]οστεφάνων
> Μοισᾶν γλυκ[ύ]δωρον ἄγαλμα, τῶν γε νῦν
> 5   αἴ τις ἐπιχθονίων,
> ὀρθῶς· φρένα δ' εὐθύδικ[ο]ν
> ἀτρέμ' ἀμπαύσας μεριμνᾶν
> δεῦρ' ⟨ἄγ'⟩ ἄθρησον νόωι.

> Blessed commander of the Syracusans
>   with charging horses,
>   you will recognize the sweet-gifted offering
>   of the violet-crowned Muses
> 5 as truly as any man now alive.
>   Rest your straight-judging
>   mind calmly from your concerns
>   and, come, direct your attention here.

Like a god, Hieron has an epithet ("blessed") and a title ("commander"). His *sedes* is Syracuse; his powers consist of martial leadership and preeminent knowledge of poetry.[5] There is even a request that he be well-disposed (φρένα ... ἀτρέμ' ἀμπαύσας μεριμνᾶν is an elaborate periphrasis of the conventional εὐμενής or πρόφρων), that he be present (δεῦρ' ⟨ἄγ'⟩, 8), and that he take heed (ἄθρησον, 8). Scholars have failed to recognize the extent to which Bakchylides treats Hieron like a god in this passage.[6] In two places Pindar approaches such language in addressing Hieron: at *Ol.* 6.98, when he hopes that Hieron (whom he has praised at length) will favorably receive Hagesias' celebration (δέξαιτο κῶμον), and at *Pyth.* 2.69-71, when he asks Hieron, as if he were a god, to look favorably upon his song.[7]

Reconsidered," who employs modern poetic concepts of imagery, emotive psychology, and associationism to uncover contrasts and resonances which create moods and articulate themes.

[5] These qualities are variations of the doublet *fortitudo et sapientia*; see above page 96 note 31.

[6] Kambylis, "Anredeformen" 146-147 finds hymnal elements in addresses to humans only in Pindar *frr.* 105, 120, and 122. See 181 note 3, where he follows Meyer, *Hymnische Stilelemente* 55 note 30 in denying that the opening of Bakch. 5 imitates hymnal addresses.

[7] Bundy, *Studia Pindarica* 78 calls the former passage a "hymn to Hieron"; for an analysis of the latter, see above page 175.

Appendix 2

Combinations of Rhapsodic and Cultic Elements

Three of Bakchylides' epinikia open in the rhapsodic tradition, and, like Pindar's, they exhibit varying degrees of complexity. Ode 3 is the most straightforward.

> Ἀριστο[κ]άρπου Σικελίας κρέουσαν
> Δ[ά]ματρα ἰοστέφανόν τε Κούραν
> ὕμνει, γλυκύδωρε Κλεοῖ, θοάς τ' Ὀ-
> λυμ]πιοδρόμους Ἱέρωνος ἵππ[ο]υς.

> Of Demeter, who rules over Sicily of bountiful harvest,
> and of violet-crowned Kore,
> sing, Kleio of sweet gifts, and of Hieron's swift
>   Olympic-running horses.

The rhapsodic core, ὕμνει Κλεοῖ (cf. ὕμνει Μοῦσα at *h. Hom.* 4.1), designates the subjects of the hymn: Demeter (whose *sedes* is Sicily), Persephone, and the horses of Hieron. The address to Kleio separates the divine subjects from the human one (tactfully introduced by τ'), which ends the strophe.

The opening of 9.1-6 is more complex.

> Δόξαν, ὦ χρυσαλάκατοι Χάρι[τ]ες,
>   πεισίμβροτον δοίητ', ἐπεί
> Μουσᾶν γε ἰοβλεφάρων θεῖος προφ[άτ]ας
> εὔτυκος Φλειοῦντά τε καὶ Νεμεαίου
> Ζηνὸς εὐθαλὲς πέδον
> 5 ὑμνεῖν, ὅθι . . .

> O Charites of the golden spindle, grant me
>   the glory that persuades men, for
> the inspired spokesman of the violet-eyed Muses
> is ready to sing of Phleious and of Nemean
> Zeus' flowering
> 5 plain, where . . .

Bakchylides expands the invocation by differentiating two aspects of poetic endeavor. The first, under the control of the Charites, seeks to endow poetry with persuasive charm (δόξαν ... πεισίμβροτον); the second, under the guidance of the Muses, seeks an accurate presentation of the substance.[8] Instead of a rhapsod-

---

[8] Cf. Homer's invocation of the Muses at *Il.* 2.485: πάρεστέ τε, ἴστέ τε πάντα and Pindar *Pa.* 6.54-55: ἴσθ' ὅτ[ι], Μο[ῖ]σαι, πάντα. For the relationship between the Charites, who provide persuasive charm, and the Muses, who know the factual truth, see above page 124.

ic imperative to the Charites (cf. Χάριτες... ὑμνεῖτε at *Nem.* 10.1-2), Bakchylides addresses a cultic prayer to them, using the explanatory clause (cf. ἐπεί, 2) to present the details of the victory.

He follows the same pattern at 12.1-7:

> Ὡσεὶ κυβερνήτας σοφός, ὑμνοάνασ-
>   σ' εὔθυνε Κλειοῖ
> νῦν φρένας ἁμετέρας,
> εἰ δή ποτε καὶ πάρος· ἐς γὰρ ὀλβίαν
> 5 ξείνοισί με πότνια Νίκα
> νᾶσον Αἰγίνας ἀπάρχει
> ἐλθόντα κοσμῆσαι θεόδματον πόλιν...

> Like a skilled helmsman, song-ruling
>   Kleio, direct
> now my thoughts,
> if ever you did so in the past, for queenly
> 5 Victory is dispatching me on behalf of guest-friends
> to the prosperous island of Aigina,
> to go and celebrate the divinely-built city...

Here he replaces the simple rhapsodic request to the Muse with a cultic prayer to Kleio, adding a brief *hypomnesis* (εἰ δή ποτε καὶ πάρος). As in the previous example, an explanatory clause (γάρ, 4) provides the poet's statement of purpose and the announcement of his theme. These cultic adaptations in Odes 9 and 12 permit the poet to add more "subjective" warmth than in the much more "objective" rhapsodic opening of Ode 3. For example, in 9 he calls himself "the divine spokesman of the Muses" and is "eager" to celebrate Nemea, while in 12 he suggests a long-standing relationship with his Muse, Kleio, and close friendship with the Aiginetans. But never does he combine rhapsodic and cultic elements with the boldness of Pindar's *Ol.* 10, *Nem.* 3, and *Isth.* 7.

APPENDIX 3

VARIATIONS ON TWO TOPICS

The more closely one observes the ways in which Pindar subtly varies every topic that he treats and how each word receives precisely calculated emphasis from its place in the developing thought and from its location in the verse, the more likely it appears that there are few (if indeed any) casual slips in his poetry, that he knowingly places each word in such a way that it contributes to the design of its passage, and eventually to the design of the whole poem.[1] Such, at least, should be the working assumption for reading any poetry written according to classical standards of composition. But it also becomes apparent that in constructing a particular poem, Pindar is also keenly aware of his other poems. There is no other indication so clear that his poems were written compositions intended to be read closely and that he conceived of his work as a whole than the fact that while he often says essentially the same thing, he never says it in precisely the same way. This is an important indication that, although he maintains a fiction of orality and spontaneity in his odes, he is a highly self-conscious artist, constantly aware of exactly what he has said in his other poems.[2]

---

[1] Cf. the description of Pindar's "austere" style by Dionysios of Halikarnassos (de Comp. 22 init.): "It requires that the words should be like columns firmly planted and placed in strong positions, so that each word should be seen on every side, and that the parts should be at appreciable distances from one another, being separated by perceptible intervals" (W. R. Roberts, trans.). Herington, "Pindar's Eleventh *Pythian* Ode," 139 note 4 reaches a similar conclusion: "I may not be alone in having found, empirically, that the archaic poets employ words as if they had the weight, substance, and reality of things; and that they locate them with a care similar to that with which a sculptor might locate a figure in a pediment."

[2] Even when he comes close to repeating himself, the similarities are more tantalizing than exact. Cf. *Ol.* 12.6a: μεταμώνια τάμνοισαι κυλίνδοντ' ἐλπίδες with *Pyth.* 3.23: μεταμώνια θηρεύων ἀκράντοις ἐλπίσιν. Both are metrically equivalent, both come at the end of their stanzas, both express the failure of futile wishes, but the differences in syntax, metaphorical expressions, emphasis, and function in their contexts are even more striking than their similarities. Cf. also *Ol.* 8.21-23 (to Aigina): ἔνθα σώτειρα Διὸς ξενίου | πάρεδρος ἀσκεῖται Θέμις with *Nem.* 11.8-9 (to Tenedos): καὶ ξενίου Διὸς ἀσκεῖται θέμις, and *Isth.* 1.28: τῶν ἀθρόοις ἀνδησάμενοι θαμάκις | ἔρνεσιν χαίτας with *Isth.* 5.8: ὄντιν' ἀθρόοι στέφανοι | χερσὶ νικάσαντ' ἀνέδησαν ἔθειραν. The fact that all these examples are dactylo-epitritic also contributes to their similarity.

Perhaps the best way of observing Pindar at work is by examining how he treats the same topic in different odes. I have chosen two of the most frequent, "appearance and action" and "the limits of human success." We shall see that in these, as throughout his work, the dominant principle is ποικιλία, constant variety, for he continually refuses to repeat himself exactly, or, to put it positively, he loves to display ever new nuances of meaning in commonplace expressions, what Dionysios of Halikarnassos (in another context) calls his μεταβολῆς ἔρως (*de Comp*. 19). Let us begin with a typical statement in praise of success that adds a *memento mori* proviso (*Nem*. 11.13-16):

> εἰ δέ τις ὄλβον ἔχων μορφᾷ παραμεύσεται ἄλλους,
> ἔν τ' ἀέθλοισιν ἀριστεύων ἐπέδειξεν βίαν,
> 15   θνατὰ μεμνάσθω περιστέλλων μέλη,
> καὶ τελευτὰν ἁπάντων γᾶν ἐπιεσσόμενος.

> If a man possessing wealth surpasses others in comeliness,
> and in contests displays his strength by winning,
> 15   let him remember that mortal are the limbs he clothes
> and that earth is the last garment of all he will wear.

This passage combines two themes that run throughout the odes and which are subjected to a rich array of variations. The topic of the first two lines concerns the relationship between appearance and action, while that of the last two lines sets forth the limits of human success. Implicit in the first half is a distinction between goods that come to the athlete from outside (wealth and beauty), and the honors he wins with his own actions. The movement of the sentence shows that there is increasing emphasis on the three items in terms of length—(1)ὄλβον ἔχων (2)μορφᾷ παραμεύσεται ἄλλους, (3)ἔν τ' ἀέθλοισιν ἀριστεύων ἐπέδειξεν βίαν—and that the last one, although introduced by a mere τ', fills an entire line and is the one of most importance in an epinician ode.[3]

Let us compare the eight occasions in the odes when Pindar uses this *topos*, as old as the *Iliad* and frequently encountered in inscriptions, which expresses the relationship between an individual's physical appearance (his κάλλος, μορφά, φύσις, εἶδος, δέμας) and his performance (his ἔργα, κράτος, ἀρετά).[4] Here are the eight passages.

---

[3] The verbal forms in the three elements are also increasingly longer and more intense: ἔχων ... παραμεύσεται ... ἀριστεύων ἐπέδειξεν. The ἔχων is a dependent participle, παραμεύσεται is a conditional subjunctive (see Gerber, "Short-Vowel Subjunctives" 84-85), whereas ἐπέδειξεν (augmented by ἀριστεύων) states a fact.

[4] The first occurrence of the topic is Homer's description of Aias at *Od*. 11.550-551:

> ... ὃς πέρι μὲν εἶδος, πέρι δ' ἔργα τέτυκτο
> τῶν ἄλλων Δαναῶν μετ' ἀμύμονα Πηλεΐωνα.

Appendix 3

1. *Ol.* 8.19:

    ἦν δ' ἐσορᾶν **καλός**, **ἔργῳ** τ' οὐ κατὰ **εἶδος** ἐλέγχων ...

    He was *beautiful* to behold, and *in action* not discrediting his *looks* ...

2. *Ol.* 9.65-66:

    ὑπέρφατον ἄνδρα **μορφᾷ** τε καί | **ἔργοισι**.

    a man beyond description in *comeliness* and | *deeds*.

3. *Ol.* 9.94:

    ὡραῖος ἐὼν καὶ **καλὸς** κάλλιστά τε **ῥέξαις**.

    being *youthful* and *beautiful* and *performing* most beautiful deeds.

4. *Nem.* 3.19:

    εἰ δ' ἐὼν **καλὸς ἔρδων** τ' ἐοικότα **μορφᾷ** ...

    If, being *beautiful* and *performing* deeds to match his *comeliness*...

5. *Nem.* 11.13-14:

    εἰ δέ τις ὄλβον ἔχων **μορφᾷ** παραμεύσεται ἄλλους,
    ἔν τ' **ἀέθλοισιν ἀριστεύων** ἐπέδειξεν βίαν ...

    If a man possessing wealth surpasses others in *comeliness*,
    and in *contests* displays his strength by *winning* ...

6. *Isth.* 7.22:

    σθένει τ' ἔκπαγλος **ἰδεῖν** τε **μορ-
    φάεις**, ἄγει τ' ἀρετὰν οὐκ αἴσχιον **φυᾶς**.

    in strength he is awesome and *hand-
    some to behold*, and he *performs* no worse than he *looks*.

Cf. the epigram on Theognetos of Aigina attributed to Simonides (11.3D = *Anth. Pal.* 16.2.3): κάλλιστον μὲν **ἰδεῖν**, **ἀθλεῖν** δ' οὐ χείρονα **μορφῆς**. The topic also exists in an early Latin epitaph: *quoius* **forma** *virtutei* **parisuma** *fuit* (*CIL* I 2.6-9, quoted in *Camb. Hist. of Classical Lit. II* 57). Cf. the famous variation at Vergil, *Aen.* 5.344: *gratior et* **pulchro** *veniens in* **corpore** *virtus*. See also Young, *Isthmian 7* 19 note 61.

7. *Ol.* 10.100-104:

100   ... τὸν εἶδον **κρατέοντα** χερὸς ἀλκᾷ
       βωμὸν παρ' Ὀλύμπιον
       κεῖνον κατὰ χρόνον
       ἰδέᾳ τε καλόν
       ὥρᾳ τε κεκραμένον ...

100   ... whom I saw *winning* with the strength of his hand
       by the altar at Olympia
       at that time,
       beautiful of *form*
       and imbued with *youthful bloom* ...

8. *Isth.* 4.49-51:

       οὐ γὰρ **φύσιν** Ὠαριωνείαν ἔλαχεν·
50   ἀλλ' ὀνοτὸς μὲν **ἰδέσθαι**,
       συμπεσεῖν δ' ἀκμᾷ βαρύς.

       For he did not have the *build* of Orion;
50   but although he was paltry *to look at*,
       to fall in with he was heavy.

Each of the eight is distinctly different from the others, not only in choice of vocabulary, but in the emphasis given to either portion of the formula. The first six examples show a very close similarity of form. The first part of each emphasizes the physical appearance and beauty of the athlete (how he *looks*: ἰδέσθαι), the second his concomitant performance (what he *does*: ἔρδειν). By choice of different vocabulary and by switching from positive to negative expressions, Pindar has varied each of them. If one compares, say, one and four, the first part is very similar (ἦν δ' ἐσορᾶν καλός = εἰ δ' ἐὼν καλός), but the first adds (negatively, in litotes) that in his performance (ἔργῳ) he did not put to shame his looks (εἶδος); the fourth states positively that he performed (ἔρδων) things equivalent to his form (μορφᾷ). A quick glance over the first six examples shows how careful Pindar is to give variety and life to each of these commonplaces.

The last two examples are even more interesting, because they deviate from the norm. With the exception of number seven, all the other examples progress from the *appearance* of the victor to his *deeds*. This order places greater emphasis on the second element by virtue of that rule of thumb in Pindaric style, whereby the last-mentioned item naturally receives greater emphasis. Such a sequence is understandable in these passages, for they occur in places where the poet wishes to emphasize the performer's achievements. In fact, this doublet anticipates the later rhetorical division of encomia into the gifts of nature and the accomplishments (πράξεις).⁵

In number seven, however, he turns from Epharmostos' achievement (κρατέοντα χερὸς ἀλκᾷ) to his beauty (καλόν) and youthfulness (ὥρᾳ). This reverses the order of the terms in all the other examples, especially in number three: ὡραῖος ἐὼν καὶ **καλὸς** κάλλιστά τε **ῥέξαις**. His reason for reversing the order of the *topos* on this one occasion becomes clear when we realize that this is the only passage which ends its ode; instead of leading up to the victor's achievement, Pindar turns away from it to the boy's youthful beauty, "which once saved Ganymede from ruthless death by the power of Aphrodite" (104-105). By ending with this vision of immortality through divine love, Pindar draws attention to a theme that is prominent in this ode, especially in the preceding lines (95-96), when he assures the youth that the Muses are preserving his immortal κλέος.

In the last example, from *Isth.* 4 to Melissos of Thebes, Pindar points to the *incongruity* between the pankratiast's appearance and his actual performance. In all seven other cases, the two halves are connected by a τε that maintains a balance between the elements (while shifting the weight to the second); here a μέν . . . δέ construction underscores the discontinuity and throws all the weight on the second element. The two infinitives, ἰδέσθαι | συμπεσεῖν, neatly emphasize the contrast between Melissos' looks and actual performance, while the chiastic adjectives ὀνοτός and βαρύς reinforce the disparity between appearance and reality.⁶

Let us take up the topic of the last two lines of *Nem.* 11.13-16:

εἰ δέ τις (1)ὄλβον ἔχων (2)μορφᾷ παραμεύσεται ἄλλους,
(3)ἔν τ' ἀέθλοισιν ἀριστεύων ἐπέδειξεν βίαν,

---

⁵ *Rhet. ad Alex.* 35.1440b16 ff. makes the distinction between goods external to arete (τὰ ἔξω τῆς ἀρετῆς ἀγαθά) and those belonging to it (τὰ ἐν αὐτῇ τῇ ἀρετῇ ὄντα). The author includes the following in the first category: εὐγένεια, ῥώμη, κάλλος, and πλοῦτος, precisely the same things Pindar praises. For a list of *loci* which treat the topic, see Caplan, *Rhet. ad Herennium* 174. Cf. also the order of encomiastic topics in Menander Rhetor's βασιλικὸς λόγος, 369.18-372.25 (on which see L. Pernot, "Les *Topoi* de l'Éloge" 33-41) and in the *progymnasmata*. For a brief review of the latter, see Miller, *Hymn to Apollo* 7 note 19.

The contrast between (rather than the parity of) the external gifts of fortune and the athlete's own good use of those aids is a subtopic of the present discussion. Cf. *Ol.* 8.67: ὃς τύχᾳ μὲν δαίμονος, ἀνορέας δ' οὐκ ἀμπλακών, where the μέν . . . δέ construction emphasizes the fact that the young man used his talents to good effect. The negative expression (οὐκ ἀμπλακών) bears its full weight (i.e., not failing—as often happens). A variation, which concerns inborn ability, is at *Isth.* 3.13-14: ἀνδρῶν δ' ἀρετὰν σύμφυτον οὐ κατελέγχει.

⁶ The model for this reversal is the description of Tydeus at *Il.* 5.801: Τυδεύς τοι μικρὸς μὲν ἔην δέμας, ἀλλὰ μαχητής, which itself became a standard topic of praise; cf. Quint. 3.7.12: *et interim confert admirationi multum etiam infirmitas, ut cum idem* [sc. *Homerus*] *Tydea parvum sed bellatorem dicit fuisse.* For the word ὀνοτός, cf. *Od.* 8.239 (also in an athletic context): ὡς ἂν σὴν ἀρετὴν βροτὸς οὔ τις ὄνοιτο.

15 (4)θνατὰ μεμνάσθω περιστέλλων μέλη,
  καὶ τελευτὰν ἁπάντων γᾶν ἐπιεσσόμενος.

It is instructive to compare this passage with *Nem.* 3.19-21:

εἰ δ' (1)ἐὼν καλὸς (2)ἔρδων τ' ἐοικότα μορφᾷ
20 (3)ἀνορέαις ὑπερτάταις ἐπέβα
  παῖς Ἀριστοφάνεος, (4)οὐκέτι πρόσω
  ἀβάταν ἅλα κιόνων ὕπερ Ἡρακλέος περᾶν εὐμαρές.

  If, (1)being beautiful (2)and performing deeds to match his comeliness,
20 (3)the son of Aristophanes has embarked
  on utmost manhood, (4)going still further
  across the untracked sea beyond the pillars of Herakles is no easy task.

The passages are grammatically similar: each consists of a protasis of three rising elements issuing into an even longer apodosis. Not only do both move from appearance to action; each implies that the athlete's achievement is so great that he needs to remember his limitations: in the first case the poet reminds him of his mortality; in the second he recalls the unsurpassable extent of Herakles' achievements. Appropriately labeled the "*ne plus ultra*" motif, it occurs some ten times in the odes. Since it puts a seal on high praise, it often follows a crescendo of rising elements, as three of the following examples illustrate:[7]

1. *Nem.* 9.46-47:

  εἰ γὰρ (1)**ἅμα κτεάνοις** πολλοῖς (2)**ἐπίδοξον** ἄρηται
  κῦδος, (3)οὐκ ἔστι πρόσωθεν θνατὸν ἔτι σκοπιᾶς
  ἄλλας ἐφάψασθαι ποδοῖν.

  For *if* (1)*along with many possessions* (2)*he wins glorious fame*, (3)*there is no further promontory upon which a mortal may set his feet.*

2. *Ol.* 5.23-24:

  ὑγίεντα δ' εἴ τις ὄλβον ἄρδει,
  ἐξαρκέων κτεάτεσσι καὶ **εὐλογίαν**
  προστιθείς, μὴ ματεύσῃ θεὸς γενέσθαι.

---

[7] The full list includes *Ol.* 1.113-114, 3.42-45, 5.23-24; *Pyth.* 10.22-30; *Nem.* 3.19-21, 9.46-47, 11.13-16; *Isth.* 4.9-13, 5.12-16, and 6.10-13. Only *Ol.* 5.23-24 and *Isth.* 4.9-13 are *not* preceded by rising elements.

Appendix 3

If a man *fosters* a sound *wealth*
by aiding others with his possessions and by *adding
praise* thereby, let him not seek to become Zeus.

3. *Isth.* 6.10-13:

10   εἰ γάρ τις ἀνθρώπων (1)δαπάνᾳ τε χαρεὶς
(2)καὶ πόνῳ πράσσει θεοδμάτους ἀρετάς
(3)σύν τέ οἱ δαίμων **φυτεύει δόξαν** ἐπήρατον, (4)ἐ-
σχατιαῖς ἤδη πρὸς ὄλβου
βάλλετ' ἄγκυραν θεότιμος ἐών.

10   For *if* a man (1)delights in expenditure
(2)and by hard work *performs heaven-inspired achievements*,
(3)and fortune *sows* for him lovely *fame*, (4)then
at the limits of happiness
he casts his anchor as one favored by the gods.

4. *Isth.* 5.12-16:

δύο δέ τοι ζωᾶς ἄωτον μοῦνα ποιμαί-
— νοντι τὸν ἄλπνιστον, εὐανθεῖ σὺν ὄλβῳ
εἴ τις (1)εὖ πάσχων (2)λόγον ἐσλὸν ἀκούῃ.
(3)μὴ μάτευε Ζεὺς γενέσθαι· πάντ' ἔχεις,
15   εἴ σε τούτων μοῖρ' ἐφίκοιτο καλῶν.
θνατὰ θνατοῖσι πρέπει.

There are only two things which foster the finest
— sweetness of life, *if*, along with flourishing wealth,
a man (1)*succeeds* (2)and *is well spoken of*.
(3)Do not seek to become Zeus; you have all there is,
15   if a portion of those good things comes to you.
Mortal things befit mortals.

Although each of these set-pieces is crafted for a specific location in its hymn of praise, their general point is essentially the same as that expressed in the concluding lines of *Pyth.* 1.99-100:

(1)τὸ δὲ παθεῖν εὖ πρῶτον ἀέθλων·
(2)εὖ δ' ἀκούειν δευτέρα μοῖρ'· (3)ἀμφοτέροισι δ' ἀνήρ
100   ὃς ἂν ἐγκύρσῃ καὶ ἕλῃ, στέφανον ὕψιστον δέδεκται.

(1)Success is the first of prizes;
(2)and renown the second portion; (3)but the man
100   who encounters both and wins them gains the highest crown.

The following table shows the variations of terms in the double crown of deeds and fame:

Pyth. 1.99-100:	εὖ παθεῖν	εὖ ἀκούειν
Nem. 9.46-47:	ἅμα κτεάνοις πολλοῖς	ἐπίδοξον ἄρηται κῦδος
Ol. 5.24:	ἐξαρκέων κτεάτεσσι	εὐλογίαν προστιθείς
Isth. 6.11-12:	πράσσει ... ἀρετάς	φυτεύει δόξαν
Isth. 5.13:	εὖ πάσχων	λόγον ἐσλὸν ἀκούῃ

In all five cases these two elements occur in the order of nature (cf. πρῶτον ... δευτέρα at *Pyth.* 1.99).

The most complex variation of this topic is at *Pyth.* 10.22-29:

>   εὐδαίμων δὲ καὶ ὑμνη-
>   τὸς οὗτος ἀνὴρ γίνεται σοφοῖς,
>   (1)ὃς ἂν χερσὶν (2)ἢ ποδῶν ἀρετᾷ κρατήσαις
>   (3)τὰ μέγιστ' ἀέθλων ἕλῃ τόλμᾳ τε καὶ σθένει,
> 25 (4)καὶ ζώων ἔτι νεαρόν
>   κατ' αἶσαν υἱὸν ἴδῃ τυχόντα στεφάνων Πυθίων.
>   (5)ὁ χάλκεος οὐρανὸς οὔ ποτ' ἀμβατὸς αὐτῷ·
>   ὅσαις δὲ βροτὸν ἔθνος ἀγλαΐαις ἁ-
>   πτόμεσθα, περαίνει πρὸς ἔσχατον
>   πλόον.

>   *Blessed* and a *subject*
>   *for song* in wise men's eyes is that man,
>   (1)who with his hands (2)or with the might of his feet achieves victory
>   (3)and wins the greatest of the contests with courage and strength,
> 25 (4)and while still living sees his son
>   appropriately win Pythian crowns.
>   (5)He will never scale the bronze heaven,
>   but of all the glories which our mortal race
>   attains, he journeys to the extent of the furthest
>   voyage.

In the previous examples Pindar used if-clauses (εἴ τις): "If a man prospers and gains fame, he reaches the limits of success." Here Pindar reverses the order by means of a conditional relative clause: "Blessed and famous is a man who does x, y, and z; he reaches the limits of success." The change allows Pindar to build to a climactic picture of the father, already blessed with two Olympic victories, who lives to see his son win a Pythian crown.

Finally, to follow the variations on the theme of limitations, as Pindar combines similar elements in ever-new arrangements, is to witness the creative energy with which Pindar imparts ever new nuances to thematic repetitions.⁸ The elements include:

1. Furthest attainment: τὸ δ' ἔσχατον κορυφοῦται (*Ol.* 1.113); ἐσχατιὰν ἀρεταῖσιν ἱκάνων ἅπτεται Ἡρακλέος σταλᾶν (*Ol.* 3.43-44); στέφανον ὕψιστον δέδεκται (*Pyth.* 1.100); περαίνει πρὸς ἔσχατον πλόον (*Pyth.* 10.28-29); ἀνορέαις ὑπερτάταις ἐπέβα (*Nem.* 3.20); ἀνορέαις δ' ἐσχάταισιν στάλαισιν ἅπτονθ' Ἡρακλείαις (*Isth.* 4.11-12); πάντ' ἔχεις (*Isth.* 5.14); ἐσχατιαῖς πρὸς ὄλβου βάλλετ' ἄγκυραν (*Isth.* 6.12-13).

2. Not seeking beyond: μηκέτι πάπταινε πόρσιον (*Ol.* 1.114); τὸ πόρσω δ' ἐστὶ ἄβατον (*Ol.* 3.44); μὴ ματεύσῃ θεὸς γενέσθαι (*Ol.* 5.24); ὁ χάλκεος οὐρανὸς οὔ ποτ' ἀμβατός (*Pyth.* 10.27); οὐκέτι πρόσω ἀβάταν ἅλα κιόνων ὕπερ Ἡρακλέος περᾶν εὐμαρές (*Nem.* 3.20-21); οὐκ ἔστι πρόσωθεν θνατὸν ἔτι σκοπιᾶς ἄλλας ἐφάψασθαι ποδοῖν (*Nem.* 9.47); μηκέτι μακροτέραν σπεύδειν ἀρετάν (*Isth.* 4.13); μὴ μάτευε Ζεὺς γενέσθαι (*Isth.* 5.14); τὰ μακρὰ δ' εἴ τις παπταίνει, βραχὺς ἐξικέσθαι χαλκόπεδον θεῶν ἕδραν (*Isth.* 7.43-44).

What is remarkable is the fact that this particular topic seems to have been a trademark of Pindar, for Bakchylides never uses it in this form, nor does any other Greek poet to my knowledge.⁹

---

⁸ One of the ways in which Pindar adds variety is by alternating positive and negative expressions; cf. *Pyth.* 10.27-30 and *Nem.* 3.20-23.
⁹ The closest Bakchylides approaches this topic is at 4.18-20 and 5.50-55. Alkm. 1.16-18 PMG warns against flying to heaven and marrying Aphrodite, but the moral is not combined with praise of achievement.

BIBLIOGRAPHY
OF WORKS CITED

Adkins, A. W. H. *Merit and Responsibility* (Oxford 1960).
Arendt, H. *The Human Condition* (Chicago 1958).
Behaghel, O. "Beziehungen zwischen Umfang und Reihenfolge von Satzgliedern," *Indogerm. Forsch.* 25 (1909) 110-142.
Bell, J. M., "God, Man, and Animal in Pindar's Second Pythian," in *Early Greek Poetry and Philosophy: Studies in Honour of Leonard Woodbury*, ed. D. E. Gerber (Chico, CA 1984) 3-31.
Benedictus, J. Πινδάρου Περίοδος (Saumur 1620).
Boeckh, A. *Pindari Opera* 2.2 (Leipzig 1821).
Bowra, C. M. *Pindar* (Oxford 1964).
—— *The Odes of Pindar* (Baltimore 1969).
Braswell, B. K. *A Commentary on the Fourth Pythian Ode of Pindar* (Berlin 1988).
Bundy, E. L. *Hesychia in Pindar* (Diss. Berkeley 1954).
—— *Studia Pindarica* (Berkeley 1962).
—— "The 'Quarrel Between Kallimachos and Apollonios' Part I: The Epilogue of Kallimachos's *Hymn to Apollo*," *CSCA* 5 (1972) 39-94.
Burnet, J. *Plato's Phaedo* (Oxford 1911).
Burnett, A. P. review of Mullen, *Choreia*, *CP* 79 (1984) 154-160.
Burton, R. W. B. *Pindar's Pythian Odes* (Oxford 1962).
Bury, J. B. *The Nemean Odes of Pindar* (London 1890).
—— *The Isthmian Odes of Pindar* (London 1892).
Caplan, H. [*Cicero*] *Ad C. Herennium* (London 1954).
Carey, C. "Pindar's Eighth Nemean Ode," *PCPhS* 22 (1976) 26-42.
—— "Pindarica," in *Dionysiaca: Nine Studies in Greek Poetry*, ed. R. D. Dawe, J. Diggle, P. E. Easterling (Cambridge 1978) 21-44.
—— "Three Myths in Pindar: *N.* 4, *O.* 9, *N.* 3," *Eranos* 78 (1980) 143-162.
—— "Bacchylides' Experiments: Ode 11," *Mnemosyne* 33 (1980) 225-243.
—— *A Commentary on Five Odes of Pindar* (Salem, NH 1981).
—— "Prosopographica Pindarica," *CQ* 39 (1989) 1-9.
—— "Two Transitions in Pindar," *CQ* 39 (1989) 287-295.
—— "The Performance of the Victory Ode," *AJP* 110 (1989) 545-565.
Cerri, G. "A proposito del futuro e della litote in Pindaro: *Nem.* 7.102 sgg.," *QUCC* 22 (1976) 83-90.

Conway, G. S. *The Odes of Pindar* (London 1972).
Cookesley, W. G. *Pindari Carmina I*² (Eton 1850).
Cope, E. M. *The Rhetoric of Aristotle*, vol. 3, ed. J. E. Sandys (Cambridge 1877).
Denniston, J. D. *Greek Particles*² (Oxford 1966).
Dissen, L. *Pindari Carmina* (Göttingen 1830).
Donaldson, J. W. *Pindar's Epinician or Triumphal Odes* (London 1841).
Dönt, M. "Zur 14. olympischen Ode Pindars," *RhM* 126 (1983) 126-135.
Dornseiff, F. *Pindars Stil* (Berlin 1921).
Drachmann, A. B. *Scholia Vetera in Pindari Carmina*, 3 vols. (Leipzig 1903, 1910, 1927).
Easterling, P. E. & Knox B. M. W. *The Cambridge History of Classical Literature I* (Cambridge 1985).
Ebert, J. *Griechische Epigramme auf Sieger an gymnischen und hippischen Agonen* (Berlin 1972).
Farnell, L. R. *The Works of Pindar II* (London 1932).
Fennell, C. A. M. *Pindar: The Olympian and Pythian Odes*² (Cambridge 1893).
—— *Pindar: The Nemean and Isthmian Odes*² (Cambridge 1899).
Finley, J. H. *Pindar and Aeschylus* (Cambridge, MA 1955).
Fraenkel, E. *Agamemnon*, 3 vols. (Oxford 1957).
Fränkel, H. *Early Greek Poetry and Philosophy*, tr. M. Hadas and J. Willis (Oxford 1975).
Galiano, M. F. *Píndaro, Olímpicas*, 2 vols. (Madrid 1944).
Gentili, B. *Poetry and Its Public in Ancient Greece: From Homer to the Fifth Century*, tr. A. T. Cole (Baltimore 1988).
Gerber, D. E. "Pindar, *Pythian* 2.56," *TAPA* 91 (1960) 100-108.
—— *A Bibliography of Pindar, 1513-1966* (Cleveland 1969).
—— "Studies in Greek Lyric Poetry: 1967-1975," *CW* 70 (1976) 132-157.
—— *Emendations in Pindar: 1513-1972* (Amsterdam 1976).
—— *Pindar's Olympian One: A Commentary* (Toronto 1982).
—— "Pindar's *Olympian* Four: A Commentary," *QUCC* 25 (1987) 7-24.
—— "Short-Vowel Subjunctives in Pindar," *HSCP* 91 (1987) 83-90.
—— review of Verdenius, *Commentaries I*, *CR* 38 (1988) 203-205.
—— "Pindar and Bacchylides 1934-1987," *Lustrum* 31 (1989) 97-269.
Gildersleeve, B. L. *Pindar: The Olympian and Pythian Odes* (New York 1885).
Greengard, C. *The Structure of Pindar's Epinician Odes* (Amsterdam 1980).
Groningen, B. A. van, *La composition littéraire archaïque grecque* (Amsterdam 1958).
Grube, G. M. A. *Aristotle On Poetry and Style* (Indianapolis 1958).
Gundert, H. *Pindar und sein Dichterberuf* (Tübingen 1935).
Hamilton, R. *Epinikion: General Form in the Odes of Pindar* (The Hague 1974).
Herington, J. "Pindar's Eleventh *Pythian* Ode and Aeschylus' *Agamemnon*," in *Early Greek Poetry and Philosophy: Studies in Honour of Leonard Woodbury*, ed. D. E. Gerber (Chico, CA 1984) 137-146.
Herman, G. *Ritualised Friendship and the Greek City* (Cambridge 1987).

Heyne, C. G. *Pindari Carmina et Fragmenta* (Göttingen 1798).
Hoffmann, M. E. *Negatio Contrarii: A Study of Latin Litotes* (Assen 1987).
Hubbard, T. K. *The Pindaric Mind* (Leiden 1985).
―― "Two Notes on the Myth of Aeacus in Pindar," *GRBS* 28 (1987) 5-22.
―― "Pindar and the Aeginetan Chorus: Nemean 3.9-13," *Phoenix* 41 (1987) 1-9.
Hurst, A. "Observations sur la deuxième Olympique de Pindare," *ZAnt* 31 (1981) 121-133.
Jebb, R. C. "Pindar," *JHS* 3 (1882) 144-193.
Johnson, W. R. *The Idea of Lyric: Lyric Modes in Ancient and Modern Poetry* (Berkeley 1982).
Kambylis, A. "Anredeformen bei Pindar," in Χάρις Κωνσταντίνῳ Ι. Βουρβέρῃ (Athens 1964) 95-199.
Kenney, E. J. & Clausen, W. V. *The Cambridge History of Classical Literature II* (Cambridge 1982).
Keyssner, K. *Gottesvorstellung und Lebensauffassung im griechischen Hymnus* (Stuttgart 1932).
Kirk, G. S. *The Iliad: A Commentary I* (Cambridge 1985).
Kirkwood, G. M. "Pythian 5.72-76, 9.90-92, and the Voice of Pindar," *ICS* 6 (1981) 12-23.
―― *Selections From Pindar* (Chico, CA 1982).
―― "Blame and Envy in the Pindaric Epinician," in *Greek Poetry and Philosophy: Studies in Honour of Leonard Woodbury*, ed. D. E. Gerber (Chico, CA 1984) 169-183.
Kleinknecht, H. *Die Gebetsparodie in der Antike* (Stuttgart 1937).
Klug, W. *Untersuchung zum Gebet in der frühgriechischen Lyrik* (Diss. Heidelberg 1954).
Köhnken, A. "Hieron und Deinomenes in Pindars erstem Pythischen Gedicht," *Hermes* 98 (1970) 1-13.
―― *Die Funktion des Mythos bei Pindar* (Berlin 1971).
―― "Gebrauch und Funktion der Litotes bei Pindar," *Glotta* 54 (1976) 62-67.
―― review of Segal, *Pindar's Mythmaking*, *JHS* 108 (1988) 223-224.
Kranz, W. "Sphragis," *RhM* 104 (1961) 3-46.
Krause, J. ΑΛΛΟΤΕ ΑΛΛΟΣ: *Untersuchung zum Motiv des Schicksalswechsels in der griechischen Dichung bis Euripides* (Munich 1976) 91-138.
Lattimore, R. *The Odes of Pindar* (Chicago 1947).
Lauer, S. *Zur Wortstellung bei Pindar* (Diss. Winterthur 1959).
Lefkowitz, M. R. "ΤΩ ΚΑΙ ΕΓΩ: The First Person in Pindar," *HSCP* 67 (1963) 177-253.
―― *The Victory Ode: An Introduction* (Park Ridge, NJ 1976).
―― "The Poet as Athlete," *Journal of Sport History* 11 (1984) 18-24.
Lobel, E. *Oxyrhynchus Papyri* XXVI (Oxford 1961).
Lonicerus, I. *Pindari Olympia, Pythia, Nemea, Isthmia* (Basel 1535).
Maehler, H. *Die Lieder des Bakchylides*, 2 vols. (Leiden 1982).

Meyer, H. *Hymnische Stilelemente in der frühgriechischen Dichtung* (Diss. Köln 1933).
Mezger, F. *Pindars Siegeslieder* (Leipzig 1880).
Miller, A. M. "*Thalia Erasimolpos*: Consolation in Pindar's *Fourteenth Olympian*," *TAPA* 107 (1977) 225-234.
—— "Pindar, Archilochus and Hieron in *P*. 2.52-56," *TAPA* (1981) 135-143.
—— "*N*. 4.33-43 and the Defense of Digressive Leisure," *CJ* 78 (1983) 202-220.
—— *From Delos to Delphi: A Literary Study of the Homeric Hymn to Apollo* (Leiden 1986).
Mineur, W. H. *Callimachus, Hymn to Delos* (Leiden 1984).
Moretti, L. *Iscrizioni Agonistiche Greche* (Rome 1953).
Most, G. W. *The Measures of Praise: Structure and Function in Pindar's Second Pythian and Seventh Nemean Odes* (Göttingen 1985).
—— "Pindar, *O*. 2.83-90," *CQ* 36 (1986) 304-316.
—— "Pindar I. 1.67-68," *RhM* 131 (1988) 101-108.
Mullen, W. *Choreia: Pindar and Dance* (Princeton 1982).
Nagy, G. *The Best of the Achaeans* (Baltimore 1979).
Nash, L. L. "The Theban Myth at *Pythian* 9,79-103," *QUCC* 11 (1982) 77-99.
Nierhaus, R. *Strophe und Inhalt im pindarischen Epinikion* (Diss. Leipzig 1936).
Nisetich, F. J. *The Poetry of Victory: A Study in the Occasional Nature of Pindar's Odes* (Diss. Harvard 1973).
—— "Olympian 1.8-11: An Epinician Metaphor," *HCSP* 79 (1975) 55-68.
—— "The Leaves of Triumph and Mortality: Transformation of a Traditional Image in Pindar's *Olympian* 12," *TAPA* 107 (1977) 235-264.
Norden, E. *Agnostos Theos* (Leipzig 1923).
Page, D. L. *Select Papyri III: Literary Papyri Poetry* (London 1941).
Papillon, T. L. "Text and Context in Pindar's *Isthmian* 8.70," *AJP* 110 (1989) 1-9.
Pelliccia, H. "Pindarus Homericus: *Pythian* 3.1-80," *HSCP* 91 (1987) 39-63.
Pernot, L. "Les *Topoi* de l'Éloge chez Ménandros le Rhéteur," *REG* 99 (1986) 33-53.
Péron, J. *Les images maritimes de Pindare* (Paris 1974).
—— "Pindare et la Victoire de Télésicrate dans la IXe Pythique (v. 76-96)," *RPh* 50 (1976) 58-78.
Podlecki, A. J. *The Early Greek Poets and Their Times* (Vancouver 1984).
Puech, E. *Pindare: Olympiques*[4] (Paris 1961).
Race, W. H. "The End of *Olympia* 2: Pindar and the *Vulgus*," *CSCA* 12 (1979) 251-267.
—— "Some Digressions and Returns in Greek Authors," *CJ* 76 (1980) 1-8.
—— "Pindar's 'Best is Water': Best of What?" *GRBS* 22 (1981) 119-124.
—— *The Classical Priamel from Homer to Boethius* (Leiden 1982).
—— "Aspects of Rhetoric and Form in Greek Hymns," *GRBS* 23 (1982) 5-14.

―――― "Two Pindaric Passages: *Pyth.* 5.55 and *Pyth.* 10.21-22," *AJP* 104 (1983) 178-188.
―――― "Pindar's Heroic Ideal at *Pyth.* 4.186-87," *AJP* 106 (1985) 350-356.
―――― *Pindar* (Boston 1986).
―――― "Pindaric Encomium and Isokrates' *Evagoras,*" *TAPA* 117 (1987) 131-155.
―――― *Classical Genres and English Poetry* (London 1988).
―――― "The Six Crowns at Pindar, *Isthmian* 1.10-12," *GRBS* 30 (1989) 27-39.
―――― "How Greek Poems Begin," *YCS* (forthcoming).
Radt, S. L. *Pindars zweiter und sechster Paian* (Amsterdam 1958).
―――― review of I.-A. Sulzer, *Zur Wortstellung und Satzbildung, Gnomon* 35 (1963) 245-247.
Rico, M. *Ensayo de bibliografía pindárica* (Madrid 1969).
Robbins, E. "The Broken Wall, the Burning Roof and Tower: Pindar *OL.* 8.31-46," *CQ* 36 (1986) 317-321.
―――― "Pindar's *Oresteia* and the Tragedians," in *Greek Tragedy and its Legacy: Essays Presented to D. J. Conacher*, ed. M. Cropp, E. Fantham, S. E. Scully (Calgary 1986) 1-11.
Rusten, J. S. "Γείτων Ἥρως, Pindar's Prayer to Heracles (*N.* 7.86-101) and Greek Popular Religion," *HSCP* 87 (1983) 289-297.
Sandys, J. E. *Pindar*³ (London 1937).
Schadewaldt, W. *Der Aufbau des pindarischen Epinikion* (Halle 1928).
Schmid, E. Πινδάρου Περίοδος (Wittenberg 1616).
Schroeder, O. *Pindars Pythien* (Leipzig 1922).
Schürch, P. *Zur Wortresponsion bei Pindar* (Bern 1971).
Segal, C. "Bacchylides Reconsidered: Epithets and the Dynamics of Lyric Narrative," *QUCC* 22 (1976) 99-130.
―――― *Pindar's Mythmaking* (Princeton 1986).
Severus, E. von, "Gebet," *RAC* 8 (1972) 1134-52.
Shorey, P. "Φύσις, Μελέτη, Ἐπιστήμη," *TAPA* 40 (1909) 185-201.
Silk, M. S. *Interaction in Poetic Imagery* (Cambridge 1974).
Skulsky, S. D. "Πολλῶν πείρατα συντανύσαις: Language and Meaning in Pythian 1," *CP* 70 (1975) 8-31.
Slater, W. J. *Lexicon to Pindar* (Berlin 1969).
―――― "Futures in Pindar," *CQ* 19 (1969) 86-94.
―――― review of Schürch, *Zur Wortresponsion, Gnomon* 45 (1973) 490-492.
Smith, B. H. *Poetic Closure: A Study of How Poems End* (Chicago 1968).
Snell, B. & Maehler, H. *Pindari Carmina, Pars I*⁸ (Leipzig 1987).
―――― *Pindari Carmina, Pars II*⁴ (Leipzig 1975).
― *Bacchylidis Carmina cum Fragmentis*¹⁰ (Leipzig 1970).
Spengel, L. *Rhetores Graeci*, 3 vols. (Leipzig 1853-1856).
Steiner, D. *The Crown of Song: Metaphor in Pindar* (Oxford 1986).
Stinton, C. W. "Si Credere Dignum Est: Some Expressions of Disbelief in Euripides and Others," *PCPS* 22 (1976) 60-89.
Stockert, W. *Klangfiguren und Wortresponsionen bei Pindar* (Vienna 1969).

Stoneman, R. "Ploughing a Garland: Metaphor and Metonymy in Pindar," *Maia* 33 (1981) 125-138.
Sulzer, A.-I. *Zur Wortstellung und Satzbildung bei Pindar* (Diss. Zürich 1961).
Swanson, R. A. *Pindar's Odes* (Indianapolis 1974).
Thummer, E. *Pindar. Die Isthmischen Gedichte I* (Heidelberg 1968).
—— *Pindar. Die Isthmischen Gedichte II* (Heidelberg 1969).
Turyn, A. *Pindari Carmina cum Fragmentis* (Cracow 1948).
Verdenius, W. J. *A Commentary on Hesiod's* Works and Days, *vv. 1-382* (Leiden 1985).
—— *Commentaries on Pindar I* (Leiden 1987).
—— *Commentaries on Pindar II* (Leiden 1988).
Wade-Gery, H. T. "Thucydides the Son of Melesias," in *Essays in Greek History* (Oxford 1958) 239-270.
Werner, O. *Pindar: Siegesgesänge und Fragmente* (München 1967).
West, M. L. *Hesiod Theogony* (Oxford 1966).
Wilkinson, L. P. *Golden Latin Artistry* (Cambridge 1963).
Wilamowitz, U. von. *Pindarus* (Berlin 1922).
Willcock, M. M. "On First Reading Pindar: *The Fifth Isthmian*," *G&R* 25 (1978) 37-45.
Williams, R. D. *The Aeneid of Virgil, Books 7-12* (Glasgow 1973).
Woloch, M. "Athenian Trainers in the Aeginetan Odes of Pindar and Bacchylides," *CW* 56 (1963) 102-104, 121.
Wünsch, R. "Hymnos," *RE* 9 (1916) 140-183.
Young, D. C. *Three Odes of Pindar: A Literary Study of Pythian 11, Pythian 3, and Olympian 7* (Leiden 1968).
—— "Pindaric Criticism," in *Pindaros und Bacchylides*, ed. W. M. Calder III & J. Stern (Darmstadt 1970) 1-95.
—— *Pindar Isthmian 7: Myth and Exempla* (Leiden 1971).
—— "The Text of Pindar Isthmian 8.70," *AJP* 94 (1973) 319-326.
—— "Pindar's Style at *Pythian* 9.87f.," *GRBS* 20 (1979) 133-143.
—— "Pindar, Aristotle, and Homer: A Study in Ancient Criticism," *CA* 2 (1983) 156-170.

INDEX LOCORUM

Aischylos
  Agamemnon: 7n12
    160-161: 106n58
  Choephoroi
    19: 86n5

Alkman (PMG)
  1.16-18: 195n9
  3: 106n57
  14: 106n57
  27: 106n57
  27.2-3: 136n49

Anakreon (PMG)
  357.8: 101n40

Anonymous
  "Hymn to the Moirai"
    1018b.3 PMG: 101n40
  CIL I 2.6-9: 188n4
  "Eulogy" LP 556 Page: 156n34

Apollonios Rhodios
  Argonautika
    1.763-767: 33n41
    3.1-5: 106n57

Aratos
  Phainomena
    1.1 ff.: 87n9

Archilochos (West)
  13.2: 101n43

Aristotle
  Poetics
    21.1457b22: 61n5
  Rhetoric
    1.1367b14: 60n4
    1.1368a13: 60n4
    2.1389b7: 78
    3.1408a1 ff.: 60
    3.1408a7: 62n10
  Rhetorica ad Alexandrum
    35.1440b16 ff.: 191n5

Aristonous "Hymn to Hestia"
  (Powell 164-165): 103n48, 105n56

Aristophanes
  Nubes
    274: 101n40

Bakchylides
  1.144-145: 157n36
  1.151: 76
  1.151-158: 40n49
  1.156-157: 144n4
  1.158: 75
  2.4: 157n36
  2.9: 63n15
  3: 167n5
  3.1-4: 185-186
  3.3: 101n41, 183n3
  3.67-68: 74
  3.93: 63n15
  4.18-20: 195n9
  5.1-8: 184
  5.4: 183n3
  5.9-10: 110n69
  5.36: 79
  5.50-55: 195n9
  5.176-182: 40n49
  5.187-190: 74
  7.6-10: 183n4
  8.27-30: 82n61
  9.1-6: 124n16, 185-186
  9.4: 93n19

11.1-14: 182-183
12.1-7: 186
12.4-7: 91n16
12.8: 101n41
13.199-202: 74
13.199-205: 75n42
14.23: 183n3
14B: 183n4
17.66: 144n5
17.109-116: 123n13
17.130-132: 120
17.132: 122, 135

[Cicero]
ad Herennium
174: 191n5

Dionysios of Halikarnassos
de Compositione
19: 188
22 *init.*: 187n1

Demosthenes
de Corona 315: 156n34

Demetrios
περὶ ἑρμηνείας
39: 11n7
50-51: 9n1
78-80: 10n6

Euripides
Alkestis
448-449: 92n17
Σ *ad Phoin.* 207: 156n32

Hermogenes
Meth. 37 (2.456.13-15 Sp): 59n2

Herodotos
1.32: 133n38
3.80.4: 60n4

Hesiod
Opera
138: 126
Theogony
58: 92n17
102-103: 160n42
430-431: 96n31
854: 93
869: 93

Homer
Iliad
1.8: 104
1.35-42: 103n50
1.37-42: 16n16, 91
1.490-491: 96n31
2.110: 16n16
2.246: 16n16
2.305 ff.: 143n2
2.484-485: 106n57
2.670: 168n7
3.150: 96n31
3.276: 16n16
3.277: 16n16
4.225: 62n9
5.801: 191n6
6.146 ff.: 65n20
9.412-416: 67
16.191: 30n35
24.60: 30n35
24.525-542: 133n38
Odyssey
1.1: 104
6.44: 62n9
8.239: 191n6
11.550-551: 188n4
14.228: 153n25
17.14-15: 155
19.354: 30n35
Homeric Hymns
1.18-19: 115
1.20: 119n2
2: 104
2.307: 126
2.353: 126
2.494: 105, 113n74, 120n3
2.495: 28n31
3: 104, 123n13
3.1: 115n80, 160n42
3.19: 104
3.179-181: 18n19
3.182-203: 100n37
3.207: 104
3.207-215: 115n81, 116
3.546: 103n49
4: 104
4.1: 106, 185
5: 104
5.93-99: 31n37
6: 104
6.19-20: 105n56, 123
7: 104

7.2: 160n42
7.58-59: 115n80
8: 103n48
9: 104
9.7: 105, 120n3
9.8: 153n26
10: 104
10.2-5: 87n6
11: 104
11.5: 119
12: 104
13: 104
13.3: 105n56, 113n75
14: 104
14.6: 120n3
15: 104
16: 104
17: 104
18: 104
18.1: 153n26
18.11: 153n26
19: 104
20: 104
22: 104
22.5-7: 122n10
23: 104
24: 103n48
24.5: 113n74
26: 104
27: 104
28: 104
29: 103n48
30: 104
30.18: 113n74, 120
31.1: 112
31.17: 113n74
32: 104
33: 104

Horace
    Carmina
        1.4.13: 102
        2.1.33-40: 57n23
        3.3.65-72: 57n23

Kallimachos
    h. Delos
        8: 115n80

Lucretius
    De Rerum Natura
        1.1 ff.: 87n9

1.15-28: 87n6
1.24: 86n5

Menander Rhetor (Spengel)
    335.13: 103n50
    369.18-372.25: 191n5

Milton
    "Lycidas": 7n12

Pindar
    Olympian Odes
        1: 2, 41
        1.1 ff.: 125
        1.1-2: 165
        1.1-7: 9-11
        1.3: 13n11
        1.3-4: 64
        1.3-7: 14n12
        1.7: 78
        1.8: 63
        1.30-34: 124n16
        1.31-32: 14n12
        1.35: 70-71
        1.37-40: 14n12
        1.46-52: 46-47
        1.52: 57
        1.52-53: 71-72
        1.81: 69-70
        1.81-84: 67-68
        1.83: 69
        1.84-85: 68
        1.87-88: 173
        1.93-94: 63, 68
        1.104: 76n48, 78
        1.108: 76
        1.110: 157n35
        1.113: 195
        1.113-114: 192n7
        1.114: 195
        1.115: 63, 121-122, 137n50
        1.115-115b: 122n8
        1.115-116: 120-121
        1.115b: 123
        1.116: 123n11
        2: 155n29
        2.1 ff.: 117
        2.1-2: 105
        2.1-7: 11-13
        2.2: 64
        2.5: 13n11
        2.5-7: 14n12

Ol. 2.6: 64
2.7: 14n12
2.9-15: 130-131
2.12-14: 20
2.12-15: 16-18, 103n50
2.13: 121n5
2.13-14: 79
2.21-22: 63
2.50: 20n21
2.51-52: 77
2.52: 8n15
2.76: 88n11
2.81-83: 57n22
2.81-85: 51n13
2.89-100: 124n15
2.93-94: 78
2.94: 74
3.1-5: 109-111
3.3: 91
3.38-41: 144
3.42-44: 11
3.42-45: 192n7
3.43: 13n11
3.43-44: 14n12, 195
3.44: 195
4: 155n29
4.1-16: 90-95
4.6-9: 20
4.6-10: 18, 144-145
4.8: 13n11, 19, 101n43
4.8-10: 14n12
4.10: 63
4.14-16: 22-23
4.15: 79n54
4.16: 14n12, 25
4.17-18: 76
4.21: 77
4.25: 96n31
5: 94n27, 95n30, 155n29
5.1 ff.: 85n4
5.1-8: 102n47
5.2: 80
5.3: 91
5.15-16: 77n50
5.21: 101n43
5.23-24: 192-193
5.24: 194-195
5 *fin.*: 119
6.4 ff.: 25n26
6.4-7: 25-26
6.6: 76
6.6-7: 74

6.9-11: 67-68
6.17: 96n31
6.19: 76
6.41-42: 88n11
6.58-59: 169-170
6.73: 63, 66
6.74-76: 74-75
6.77-81: 143-144
6.81: 74
6.89-90: 70, 77
6.91: 64
6.92-96: 76n47
6.92-97: 79
6.96-97: 76
6.97: 129-130, 149
6.98: 184
6.101: 103n50
6.101-105: 121-123
6.103-105: 135
6.105: 63
6 *fin.*: 125
7: 7n12
7.19: 48n11
7.20-21: 109n62
7.21: 126n21
7.43: 168n7
7.49-51: 168
7.68-69: 144n6
7.80-87: 20n21
7.86-87: 81n59
7.87-89: 18-19
7.87-95: 124-127
7.90: 75
7.93-94: 101
7.94-95: 102n44
7 *fin.*: 119
8: 2, 140-164
8.1-11: 102n47
8.9: 93n20, 93n21
8.10: 63, 86
8.15-18: 14n12
8.16: 63
8.19: 78n52, 189-190
8.21-23: 187n2
8.22: 88n11
8.25: 97n33
8.28-29: 79, 129
8.45: 76n45
8.46: 8n15
8.46-52: 170
8.55: 75n44
8.67: 191n5

Ol. 8.67-71: 65-67
8.74: 69n30
8.82-83: 63
8.84-88: 127n24
8.87: 121n5
8 fin.: 119
9: 41, 155n29
9.17: 147n13
9.19: 160n43
9.29-42: 54-56
9.31-33: 57
9.35-36: 57
9.37-38: 71n35
9.65-66: 189
9.67-70: 14-15
9.69-70: 14n12
9.76-83: 48-49
9.77-78: 76n45
9.80: 57
9.81: 57
9.82-83: 83
9.83-84: 57
9.83-100: 20n21
9.89-94: 56n21
9.94: 189, 191
9.104: 70n33
9.109: 64
10: 155n29
10.1 ff.: 108, 186
10.3: 93n21
10.4: 144n6
10.7-12: 175n16
10.11-13: 126n22
10.12: 175n17
10.53-55: 144
10.54: 144n6
10.100-104: 190-191
11: 7
11.1-6: 13-14
11.4-6: 14n12
11.7: 74
11.16-19: 77-78, 113n73
11.17: 76-77
11.17-19: 23n24
11.18: 76
11.19: 14n12, 96n31
11.19-20: 171
11 fin.: 171n10
12.1-4: 95-97
12.4-5: 19
12.6a: 187n2
12.14: 68, 69n28

12.14-19: 65
12.15: 66, 68
13.2-3: 39n47
13.14: 63
13.22-26: 48n11
13.24-29: 79
13.24-30: 131-132
13.27: 121n5
13.29: 101n41
13.29-46: 20n21
13.30-31: 78
13.31: 160n44
13.34: 81n59
13.44-45: 124n17
13.49-60: 179-180
13.52: 76
13.53: 8n15
13.84: 97n33
13.87-91: 40n49
13.87-92: 51-52
13.91: 57
13.92: 57
13.93-100: 124n15
13.94: 57
13.96: 57
13.97: 57
13.98-114: 20n21
13.102: 160n45
13.115: 122, 135
14: 97-102, 103n48, 155n29
14.2: 88n11
14.5-7: 21
14.8: 76
14.10: 88n11
14.21: 64
Pythian Odes
1: 5n9
1.1 ff.: 85n4, 173, 181
1.1-12: 86, 100n37, 102n47, 103n50, 146n11
1.5-10: 144n5
1.13: 61
1.13-16: 27
1.15-16: 14n12
1.15-29: 127
1.22-24: 165
1.26: 165n1
1.27-31: 41-42
1.29: 45n6, 57, 136
1.32: 64
1.33: 157n35
1.35-38: 166

Pyth. 1.38: 62
1.39: 101n41
1.39-40: 17-18, 136
1.40: 14n12
1.41-42: 21
1.42-45: 124n15
1.43-46: 136-137
1.46: 103n50
1.47-55: 137-138
1.49: 78
1.50-55: 167n5
1.56-57: 138
1.57: 121n5
1.58-60: 139
1.59: 76
1.60: 175n17
1.61-66: 48n11
1.67-70: 139
1.71: 129n29
1.71-73: 140
1.75-80: 15-16, 56-57
1.75-84: 140
1.77-78: 35n42
1.79: 174n14
1.79-80: 14n12
1.81: 57
1.82: 70
1.82-84: 166-167
1.84 ff.: 83n64
1.85-100: 80n56
1.90: 60, 79n54
1.90-92: 60n3
1.92: 108n60
1.94: 64n20
1.94-98: 167-168
1.99: 122n8, 172n12
1.99-100: 193-194
1.100: 63, 195
2.1-2: 20n20
2.1-8: 111n71
2.2: 13n11, 38n46
2.6: 63
2.7: 76
2.19: 64
2.32: 76n45
2.36: 97n33
2.42-43: 61
2.49 ff.: 27
2.49-52: 21-22
2.51: 13n11
2.52-53: 77
2.52-56: 72-73

2.60: 78
2.63-65: 96n31, 172n12
2.64: 97n33
2.67-71: 175
2.69-71: 184
2.70: 175n17
2.73-96: 80n56
2.74: 60n4
2.81-83: 127
2.86-88: 21
2.88: 14n12
2.93-96: 128n26
2.96: 121n5, 127n24
3: 6n11
3.23: 187n2
3.43: 153n24
3.55: 97n33
3.57: 57, 129n29
3.57-62: 42-44, 46n7
3.61-62: 57
3.61-76: 9, 37-39
3.71: 60n4, 74
3.73: 145n8
3.103: 144n6
3.111: 63
3.112: 168n6
4.1: 112n72, 122n7, 158
4.1-3: 107-108
4.1-4: 114
4.3: 101n41
4.5: 76
4.13-57: 152n21
4.23: 129n29
4.32: 66
4.67-68: 107n59
4.70-71: 107n59
4.87-92: 31-32
4.88-89: 35n42, 147n13
4.89: 33n39
4.90-92: 14n12
4.118: 76
4.171-183: 32-33, 36
4.176-177: 35
4.178-179: 35n42
4.185-187: 68-69
4.186: 68
4.193-202: 143n2
4.194-198: 144n5
4.248: 124n17
4.253: 63n15
4.261: 134
4.264-269: 177-178

Index Locorum 209

Pyth. 4.272-274: 178n18
4.276: 162n52
4.279-299: 178
4.283: 61n5
4.284: 75
4.299: 178
5.45-49: 67n27
5.76: 76
5.109-117: 20n21
5.117-124: 127n24
5.119: 96n31
5.120-121: 65n20, 79
5.124: 162n50
5 fin.: 119
6.14: 63
6.18: 64
6.44: 97n33
6.46-54: 21n22, 33n40
6.47-49: 78
6.48: 61
6.50-51: 35n42, 147n13
7: 85n1
7.5-8: 105n54
7.7: 63
8: 4, 154
8.1 ff.: 85n4, 181
8.1-5: 19-20
8.1-8: 102n47
8.3: 96n31
8.5: 13n11, 93n22
8.6-12: 172-173
8.17: 93
8.19-20: 145n8, 146n10
8.19-84: 135
8.21: 76
8.33-35: 134n43
8.36: 78n52
8.44-56: 152n21
8.56-72: 133-135
8.67-72: 79
8.73: 67n27
8.78-84: 23-24
8.80: 67n27
8.81-87: 66-67, 159n41
8.81-97: 80n56
8.85-86: 64n18
8.90-91: 67
8.93: 65n20
8.95: 67n24
8.98-100: 127n24
8 fin.: 119
9.1-5: 108-110

9.44: 135
9.51-66: 152n21
9.58: 76
9.67-68: 153n24
9.70-103: 59, 80-84
9.73: 63
9.78: 70n33
9.79-103: 20n21
9.80: 77n49
9.89a-90: 135n46
9.90: 76
9.91: 8n15
9.92: 59n1
9.93-94: 65, 126
9.103-125: 84
9.104-105: 69n30
10: 4
10.2: 172n12
10.8-9: 64
10.12-22: 132
10.17-22: 79-80
10.21-22: 162n52
10.22 ff.: 25n26
10.22-29: 194
10.22-30: 192n7
10.23: 4
10.23-26: 24-25
10.25: 25
10.25-26: 14n12
10.27: 195
10.27-30: 195n8
10.28-29: 63, 195
10.37: 59n1, 76
10.40: 102n45
10.46-52: 45-47
10.48: 57
10.49: 57
10.51: 57
10.59: 14n12
11: 6n11, 41
11.1 ff.: 85n4
11.1-16: 102n47
11.2: 14n12
11.22-28: 178-179
11.28: 61n5
11.36-41: 47
11.37: 53n16, 179n19
11.38: 57, 57
11.41: 57
11.43-45: 172n12
11.59-64: 169n8
12.1 ff.: 85n4

Pyth. 12.1-6: 102n47
12.5: 86
12.5-6: 93n22
12.28-29: 76n45
Nemean Odes
1: 4
1.1 ff.: 85n4, 111n71
1.16-17: 129n29
1.18: 76
1.23: 76
1.26-30: 172
1.31: 69n28
1.31-32: 65n19
1.32: 122n8
1.34: 180n20
1.48-58: 165
1.61-72: 152n21
1.62-63: 4
1.62-69: 33-34, 53n16
2: 85n1
2.1-3: 87n8
2.12: 76
2.19-24: 20n21
2.22: 160n45
2.24: 66
3.1 ff. : 181, 186
3.1-17: 111-113
3.3: 86
3.8: 166n3
3.9: 74
3.15: 78n52
3.17: 157n35
3.19: 189-190
3.19-21: 192
3.20: 195
3.20-21: 195
3.20-23: 195n8
3.22-28: 55n20
3.50: 168
3.53-58: 30
3.54-55: 35n42
3.56-58: 14n12
3.76: 76
4.6-8: 94n25
4.10: 101n41
4.17-24: 27n29
4.19: 101n41
4.21: 81n59
4.25-35: 52n15
4.27: 14n12
4.33-35: 29
4.35: 8n15, 14n12

4.39: 8n15, 75
4.41: 65n20
4.44-45: 175n17
4.46-56: 34-35
4.54-58: 14n12
4.66-70: 43n4, 44n5, 46n7
4.74: 52n15
4.75: 101n41
4.77: 75
4.95-96: 173n13
5.1: 69n30
5.2-3: 63
5.14-20: 52n14
5.16: 57-57, 70n33
5.16-17: 124n16
5.17: 144n6
5.18: 70n33
5.50-51: 60n3
5.50-54: 28n32
5.52-54: 14n12
5.54: 76
6.2: 172n12
6.13b: 63
6.20-21: 69
6.21: 8n15
6.25: 78
6.26-28: 124n15
6.31: 75
6.39-41: 81n59
6.50-57: 47-48
6.54: 57
6.57b: 57
7.1 ff.: 181
7.1-8: 87-89, 181-183
7.2: 86
7.2-3: 76
7.7: 64, 97n33
7.12-13: 70
7.14: 71
7.25: 144n6
7.49: 76
7.54-82: 80n56
7.61: 76
7.61-62: 62n11, 60n3
7.61-63: 70-71
7.63: 70
7.64: 70
7.66: 59n1
7.67-68: 129
7.70-73: 67n27
7.71: 157n37
7.76: 76

Index Locorum 211

Nem. 7.77-79: 1
7.78-79: 40
7.79: 14n12
7.89-101: 127n24
7.90: 160n44
7.98-100: 121n5
7.102 ff.: 61n6
7 fin.: 119
8.1 ff.: 20n20, 85n4, 181
8.1-5: 86, 103n50
8.1-7: 102n47
8.3: 14n12
8.6: 97n33
8.8: 96n31
8.18: 97n33
8.23: 97n33
8.26-34: 15n14
8.32-37: 45n6
8.35: 57, 128
8.36-37: 70
8.37-39: 15
8.38: 13n11
8.39: 2n3, 71
8.40: 15n14
8.48-49: 73n39
8.49: 64
9.1: 86
9.1-3: 108n61, 113n73
9.3: 93n21
9.6-7: 65, 126
9.7: 64
9.19: 129n29
9.22-23: 66
9.24-32: 44-45
9.27: 57, 140
9.28: 57
9.28-32: 57n22
9.28-33: 128-129
9.29: 57
9.39: 96n31
9.39-42: 173-174
9.46-47: 192, 194
9.47: 195
9.48-53: 174
9.53-55: 123-124
9.55: 121n5
10.1 ff.: 115n81
10.1-2: 106, 186
10.1-12: 113-115
10.1-24: 37n44
10.2: 63, 116n83
10.2-20: 20n21

10.13-15: 35n42
10.18-19: 43n4
10.27-29: 177
10.30-36: 135n47
10.40-41: 59n1
10.41-48: 20n21
10.49-54: 144n4
10.76: 129n29
10.89: 162n52
11.1 ff.: 183n4
11.1-10: 102n47
11.8-9: 187n2
11.9: 93n21
11.12: 96n31
11.13-14: 189
11.13-16: 188, 191-192
11.14: 14n12, 63
11.20: 63
11.24-26: 176-177
11.26: 67n26
11.28: 102n45
11.29-32: 174-175
Isthmian Odes
1: 6n11, 7
1.1 ff.: 85n4, 155-156, 181
1.3: 162n52
1.5: 161n46
1.6: 172n12
1.12-14: 55n20
1.14: 57, 153n26
1.14-34: 109n64
1.15: 76
1.15-34: 103n49
1.17-31: 27
1.22: 63
1.28: 187n2
1.30-32: 168-169
1.32-33: 7n13
1.32-34: 170
1.32-35: 27-28
1.33-34: 14n12
1.34: 180n20
1.41-45: 73-74
1.52-63: 20n21
1.63: 70n33
1.64: 63, 127n24
1.64-67: 121n5
1.64-68: 64-65, 67, 127n23
1.65-67: 176
1.66: 102n45
1.67: 68
1.68: 68

Isth. 1 *fin.*: 119
  2.10: 144n6
  2.12-29: 20n21
  2.17: 157n35
  2.18: 81n59
  2.19-22: 35n42
  2.20: 70
  2.24: 82n61
  2.30: 76
  2.37-42: 23n24
  2.38: 157n35
  2.43: 75
  2.46: 69n30
  3: 8n15, 85n1
  3.6: 66n23
  3.11-13: 176
  3.12: 64
  3.13: 157n35
  3.13-14: 191n5
  3.14: 78n52
  4: 8n15
  4.2: 63
  4.2-3: 59n1, 83n63
  4.5: 76
  4.8-9: 61n5, 75
  4.9-13: 192n7
  4.10: 170n9
  4.11-12: 195
  4.13: 195
  4.16-17b: 161n48
  4.19-20: 170
  4.22: 63
  4.22-23: 69
  4.29: 79n54
  4.35b: 160n44
  4.38: 63
  4.44: 97n33
  4.45-47: 171-172
  4.49-51: 190-191
  5.1: 116n83
  5.1 ff.: 181
  5.1-10: 5n9, 102n47
  5.2-3: 10n4
  5.7: 101n41
  5.8: 187n2
  5.12-16: 192n7, 193
  5.13: 122n8, 194
  5.14: 195
  5.17: 63
  5.20: 76
  5.21: 110
  5.22-25: 73
  5.23: 66
  5.30-35: 33n40
  5.39-42: 30n36
  5.46-53: 57n22
  5.46-54: 53-54
  5.49: 57
  5.51: 57
  5.52: 54n17
  5.59: 97n33
  5.61: 96n31
  5.61-62: 5n9
  5.62-63: 28-29
  5.63: 14n12
  6.3-9: 26
  6.10: 79n54
  6.10-13: 192n7, 193
  6.11-12: 194
  6.12-13: 195
  6.27-28: 50n12
  6.31-36: 49-50
  6.42-51: 143n2
  6.50: 144n5
  6.52-56: 152n21
  6.52-57: 50-51
  6.56: 57
  6.57: 57,
  6.72: 61
  7: 6n11
  7.1 ff.: 181, 186
  7.1-21: 115-117
  7.3-15: 35-37
  7.10-12: 35n42
  7.12-15: 14n12
  7.16: 69
  7.17-19: 62n11
  7.21: 97n33
  7.22: 189
  7.25 ff.: 161n48
  7.30: 170n9
  7.37-42: 132-133
  7.43-44: 195
  7.49-55: 127n24, 162n50
  7 *fin.*: 119
  8: 85n1
  8.6a: 75
  8.19-23: 169
  8.35a-45a: 152n21
  8.49-55: 20n21
  8.56: 63
  8.65a: 78n52
  8.70: 65n19, 76
  8.70-71: 69

Index Locorum

9: 85n1
Paians
  2.1-5: 111n71
  2.25-27: 130
  2.68: 63
  6.1-11: 102n47
  6.8-9: 75
  6.127-131: 61-62
  6.128-129: 71, 146
  6.131: 113n73
  6.132-134: 54n17
  12.17: 88n11
Partheneia
  1.8-14: 127n25
  1.9-10: 69
Threnoi
  7.7: 63
Fragments
  2: 63
  29.1-5: 104-105
  32: 63n15
  42: 65n21
  75.1: 86
  75.1-12: 102n47
  75.7-8: 101n42
  81.2-3: 61
  89a: 105n54
  105: 184n6
  120: 184n6
  121: 69
  122: 184n6
  122.1-8: 20n20
  141: 54n17
  198a.2: 76
  228: 69
  229: 69

Plato
  Phaido
    58B: 152n22
    60D: 87n8
  Phaidros
    237A: 106n57, 106n58

Quintilian
  3.7.7: 87n7
  3.7.12: 191n6

Sappho
  1.25: 103
  1.28: 86n5, 103

Semonides (West)
  10: 156n32

Shakespeare
  Hamlet: 7n12

Simonides
  85.4D: 60n4
  11.3D (= A.P. 16.2.3): 188n4

Sophokles
  Antigone
    781-801: 87n9

Thebaid
  1: 106

Theognis
  1-2: 115n80
  341-342: 82n61

Theophrastos
  Characters
    28.1: 71n36

Thoukydides
  2.35.2: 73
  2.35.2-3: 70n33
  3.104: 87n8

Vergil
  Aeneid
    5.344: 188n4
    8.630: 97n33

Xenophon
  Agesilaos
    7.1-3: 94n27

General Index

anticlimax: 40n49
apology/apologetic: 54, 108, 154-156
appearance and action: 2, 147-148, 187-191
associationism: 3, 5, 183n4
asyndeton: 42-44, 45n6, 46, 48n11, 49, 51n13, 52, 55, 57, 84, 127-128, 132, 140, 162
beyond expectations ($παρὰ\ τὸ\ προσῆκον$): 60n4, 70, 77n49
break-offs: 7, 41-57; asyndeton in: 41, 43, 45-46, 48-49, 51-52, 55, 57; death or suffering in: 41-48, 52-53, 55, 57; divine presence in: 41, 43-44, 46, 50, 52-53, 57; emphasis in: 41, 43-44, 46-48, 50, 52, 55, 57; gnomes in: 43-44, 46n7, 52n14; self-exhortation in: 37, 41, 43, 44n5, 46, 52, 57; statement of encomiastic role in: 47-52, 57; weapons in: 47-49; too much to tell in: 51n13, 52
catalogues: 20-37, 43n4, 51n13, 52n15, 53n16, 56n21, 60, 78, 80, 81n59, 83-84, 115n81, 116n84, 116n85, 124, 135, 177, 181; climactic elements in: 20-37; elaboration of $πᾶς$: 20-22; elaboration of penultimate item: 35n42; low point in: 33, 35-36; of individual accomplishments: 22-26; of victories: 20n21, 23-24
charis ($χάρις$): 3, 64n18, 66, 71, 73, 83, 92-93, 99n35, 113n77, 119, 122, 124n16
Charites: 91n16, 94n25, 99-101, 102n45, 109-110, 115n81, 124, 185-186; distinguished from the Muses: 124, 185
climax/climactic: 2-3, 6-7, 9, 11, 12n10, 13-17, 18n19, 19-20, 21n22, 22, 23n24, 24-27, 29-39, 46, 48n11, 50, 55-57, 60, 62, 69, 74, 76n47, 77, 78n51, 80, 82-84, 91-92, 93n22, 94n28, 95n30, 97n32, 97n33, 101n43, 110, 116n85, 120, 122-123, 125n19, 129n30, 131-132, 135n48, 141, 147, 148n14, 152, 157, 159, 163, 165, 169, 171-174, 176-177, 179-180, 194; climactic pairs: 165-180; ending of odes: 28-29; genealogy in: 17-19, 88, 91, 93, 99, 101, 103n50, 109, 130; indicators of climax: 10n5, 62n9; in *Pyth.* 3.61-76: 37-39; introduced at beginning of line: 14n12; introduction of new theme: 27-28; movement from divine to human: 13-14, 147; proper names in: 10, 13, 15-17, 19, 27-28, 31n36, 33, 35, 81-82, 91-92, 94, 97n33, 99, 101-102, 109, 113n73, 122, 132, 138, 147, 158, 177
colometry: 8n14, 9
crescendo: 6-7, 38-39, 83, 192; (see also climax)
cultic hymns: (see under hymns)
decreasing elements: 40n49
deeds of war/deeds of peace: 44-45, 50, 53, 56-57, 139
double crown of success ($εὖ\ παθεῖν, εὖ\ ἀκούειν$): 122-125, 166, 192-194
ekphrasis: 27, 33n41, 41, 86, 91, 100
emphasis/emphatic placement: 1, 7, 9, 11, 13-16, 18-19, 20n20, 21-30, 33, 35-36, 38, 40-41, 43-44, 46-48, 50, 52, 55, 57, 62n12, 71, 78, 91, 93n22, 94-96, 97n32, 102-103, 113, 120, 123, 125n18, 126n22, 130, 134, 137-138, 143, 147, 149n15, 152-153, 157n37, 158-160, 187-188, 190-191; of second of a pair: 165-180
enjambment: 3, 4n6, 15, 50, 55, 149,

215

152, 157, 176
first personal statements: 10, 11n9, 41, 44n5, 46, 57, 104, 122, 133n41, 153n26, 175
Gesetz der wachsenden Glieder: 4-5, 10; (see also increasing length)
hard-earned victory: 67, 159
hendiadys: 145, 166
hymns (opening): 85-117; *charis* in: 92-94, 113n77; cultic hymns: 87-102; combinations of rhapsodic and cultic features in: 111-117; companion deities in: 86, 88, 89n14, 91n16, 99; *ekphrasis* in: 86, 91, 100; elements of style in: 85-86, 88, 99; hymns in Bakchylides: 181-186; *hypomnesis* in: 18, 86, 91, 93-94, 99, 106, 116, 186; invocations and requests: 16-20; invocations in Homer: 16n16, 18n19; movement from general to particular in: 87, 91, 97; re-invocations in: 91, 93, 100-101, 144-146; relative clauses in: 18, 22, 91n16, 109, 113, 142; rhapsodic and cultic elements distinguished: 102-106; rhapsodic elements in: 106-111; rhetorical functions of: 86-87; *sedes* of the god in: 17-19, 28, 86, 88, 91, 93, 99, 103n50, 130, 134, 170, 184-185; sequential reading of: 87, 91
imagery: 2n2, 3, 5, 6n11, 7n12, 126, 183n4
impromptu qualities: (see spontaneity)
increasing length: 4, 5n9, 9-13, 16-19, 20n20, 22, 25, 29, 31n37, 34, 38, 47n10, 55, 100, 120, 122, 131, 134, 146-147, 152, 159, 188, 192; in hymnal invocations and requests: 16-20; of pairs: 165-180
increasing relevance: 7, 9, 11, 15-18, 28, 40n49, 116n85, 130, 177
increasing specification: 7, 9-19, 20n20, 22, 25-27, 30, 31n37, 33-34, 36, 38-39, 50, 87, 89, 91-92, 94, 97, 100, 101n41, 117, 122, 131-132, 146-147, 152, 183n2
intensification: 7, 9-13, 15, 17, 22, 23n24, 27, 29, 38-39, 89, 100-101, 117n86, 122, 129, 147, 165, 167, 188n3
last-mentioned item: 11n7, 16, 137, 190
limits of human success: 2, 191-195

linear development: 5-6; (see also sequential reading)
litotes: 50, 59n2, 59n3, 66, 70, 74, 76, 80, 126, 131, 135, 190; in vaunts: 77-78
metaphor: 2n2, 3, 5, 6n11, 10n6, 44n5, 60, 61n5, 62-64, 65n20, 75, 88n11, 122n10, 124, 126n22, 134, 187n2; in negative expressions: 62-71
Muses: 1, 40, 47, 52, 57, 76, 99n35, 103-104, 106-114, 124, 138-139, 183n3, 185-186, 191; distinguished from Charites: 124, 185; in break-offs: 52, 57
ne plus ultra: (see limits of human success)
negative examples: 42, 44, 45n6, 47, 127, 167-168
negative expressions: 2, 38-39, 59-84, 141, 147, 149, 154, 157, 159, 163, 190, 191n5, 195n8; ἀ-privatives in: 60-61, 68, 76-77, 163; ethical proof in: 2, 60-61, 77-78; followed by positive climactic assertion: 15n14, 22, 23n24, 38-39, 42, 47, 57, 60, 62, 65, 68-69, 73-74, 77-78, 83-84, 89, 97n32, 123, 127-128, 132, 137, 150, 157, 163; in achievement and its celebration: 62-70; in praise and blame: 70-73; in prayers: 78-80, 82, 123, 129, 131-132, 137, 150, 154, 163; in vaunts: 76-78; involving association: 75-77; involving kindness and envy: 73-75; involving perception: 62-65; metaphors in: 62-71; ὅπως οὐκ ἔχει in: 60, 84, 168; στέρησις → ἕξις in: 60, 62; variety achieved by: 59-60, 77, 80
particularizing καί: 89, 97n33, 149n16
Partizipialstil: 17, 86
phthonos (φθόνος): 54, 73-75, 79-80, 127n25, 131, 133, 154, 156, 167
praeteritio: 40n49, 52, 82
prayers: 2, 16-20, 49, 60, 78-80, 82-83, 94-95, 101n40, 106n57, 112, 119-140, 149-150, 161-163, 186; asyndeton in: 42, 44, 45n6, 48n11, 49, 57, 127-130, 132, 140, 162; climactic elements in requests: 120-125, 163; concluding prayers: 119-127; distinction from cultic hymns: 103n50; in *Pyth.* 1: 136-140; medial prayers: 127-140; negative expressions in: 78-

80, 123, 129, 131-132, 137; participles in: 121n5, 123n11; used to break from negative example: 42, 44-45, 57, 127-129; used to end praise: 48-49, 129-130, 149
previous studies of Pindaric style: (see under style)
priamel: 3, 7, 9-16, 30, 97n33, 99, 107, 113, 116, 117n86, 146-147, 153, 172n12, 180
proper names: (see under climax)
readings differing from S-M⁸: 8n15
recurrent words: 2, 3n4, 4
Relativstil: 18, 86; (see also hymns, relative clauses in)
responsion: (see recurrent words)
rhapsodic hymns: (see under hymns)
rhetoric: 2, 5, 7n12, 9, 17n17, 42, 50n12, 53-54, 59-62, 72, 74, 82, 84, 86-87, 103, 110, 111n70, 124n16, 141, 149-150, 154-156, 165, 169, 191; function of ἐσλὸν αἰνεῖν: 2, 59, 65; of hymns: 86-87; of negative expressions: 59-62; tropes and figures: 3; (see also apology, beyond expectations, break-offs, hendiadys, litotes, negative examples, priamel, *thauma*)
rising elements: 9, 14, 15n14, 16, 20-22, 23n24, 27-28, 30n36, 31, 38-39, 56, 100, 136n49, 192; elaborating πᾶς: 20-22; in hymnal invocations and requests: 16-20, 100; linked in mid-line: 14, 16, 19, 147, 159
sapientia et fortitudo: 78, 89, 96n31, 171-172, 179-180, 184n5
second personal statements: 33, 36, 62n11, 103, 147n13
sequential reading: 6-7, 87, 91; (see also linear development)
spontaneity: 41-42, 150n17, 187
stephanaphoria (στεφαναφορία): 145-146
style, previous studies of: 2-5; principles of: (see emphasis, increasing length, increasing relevance, increasing specification, intensification, rising elements); (see also asyndeton, climax, emphasis, enjambment, litotes, negative expressions, variety)
syllable count: 5n9, 7n13, 10-15, 17, 20n20, 20n21, 25-26, 33, 36, 40n49, 101, 147; (see also word count)
symmetry: 4n7, 5, 6n11

thauma (θαῦμα): 33n41, 43n4, 46, 52, 57, 166
variety (ποικιλία): 11, 33n39, 59-60, 61n5, 75, 80, 92, 147, 188, 190, 195n8
Vergleich ohne wie: 3, 10
word count, problems of: 5, 7n13; (see also syllable count)

www.ingramcontent.com/pod-product-compliance
Ingram Content Group UK Ltd.
Pitfield, Milton Keynes, MK11 3LW, UK
UKHW041430180426
11947UKWH00007B/368